17349/

ADULT LEARNING

ADULT LEARNING
Research and Practice

HUEY B. LONG

CAMBRIDGE
The Adult Education Company
888 Seventh Avenue, New York, New York 10106

Excerpts on the following pages reprinted by permission:
   26: *Democracy and Education* by John Dewey, copyright 1916 by Macmillan Publishing Co.,
      Inc., renewed 1944 by John Dewey.
   191, 192: "A Comprehensive Model of Assessing the Training Needs of Local Governmental
      Staff" by Edmund Sheridan and Daniel W. Shannon, University of Washington, 1979.

Designed by Muriel Underwood

Library of Congress Cataloging in Publication Data

Long, Huey B.
   Adult learning, research and practice.

   Bibliography: p.
   Includes index.
   1. Adult education.   2. Adult education—Research.
I. Title.
LC5215.L57   1983   374   83-2703
ISBN 0-695-81666-7

9 8 7 6 5 4 3 2 1

Contents

List of Figures

List of Tables

Acknowledgments

In preparing this volume, I sought and obtained invaluable assistance from a number of colleagues. It is with deep gratitude and appreciation that the personal contributions made by a number of educators of adults are acknowledged here. Assistance was provided in many forms. A number of colleagues freely shared their research with appropriate suggestions and comments. Others recommended sources that may have been overlooked, and yet others took valuable time to review all or parts of the manuscript. Whatever merit *Adult Learning: Research and Practice* has must be attributed in large measure to the assistance obtained from my colleagues and fellow learners. Singular encouragement from the following colleagues is gratefully recognized: Stephen Agyekum, Jerold Apps, George Brooks, William Dowling, Betsy Goodnow, Mary Jane Even, Roger Hiemstra, Tom Sork, and Curtis Ulmer. Appreciation is also expressed to some special mentors in my professional life: George Aker, Cy Houle, Malcolm Knowles, Howard McClusky, Wayne Schroeder, and Ralph Spence.

The completion of the manuscript during a time of professional change would not have been possible without the encouragement and support of some very special women: my colleague and righthand support for almost nine years, Mrs. Cathy Morris; and my wife, Marie. To both these very special people I continue to be indebted.

Huey B. Long

Introduction

Adult Learning: Research and Practice is designed to report and discuss recent research, primarily completed since 1965, that contributes to understanding and application in the practice and study of the field. The emphasis is twofold: upon questions of practice and upon conceptualizations. The research selected for identification and discussion was selected because it appears to address some of the persistent issues of education of adults. The work cited is perceived to have the potential of influencing practice or theory. Of thousands of abstracts, dissertations, journal articles, research papers, and research, only a small percentage was selected for citation purposes. The majority of the work reviewed and subsequently cited originated in North America; selected supporting research from the United Kingdom, the Nordic countries, Australia, and Latin America is occasionally cited.

The classic *Overview of Adult Education Research* by Brunner et al. inspired this work. The purposes and structures of the two volumes are different, however, and comparisons should be made with caution. It is not, therefore, the goal of *Adult Learning: Research and Practice* to *up-date* Brunner's work in a literal sense. Certain topics discussed in the earlier work, such as group processes and comparisons between lecture and group discussion, are not explicated in detail here. In contrast, topics that were only beginning to emerge, or not present at all, in the literature reviewed by Brunner are included. Such topics include cognitive/learning styles, cognitive structure, crystallized and fluid intelligence, brain hemispheric research, marketing adult education, and computer-assisted learning.

Even with the results of thousands of investigations annually reported, the education of adults is a long way from being a science. Such important questions as "How *do* adults learn?" "What is the best program planning/implementation process?" and "What are the necessary sufficient competencies of the educator of adults?" remain. The rapid expansion of the research and dissemination activity in the field is illustrated adequately in Chapter 1, but an additional illustration is provided by the publication of Cross's *Adults as Learners* (1981), Boyle's *Planning Better Programs* (1981), and other works during the preparation of this volume.

The review conducted for this book actually began almost ten years ago. It has come to a climax with approximately twenty-four months of intensive effort. The task revealed several things. First, such reviews in the future will likely require a team of reviewers. Second, there is a dearth of good on-going reviews of selected research topics. (The work on participation is a singular exception.) Third, no investigator has followed Verner's example of encouraging intensive reviews of the corpus of existing research on selected topics (meta-research). Fourth, there is an increasing need for better international dissemination and translation. Fifth, the quality of adult education research compares favorably with that of other educational and social science areas.

Adult Learning: Research and Practice is divided into six major divisions and 14 chapters as follows:

Part I: Informing Practice This division contains a single chapter, the purpose of which is to develop an understanding of the status of research in the broad field that is concerned with the education of adults. Criticism and evaluation of research are discussed. In addition, concepts of research in adult education and other topics are explicated.

Part II: Adult Learning Ability The second division contains two chapters concerning the ability of adults to learn. Research foundations that support the growing acceptance of the concept that age is an empty variable in explaining adult learning ability are noted. Chapter 2 also identifies some conceptual structures and appropriate research concerning questions of adult learning ability. It is believed that such concepts as crystallized and fluid intelligence, cognitive styles, and cognitive structures may be more informative than age as explanatory factors. Other factors that are associated with learning ability for which research is discussed include health, response-reaction time, personality variables, and social class. Chapter 3 turns to a futuristic area of research: the focus is upon morphology and biology as variables that may exert certain limits upon learning.

Part III: Participation of Adults in Educational Activities The third division of the volume contains three chapters concerned with participation questions and research findings. Chapter 4 reports "reasons" for participation and perceived obstacles as identified by a number of studies using analytical, statistical, or psychometric procedures. Chapter 5 examines the analytical research designed to explicate the "motives" for participation. Chapter 5 also reports several models used in the study of participation of adults in educational activities. Chapter 6 discusses dropout or wastage studies and identifies some of the characteristics that have been associated with the phenomenon.

Part IV: Program Development Part IV contains three chapters devoted to research concerning selected elements of the program development and implementation process. Chapter 7 provides a discussion of program elements as identified in the literature, the conceptual base for program development, and five different concepts or models of planning. In addition, research concerning participation in planning, program evaluation, and facilities is discussed here. Chapter 8 addresses a specific program planning element: needs assessment. The chapter reports and discusses research concerning different needs assessment concepts and procedures. The third chapter in the section, Chapter 9, identifies and reviews selected research that is concerned with promoting, marketing, and recruiting adults for educational activities.

Part V: The Teaching-Learning Transaction The fifth major division of the volume contains two chapters about the teaching-learning transaction. Chapter 10 reports and discusses the literature on the learning process, learning models, and some common personal variables that should be considered in the teaching-learning transaction. The latter topical area includes intelligence, cognitive/learning style, experience, anxiety, curiosity, and motivation. Chapter 11 is concerned with other variables in the teaching-learning transaction. Variables included are the social environment of the learning context and a variety of learning activities and formats, including telecommunications and media- and computer-assisted learning.

Part VI: The Field of Adult Education The concluding division contains three chapters. The first chapter in this section discusses selected research concerning adult education as a field of practice and study. Topics such as historical foundations, concepts and terminology, parameters of the field, purposes, content, and professionalization are examined in Chapter 12. Chapter 13 reviews the philosophical literature in the field. The final chapter of the section and the book provides a brief summary of the entire volume.

The following procedure was used to select research for citation in *Adult Learning: Research and Practice*. First, the general topical content of research emerged through my continuing review of material published in *Adult Education* and papers presented annually at the Adult Education Research Conference and the Lifelong Learning Research Conference. These sources provided a basis for fourteen chapter topics. After deciding upon the topics to be discussed in the book, topical searches were initiated. This search led in several directions, including English-language journals published in other countries and adult education publications of all kinds in the United States, including books, magazines, journals, newsletters, and ERIC sources. In addition, literature in related areas such as educational psychology, gerontology, psychology, social psychology, and sociology was examined. Ultimately, the items selected for citation were judged against the following criteria:

1. Strength of the research design
2. Appropriateness to the topic
3. General availability for further review by the interested reader
4. Reputation of the investigator
5. Significance of a particular investigation

Two problems are apparent. First, there are a large number of articles on some topics such as participation. To cite all the reported studies would be redundant. Therefore, the ones cited were selected according to the above criteria. Second, on some topics, such as the study of learner participation in goal setting and management of the learning experience, only a few studies could be identified. Most of these studies have design flaws, but because of the importance of the topic to educators of adults, they are cited nonetheless. In addition, even though the emphasis is on research published since 1965, some investigators such as Thorndike, Lorge, and Owens are cited because of the historical significance of their research. Thus, in some instances, it seemed desirable to look backward a few years to provide a context for understanding the more recent research.

More than 600 sources are cited here. They represent approximately 10 to 15 percent of the items reviewed in the development of the manuscript. Approximately fifty of the references were published in countries other than the United States. A number of the articles printed in the United States were authored by Canadians, Britons, Scandinavians, and others on research in their own countries, but also are of interest in the United States. Because of the availability of materials in English, the majority of the publications issued in other countries originated in Canada and the United Kingdom. The same criteria were used in selection of the "international" sources. The corpus of research reports published outside the United States that was read numbered more than 500.

I · Informing Practice

1 · Research: A Foundation for Practice

STUDENTS, PRACTITIONERS, AND RESEARCHERS interested in the education of adults are challenged by two general questions:

1. How can practice be improved?
2. How are we to address the questions of practice?

For example, educators of adults in all kinds of settings seek answers to questions such as these:

How do adults learn?
Why do adults learn?
How does one best teach adults?
How does one best organize and administer educational programs for adults?
Why should educational programs be made available to adults?

But, as basic as these questions are, an even more fundamental question needs to be asked: By what means shall the above questions be answered?

Several alternatives, independently and collectively, may be used by educators of adults to secure the answers to questions of practice that perplex them. These sources include authority, experience, intuition, and science. As was the case in many fields, during the development of adult education as a field of practice, educators of adults were primarily informed by the experience of respected longtime practitioners. Tubb (1966), however, warns that basing practice on traditional educational approaches of using fortuitously absorbed commonsense educational theories picked up through intelligent reflection or wide and lengthy experience is no longer appropriate. He says that practices based on such sources are not adequate for a mass society undergoing an explosion of knowledge no matter how well they may have worked in the past or how well they may seem to work when judged only by the people who use them. If, as Tubb suggests, the value of intuition and experience as means of informing the practice of adult education has been reduced by the knowledge explosion, the expansion of educational programs for adults, and the increasing numbers of professionally trained practitioners, how shall theory and practice be strengthened?

Scientific and philosophical investigations provide one means for overcoming the limitations of prescientific intuitive activities and uncritical acceptance of experience as a means for informing the field of practice. Literally thousands of scientific and philosophical inquiries are available to inform the practice of educators of adults in a multitude of settings and conditions, from highly independent distance-learning situations to voluntary study circles. The bulk of this work is also a disadvantage. The quantity of research concerning the education of adults is expanding at such a rapid rate that not since 1959 has an effort been made to provide an extensive and intensive organized review of the broad field. Indeed, the present effort may be the last such attempt.

Expansion of research activity and publication of investigations concerned with questions about the education of adults have been of such dimensions that it is highly unlikely that I shall be able to accurately and adequately describe the phenomenon here. The volume of worldwide research in the multitude of related disciplines is too great to even inventory. *Adult Learning: Research and Practice,* however, provides a selective sampling of U.S., Western European, and South American research that has implications for several important areas of practice.

This introductory chapter is designed to accomplish several objectives. First, it seeks to place the status and criticism of adult education research in an appropriate perspective. Second, attention shifts to the issue of "who" is to do the research in adult education. This question concerns the relationship between the field of adult education and other disciplines. Specifically, it is concerned with the contributions that researchers in other fields may make to adult education as a field of study and practice. Third, attention is directed to the question "What is research?" The section is concerned with the issue surrounding the methods of research and the controversy related to the alleged overemphasis on empirical scientific methods at the expense of other ways of knowing, including philosophy. Fourth, I discuss some of the means of disseminating research to adult educators, namely, *Adult Education* and an important annual research conference. A tenuous step is then taken into the future before the presentation of some general observations.

STATUS AND CRITICISM

Two contrasting perceptions of the attitudes of adult educators about research appear in the literature. Bittner (1950) was rather pessimistic about the ability of adult educators to conduct useful research, and Brunner and his associates (1959) implied that, at least up to 1957, adult educators had not conducted much effective research. On the other hand, Knox and others suggest that adult educators have for a number of years concerned themselves with how to improve practice in adult education through improved research activities. Much of this chapter explicates this continuum about research in adult education that ranges from optimism to pessimism. The clustering of scholars and practitioners along several continua on a variety of issues such as the quality of research, the usefulness of research, the appropriate conductors of research, the purpose of research, and research methodology will become apparent in the following pages.[1]

The contemporary status and criticisms of research concerning the education of adults seem to be understood best by beginning in the 1960s, when two important books were published within a five-year period.

Whereas the education of adults and the concept of lifelong learning have a rich and lengthy history, adult education as a professional discipline or field of practice is a very recent phenomenon. The youthfulness of the field is suggested by the title of an important book published by the Adult Education Association in 1964: *Adult Education: Outlines of an Emerging Field of University Study* (Jensen, Liveright, and Hallenbeck 1964).

Since adult education is still a developing field of study and practice, there remains a continuing interest in the rational basis of the practices that characterize the field. A review of the literature on research in adult education over the last thirty years reveals the practitioner's concern for empirical justification and theoretical explanations for certain practices.

Brunner's classic work continues to serve as a reference point for professional adult educators. It is durable and continues to be a useful source of information concerning selected topics such as adult learning, adult interests, and instructional techniques. Over a two-year period, Brunner and his colleagues surveyed between 4,000 and 5,000 titles, some 600 of which were cited in the report. They arrived at several important conclusions concerning the nature and status of adult education research.

It is instructive to review, within the context of the current situation, four important observations that were noted by Brunner.

First, Brunner and associates noted the omission of a number of topics from the review because of inadequate research procedures or contradictory findings.

Second, research in adult education was described as chaotic because some topics such as adult learning had been explored more thoroughly than others. In retrospect, the term *unevenness* is preferred over *chaotic* as a descriptor. The adjective *chaotic* seems to be a little strong if it was used only because of varying emphasis upon diverse topics. However, if it was the best word to describe the situation in 1959, it continues to qualify. Topics such as adult learning and participation have received much more attention from researchers than have other topics such as comparative (international) adult education and historical research.

Third, Brunner and his colleagues were of the opinion that the *effective* bodies of available research, other than in methods, were contributed by social scientists rather than adult educators. The comment implies at least one, and possibly two, things: (1) that only social scientists (i.e., others rather than adult educators) were conducting research useful to adult educators, and (2) that only social scientists were conducting *useful* research (i.e., research of adult educators was not "effective"). Pessimism concerning research in the field has not been restricted to Brunner and his associates or to the 1950s. Bittner (1950) and Kreitlow (1960, 1964, 1970) in the United States are joined by Easting (1979) of Great Britain, who is of the opinion that adult education as a discipline is sadly lacking in high-powered research. Furthermore, according to Easting, much of the research is of mediocre quality and has made no impact upon the process of adult education. In much stronger language he asserts that much of the research work is entirely wasted in terms of any contribution to the principles or practice of adult education.

Easting's rather harsh negative view is, however, softened by the observations of Legge (1979), also of Britain, who is of the opinion that suspicion and hostility toward research in adult education has existed for some time. He considers the main source of disaffection to be those who have perceived adult education as a mission dependent only upon inspired teachers. Furthermore, he believes that such pessimistic views of adult education research are partly explained as a defense mechanism of those overworked teachers and partly by the mystical unrealistic expectations that some hold for research.

Griffith (1979) has identified five reasons for dissatisfaction with traditional adult education research:

1. The research is poorly done.
2. Inappropriate methods are used.
3. Emphasis is on production of knowledge rather than on improvement of the quality of life.
4. Use of research is hindered in some way.
5. Research findings are sometimes used to exploit the population or people of a given area or culture.

Being able to point to the handicaps of another does not make one whole; however, it is sometimes comforting for us to realize that others also have similar challenges. Educators of adults are not unique in their dissatisfaction with the fruits of their research efforts. The heat of the issue of contributions to educational practice via research was sufficient in 1967 to lead to an article entitled "When Will Research Improve Education?" (Cross 1967). A series of publications critical of the accomplishments and values of education research appeared in the 1970s (Committee for Economic Development 1969; Cronback and Suppes 1969; Glennan 1973). Criticisms of research in the broad field of education include a number of specific charges such as being "too basic," insufficiently applicable, too narrow, insignificant, methodologically tight, and substantively weak (Fincher 1974).

It is of course possible that the above charges are accurate and even too kind in many instances. It is also probable that the charges are overly broad and too caustic. For example, it has been suggested (Westfall 1973) that Newton's use and analysis of data that led to his law of universal gravitation, the determination of the velocity of sound, and the calculation of the precession of the equinoxes could never have passed a system of research control proposed by some.

Fourth, Brunner and his associates noted five factors that were believed to interfere with the production of effective research by adult educators: (1) pressures of large enrollments, (2) newness of the profession, (3) the profusion of agencies involved, (4) lack of funds, and (5) emphasis on descriptive studies.

In the period since Brunner's work, some things have remained the same, but others have changed.

At the time of the publication of *An Overview of Adult Education Research* there were fewer than 25 professors of adult education in the United States. Today, there are more than 200. It is estimated that more than 1,700 doctorates in adult education have been awarded in the United States and Canada since 1970. Adult and continuing education activities have also increased rapidly, with higher education institutions and numerous other agencies very actively seeking to develop even larger enrollments.

Only one of the five reasons Brunner cited for the lack of visibility of adult educators in the production of what he labeled effective bodies of research has changed: the field has become a little older. Age seems to have brought some maturity. The last twenty years have proved to be important in the development of a research base for adult education. My study of publication practices of professors of adult education generated data that suggest that the field experienced a significant spurt of growth beginning about 1966 and has only recently begun to slow its rate of growth. Between 1950 and 1973, 81 of the 172 members of the 1972 Commission of Professors of Adult Education (CPAE) produced 2,098 publications, with most of them being published after Brunner's review appeared (Long 1977). Today, the body of research concerning adult education topics is probably several times larger than that available to Brunner and his colleagues. The *annual* production of research in the years between 1970 and 1980 was probably close to the *total* corpus of research that they reviewed.

The expansion of research parallels the momentous growth experienced in related higher education disciplines, psychology, sociology, and gerontology between 1960 and 1975. More than 600 articles and research papers were published in *Adult Education* or presented at the now-annual Adult Education Research Conferences and Lifelong Learning Research Conferences between 1971 and 1980. During the same period, a number of research articles were published in such regional journals as the *Mountain Plains Journal of Adult Education, Tennessee Adult Educator,* and *Mississippi Adult Educator.*

Significant events in adult education also took place in Western Europe, the U.S.S.R., the People's Republic of China, and other nations. UNESCO, the World Bank, and other international as well as national organizations have spent millions of dollars on behalf of adult education. The growth and development of adult education internationally is indicated by the publication of a number of national and international journals of adult education such as *Convergence, The Indian Journal of Adult Education, Adult Education* (London), *Studies in Adult Education* (Great Britain), and *Australian Journal of Adult Education.*

This evidence makes clear that educators of adults have chosen to plan, conduct, and report activities designed to answer questions of practice. They continue to be assisted by scholars in other fields, however, and do not hesitate to use theoretical underpinnings developed in other disciplines.

WHO WILL DO ADULT EDUCATION RESEARCH?

The debate concerning whether adult education research will be done by adult educators or by social scientists and others from related disciplines is not new, nor will it be resolved within the parameters of this discussion. Research that is of interest to both professional and volunteer adult education workers must by its nature be conducted by competent investigators in a variety of fields. Professors of adult education—those who are expected to conduct the larger proportion of adult education research—usually do not have the requisite background to conduct biological, physiological, economic, and psychological studies. The trend indicates that the problem will become more acute. For example, Harris (1980) recently expressed an opinion that any valid psychological research concerning aging that involves cognitive and intellectual functioning will require the investigator to know the biological strata and function of the brain. He believes that the researcher can no longer accept a subject as "normal" without the aid of an electroencephalogram, a brain scan, an echoencephalogram, and even a computerized axial tomography (CAT) brain scan.

The research of adult education is conceptualized as falling into 4 cells, based on two dimensions, according to (1) who does the research and (2) the purpose of the research. The research of adult education has not been inventoried according to this concept, but it can be speculated that the bulk of the basic work has been and will continue to be conducted by professionals from fields other than adult education. Adult education personnel are believed to focus mainly on the applied aspects of research.

The importance of borrowing research from related fields was clearly articulated by the Commission of Professors of Adult Education (CPAE) in 1961. They indicated that for the first thirty-five years following the founding of the American Association for Adult Education adult education knowledge and practice was largely borrowed from that of youth education. The Commission in 1961, however, believed that progress had been made in the development of the body of theory, knowledge, and practice through the process of borrowing and adapting from others.

The professors, however, were also aware that borrowing and adapting had limitations. The other fields with their competent investigators could not, and cannot to this date, answer all the questions of adult educators, and even some of the answers offered do not directly address the uniqueness of the adult education situation. Therefore, the call of individuals such as Mezirow (1971) and I (Long 1980b) for strengthening adult education research from the perspective of the adult educator has merit. It is recognized that such research cannot meet all the needs of the field today, but neither can complete dependence on research conducted by personnel from other disciplines meet all the needs.

Even though the necessity (and even the desirability) of borrowing from other disciplines is frequently noted in the literature of adult education, criteria for such activity are very limited. Only Jensen (1964) and Verner (1978) have been cited as individuals who proposed definite procedures or guidelines for determining the usefulness of information from other fields to adult education. Verner believed that the categories of knowledge at the heart of adult education are adult learning, psychology of adults, physiology of aging, adult instruction, instructional processes, instructional devices, the client system, the organizational system, the social setting, the role of adult education, and historical foundations. Knowledge from other disciplines to develop the above categories would be borrowed and used according to how well it met the following seven criteria (Verner 1978):

1. It helps to explain some phenomenon encountered in the field or discipline.
2. It helps in the solution of practical problems encountered in the field.
3. It can be translated into operational principles that will contribute to greater efficiency and effectiveness in adult educational programming.
4. It contributes to the development of essential attitudes, values, or skills important to the field.
5. It can be reformulated so that it is applicable to adult education.
6. It is derived solely from adult populations.
7. It relates to systematic education for adults.

WHAT IS RESEARCH?

Educators of adults are greatly interested in the question "What is research?" The question is not an academic one in which only a few "ivory tower" types are interested. It is a basic question that at times separates colleague from colleague, practitioner from professor, and administrator from teacher. It has been suggested that human beings seek to arrive at truth by many paths. The different routes often used include theology, philosophy, experience, and science. Each of the different pathways to knowledge and truth has its own set of definitions and advocates. It is possible that each of the different means of ascertaining truth is most appropriate to special kinds of questions.

For example, theology appears to be the most appropriate pathway for developing an understanding of God, while philosophical inquiry is especially suited to determining value and definitional questions. Other issues recommend the scientific approach. In this volume, we are particularly interested in what is defined as scientific and philosophical research. Research here is defined as "systematic observation and interpretation of data associated with the process of problem definition, observation, data collection, interpretation, and conclusion." For the purposes of definition, the character of the observation and the nature of the data are not critical issues here. Such issues within themselves deserve the attention of philosophers.

The literature concerning research in adult education contains a number of references about the need for alternative research approaches. Apps (1972) is among the more prominent adult educators who have called for a broader definition of research. He wants a definition that moves beyond empirical inquiry. He pictures adult educators as having been caught up in believing that all knowledge comes from empirical research. Therefore, he recommends that educators of adults consider other paths to knowledge, such as thinking, synthesizing, sensing, and accepting—or, in Royce's 1964 terms, rationalism, intuitionism, empiricism, and authoritarianism. Addressing himself specifically to empiricism, Apps notes that a ritualistic approach to empiricism could be limiting. Others who have issued similar warnings to adult educators concerning research include Forest (1972) and Schillace (1973).

What is the defining characteristic of empirical research that Apps, Forest, and Schillace find unacceptable? Unfortunately, comments on the topic do not always clearly identify the undesirable aspects of empiricism. Forest implies that acceptance of empiricism hinders the development of other kinds of research. For example, he encourages greater acceptance of personal reports and expanded use of systematic and logical analysis. Schillace's argument appears to focus on the expected rigor of "scientific" study, which limits the opportunity for creativity and innovation. Apps's major criticism of the use of the scientific method of adult education research seems to be based on what he sees as a conflict between the requirements of the research procedures and fundamental positions of the field of adult education (Apps 1979). The observations suggest the possibility that empiricism may be variously defined. For example, Forest's call for expanded use of personal reports and systematic and logical analysis also could be issued by an advocate of empirical research. It seems that Forest may be calling for what has come to be referred to as qualitative research as opposed to quantitative research. More is said on this topic later; now it may be helpful to share a few observations about the empirical approach and other research methods.

Empirical Approach

The idea that knowledge is derived from practical experience as well as rational empirical sources has a long history. The debate concerning the relative values of rational thought and practical activity can be traced to classical Athens, where both Plato and Aristotle identified experience with purely practical concerns and, hence, with material interests as to its purpose and with the body as its organ. In contrast, knowledge exists for its own sake, free from practical reference, with its source and organ a purely immaterial mind. Knowledge has to do with spiritual or ideal interest. Experience is represented as never self-sufficient, whereas rational knowing is perceived to be complete and comprehensive within itself (Dewey 1966).

The relative merits of rational empiricism, or the scientific method, and experience as a conglomerate of unsystematic relationships among sense impressions are elegantly discussed by Dewey. He shows how experience was first defined as empiricism as opposed to rational systematic and logical mental activity. Knowledge based on experience was thus inconsistent, conflicting, and unstable. Intellectual knowledge developed during this period as something to be preferred over experiential knowledge because it offered consistency and some dimensions of universality and permanence. The development of experimentation as a method of obtaining knowledge altered the importance or value of "experience." Experience within the experimental method thus became a name for something intellectual and cognitive. Sensationalism emerged as the counterbalance to experience. Sensationalism emphasized a concrete firsthand source of knowledge based on the impact of an activity on the individual. By the twentieth century, we thus had "experimental empiricism" and "sensational empiricism."

Experimental empiricism also may be identified as rational empiricism to note the use of the scientific methods of observations, controls, hypotheses, and conclusions. The following observation of Dewey (1916, p. 276) is particularly instructive to those who seek to understand the historical dimensions of the debate.

> The modern age began . . . with an appeal to experience, and an attack upon so-called purely rational concepts on the ground that they either needed to be ballasted by the results of concrete experiences, or else were mere expressions of prejudice and institutionalized class interest, calling themselves rational for protection. But various circumstances led to considering experience as pure cognition, leaving out of account its intrinsic active and emotional phases, and to identifying it with a passive reception of isolated "sensations." . . .
>
> Meantime, the advance of psychology, of industrial methods, and of the experimental method in science makes another conception of experience explicitly desirable and possible. This theory reinstates the idea of the ancients that experience is primarily practical, not cognitive—a matter of doing and undergoing the consequences of doing. But the ancient theory is transformed by realizing that doing may be directed so as to take up into its own content all which thought suggests, and so as to result in securely tested knowledge. "Experience" then ceases to be empirical and becomes experimental. Reason ceases to be a remote and ideal faculty, and signifies all the resources by which activity is made fruitful in meaning.

Guidelines for Alternative Methods

The previous discussion included observations concerning the call for alternative approaches to research in adult education. It was noted that investigators should be free to choose alternative methods of inquiry. Few criteria, however, are available to guide the investigator in the determination and selection of optional procedures. One of the few lists of criteria to help the researcher select an alternative to the empirical method is provided by Apps (1979):

1. Recognize that knowledge does not exist apart from values.
2. Examine research assumptions and make them explicit.
3. Conduct research that furthers the purposes of continuing education.
4. The subject should be "involved" in the process as opposed to being an object of research.
5. Results of research should be of assistance to those studied while having the potential for adding to a body of knowledge.
6. Practice and research should be linked.
7. Knowledge should be viewed broadly.

Empiricism has also become another name for the scientific method. Unfortunately a broad brush is frequently used to smear both terms. For example, there is no reason for "empirical" or "scientific" research to be conceptually restricted to laboratory, experimental, and quantitative investigations. Proponents of field-based research procedures employed in honorable areas such as anthropology and ethnology should find little cause to reject the appellation "scientific." It is incumbent upon the scholar-practitioner to remember that the different methods of inquiry may be used for different purposes in diverse settings for a variety of reasons.

Adult educators in the United States and Great Britain have urged greater acceptance of what are currently referred to as "qualitative" methods of inquiry. British publications reflect wider acceptance of qualitative methods than U.S. publications do, even though such individuals as Apps (1972, 1979) and I myself (Long 1980b) have encouraged such research. Brookfield's 1982 analysis of research philosophies in the two nations indicates that qualitative methods have yet to be widely reported in published research. Some exceptions are evident in the dissertation research of American doctoral students and a few works such as *Last Gamble on Education* (Mezirow, Darkenwald, and Knox 1975).

Participatory Research

Some adult educators indicate that scholars have been guilty of separating knowledge into rational empirical and intuitive modes. Those who are identified with the former are called scientists, and those who are identified with the latter are referred to as artists. Succinctly put, the two are distinguished by the process through which they are developed. The rational empirical mode is a referential and inferential process that sequentially considers the stuff of decisions. In contrast, intuitive modes reflect a holistic, simultaneous grasping of a situation to come to a conclusion. The process is sometimes referred to as "insight."

An effort has been made to combine the elements of rational empirical research with intuitive research under the banner of "participatory research" (Apps 1979). Guidelines for participatory research emphasize the value of the research to the subjects involved as opposed to more general theoretical goals. While participatory research is sometimes hailed as a new approach to research in adult education, it is hauntingly similar to community problem-solving approaches used by adult educators involved in community development twenty years ago.

The principles of participatory research identified by Budd Hall (n.d.) are striking in their similarity to principles of action research. Five of the principles of action research as often used in community self-studies and studies of community facilities and needs all emphasize the active and central role of the community in the process. They specify that the community is fundamental in the origin, process, and results of action research (Carter 1959).

Action research has been historically traced to the Tavistock Institute in Human Relations in London (Voth 1979). An article by Curle (1949) is identified as one of the earliest articles describing the action research process. Others who have been identified with this kind of research include Kurt Lewin and a number of anthropologists, including William F. Whyte (Voth 1979). Voth notes that among advocates of action research there is some disagreement on the appropriate balance between applied objectives and the objective of con-

tributing to social science theory and research. He observes that the process
has usefulness in achieving both kinds of objectives.

These comments do not denigrate the principles of participatory research
as identified by Hall and others. They do, however, underscore two of the
difficulties that seem to plague adult educators: (1) lack of awareness of other
important developments such as action research and its established base and
(2) a proclivity to prefer new labels. Both tendencies have disadvantages and
contribute to what may be identified as minimal progress in the field.

Philosophical Research

Philosophy as a way of knowing has a long history. Adult educators have
preferred other ways of knowing to philosophical inquiry. The scientific
method, broadly defined to include case studies and other qualitative research,
has been the preferred method of investigation. The scientific method and
philosophy, however, are perceived to be concerned with different kinds of
questions. The scientific method can be useful in defining what is, how something came to be or may be done, when something happened or should occur,
and with where questions. Why questions and some how, when, and where
questions, however, are also open to philosophical inquiry.

Modern analytic philosophy has greatly influenced educational theory.
Individual philosophers, including the British philosophers Charles Hardie
and Richard S. Peters, have made important contributions to the study of
education. Philosophical inquiry into the purposes, process, and elements of
adult education is promising. And—as is discussed in Chapter 13—additional
philosophical efforts should be encouraged.

DISSEMINATION OF ADULT EDUCATION RESEARCH

Investigations using adult subjects and designed to examine various aspects of
the adult condition are conducted by scholars from a variety of fields that
include, among others, medicine, pharmacology, social psychology, biology,
psychology, anthropology, political science, and sociology. Such research activities often are not even indirectly related to adult education; some are,
however, and some have important implications for adult education as did
Havighurst's Kansas City Studies, Levinson's study of male development, and
a multitude of learning studies. Reports of research from across these disciplines are reported annually by the hundreds at numerous international, national, regional, and state professional association conferences. They are also
scattered among hundreds of journals.

The situation concerning research that is specifically designed to examine
particular adult education problems is less demanding. Even though there is
an increasing number of national and international journals and even an increasing number of organizations such as the International Council for Adult
Education, the Interamerican Congress of Andragogy (in South America), the
African Adult Education Association, the European Bureau of Adult Education, and the Documentation Center for Education (in Europe), the variety and
number remain conceptually manageable.

Dissemination of adult education research in the United States has been primarily handled by two organs: the journal *Adult Education* and the annual Adult Education Research Conference. Recently an annual research conference on lifelong learning, conducted at the University of Maryland, has gained increasing popularity with adult educators. While there is no assurance that *Adult Education* and the Adult Education Research Conference faithfully reflect the condition, trends, and dimensions of adult education research in the United States, there is some justification for the opinion that together they provide satisfactory representation of adult education research here.

THE FUTURE

The past as prologue provides some suggestions concerning future needs and directions for research in the education of adults. If research is to adequately inform the practice and study of the education of adults in the future, several things must happen. First, changes must occur in the approach that researchers use; systematic programs of research much be undertaken. Second, different kinds of research must be conducted in connection with improved conceptualization. Third, diverse research methods are recommended. These topics are expanded upon in the following sections.

Programs of Research

The potential contributions of research to practice in the future seem to be associated with the prospects of developing research programs, rather than the unsystematic approaches that currently exist.[2] By programs of research we refer to systematically planned and purposive investigations of specific research questions. Individual researchers and graduate departments of adult education are encouraged to increase their specialization in appropriate substantive research issues, over a number of years and including a number of graduate students. The advantages of developing programs of research are many. Some of them follow.

1. Institutional resources could be developed in depth. (For example, library holdings and departmental resources on a given topic such as cognitive structure in adults or history of adult education or teaching techniques and personality traits could be strengthened.)
2. Beginning from a given position, research in the selected areas could proceed in a linear fashion.
3. Student investigators would benefit from the regular involvement with other researchers and would possess a greater level of sophistication prior to initiating their own research.
4. Student investigators could cooperate in research activities in such a way as to improve the substantive, methodological, and applied aspects of research.
5. Through greater specialization, individual faculty members would strengthen their own scholarship and improve their abilities to lead, direct, and supervise unfolding research.

Reviews of the research contributions from the major producers of published research in the United States and Canada do not reveal the current existence of research programs. There are a few instances where there are suggestions of the possibility of a kind of informal effort in this direction. Allen Tough's personal investigations concerning the self-directed learner are associated with a number of similar investigations conducted by students at the Ontario Institute for Studies in Education. Roger Boshier's follow-up to Verner's interest in participation and other studies of this topic are identified with the University of British Columbia. Gary Dickinson and his students, also at the University of British Columbia, have been identified with teaching issues. Alan Knox, associated with the University of Wisconsin, has been identified personally with a number of investigations related to the adult learner and adult development and administration. Roger Hiemstra of Syracuse University has initiated an exciting program of research concerning self-directed learning. I myself, at the University of Georgia, have contributed to historical studies of the colonial period of America.

The idea of research programs is not without its disadvantages. For one, it is not unusual for professors to feel that individual students should be given great freedom in the identification and selection of research topics for dissertations. Limiting the opportunities for research topics is perceived to be inconsistent with a basic philosophical position concerning the importance of personal choice, self-direction, and human worth. To require that a student conduct research in a preselected topical area somehow seems offensive. A second disadvantage is associated with the possibility that faculty members would become too narrow in their specialization and hence lose a broad perception of the field of adult education.

These two major disadvantages can be addressed. First, students can be well informed of the focus of a department and individual faculty members prior to admission. If the program is not consistent with the student's academic and professional goals, other institutions that specialize in the appropriate areas (as far as the specific student is concerned) can be identified. The problem of potential overspecialization by an individual faculty member can be addressed by the opportunity to have a major area of specialization such as adult learning and a minor area of inquiry such as history. The second topic could be used by the individual professor as an alternate area when he or she temporarily becomes fatigued through emphasis in the first area of research. Taking both the advantages and disadvantages into consideration, it seems that the development of research programs in graduate departments of adult education is commendable.

Recommending the development of programs of research by individuals and departments does not mean that professors or institutions should limit themselves in conceptualizing research needs. For example, educational and social science research generally appears to suffer from two great weaknesses. One object of criticism is the one-shot kind of research in which a single minor topic is selected with little reference to previous and related research. The investigation is completed and reported, but no further progress is made with the findings, and the general research questions are left undeveloped. The other problem concerns the tendency to select a particular topic and procedure and replicate previous work without a systematic goal in mind. Consequently, ten studies of participation or some other topic appear in the literature without conceptual refinement or progress; only the subjects have been changed.

An example of the phenomenon of neglecting one area while tending to overrepeat research in another is participation studies. Miller's "force field analyis" concept has been virtually ignored by investigators even though it is based on the reputable work of Lewin. At the same time, numerous factor-analytic studies that seem to provide few new insights or explanation for participation phenomena continue to be reported.

Neither does the proposal for research programs negate the need for creative and innovative approaches to educational issues in the education of adults. For example, is it not possible to identify an important research question that can be investigated simultaneously by several investigators using different research approaches—for example, philosophy, experimentation, and grounded theory? Topics for research should not be limited to those that are considered to be safe, popular, or likely to be approved by a screening committee for reporting at a research conference or in a publication. Some research, particularly that presenting new conceptualizations, new analyses, and new variables, requires development over several years. In such cases the first few studies may have little meaning except as a potential foundation for later work.

Different Kinds of Research

Adult education as a field of study and practice also has a need for different kinds of research. The field is not sufficiently mature to be presented as having no additional needs for some of the kinds of research that are already found in the research literature.

For the purposes of this book, I recently conducted a survey of individuals who have served on editorial and publications committees of the Adult Education Association of the U.S.A. The survey revealed several perceptions of research in adult education. The respondents indicated that they believe that some of the research concerning the education of adults is useful and that its greatest contribution has been in describing the field. To be more useful in the future, research should, said the respondents, emphasize development of theory over application and basic research.

My personal opinion differs from the survey results, which also indicated that research has not been helpful in influencing practice. It seems that if the research concerning the education of adults has not been helpful in influencing practice, as indicated by the respondents, the greatest need in adult education studies does not lie in the further development of theoretical positions but in the translation of theory and research findings into applied practice.

The expansion of the body of research findings now available to practitioners recommends the development of a cadre of researchers involved in meta-research. Six types of meta-research concerning adult education research have been identified by Sork (1980):

1. Inventories of research
2. General reviews of research
3. Critical reviews of specific topics
4. Research agendas or taxonomies of needed research

5. Focused critiques of research methodology
6. Frameworks or paradigms for understanding and improving research

This volume represents each of the above types to some degree. However, the task of preparing *Adult Learning: Research and Practice* revealed the great need for more and better meta-research. Research agendas or taxonomies of needed research, however, seem not to be generally useful; there is reason to believe that few researchers are influenced by a list of needed research topics developed by others. On the other hand, the other five types of meta-research listed by Sork seem to have general usefulness. They inform both practitioners and researchers of the development of research trends and methods.

In addition to the need for interpretation of existing research for purposes of application, the field of adult education requires a number of specialists who are competent to analyze and synthesize the larger bodies of research on diverse topics. Some of the needs in this area were identified in 1965 by Kreitlow. We continue to have a need (1) to integrate past research in adult education with more recent findings, (2) to selectively review recent research in the fields of psychology, sociology, anthropology, vocational education, and communications for findings pertinent to the process of educating adults, (3) to integrate the adult education literature with relevant material from other fields, and (4) to relate the integrated research literature from the various disciplines to existing theory in adult education.

Kreitlow's observations, plus impressions gained in the process of reviewing thousands of research reports and abstracts for the purpose of this book, suggest to me that educators of adults should turn some of their attention to the process of synthesizing the vast body of research currently available. In essence, this volume represents such an effort. There is, however, a continuing need for scholars in the field to remain current in specific topical areas in much the same ways that Verner attempted to develop selected areas through collaboration with his students. Some examples of the kinds of reviews and summaries of research that provide at least the first step in such a direction are listed below, with the names of researchers closely identified with them:

1. Adult Development—Knox
2. British Research—Charnley, Legge
3. Cognitive Development—Long
4. Lecture—Verner and Dickinson
5. Needs—McMahon, Monnett
6. Nordic Research on Recruitment and Participation—Rubenson
7. Participation—Boshier, Cross
8. Philosophy—Apps
9. Research and Publication in Adult Education—Dickinson and Rusnell; Kreitlow; Long and Agyekum
10. Self-Directed Learning—Tough, Hiemstra

Diverse Methods

A review of what has been said about adult education research by those who seem to be most actively involved indicates that the future will include a greater variety of research methods. Adult education as a field of study is located in higher education institutions that seem to be gradually expanding research options. This observation does not indicate that the popular quantified experimental research of earlier decades will fade from the scene. Rather, it seems as if there is a slowly developing recognition that other research methods also have respectable places in graduate and post-graduate investigations. Actually, we should have increasing development of quantification methods due to the increasing competence in computer science and the speed at which electronic data processors can examine, order, and treat masses of data. While developments are progressing in the mathematical and computer-based areas of quantified research methods, similar advances are likely to occur in the qualitative methods, with grounded theory and other anthropological-ethnographic procedures gaining adherents for specific kinds of research. It is likely that scholars will creatively combine the capability of computers and qualitative research procedures in new and novel ways that will greatly enhance this area of research.

It is also likely that educators of adults will show increasing interest in a number of research methods that are already available but that have been relatively neglected in the past. These include philosophical inquiry and historical analysis, including interpretation as well as original source work. Other potentially useful but seldom used methods include path analysis and critical-incident research procedures. Overall, it appears that a general opening up of higher education to the acceptance of diverse research methods will have favorable effects on adult education research, provided the leaders of the field are sufficiently open to encourage and support such developments.

OBSERVATIONS

This chapter and this volume are both predicated upon the assumption that the scientific method of inquiry is a useful means for informing the practice of the education of adults. It is believed that prescientific methods based on on-the-job training have value, but that ultimately these experiences too must be evaluated and tested in a logical and rational manner that is best exemplified by the scientific method. Scientific method is broadly interpreted here to include such activities as historical investigations, case studies, field work modeled after anthropological and ethnographic procedures, and formal philosophical inquiry. The common elements in this process include (1) recognition of a "problem," (2) systematic observation, (3) systematic recording of observations, (4) appropriate controls, (5) rational and objective analysis of the collected data according to orderly and consistent procedures, and (6) judicious interpretation.

As an expanding field of practice and study, adult education is challenged to review the research foundations upon which the practice is based. Accordingly, such a review should consider the potential and the limitations of research as a means to inform practice. First, the limitations of research in general as it applies to the education of people, young and old, and to social science inquiry must be recognized. Failure to understand the limitations of the process increases the possibility of developing an unrealistic expectation for research and according the process honor that it does not deserve. In contrast, too much pessimism about the shortcomings of research in general or of specific investigations is equally unrealistic and is perceived to be a part of the original problem concerning expectations. Research, at best, is a series of compromises that points us toward the truth. At any stage and time, it is as close an approximation of truth as can be known at the time. But the strength of the process is the central concept that disproof is not a disservice but a contribution in its own right to the continuing search for knowledge and truth.

Despite the progress in adult education in the last twenty years (or perhaps because of it), adult educators continue to be very dependent upon scholars from a number of disciplines to provide basic research for our application. The research reviewed in this volume draws heavily from the work of psychologists and others who might be referred to as behavioral scientists. This is not to indicate that adult educators are not conducting research or that it is too poor in quality to be seriously considered or that there is not a field of study that requires a distinctive approach that the adult educator is most competent to take. Advances in all areas of life, however, indicate that techniques and equipment used in such specialized kinds of investigations as psychological and physiological studies may eventually be outside the competence of most adult educators and that the researchers who do conduct such studies may have to have additional educational preparation in the specialized areas.

The growth and expansion of the research activity in the field of adult education is obvious to those who have observed the publications and conference activity in the past decade. More than 600 dissertations were reported in a recent three-year period in the United States; in a ten-year period, another 600 research articles and research papers were published or presented by one journal and two conferences conducted annually (one of the conferences was in existence only during the most recent three-year period). In addition, many research articles have been published in other magazines and educational journals such as *Convergence* (printed in Canada), *Adult Literacy and Basic Education*, and *Lifelong Learning: The Adult Years* and its predecessor, *Adult Leadership*. My own 1977 study of publication activity of members of the Commission of Professors of Adult Education revealed that 81 of the professors published more than 2,000 publications including books, articles, and reports. Most of the material was published between 1960 and 1972.

Research production does not exist in a vacuum. The methods, priorities, and volume of inquiry and dissemination are associated with other social development. The Adult Performance Level (APL) Program (Griffith and Cervero 1977) illustrates how social, political, and educational issues converged to produce a major research project. This particular research activity has been the subject of both praise and condemnation. The review and analysis of the APL Program by Griffith and Cervero also illustrates appropriate use of research procedures to test the efficacy of other research conclusions. Other factors that influence research priorities are researcher interests, emphasis and gaps in available research findings, preferences of leader problems in practice that call for additional study, and preferences of organizations that support research (Knox 1977b). Factors that I have identified as influencing the volume of research include our relatively limited knowledge of adulthood; the peculiarities of adulthood, which suggest a subtle distinctiveness of inquiries based on adult samples; the rapid expansion of programs designed to address educational needs of adults; increased public support for study and teaching of adults; and increasing numbers of scholars and advanced students whose primary responsibilities include adults as learners (Long 1980b).

Educators of adults experience problems associated with the dissemination of the research in the field both as consumers and as producers of research. As consumers they face a high probability of missing a number of research reports on a variety of topics because of the great numbers of different publications that include occasional articles of interest to adult educators. For example, 81 professors of adult education published in 338 journals (Long 1977). There is also limited translation of much important work, so that most Americans and others limited to English have very little opportunity to be informed by the research conducted in France and Germany and many Spanish and Arab nations. Some regular translation of limited work in the Nordic countries has been increasingly available in English.

Overall, even though it is possible to be critical of much of the research conducted in adult education, including much of that reviewed here, a body of knowledge informed by research is emerging.

NOTES

1. Kjell Rubenson (1982) critically comments on several aspects of adult education research. He suggests that the territory of adult education research has been too narrowly defined in terms of learner characteristics of a psychological nature. Consequently, he is of the opinion that "reductionism" in combination with a stress on sophisticated methodology and inadequate conceptualization has interfered with the development of adult education as a discipline.

2. Geoffrey Easting (1979) has also recommended the development of "research programs."

II · Adult Learning Ability

2 · Adult Learning

IT IS DIFFICULT to identify a topic of more enduring interest to adult educators than the question of adult ability to learn. Fortunately for adult educators, the topic has also been very popular with psychologists. Efforts to answer a number of specific questions concerning adult ability can be directly traced to the pioneer work of Francis Galton (1822–1911), whose interests included strengths and physical abilities of adults. Others studied the adult's ability to learn a variety of tasks, but E. L. Thorndike (1928) is most frequently credited with reporting early optimistic research concerning the ability of adults to learn.

Brunner's 1959 discussion of adult intelligence and capacity to learn was based on the conclusions of Thorndike, Lorge, and a few others (Auch 1934; Sorenson 1938). Even though their research designs differed in important ways, both Thorndike (1928) and Lorge (1936) agreed that adults can learn up to age 70. Thorndike's design emphasized *rate* of learning, while Lorge designed his investigations to examine *power* to learn; hence, Thorndike used timed tests and Lorge worked with untimed activities. As a result, Lorge's findings seemed more "favorable" than those of Thorndike. Lorge applied a mathematical adjustment to timed intelligence tests and reduced the differences between old and young subjects noted by Thorndike.

Thorndike's test included a variety of tasks such as learning to write with the unpracticed hand, translating messages into code, learning an artificial language, making judgments, and memorizing poetry (Kidd 1975). Lorge gave his subjects a similar test of writing with the unpracticed hand, in which he used two criteria in his analysis: number of letters per minute and quality of the letters. Based on the criterion of time, younger subjects outperformed the older (35 years of age and older) subjects. When quality was considered, performance did not reveal a decline according to age.

Three critical conclusions came from Thorndike's work. Based on the reported data, it was suggested that learning ability is at its peak during the period between twenty and twenty-five years of age. Thorndike also identified a decline in learning ability of about 1 percent per year from age twenty-five to about age forty-two. Finally, Thorndike's data suggested that the curve of ability to learn is only slightly related to age (Kidd 1975).

Present-day reviewers of Thorndike's work are aware of several design weaknesses that reduce both the internal and external validity of his findings (Kidd 1975). For example, his results were based on rate or speed of performance; subjects were selected based on the assumption that they were equal in all respects save chronological age. Tasks employed in the research were laboratory or school related rather than real-life tasks. Practice is indicated as being more important than the quality or character of instruction.

A great quantity of high-quality research on adult learning was produced in the years between Thorndike's and Lorge's early work and 1965. These studies provided the nucleus of a body of research related to a number of questions with important applied ramifications. For example, is there an association between learning ability and education? How do the results of cross-sectional and longitudinal designs differ? Do high performers maintain their relative edge over low performers across the life span? What other variables, if any, are associated with performance? These and other questions are addressed in the following pages.

FACTORS IN ASSESSING LEARNING ABILITY

As suggested by the differences between Lorge and Thorndike, the task of assessing learning ability is not a simple straightforward one. It is confounded by a number of variables, including the difficulty of conceptualizing learning ability. For example, learning ability may be thought of as potential, as actual measured performance, as power to learn, or as speed of learning. Other factors that complicate measurement and discussion of learning ability include the association between learning ability and educational level, the research design (longitudinal or cross-sectional), and stability of the variable.

Learning ability is usually discussed in terms of performance. Even though conceptually it may be desirable to divide the concept into actual measured performance and potential performance, there appears to be no way, at this time, to measure potential independent of performance.

Learning ability has also been conceptualized along the power/rate dimension referred to earlier. Consequently, the same individual may receive two very different scores. Thorndike's work emphasized rate. Lorge distinguished between rate and power.

As a consequence Thorndike developed his general curve of what has been called "ability to learn in relation to age." The curve was based on the quantity of performance per unit of time as related to chronological age. Thus, the popular curve of learning in relation to age primarily describes learning efficiency. For example, the curve indicates for different age groups the relative values for the amount performed in a given unit of time. Hypothetically, if the amount performed by the average 20- to 24-year-old age group were considered 100 percent efficiency, then the average performance per time unit for other age groups would be as follows: 14–16, 59 percent; 17–19, 85 percent; 25–29, 89 percent; 30–35, 87 percent. Such an illustration suggests how Thorndike arrived at his conclusion that learning (rate) declines about 1 percent per year from age 25 years to about 50 years.

Analysis of Thorndike's findings illustrates the importance of understanding that he primarily measured the rate of learning within a specified time unit. Thorndike's studies were also restricted to subjects 50 years of age or less. Others such as Miles (1934) and Jones and Conrad (1933) extended the upper age limits and generated findings that have been interpreted as suggesting that the decline in performance per hour is not much more rapid than 1 percent per year in the age range from 45 to 70 years. The use of Thorndike's concept of amount per hour clearly distinguishes between learning rate and learning ability. The distinction between the two concepts has more than theoretical significance.

Lorge (1963) has said that learning is the power to learn, while learning performance is a function of the circumstances under which a person performs. The distinction becomes apparent when one observes the performance of an individual who perceives the assigned learning task as being silly or unreasonable. Two other factors that might similarly influence performance are perception of the primary objective as being quantity or quality and physiological impairment. Any of the above may significantly affect learning performance independent of the subject's potential.

Lorge, using a cross-sectional approach, demonstrated that when individuals were equated for "power intelligence ability," their mental performance based on mixed speed-power intelligence scales was related to chronological age.

To evaluate the influence of the nature of the test upon estimates of the ability being measured, three different age groups were selected: Group I, 20–25 years of age; Group II, 27.5–37.5 years of age; and Group III, 40–70 years of age. The subjects from the three groups were matched on the power score, thus creating artificial triplets differing in age. Although they were equivalent in so-called power ability, the averages of the three groups differed on tests mixing speed and power. For example, on the Army Alpha Examination, Group I made a (mean) score of 150; Group II, 142; and Group III, 129. The corresponding scores on the Otis Self Administering Test of Mental Ability were 44, 39, and 33. The speed-power "penalty" was noted on all test results.

Based on his results, Lorge computed a correction that represents the penalty that age places on such speed-power test scores. He then applied the correction to data generated by Miles and Miles (1949) and Jones and Conrad (1933). The adjusted scores do not show the declines reported originally. Lorge (1963) says that his correction is not really a correction for age but is a correction for slowness, remoteness from schooling, disuse of practice with school functions, and lack of motivation.

Educational Level

Educational level reflects one's long-term association with certain schooling tasks such as reading, writing, and computation. The tasks usually include other components such as comprehension, application of rules, logic, and vocabulary. In turn, such competencies often constitute the substance of intelligence tests and other scales used to assess learning ability. The association between educational level and mental performance, along with its impact on longitudinal data, is one of the most visible and popular criticisms of earlier studies of adult learning ability.

It is obvious that in a sample where educational achievement is not controlled it is likely that older adult subjects will have less education than younger adult subjects. Blum and Jarvik (1974) are among the investigators who have concluded that there is a positive association between educational achievement level and intellectual functioning.

Within the applied area of adult education practice, Knox and Sjogren (1965) studied adult learners to determine the association between prior learning and learning in selected content areas. Their study concerning the association of learning achievement with age, level of education, and degree of prior adult education participation is reported below in some detail because of its significance to the field. It is significant because it marks a turning point in adult education research of this kind. Prior to Knox and Sjogren's work few adult educators had conducted studies of adult learning; most studies of this nature had been done by psychologists.

Knox and Sjogren's study was designed to provide a representative sample of adults eighteen through seventy-five years of age, to allow generalization to the adult population. From 650 volunteers they developed a stratified design that resulted in the selection of 211 subjects, 208 of whom completed the six-month project. The subjects engaged in four learning experiments that were replicated several times using different content. The subjects took a pretest, engaged in specific learning activity under established conditions, took a posttest, and finally took a retest after several weeks.

Three major findings were reported. The first set of findings concerned learning ability and its relationship to age. Age was not found to be associated with performance on the learning activities. Furthermore, there was no observed difference between older and younger subjects on the Wechsler Adult Intelligence Scale (WAIS). Knox and Sjogren believed their findings on these points were explained by the comparative educational achievement of older and younger subjects. Finally, they also observed a significant positive relationship between achievement and educational level.

Second, the investigators emphasized the influence of prior adult education participation on learning ability. Half the subjects had participated in some adult education activity in previous years, whereas the others had not done so in the previous five years. There were no differences between the two groups according to age, intelligence, level of formal education, proportion of men and women, or interests, yet topic pretest scores for participants differed significantly from nonparticipant's scores. These findings are interpreted as supporting the opinion that learning ability can decline with disuse.

The third finding discussed by Knox and Sjogren concerns the pace of learning. Three different learning situations involving "pacing" were studied: at the learners's own pace, faster than the learner's pace, and slower than the learner's pace. Learners performed best at their own pace. When they were required to learn at a pace faster or slower than their own preferred pace, achievement declined to about the same extent for all age groups. When the subjects were permitted to proceed at their own pace, the older subjects, those with less formal education, and those who had not recently participated in adult education recorded the slowest performance. In general, those who set a faster pace were those individuals who achieved significantly better.

Sharon's (1971) study of test score performance of 43,877 military people on the General Examinations of the College-Level Examination Program (CLEP) revealed that 12 to 27 percent of the subjects, without the benefit of post-high-school study, did as well as the average college sophomore. As expected, a significant positive relationship was found between formal college education and academic knowledge. The pattern of the scores in different disciplines changed as a function of age. Performance on tests of humanities, social science, and history improved with age, while achievement in mathematics and the natural sciences declined.

Following Sorenson's classic 1938 investigation of adult learning ability, Knox, Grotelueschen, and Sjogren (1968) investigated the association between learning ability and recent participation in a learning activity. Their findings were interpreted as supporting Sorenson's conclusion that recency of participation in an educational activity is related to an adult's ability to learn. Explanations offered for the results are as follows. First, participants may have developed their study skills to a higher level—they have learned to learn. A second explanation suggests that the level of formal education included in one's socioeconomic classification provides only a gross estimate of learning background, e.g., participants may actually have higher intelligence and more prior knowledge about selected topics, which enables them to learn more effectively. A third suggestion is that adult participants in learning activities are more highly motivated in a learning situation; in the present study, however, there was no reason to believe that a difference in attitude or motivation existed between participants and nonparticipants.

Knox, Grotelueschen, and Sjogren concluded that the participants learned more effectively for two reasons: (1) the adult who has not recently participated in education may have become less able in the use of study skills, and (2) participants may have achieved a broader background of knowledge and information that enables them to more readily acquire and retain new information. The relative contribution of each factor was not determined.

Following the idea that learning ability is content based and that ability is associated with interest or application, Monge and Gardner (1972) pursued an investigation of adult differences in cognitive performance. They justified their study by indicating that the application of productive abilities of adults at different ages in various work situations and the degree to which they can be retrained for new types of jobs depend on knowledge of their intellectual resources and learning ability. The Monge and Gardner study was designed to differ from other investigations that had focused on laboratory tasks of academic school-based content.

At the time of their study, they observed that little research had been done on more meaningful (practical) types of research materials. Furthermore, they were of the opinion that neither has there been much research directed toward an analysis of the types of variables, particularly personal variables, that might differentially influence learning and performance during young adulthood, middle age, and the older years. Accordingly, Monge and Gardner developed twenty-eight tests that were specifically designed to discern differential age trends among adults. Some of their more interesting findings are noted below.

Younger adults performed better than older adults on tests of an educational nature, with the exception of spelling, where the maximum mean score was obtained by the 50-to-59-year-old male group and the 40-to-49-year-old female group. They concluded that proficiency in the basic skills taught in school is at its highest around 30 years of age and then declines for the successive age groups.

Cognitive functioning for all variables is not at a maximum for groups of males and females less than 40 years of age. Data reported by Monge and Gardner show that for most of the variables they studied, the largest mean scores were obtained by groups of much older subjects. They also report variability among the variables (transportation, finance, slang, and death and disease) concerning the age at which the maximum mean score is observed for both sexes.

The findings of Knox and others thus provide evidence that seems to confirm a possible association between prior knowledge and performance on achievement- and intelligence-type examinations. The relative performance of individuals, according to prior achievement, is discussed further in the section on stability.

Design

The issue concerning the association between educational achievement and intellectual ability of adults is closely related to the validity of the research findings based on the cross-sectional design. Sociologically oriented scholars point out that differences in education across one or more decades is only one cultural difference that may be discovered within an adult sample. For example, a 1980 sample including one 30-year-old, one 40-year-old, one 50-year-old, and one 60-year-old subject would include an individual who lived in the post-World War I boom, two who experienced the Great Depression, three who lived during World War II, and four who experienced the Korean War and the internal political stability of the United States during the 1950s. Television became a popular cultural item during the childhood of one, the adolescence of another, the young adulthood of the third, and in the middle life span of the fourth. Coal-burning locomotives faded from the scene during the early childhood of the youngest; jet airplanes and diesel locomotives joined TV as common cultural items. Numerous other advances occurred in medicine, health care, telecommunications, and other areas.

Responding to the criticism of the impact of a cultural bias on cross-sectional studies of adult learners, investigators such as Owens (1966) and Bayley and Oden (1955) reported some interesting longitudinal studies. But just as the cross-sectional designs have external validity weaknesses, the longitudinal designs are victimized by internal weaknesses. Critics of the longitudinal designs point out that there is often a problem associated with subject survival in the studies. They contend that the healthier and most able subjects tend to survive longitudinal designs better than their less healthy and less able cohorts. Consequently, at the end of a longitudinal study, superlative subjects are overrepresented in the research. The data are thus an inaccurate reflection of the abilities that would be measured in a normal or random sample.

Because of the differences between the characteristic findings of the cross-sectional and longitudinal studies, it appears that the two designs attract different kinds of scholars, with different attitudes concerning the ability of adult learners. The more traditional scholars have seemed to favor the cross-sectional studies that produce evidence of a moderate but noticeable decline in performance across the life span as noted by Thorndike, viz., after age twenty-five the decline is approximately 1 percent per year. In contrast, longitudinal studies such as Owens's indicate that abilities persevere and may even increase into the seventh decade of life. This view seems to be shared by many, if not most, adult educators and younger psychologists.

A different design, structured to resolve the major criticisms of both the cross-sectional and longitudinal approaches, has been used by Baltes and Schaie (1974). Known as the cross-sequential design, it combines cross-sectional and longitudinal elements. Based on the use of the cross-sequential design, their work found that the upward limits of adult ability were even higher than those reported earlier by Thorndike and even Lorge.

Baltes and Schaie seemed to have debunked general intellectual decline; they labeled the idea a myth.[1] They base the assertion on results of a cross-sequential study initiated in 1956 and followed up in 1963, employing measures of four general, fairly independent dimensions of intelligence: (1) crystallized intelligence (includes the kinds of skills acquired through education and acculturation, such as verbal comprehension, numerical skills, and inductive reasoning), (2) cognitive flexibility (measures the ability to change from one way of thinking to another within the context of a familiar intellectual operation), (3) visuo-motor flexibility (measures a similar but independent ability, the one concerned with shifting from familiar to unfamiliar patterns in tasks that require coordination between visual and motor abilities), and (4) visualization (measures the ability to organize and process visual materials and involves tasks such as finding a simple figure contained in a complex one or identifying an incomplete picture). A definite decline was noted by Baltes and Schaie in only one of the four areas of intelligence examined: visuo-motor flexibility. They found no age-related change in cognitive flexibility.

Baltes and Schaie's work is probably as significant for contemporary adult educators as was the work of Thorndike and Lorge about fifty years ago. Using a combination of cross-sectional and longitudinal designs, their work produced two useful conclusions: (1) When a cross-sectional design is used, the younger group performs better than the older group, and (2) when a longitudinal design is used, crystallized intelligence and visualization increase with age, at least into the seventh decade.

Stability

The question of stability or relative performance differentials between the more able and the less able includes two concerns. The first of these, i.e., does performance decline across the life span?, was addressed in the preceding section. The second is the relative performance question, i.e., how do the changes in performance among the more capable and the less capable compare?

The answer to this question is related to the design issue discussed earlier. Studies based on cross-sectional designs generate one kind of data that leads to one set of conclusions, and longitudinal studies result in different decisions. Based on cross-sectional studies, there is evidence that there is an increasing range of individual differences in learning abilities, at least until about age sixty. These data suggest that the more intellectually able individuals show greater increases during childhood and adolescence, reach a higher plateau later in young adulthood, and increase their learning ability gradually or maintain the ability longer during adulthood. In contrast, the least able seem to develop more slowly, reach a lower plateau earlier, and decline more rapidly.

Longitudinally designed investigations of adult learning ability, primarily based on readministration of intelligence tests, have generated results that support the conclusion of a high degree of stability in performance (Furry and Baltes 1973). Many of the longitudinal studies have been based on selected samples, e.g., college students or the intellectually gifted (Bayley and Oden 1955). These are the kinds of people who tend to learn more rapidly and who seem to learn more complex tasks with greater alacrity. Then there is evidence, based on longitudinal data, of a greater increase or stability in the learning ability of the more able individuals in contrast with the general adult population. Individual differences according to age occurred at all ability levels (Knox 1977a).

SOME CONCEPTUAL STRUCTURES

In addition to concepts such as learning ability and intelligence, investigators of adult learning have turned to other explanatory structures. Three such conceptualizations that have emerged in the literature since 1960 are crystallized and fluid intelligence, cognitive styles, and cognitive structure. None of these terms were used in Brunner's discussion of research concerning adult learning.

Crystallized and Fluid Intelligence

There are two bodies of research relevant to age and performance. The first, with some exceptions, generally suggests that age should not be seriously considered as an obstacle to adult learning; some performance areas actually increase with age up to age 70. The second indicates that the sensory mechanisms and perhaps other human physical and biological elements show important negative changes over the course of life. How are these two bodies of findings reconciled?

Cattell (1965) has offered a concept of intelligence that is useful in interpreting the interplay between improved performance on verbal tests and declining performance on visual and reaction measures. He has introduced the idea of two kinds of intelligence or at least two different bases of intelligence. He calls them crystallized intelligence and fluid intelligence. Crystallized intelligence, as was noted earlier, includes acquired abilities such as verbal comprehension, numerical skills, and inductive reasoning. Fluid intelligence is perceived as being primarily innate and adaptive toward all types of problem solving. In contrast to crystallized intelligence, which appears to be culturally based and is best applied to bodies of information such as school subjects, fluid intelligence is biologically based and is heavily dependent upon neurophysiological structures. The neurophysiological base of fluid intelligence has been identified by J. L. Horn (1970), a close associate of Cattell's, as being the main ingredient in the anlage function. Anlage refers to very basic, unlearned central organizing functions in all behavior that can be said to involve intelligence. (Intelligence is used here to refer to all of the abilities to which psychologists refer when they use such terms as *intelligence, general aptitude,* and *"g."*) Anlage is a function that can operate in performance at a late stage of development; even unlearned reactivities and capacities influence the behavior of mature adults. Thus, anlage refers not only to conditions imposed on the development of abilities but also to conditions that operate in the expression of an ability. Short-term memory is perhaps the most outstanding example of anlage function. Physiological condition is determined by two factors: heredity and the accumulation of insult or injury to neural structures caused by disease, severe shocks, poisons, drugs, and bodily injuries. Fluid intelligence is described as being relatively formless and independent of experience and education. Examples of activities classified as fluid include rote memory, common word analogies, matrices, and verbal reasoning.

Essentially, fluid intelligence is reflective of neurophysiological structure and is relatively free from the influence of experience and education, while crystallized intelligence is very dependent on experience, cultural influences, and formal schooling. Crystallized abilities are bolstered by aids—techniques, frequently acquired within the context of an individual's culture, that enable him or her to surpass anlage (fluid) limitations. Horn has suggested that aids may be analogous to Piaget's operations construct. This view is countered in the influential article by Hooper, Fitzgerald, and Papalia (1971), who instead argue that Piagetian operations are essentially congruent with fluid aspects of cognition.

Subsequent research is divided about which theory is correct. Papalia and Bielby (1974) report that the scores made by the college-aged and elderly female subjects on Piaget's pendulum task[2] had a significant positive correlation with these subjects' scores on the Raven Progressive Matrices test, a measure of fluid intelligence. On the other hand, it is possible that formal operations depend mainly on crystallized intelligence because vocabulary scores, reflective of crystallized intelligence, correlated most strongly with formal operations scores, and because, whereas fluid intelligence declines rapidly, formal operational performance in their study did not exhibit such a decline but remained stable over age, like the measure of crystallized intelligence. Storck's 1974 cross-sequential life-span study of 298 subjects aged 6 to 91 years produced results having unclear significance: scores from the volume conservation task and the task of combinatorial reasoning had a significant positive correlation with measures of both fluid and crystallized intelligence. However, in an earlier study that tested adults aged 55 to 79, Storck, Lott, and Hooper (1972) found a different result: no significant correlation was found between results from the volume conservation task and tests of crystallized and fluid intelligence. Finally, one study (Coleman 1973) of 100 females aged 20 to 94 years found one formal ability, combinatorial thought, to be highly related to crystallized intelligence. Therefore, research in this area can be seen to provide only an equivocal response to the question of whether environmental stimulation affects level of cognitive functioning.

The seventh and eighth decades of this century have witnessed the publication of a number of additional studies concerning adult learning ability. For years following Thorndike's important study adult educators and psychologists have debated the effect of variables such as design (cross-sectional vs. longitudinal) and educational achievement level on the results of adult ability studies. Furthermore, scholars such as Owens and Bayley conducted studies that indicated differential performance according to the nature of the criterion used to measure adult performance. Owens's longitudinal study revealed that the performance of some subjects in areas such as the verbal ones actually improved across the life span, at least to age sixty. The subsequent research on adult ability conducted during the 1970s is exciting and confirms an increasingly "optimistic" perception of adult learning ability.

Cognitive Styles

A second development in the study of the ability of adults to learn has been a shift from the classic intelligence-test-based studies to analyses of cognitive styles. The concern with cognitive styles appears to have originated with the recognition that people differ in their learning behavior, i.e., some people learn some things such as math better than others such as language, whereas other individuals have the opposite propensities. Not only do individuals differ in their learning efficiency according to content, but they also differ according to their approach to the learning task. In common language, cognitive style is no more than the characteristic way in which individuals use their minds. According to Witkin, Dyk, et al. (1962), cognitive style is, however, quite a powerful variable in the academic choices and vocational preferences of individuals, in their academic development, in how students learn and how teachers teach and how they interact in the classroom. Unfortunately, according to Cross (1976), very few teachers and counselors know anything about cognitive styles, even though the research has been going on for more than twenty-five years. Only recently has a concerted attempt been made to bridge the gap between cognitive style research and learning practice.

Terminology in the area is somewhat confused; terms such as *cognitive style, learning style, cognitive maps,* and *learning modalities* are all used in the literature. Following Cross, the term *cognitive style* is used here to refer to those concepts concerning cognitive functioning that have a laboratory research base.

At least ten cognitive styles are frequently reported in the literature. Messick (1970) has provided a good description of nine styles:

1. Field independence versus field dependence
2. Scanning
3. Breadth of categorizing
4. Conceptualizing styles

5. Cognitive complexity versus simplicity
6. Reflectiveness versus impulsivity
7. Leveling versus sharpening
8. Constricted versus flexible control
9. Tolerance for incongruous or unrealistic experiences

Kagan's (1965) risk-taking versus cautiousness brings the total to ten.

Field Independence versus Field Dependence

The most developed body of research literature focuses on the first of the nine styles identified by Messick. Witkin is acknowledged as the leading expert on the concept of field independence versus field dependence as a cognitive style. Briefly distinguished, field-dependent people tend to be influenced by the environment; they are more "other directed" than field-independent people, who are described as being inner directed. The origin of a cognitive style has not been satisfactorily determined. Witkin and Berry (1975) reviewed almost 200 cross-cultural studies of cognitive style and arrived at the following conclusions:

1. Direction is toward field independence up to early adolescence, followed by a plateau, with a movement toward field dependence at around fifty years of age. Individuals show stability throughout life with respect to their *relative* position on the continuum.

2. Field-dependent styles seem to be favored in cultures that emphasize sharp, clear role definition and social control; cultures that place greater emphasis on self-control and independence encourage field independence.

3. Field dependence is also associated with cultures that follow strict child-rearing practices that emphasize obedience and parental authority; practices that encourage individual autonomy and are tolerant of violation of parental authority are associated with field independence.

The dimension of field dependence–field independence does not seem to be associated in any meaningful way with general intelligence. Field independence, however, seems to be positively associated with analytical ability. Field independents seem to favor the sciences and math in academic course work and also appear to have fewer learning problems than field dependents (Keogh and Donlon 1972). The possibility that learning difficulties may be more of a function of the way learning is structured than of intelligence is an important consideration in the instruction of adults.

Applications

One of the best-known efforts to apply cognitive style theory to instruction is Hill's Cognitive Mapping, as conducted through the use of his Cognitive Style Inventory (Hill 1971). Designed to yield a cognitive style profile or a "cognitive map" of individuals who complete the Cognitive Style Inventory, the instrument has been perceived as a means to help teachers of adults select appropriate learning activities for their students. Sheriff (1979), however, warns that the instrument is of questionable value. His factor analysis of the results of inventory forms completed by 4,437 community college students led him to question the descriptive and diagnostic features of the instrument. Sheriff is of the opinion that the Cognitive Style Inventory does not yield empirical evidence to support the theoretical foundation of the instrument.

Cawley, Miller, and Milligan (1976) report an investigation of conceptual styles based on the work of Kagan, Moss, and Siegel (1963) and Cohen (1969). They describe the polar styles studied in their research as analytic and global-relational—styles that compare in many respects with the field independence–field dependence continuum discussed above.

Based on their study of a small sample (11) of graduate students in adult education, Cawley, Miller, and Milligan report the following findings concerning analytic-relational cognitive styles:

1. Even within a small sample individuals tended to fall along the continuum from one extreme to the other.
2. Two individuals appear to have revealed conflicting styles as measured by two different instruments.
3. Analytic individuals tend to prefer more formal learning environments, whereas the global-relational types seem to prefer more informal environments.
4. The data also suggest that cognitive style may reflect a change in life-style, with an individual who formerly was more analytical becoming more global-relational if the appropriate change in life-style occurred.

Cawley, Miller, and Milligan's findings are interesting and, if confirmed by further research, should be helpful to teachers of adults. The results, however, should be used carefully for several reasons. First, the size of the sample is very small. Second, the nature of the sample limits external validity. Third, the investigators express some reservations about the Cognitive Style Inventory and its apparent bias favoring the individual reflecting an analytic style.

Pigg, Busch, and Lacy (1980), building upon the concept of an experiential learning model attributed to Kolb, suggest that four integrated stages are observable: (1) concrete experience, (2) observation and reflection, (3) formation of abstract concepts and generalization, and (4) testing implications of concepts in new situations. These components have been used as important elements in the development of cognitive field theory (Perkins 1974). According to the conceptual framework, the effective learner needs four kinds of abilities: (1) the ability to involve himself or herself fully and openly in new experiences (concrete experience abilities), (2) the ability to consider the experiences from many perspectives (reflective observation abilities), (3) the ability to create concepts that integrate observations into sound theories (abstraction abilities), and (4) the ability to use such new theories to make decisions and solve problems (active experimentation abilities). The theory thus yields two dimensions, each with abilities that are polar opposites. One dimension concerns the distinction between concrete experience and abstract conceptualization, whereas the other distinguishes between reflective observation and active experimentation. Finally, the model represented here suggests that learning occurs in an environment reflecting the resolution of dialectical tensions between the identified sets of opposing characteristics. People tend to resolve the tension in a rather consistent and stable pattern through the development of learning styles that emphasize some learning abilities over others.

Using Kolb's Learning Style Inventory (LSI), Pigg, Busch, and Lacy surveyed the Cooperative Extension agents in Kentucky to identify learning styles and implications for designing education programs for those individuals. The research resulted in the identification of all four learning styles suggested by Kolb: those of accommodators, divergers, assimilators, and convergers. Three conclusions are reported by the investigators: (1) no relationship between learning style and preferred learning activity was observed, (2) educators should not plan educational activities based on the LSI alone, and (3) the LSI may be useful in helping individuals become more sensitive to particular learning behaviors.

Denis (1979) examined a different dimension of learning styles when she investigated intuitive learning using an adult sample. Adult educational practice, reflection, and research are viewed by Denis as being preoccupied with the rational mode of learning and its attendant dynamics of logical progression, linear processes, objective setting, and attainment of objectives. Using interviews, she probed the intuitive mode of learning and thereby identified and described eighteen different processes that are operative in intuitive learning. In addition to suggesting that the identified processes contain important implications for adult learning and research in the field of adult education, she believes that understanding the phenomenon of intuitive learning is relating reflective analysis, which by definition takes place in the rational mode, to experience, which takes place in the intuitive mode.

Cognitive Structure

It has been observed (Long 1980b) that the admission of adults in expanding numbers to an increasing variety of traditional and nontraditional educational programs emphasizes questions of cognitive development in adulthood that received limited attention only a short while ago. Cattell (1965) and Horn (1970) discuss ideas concerning the development and maintenance of intelligence into and throughout adulthood that suggest a dynamic system that expands and contracts within established parameters according to the interaction of the various neurophysiological structures and sociophysical-cultural environmental structures. The framework of cognition and the development of cognitive skills, thus, seem to be explained by the interaction of morphogenetic features with an individual's personal experiences. This concept seems to be further supported by Flavell (1970), who notes that much of what he finds to be interesting and distinctive about preadulthood intellectual changes results from these changes' being guaranteed in fact and significantly constrained in form by biological-maturational factors. Consequently, cognitive change is inevitable in all neurologically intact growing children.

As perceived by Flavell, adult cognitive change seems to be quite different from childhood changes because of the underlying absence, in adulthood, of the biological growth process that contributes to childhood changes. Thus, there is something missing in adulthood that is present in childhood. It is that morphogenetic base that earlier provided an impetus to changes that were inevitable, significant, clearly directional, uniform, and irreversible. Flavell observes that it is not obvious that there is any biological process indigenous to the adult part of life that imposes such constraints on intellectual change. He cautions that the claim is not made that adult cognitive changes cannot and do not occur. Instead, it is suggested that adult biological changes are different and that because of these differences cognitive changes associated with them would not have the same morphogenetic features that childhood cognitive changes have.

Because of the questions that Flavell has about the inevitable and necessary directionality of adult cognitive development based on biological processes, we might be encouraged to look more carefully at the role of experience or environmental stimulation. In fact, Flavell strongly suggests that experience is a far more promising source of interesting adult cognitive changes than are biological events. Furthermore, he observes that the cognitive changes influenced by experience might prove to be more similar to the childhood prototypes in their morphogenetic features. These kinds of cognitions, according to Flavell, have to do with judgments, attitudes, and beliefs rather than with the kinds of skills usually measured on typical psychometric tests. Interestingly, cognitions of this kind are believed by Flavell to be appropriate at Piaget's concrete operations level.

Flavell's observations concerning the kinds of adult cognitions affected by experience and the operational level appropriate to these kinds of cognitions are provocative. They are not unlike an observation made by Bligh (1977), who notes that the major objectives of post-secondary education are primarily concerned with the development of patterns of thought, attitudes, and motivation. Both men, however, seem to have adopted an extremely narrow view of the cognitive activities of adults in and out of post-secondary education. Nevertheless, Flavell's most important point concerns the importance of experience in adult cognition that is a kind of delayed parallel to the role of biology in childhood cognition. This view does not seem to be too different from the concept of crystallized intelligence that is assumed to be a precipitate of experience and is largely due to the subject-related differences in experiential processes associated with the course of acculturation. Eisdorfer and Lawton (1973) also note that a further implication of the data on personality and social development seems to be the suggestion that adjustment mechanisms used in old age may represent individual responses to environmentally programmed conditions required of older people rather than maturationally required responses.

Piaget and Cognitive Development

Long, McCrary, and Ackerman (1979) provide a useful and detailed review of Piaget's theory of cognitive development, and the reader is referred there for additional information. However, a brief review of the four stages is presented here to facilitate interpretation of research reported in the following pages:

1. *Sensori-motor stage* (birth to about two years). This stage is called "sensori-motor" because the child still lacks the symbolic function; that is, does not

have representation, by which he or she can evoke objects in their absence. But during this period, the child constructs all the cognitive substructures that will serve as a point of departure or readiness for later perceptive and intellectual development.

2. *Pre-operational stage* (2 to 6 years). With the acquisition of language, formation of symbolic play, and mental imagery, actions are internalized and become representative. However, the logic of this period remains incomplete until the child is seven or eight years old. Conceptualization begins at this stage, but thought is still prelogical and preoperational, lacking reversibility and conservation.

3. *Operational stage* (approximately 7 to 11 years). Mental operations in this stage become functional. The emergence and coordination of operations and relations enable the child to conserve quantity, weight, and volume. Thought, however, is still tied to concrete objects. Ability to reason in terms of hypotheses before knowing that they are true or false is not possible.

4. *Formal stage* (approximately 12 to 15 years). The formal stage, the highest stage in the cognitive structure, is characterized by the ability to reason hypothetically. Hypothetical reasoning implies the subordination of the real to the realm of the possible, and consequently, the linking of all possibilities by necessary implications that encompass the real, but at the same time go beyond it.

Since Piaget's concept of cognitive development is based on an interaction of the biological with the environmental, it too bears some relationship to the aforementioned ideas concerning experience and neurophysiological structures. Piaget's work and theorizing have focused on the child, and undoubtedly he considered those morphogenetic changes that Flavell mentions. However, Piaget's emphasis on assimilation and accommodation, along with the concept of information as an "aliment" that nourishes cognitive structures, seems to provide a sufficient range of opportunity for consideration of adult experience in a theory of adult cognition even though Flavell suggests that a Piagetian view is more limited to the biological. Had Flavell had access to a 1972 article of Piaget's, his views may have been different.

Piaget's major concession concerning progression through the four stages of cognitive development concerns the rate and consistency of attainment of the fourth and highest stage, according to his concept. He observes that his work with children in Geneva may lack generalizability due to the nature of his select samples. Differences between his findings and the work of others thus require explanation.

A first possibility to explain the different findings is to posit a difference in speed of development without any modification of the order of succession of the stages. Differences in speed would be attributable to the quality and frequency of intellectual stimulation received from adults or from the environment. Poor stimulation could thus explain a reduction in the speed of development. It could be proposed that formal thought would therefore suffer from the cumulative effect and would not be formed until 15 or 20 years of age; or that in extremely disadvantaged conditions formal thought would never occur, or would develop only in those individuals who change their environment while development is possible.

This observation by Piaget (1972) appears to place a heavier emphasis on environment and lighter emphasis on biological development than formerly reported. He offers a moderating notation indicating that in his opinion formal structures are not exclusively the result of social transmission and that we are, therefore, required to consider the "spontaneous and endogenous" factors of construction proper to each normal subject. Yet the formation and completion of cognitive structures imply a series of exchanges and a stimulating environment. According to this proposition, all normal individuals are capable of reaching the level of formal operations provided that the social environment and acquired experience yield the cognitive nourishment and intellectual stimulation necessary for such a construction.

A second possibility offered by Piaget to explain the differences would take into account the diversification of aptitudes with age. This second possibility is not without difficulties, as it means excluding certain categories of normal individuals, even in favorable environments, from the possibility of reaching the formal level of thought. Consistent with this second possibility, it would be hypothesized that if all normal children, by age 15, do not demonstrate formal thought and demonstrate a less general distribution of concrete thought than children from age 7 to 10 years, this could be the result of the diversification of aptitudes with age. If this interpretation is accepted, however, we should have to admit that only individuals with aptitudes for logic, mathematics, and physics would manage to construct the formal structures, whereas those individuals with literary, artistic, and practical aptitudes would be incapable of doing so. It would not then be a problem of retarded development but more simply a growing diversification in individuals with the span of aptitudes increasing progressively with age. Such an interpretation places the fourth level beyond the characterization of a proper stage and describes it as a structural advancement in the direction of specialization.

A third hypothesis suggested by Piaget (and which he accepts as the most probable) allows us to reconcile the concept of stages with the idea of progressively differentiating aptitudes. This hypothesis states that all normal individuals do attain the formal operations stage—if not between the ages of 11 and 15, then in any case between 15 and 20 years—but they reach this stage in different content areas consistent with their aptitudes and specializations; the way in which these formal structures are used, however, is not necessarily the same in all cases.

Based on Piaget's 1972 paper, it seems as though he is saying that (1) there are four distinct cognitive structural levels, (2) all normal people attain the highest level at least by age 20 (instead of between 11 and 15), (3) demonstration of formal operations may differ among individuals according to area of specialization, and (4) formal operations, unlike concrete operations, are free from their concrete content, but this is true only on the condition that for subjects the situations involve equal aptitudes or comparable vital interests. The latter phrase opens the door for continued speculation concerning the role of reality, concrete content, or experience in the cognitive performance of adults.

Traditional Piagetian theory regards the stage of formal operations as a necessary final stage of cognition, characteristic of the years from middle adolescence through adulthood. The necessity ascribed by Piaget to the stage of formal operations, as well as to the earlier three stages, is not initially present in the infant but arises during the developmental process. Piaget (1971) explains this constructed yet unpredetermined necessity in this fashion (p. 9):

> For example, the formal structures become necessary once the child possesses the concrete operations. As soon as he can perform the concrete operations, sooner or later he will begin to coordinate reversibility by inversion with reversibility by reciprocity and hence construct the group of four transformations. Similarly, once he is able to manipulate the classifications, sooner or later he will construct a classification of all the classifications, and thus he will end up by producing the combinatorial, which is a necessary form of formal thought.

Piagetian-Based Research in Adulthood

Some studies based on adolescent samples support the traditional Piagetian position concerning youthful development and maintenance of the formal operations stage. A few studies based on adult samples that support the traditional view also have been reported, but the bulk of the research using adult subjects is at variance with the traditional position that formal operations are necessarily attained in adolescence and are maintained through adulthood.

Studies indicating that formal operations are not necessarily attained or maintained by late adolescence include studies of the performance of college students. Arlin (1975), Elkind (1962), McKinnon and Renner (1971), Papalia (1972), Renner and Stafford (1972), and Wason (1968) all found that a sizable proportion of their subjects failed to meet formal operations criteria.

Research findings based on older adult subjects also contribute to questions about traditional Piagetian theory concerning the necessity of and maintenance of formal operations. Chiappetta (1975) administered Piaget's balance task to 15 K–8 female teachers and found 47 percent performing at the level of formal operations. Coleman (1973) studied 25 women aged 20 to 44, and 25 women aged 45 to 68, as a part of a larger life-span study. Three measures of formal thought were used: conservation of volume, a logical inference test, and a test of combinatorial thought. Both groups exhibited a suitably high percentage of formal operations on conservation of volume, and the younger group demonstrated a high level of formal operational thought on the combinatorial task. Nevertheless, less than 60 percent of the 45-to-68 age group performed formally on the combinatorial task, and only 20 percent of that group achieved a formal score on the logical inference task; 40 percent of the younger group performed formally on the latter task.

Others who report findings that fail to support the traditional Piagetian position concerning formal operations attainment and maintenance include Dulit (1972), Flavell (1963), Goodnow (1962), Graves (1972), Mirza (1975), and Peluffo (1967).

Based on Piaget's premise that severe cultural deprivation, cultural differences, emotional problems, and physical and mental handicaps could delay cognitive development, at least into early adulthood, Sequin (1980) designed an investigation to identify levels of cognitive development among a group of adult basic education students. She based her inquiry on the use of Gray's 1973 test of cognitive development and the California Test of Adult Basic Education.

Gray's "How's Your Logic?" test contains 13 items specifically designed to measure different kinds of logical solutions to problems. Sequin interpreted the results as indicating the subjects' performance on the test to be consistent with classroom performance in the area of comprehension and problem solving, but sometimes at variance with scores on the California Test of Adult Basic Education. She found that none of the students were operating consistently at the level of formal operations; many were functioning at the preoperational level and at the beginning concrete operational level.

On the other hand, support for Piaget's conjectures concerning the necessity and maintenance of formal operations has been recently reported in three investigations. Whitbourne and Weinstock (1979) accept the findings of Rubin (1976) and Tesch, Whitbourne, and Nehrke (1978) as adequate proof that regression in later adulthood to the cognitive level of childhood does not occur. Additional study, including more longitudinal investigations and better controlled research, is required before the question of regression can be fully answered.

In addition to the necessity and maintenance of the stage of formal operations, traditional Piagetian theory has been shown to reflect the belief that formal operations is the final stage of development. Again, there are research findings that differ with the traditional position. Papalia (1972) clearly shows that, within the Piagetian framework, development continues beyond adolescence; in this life-span study of conservation of number, substance, weight, and volume, the subjects in the 55-to-64-year-old group, instead of those in the college-age group, attained the highest overall mean performance level. Mirza (1975) offers perhaps the best example of cognitive attainment beyond the formal operational level as stated by Piaget. Mirza classifies the performances of her subjects, who range in age from 1 to 64 years, into four formal substages, A through D. The performances of her subjects at Substage C are a little better than those reflected in the protocols reported by Inhelder and Piaget (1958) for Stage IIIB, while subjects at Mirza's Substage D are definitely superior to Piaget's Stage IIIB. Mirza compares her protocols with those of Piaget to establish that her subjects' protocols are definitely superior in three respects: (1) her subjects show "a superior ability to organize and generalize their conclusions," (2) they use better procedures to test variables, and (3) they have "better and more comprehensive understanding of the relationship among the various liquids" in the chemicals task. She concluded that cognitive growth continued beyond Stage IIIB, which was identified by Piaget as the culminating stage for cognitive development. See Table 2.1.

Within the last ten years, a number of individuals have proposed the possibility of extending Piaget's stages of cognitive development to include a fifth stage. Noteworthy suggestions have been made by Arlin, Koplowitz, Dulit, and Riegel. Koplowitz's 1978 proposition is the most recent of the three noted here. According to Koplowitz's theorizing, there is a fifth level of cognitive development in the scheme of Piaget, one that he labels "unitary operations." This stage is characterized by conceptualization of reality in a systems framework. It is synergistic and gestaltist in nature as the whole is always greater than the sum of its parts. Metaphorically he relates the concept to Einstein's theory of relativity and family systems. He emphasizes holistic concepts, personal knowledge, and qualitative analysis, following Patton's work (1980).

Arlin (1975) hypothesizes that there is a fifth stage of cognitive develop-

Table 2.1
Summary of the Various Substages of Piaget's Formal Operations Stage

Characteristics	A	B	C	D
Procedure to solve the liquids test	Use of hierarchical procedure but in combination with the system of addition and subtraction of one variable and random attempts.	Mostly used the hierarchical procedure with a minor use of other systems here and there.	Exclusive use of hierarchical procedure with unsystematic random attempts ranging from zero to three.	Exclusive use of hierarchical procedure with complete absence of random trials.
Procedure to solve the pendulum test	Able to hold three variables constant but not all the time. Procedure not systematic.	Able to hold three variables constant to test the fourth one. More systematic. Tested some interactions.	Able to hold three variables constant. Tested each variable by a separate pair of combinations. Tested two to four interactions.	Highly efficient—concise and comprehensive. Tested all variables in five combinations only.
Organizational continuum	Not well organized. Made many repetitions. Sometimes the number of attempts reached up to 50.	Better organization and memory. Number of repetitions decreased. 24 maximum attempts.	Highly organized system. Maximum number of repetitions was five.	Highly organized. No repetitions at all.
Critical observation	Critical observation almost nil. Number of combinations without G ranged from 6 to 13.	Presence of critical observation for various combinations and the directions given by the experimenter.	High degree of critical observation. Volunteered statements about the noticed results.	Very careful observation. Spontaneous statements about critical combinations.
Analysis, synthesis, conclusions	Able to relate information for synthesis but logic still incomplete.	Able to relate even complex data. No erroneous conclusions.	High ability to relate and synthesize information to arrive at conclusions.	Very careful analysis and synthesis. Proved conclusions with supporting data. Made generalizations based on the empirical data.
Exclusion of variables	Unable to exclude all inoperant variables. Generally could not separate the effect of weight and string.	Able to isolate the effect of each variable. Excluded all inoperant ones, not necessarily explicitly.	Isolated the effect of each variable. Excluded all inoperant variables explicitly.	Isolated the effect of each variable. Excluded the inoperant ones explicitly.
Quality of concluding statements	Statement of the conclusions includes irrelevant and untested speculations.	Statements specific to observation but not very organized.	Statements organized and logical. Still not very comprehensive.	Highly organized, logical and comprehensive statements.

Source: Mirza 1975, pp. 74–75.

ment in adulthood, another yet higher formal stage that is problem-finding as opposed to traditional formal operations, which is problem-solving. She administered problem-solving and problem-finding tasks to 60 female college seniors in order to test this hypothesis. Results indicate that the problem-solving stage is a necessary, but not a sufficient, condition for the problem-finding stage. The data supported the primacy of relations and systems questions, which are seen as related to combinatorial thinking and the systematic manipulation of one variable in a set with all other variables held constant. The relations and systems question in turn seems to occur logically prior to implication and transformation questions, which are characteristic of high problem-finders.

Two other researchers make proposals similar to Arlin's: Dulit (1972) and Riegel (1976). Dulit discusses the possibility of alternatives to the single-path theory of development at adolescence, pointing out the need to introduce into the model concepts such as "dropout rate" or branching into parallel tracks. He concludes that two alternate tracks were observed during his study. These are exemplified by (1) the "standard method type," a subject "who failed to function at a full formal level but who tried instead to match the problem at hand to some repertoire of 'standard problems with their standard solution,' " and (2) the "inspirational type," a subject who experienced answers leaping into his or her mind but who could give very little explanation for these answers. Since fully formal subjects in this study tended to exhibit a more convergent style, Dulit suggests a second alternative similar to Arlin's view: "It may well be that the concept of the formal stage itself is much more appropriate and useful as a model for convergent styles of thought." Riegel, like Arlin, proposes a fifth stage that would take into account creative, divergent thought. He labels the stage "dialectic operations" and emphasizes that a person at any developmental level can directly enter a corresponding stage of dialectic operations and, hence, acquire a mature mode of thought. According to Riegel, the most significant developmental changes take place when the individual is in a state of disequilibrium. Consequently, his dialectical interpretation of human development contrasts with Piaget's theory, which emphasizes the plateaus at which equilibrium is achieved. The stage of formal operations according to Riegel's position thus becomes not a stable one but a stage where the possibility for change remains.

Formal operations are not a necessary prerequisite to dialectic maturity according to Riegel. He also expresses new possibilities for intraindividual variation encompassed in his theory. He suggests that the proposed fifth stage of dialectic operations would allow mature thinkers to accept and live with dialectic conflicts and contradictions, viewing these as fundamental properties of thought and creativity, a position that is in opposition to the one that claims that formal operations is a final equilibrium in which conflicts and contradictions are equilibrated. In short, the stated purpose for proposing a fifth stage is "to reintroduce dialecticism into Piaget's theory of cognitive development."

Thibodeau (1980) studied four questions: (1) What are some of the differences and/or similarities in the problem-solving process used by late adolescents, young adults, and middle-aged adults? (2) Does cognitive performance have a relationship to task content? (3) Does cognitive performance have a relationship to age and stage of career development? and (4) Is there a relationship between cognitive development and cognitive style? She reports that the cognitive performance of late adolescents was better than the performance of young and middle-aged adults in her study. The use of formal operations varied among the experimental groups according to content; late adolescents used formal operations more than the young adults and middle-aged adults when solving the equilibrium task, whereas young adults used formal operations more than the other two groups on the nursing analogue task. No relationship between cognitive performance and age and career development was found. Finally, Thibodeau reported that a positive relationship exists between field independence and formal operations, but no relationship was discovered between formal operations and reflective cognitive style. Distinct differences in learning preferences among the three age groups were identified. Table 2.2 provides a detailed summary of differences among the experimental groups.

The focus of this discussion has been on cognitive structure rather than on Piaget. However, Piaget has so influenced the literature concerning cognitive structure that his theory is the dominant one. Consequently, most other theories are contrasted in some way with Piaget's position. The concept of structure is found in the writing of Lewin (Hall and Lindzey 1957) and Rokeach (1960). Others such as Baldwin (1915), Werner (1957), and Cassirer (1957) have addressed theoretical aspects of genetic epistemology and development. Nevertheless, space limitations frequently require authors to limit their discussion to Piaget or to discuss other theoretical positions from a comparative perspective.

MEMORY

Research into the several dimensions of memory is closely related conceptually to learning. The processes of memory and learning are so closely related and interdependent that it is often difficult to determine whether we are concerned with one phenomenon or two. The association is obvious, as one who does not learn has nothing to remember, and without memory there is no evidence of learning. Therefore, the wisdom of separating learning and memory may be questioned; the separation may be unreasonably artificial and even inappropriate. There are, however, some data and theory bases that suggest the independence of each cognitive ability; consequently, memory and learning have been examined independently and together (Botwinick 1967).

Memory is one of five operations in the structure of intellect identified by Guilford (1971). According to his model, there are twenty-four projected memory abilities, twelve of which have been demonstrated by research. Learning ability and memory ability are closely associated processes, and both are included in the act of cognition. However, Guilford has distinguished cognitive ability and memory: Cognitive ability is related to how much an individual knows or can know at a specific time, while memory pertains to how much the individual can remember, given a standard exposure to information.

The memory process has been conceptualized traditionally as occurring in stages. The first stage is the act of receiving an impression, or registration. New information, obtained by the use of the various senses, must be recorded if it is to be available for later use. The second stage in the process is retention,

Table 2.2
Summary of the Differences of Group Responses to Posttest Interview

Response	Late Adolescents	Young Adults	Middle-Aged Adults
Task perceived as easiest	Balance (67%)*	Nursing (67%)	Personal Data (50%)
Ability to perceive commonalities among tasks	No (83%)	No (83%)	Yes (50%)
Effect of diagram on ability to solve balance task	Helpful (83%)	No effect (83%)	Helpful (50%)
Effect of talking out loud while solving problems	No effect (67%)	No effect (67%)	Helpful (100%)
Experiences perceived to help learning	Independence, active participation, concrete examples	Demonstration, methods to save time, explicit expectations, principles vs. facts	Visual presentations, practical information, relaxed atmosphere, working with same level learners, experience valued, planning of own learnings
Experiences perceived to hinder learning	Demonstration, being given answers, lack of positive feedback, dependence	Abstract presentations, too much structure, no input in planning	Being rushed, non-relevant information, condescending approach
Changes in learning with age	More efficient; better organized, better able to perceive relationships, learning is easier	Motivation, commitment, concentration, depth of preparation and self-expectations are increased	Takes more time; need more reinforcement, more relaxed; more fun, more self-directed, better use of experience
Preferred methodologies	Lecture, individual study	Demonstration, small group discussion, group study	Visual presentation, "hands on" experience, 1:1 student-teacher relationship

*Percentages indicate the percentage of the six subjects in each group who gave the indicated responses.

Source: Thibodeau 1980. Reproduced by permission.

which is conceived of as the consolidation of the registered bits of information. As suggested by the term *retention,* the second stage is believed to involve a more or less long-term quality of the input. Studies of the registration process include measurements immediately after learning, while tests of the retention process involve later measurement: short-term versus long-term processes. There is no agreement as to whether the two stages are independent or related.

The third stage of memory is identified by two terms that reflect different processes: recall and recognition. After information has been registered and retained, it may be recalled for use.

The independence of the three stages has been debated in the literature. There is some rather strong opinion concerning the independence of the first two stages, registration and retention. Talland (1965) thought of retention as a separate process that was the effect of registration. Melton (1963) argued that registration and retention are a single process. Botwinick hypothesizes that the stages of registration and retention are independent of the stage of recall and recognition. For example, he suggests that if the recall stage is one that involves scanning, searching, and selecting from among many items of stored information, then it is possible to hypothesize a flaw in that process without similarly hypothesizing a defect in the retention process. Operationally, however, recall is not independent of the first stages. We are informed about registration and retention based upon studies of recall. It is suggested that the inability to recall an experience does not necessarily mean that retention did not take place at a specific test of recall.

Research literature on memory includes two general kinds of studies. One kind of study involves the recall of experiences that occurred prior to the time of the data collection. These studies can include the recall of recent events or of experiences in the more distant past. Memories of the distant past that have been recalled and considered often are referred to as "old memories." Those memories which have not been recalled, or rehearsed only briefly, are called "remote memories." A second type of investigation of memory is based on the recall of information learned at the time of the study. It often includes teaching new material in a systematic and controlled manner and testing for recall afterward. The tests of recall may immediately follow the learning experience or take place much later to study delayed recall.

Studies of memory in adulthood are complicated by an apparent relationship between immediate and delayed recall. There are numerous studies (for example, Schonfield 1967; Schonfield and Robertson 1975; Hulicka and Weiss 1965) that have generated similar data that indicate a decline in immediate recall across the life span, but the results of tests of delayed recall are less clear. Therefore, it is important to guard against an incorrect inference that retention ability declines with age when it may be the acquisition or registration ability that has declined. Age deficits in immediate recall may also be explained by noncognitive factors rather than cognitive ones.

Short-term Memory

Several different approaches are reported in the literature to explain the apparent age-associated deficit in retrieval from short-term memory. Sternberg (1969), for example, has indicated that the recall process is carried out at high speed, in a serial and exhaustive manner. In other words, the memory bank is scanned at a high speed in an orderly and complete manner. Anders, Fozard, and Lillyquist's 1972 results were interpreted as supporting Sternberg's position. However, they attributed age-related differences in retrieval to a slower scanning process associated with the age of their subjects. Based on their interpretation of the results, Anders and his colleagues speculate that the slower retrieval time of older adults may also explain poorer performance on paced tasks, tasks that require constant switching of attention, and tasks that require frequent changes of "set."

Many studies of short-term memory processes have been concerned with estimating storage capacity. A popular experimental design involves the presentation of a series of items in some specified order. Subjects are then requested either to recall the entire series (in order or irrespective of order) or to recall selected parts of the series. Typically little decline with age is reported in studies using this paradigm.

A different approach to the study of short-term memory is concerned with the processes involved in the *organization* of input and output rather than with how much adults of different ages can store. For example, the investigation may be concerned with how adults of different ages transform the stimulus into a system or code that increases registration capacity. The objective in many of these study designs is not limited to comparing absolute levels of encoding performance between old and young persons. Instead, emphasis is on observing and comparing relationships among input-output variables within age groups. In other words, the purpose of the research is to identify and describe patterns within age groups. In a recent study of this kind (Hultsch 1975), subjects were requested to recall and write down forty words from ten categories and to do so under conditions where category names either were or were not provided. Young subjects (mean age 20.24 years) recalled more words than older subjects (mean age 70.25 years). The main concern of the study was not the level of performance; it was the relative degree of improvement noted within age groups according to cued or uncued conditions. The older adults seemed to increase their performance more than young adults when the cues were made available. In Taub's 1975 study based on the visual version of the forward digit span subtest from the Wechsler Adult Intelligence Scale (WAIS), he discovered that his experimental groups did not differ with respect to age or education level.

Other investigators have suggested that memory deficits among older subjects are associated with the failure of older individuals to use a systematic or structured approach to organize their learning. The problem is conceptualized differently, however, by different investigators. McNulty and Caird (1967) have sought to explain it in terms of greater difficulty in getting things into memory storage in the first place. Schonfield (1967) suggests that the problem is one of retrieval from storage. Laurence (1967) employed Schonfield's strategies to examine the relative efficacy of rehearsal and of increasing cues for recall. Tentative conclusions derived from Laurence's study indicate that cues at the time of recall may be more potent than advance cues. Additional study, however, is recommended by Laurence. Glynn and DiVesta's 1977 use of advance organizers indicates that providing a structural outline prior to a reading exercise facilitates reproductive recall of factual material.

The concept of organization is further conceptually divided among theorists into hierarchical and nonhierarchical networks. Anderson (1976) favors a nonhierarchical network concept, whereas Collins and Quillian (1972) propose a hierarchical model. The relative efficacy of the two concepts has yet to be determined; both appear to be associated with improved recall.

Memory Decline

Age-related memory decline is generally revealed more frequently in studies designed to test recall (e.g., essay-type tests) than in studies requiring recognition of stimuli (e.g., multiple-choice tests). These findings have prompted debates concerning whether storage mechanisms are deficient in the elderly adult, or whether information is available but not as readily accessible as in the younger adult. One study (Schonfield and Robertson 1975) reported results that showed a consistent decline with age in recall and no significant decline with age in recognition. Subjects involved in this study were from 20 to 60 years of age. No decline with age was noted for recognition, but a decline with age, of almost 50 percent, was noted on the recall scores. These results were interpreted as indicating that accessibility of stored information and the storage process were impaired by aging. McNulty and Caird (1966) have suggested that the amount of information learned or stored may decrease with age but that procedures designed to measure performance on recognition tasks may not be sufficiently sensitive to note the decline. This argument was based on McNulty's 1965 study, which revealed that only part of the stimulus need be stored to produce correct recognition.

The ability to retain information in immediate-access and short-term memory storage tends to be relatively stable during most of adulthood if the material used in the experiments is meaningful, if the criterion for learning is errorless acquisition of all material, and if the amount of information to be stored is too large for immediate-access memory (Clark and Knowles 1973). When the material is not meaningful and the criterion for acquisition is a fixed number of trials, however, there is a marked decline in retention with age (Smith 1975). There is reason to believe that with advancing age there is an increasing registration deficit.

According to Rees and Botwinick (1972), recall or retrieval of information is greatest when the material is meaningful and when the recall conditions are similar to those under which the original registration occurred. The importance of the recall conditions seems to be greater for older adults; there appears to be some conflict between the processes of responding and storing new information at the same time that one is trying to recall stored information. This kind of situation exists when something stimulates old memories and the subject is temporarily distracted. Over the years, as adults acquire more information associated with larger numbers of topics, there is the possibility of making more cross-references and potential connections between new inputs and existing stored information. Consequently, older adults appear to expand the scope of search required to recall information. Such a process takes more time and may result in greater interference with the new material that is being learned. There is also indication that there is an age trend toward greater caution. As a result, errors in recall by older adults tend to be errors of omission caused by forgetting of items rather than errors of commission.

Most of the tested knowledge of the association between adult memory and age concerns immediate and short-term memory. As reported, the memory process seems to be related to the effectiveness with which the individual organizes and structures stored information. Individuals who organize information on the basis of categorical or associative relationships reveal greater recall abilities for information that is so organized. However, there seems to be a negative relationship between age and the use of organizational processes. Consequently, older adults experience a decline in recall performance. When conditions that maximize the possibility for improved organization are provided, older adults show less of a recall deficit.

For material that is once learned, decline with age in extent of immediate recall from short-term memory is much greater than the decline in recall of old material from long-term memory. Forgetting seems to depend on the strength of the original registration of information and on factors such as disuse and interference. The strength of registration results from frequency, intensity, and importance of exposure and tends to require more time for older adults, according to Knox (1977a).

OTHER FACTORS IN LEARNING ABILITY

It is generally noted that learning ability is a function of many factors. Guilford (1971) has provided an elegant model that distinguishes between operations, such as cognition and memory; products, such as units and transformations; and content, such as figural and behavioral. Both Knox (1977a) and Long (1971), among others, have indicated that other factors such as social, physiological, and personality variables should be considered in models of adult learning performance.

In the last ten years adult educators, gerontologists, and psychologists have shown increasing interest in the association of variables other than age with learning ability. These include physical conditions (for example, health, energy levels, and sensory integrity), personality variables (including interests and motives), and social class.

Physiological Factors

The aging process is associated with a variety of physiological changes in addition to visual and aural ones that may influence learning behavior of adults. Research findings and conclusions concerning some of the more important changes that may be associated with learning behavior are discussed in the following pages.

Problems in studying physiological or biological changes across the age span, according to Eisdorfer and Cohen (1980), are methodological and conceptual. Following Busse (1969), they support a construct that introduces primary and secondary aging. Primary aging is those events and developments that occur simply with the passage of time. Secondary aging includes those events such as disease and trauma, related to longevity, that individuals randomly experience and accumulate with longer life. According to this concept,

biological changes across the life span are related to age and age-disease interactions. Harris (1980) suggests that the practice of comparing older adults
with children should be changed to a practice of comparing older adults with
mature (younger) adults. Maturity is defined as that stage when growth and
development stop.

Thus, even though there is a wealth of information available that reports
health, disease, and illness data for different age groups (for example, that
75.80 percent of all persons 65 years of age and older have had at least one
chronic disease and that 47 percent of older Americans report some limitation
in their daily activities), the practical and theoretical implications for adult
intellectual functioning are unclear. Furthermore, the association of the data
to program development, recruitment for education, and instruction remains
vague, except for the obvious overrepresentation of individuals suffering from
illness and its related effects among older samples. This is one of those areas
referred to in Chapter 1 that will require basic research from biologists and
individuals with similar appropriate education while the applied research is
pursued by adult educators and related specialists.

Health and Physical Condition

Wilkie and Eisdorfer (1971) provide one of the better investigations concerning the relationship between health and cognitive change across time.
According to their study, elevated diastolic blood pressure rather than age was
identified as a factor in the intellectual decline of a group of older subjects first
tested at ages 60–69 and then studied over a ten-year period using the Wechsler Adult Intelligence Scale (WAIS). The subjects showed no decline in intellectual performance at least through the eighth decade of life if they had
normal or slightly elevated diastolic blood pressure.

The complete association between physical condition and intellectual
functioning has not been fully explicated. The concept of crystallized and fluid
intelligence as proposed by Cattell sheds some light on the possible relationship between physiological functioning and learning ability. While debate
rages on the magnitude and direction of intellectual ability changes across the
life span, no such debate characterizes the literature on physiological change.

Response and Reaction Time

The evidence that psychomotor responses such as handwriting and auto-
mobile driving skills slow with age is overwhelming. The gradual diminution
of response time does not seem to be readily discernible until about age forty.
After forty, increasing psychomotor slowness is often an important factor in
explaining individual performance. Much of the difference in performance
between young adults and older adults on timed intelligence tests that require
sharp perception and complex and speedy decisions has been explained by
slowed psychomotor performance of older people.

Response time as measured in most of the basic research on psychomotor
performance involves one of two kinds of activities: those that involve simple
response time—a measure of the time it takes a subject to respond to the onset
of a simple stimulus such as throwing a switch on a given signal; and those
that involve choice response time or disjunctive response time—a measure of
the time it requires the subject to make a decision about how to respond to the

stimulus. Evidence in the literature supports the idea that there is relatively little difference between healthy older people and young subjects on simple response time. There are, however, observable increases in simple response time by middle age for each of the following conditions: (Elias, Elias, and Elias 1977):

1. A choice that requires the individual to withhold a response
2. A situation that requires the individual to make one response and withhold another
3. A task that involves a series of responses
4. A situation that requires the individual to correctly match one stimulus to another in order to make the right response.

The more complex test situations emphasize differences between young adults and middle-aged adults. Differences are most significant when there is a need to make a complex decision in a rapid manner.

Two classic types of experiments on psychomotor performance are digit and word copying exercises and execution of unfamiliar tasks. In experiments of both types, older subjects usually do less well than younger subjects. For example, Birren and Botwinick (1951) reported that between the ages of twenty and sixty there is a 97 percent increase in the time required for a task like copying.

In my 1972 book, I considered the two possible sources of the slowing of psychomotor responses with age. One of these is the muscular movements themselves, but the more likely source is the central nervous system. Interpretation of experimental research data (Welford 1951) suggests that the central processes that guide hand movements, for example, to a small target are a more serious source of limitation than the actual muscular movements. Furthermore, it appears that when accuracy is required, any reduction of speed in the actual movements can be accounted for by the effect of control mechanisms.

Two interesting lines of experimental activity are currently progressing in the study of response time. The first of these is focusing on the slowing of the alpha rhythm with age. Alpha rhythm is the pattern of regular brainwaves present during relaxation; it has a frequency of 9 to 12 cycles per second. A positive association has been found between both simple and choice response times and the frequency of the alpha rhythm. Experiments that control for frequency of the alpha rhythm have reported nonsignificant associations between age and response time (Stevens-Long 1979).

A normal young person has an alpha rhythm frequency of about 8 to 13 cycles per second, with the mean falling in the range of 10.2 to 10.5 cycles per second. In contrast, at age seventy, the mean alpha rhythm for a group of experimental subjects may be as low as 8.0 to 9.7 cycles per second. The importance of the data is obvious if it is true, as Stevens-Long reports, that information can be processed only during a specific part of the alpha cycle and that the reduction in cycles per second by older individuals requires a longer time to fit the stimulus with the appropriate phase of the alpha cycle.

Woodruff's 1972 research seems to confirm the nature of the problem. In her experiment, older subjects learned to increase alpha rhythm through biofeedback procedures. Faster response time was positively associated with increases in alpha. The increase in response time did not, however, completely compensate for the slowness of older people. Factors other than alpha frequency must also be influencing response time. Marsh and Thompson (1977) believe this to be so as they suggest that age-related changes in sensory input might contribute to changes in response time in such a way that the relationship between brainwaves and response time is more important for older people. Furthermore, Woodruff's study does not confirm that a reduction in alpha causes an incremental reduction in the speed of response time, i.e., a causal relationship has not been demonstrated. Other explanations include changes in the vascular system that are simultaneously associated with slowed alpha and slowed response time.

A second line of inquiry focuses on the possibility of "neural noise" that interferes in the sensory reception and cognition of older people. Neural noise is the result of an increasing random activity of the neurons. It is assumed, according to this experimental logic, that random activity of the neurons in the brain increases with age and consequently causes a reduction in the strength of sensory signals that are received. Furthermore, the theory suggests that stimulation may produce longer aftereffects with age, setting up a kind of chain reaction that begins to interfere with the cognitive processes associated with each succeeding stimulation. This part of the theory is based on the results of studies of perceptual masking that seem to support the view that the duration of the aftereffects increases with age.

Perceptual masking occurs when a second stimulus, known to "erase" the perception of the first visual stimulus, is presented to a subject. Studies of perceptual masking have generated data that support the idea that older subjects require more time to recover the first figure. Furthermore, the neural noise theory also considers the possibility that older people may take more time to monitor incoming signals before they respond. It is also possible that older people tend to fix on a given stimulus, i.e., they tend not to be able or willing to stop monitoring previous stimuli and responses before moving on to the next task. It is likely that increased monitoring may be a form of cautiousness that may be invoked to compensate for increased neural noise and reduced signal strength.

The general view of the physical condition of the aging individual is one of diminishing sensory integrity. The average older individual is perceived as being at a disadvantage when contrasted with the average younger individual on vision, hearing, and response time. These variables are important in timed tests of performance.

Carpenter (1971) reported the results of an interesting investigation designed to determine the association between age and the information processing capacity of adults. Based on the assumption that physiological changes associated with aging contribute to the decline in performance of adults in areas such as reaction time, card sorting tasks, and learning activities, he planned his study on a visual information processing model. In most of his tests a decline in information processing was observed with advancing age; the decline was statistically significant in some. However, the study also confirmed the ability of adults above age fifty to make precise judgments, even under the stress of severe testing conditions.

Personality Variables

Personality is a complex topic and includes a number of concepts such as feelings, attitudes, and interests. There is little question concerning the association between personality and learning performance. An individual's personality can greatly influence the approach that he or she takes to execute a learning task. Alienation, hopelessness, and defensiveness are identified as obstacles to risk-taking associated with learning something new (Knox 1977a).

Scholars and practitioners interested in the education of adults have identified several personality variables that are believed to be associated with the intellectual performance of adults.

Monge and Gardner (1976) noted that the extent to which older adults are either positively inclined or negatively oriented toward new learning experiences is more important, in a practical sense, than the specific abilities that they bring to a learning situation. Several important factors that they identified as contributing to the attitude toward learning for different age groups were achievement motivation, learning apprehension (anxiety), life-style, and dogmatism. Anxiety is discussed in a later chapter; dogmatism is briefly mentioned here as an example of the implications that personality variables carry in a learning situation.

Most of the studies reviewed for this section indicate that higher dogmatism scores are associated with increasing age, that increased rigidity is associated with older age, and that cautiousness is associated with aging. The explanations for these findings, however, are quite wide ranging, and the practical implications of the observed phenomena are unclear. There is reason to believe that dogmatism and increasing rigidity may interfere with problem solving. Similarly, there are suggestions that while older adults may manifest accuracy in untimed test situations, the results indicate a loss of competency (ability to perform the specified task). A related negative interpretation suggests that cautiousness is a reflection of declining competency.

The conceptual complexity of dogmatism, rigidity, and cautiousness as personality variables requires additional specification and explications for theoretical purposes. Practical application of the findings is not overly complex; however, it should be remembered that theoretical clarification may modify the practical applications in the future.

Social Class and Life-style

Social class is a factor that requires consideration when discussing adult learning ability. Social class subsumes a number of other variables such as educational opportunity, home environment, cultural experiences, diet, and health care. Education has been selected from among the social class variables and as mentioned previously, Blum and Jarvik (1974) established a positive association between education and intellectual functioning. In fact, education is believed to be more important than age (Fozard and Nuttall 1971).

Because of the many variables that are included in definitions of social class, few studies have been designed to classify developmental trends by detailed social class level. Two broad levels of social class are usually used in adult education studies in the Western industrialized nations: white collar and blue collar. The white collar division of social class includes adults with at least two years of college or individuals in the top three of seven levels of occupational prestige. Many individuals in this level occupy the upper income ranges. In contrast, the blue collar level of social class often includes the remaining adults who have lower levels of education, income, and occupational prestige. Examples of such studies cited in this volume are Bergsten's Nordic work, Haldane's in Great Britain, Robinson's research in Wisconsin, and London's work in California.

Comparisons between the two major social classes are further complicated by education, geographic mobility, mass media, and other cultural changes. Knox issues words of caution to those attempting to interpret studies of social class comparisons. Moderate changes across a few years become cumulative and often have much greater impact than one might expect. For example, the educational level of Americans of all social classes has generally increased since 1900. More blue collar family members thus have higher levels of education than did their ancestors.

An increasing accumulation of research concerning social class and life-styles indicates a strong relationship of educational level with both variables. Education as noted above is one of the key criteria for social class specification; higher levels of education are associated with higher social class. Education also seems to be associated with active and passive life-styles. Consequently, a passive life-style is related to low educational achievement and is perceived to be an important obstacle to continuing education (London and Wenkert 1969).

The difficulty of attributing differences between social classes concerning adult education preferences is not always a simple one. For example, Buttedahl and Verner's 1965 study generates findings that complicate conclusions that social class and institutional preferences for educational activities are related.

Buttedahl and Verner report different social characteristics among participants in adult education programs using two different methods of instruction. It is noted that other researchers have found that different institutions involve different kinds of people in continuing education; university programs attract a higher status participant than public school programs, for example. Three variables in comparative participation studies are discussed: differences in the sponsoring institution, differences in instructional method, and differences in content areas. Buttedahl and Verner chose to study methodology; the authors assume that differences among participants might result from choice of method rather than of content or of institution.

The proposition of a life-style association with social class is generally supported by the findings of Robson, Robinson, and myself cited in Chapter 4, concerned with participation. Robson's and Robinson's studies were based on a working class population, while my own investigation focused on a white-collar technical community.

OBSERVATIONS

It was natural that the increasing academic interest in the education of adults that developed in the 1920s in the United States would be accompanied by a parallel interest in questions about the adult's ability to learn. A number of scholars had used adult subjects in a variety of learning experiments between 1890 and 1930. However, E. L. Thorndike's status as a psychologist with an international reputation gave legitimacy to research concerning adult learning ability. Thus, Thorndike's investigations of learning rate were favorably received by an academic system that was beginning to extend educational services to adults. Others such as Lorge and Sorenson gave additional credence to Thorndike's general conclusions. Actually, Lorge believed that Thorndike's findings *underestimated* the adult's power to learn by the emphasis on learning *rate.*

The debate was thus joined with three different views being represented: (1) that the learning ability of adults declines significantly with advancing age, (2) that adult learning ability (rate) declines slowly with advancing age, and (3) that adult learning ability (power) does not decline significantly with age. Other arguments include other concerns with design. Research designs should not be planned to examine rate, according to Lorge. Others indicated that cross-sectional designs have low external validity and that cultural change, including rising educational levels, explained much of the performance difference between younger and older subjects. Those who supported cross-sectional designs criticized the few longitudinal designs for low internal validity and said that higher performance in retest experience was the consequence of the survival of the most able subjects.

The debate, however, has almost been shut off with the dominant view favoring the conclusion that ability to learn is not negatively associated with aging. The position favors a search for other variables that may be more strongly associated with learning than age. Consequently, other explanations and constructs have emerged to attract the attention of psychologists and educators of adults. Two such concepts are crystallized and fluid intelligence and cognitive style. Other variables in adult learning ability that have been the topic of research include health and physiological changes in hearing and vision, cognitive development, personality characteristics, and social class.

Adult educators have deferred to the psychologists for basic theoretical research in most of the above areas. Dogmatism, cognitive development, and social class have each received the limited attention of a few adult educators. I would judge the research in each of the identified areas to be of acceptable quality. As in most research, however, the findings of these studies must be considered within appropriate limitations. For example, most studies of dogmatism and cognitive development conducted by adult educators have been cross-sectional. Hence, findings of any significant relationships between age and either of the variables are open to challenge by alternative hypotheses. For example, a positive relationship between age and dogmatism must be explained in a manner that logically considers findings of a negative association between educational achievement level and dogmatism. Given the cultural reality of regularly increasing educational achievement levels across the last fifty years, is the purported relationship explained by age or educational differences?

Memory, generally recognized as being an integral element in learning, and its relationship to learning seem to present a conceptual challenge. Yet there is a need, from a theoretical research perspective, to separate memory out for the purposes of investigation and analysis. Some provocative applied work that has direct implications for academic or structured learning ability is also in progress. Findings concerning the use of organizational structures for improving reproductive and productive memory are particularly appropriate for consideration by educators of adults.

Some of the problems of conceptualizing and specifying criteria for detailed comparisons among social classes have already been mentioned. The difficulties encountered by investigators of adult learning ability are not imaginary. A solution to the conceptual and design problems, however, may be well worth continuing efforts. Increasing numbers of adult learners, studying more and engaging in educational activities throughout life, represent adequate justification for educators of adults to continue to build upon the research foundations reported here.

NOTES

1. Horn and Donaldson (1976) take a more conservative position than Baltes and Schaie concerning the relationship between age and ability.

2. Inhelder and Piaget (1958) report a number of different scientific approaches to measuring and describing the activities of subjects who have been examined in studies of cognitive structure. The pendulum test consists of providing the subject with a stand and a horizontal bar to which strings of different lengths may be tied and a variety of weights that may be affixed to the lower ends of the strings. The subject is asked to determine which variable contributes to the frequency of the oscillation of the pendulum: the length of the string, the weight used, the amplitude (point of release), or the force of the release.

3 · Anatomical and Chemical Factors in Learning and Memory

MOST OF THE TRADITIONAL RESEARCH and consequent application of the results of investigations into learning abilities and processes of interest to educators of adults has focused on psychological and personological areas. Increasingly, however, there seems to be a growing awareness of, and sensitivity to, the physiological basis of the psychological and intellectual processes that are associated with, or result in, learning. The nature and foci of these new research thrusts are quite varied, but the work generally examines neurophysiological structures and processes, electrochemical activity, and hormonal and enzymatic properties of the human organism. The application of research findings in some of these areas seems to be years in the future, as scholars and practitioners strive to identify educational implications of the research.

The challenge of deriving implications for educational practice from the new wave of neurobiological studies as well as additional inquiries into other physiological and biological topics is further compounded by the esoteric nature of the research and the continuing dependence upon animals for laboratory subjects. There is increasing justification, however, for educators of adults to become acquainted with this area of research.

More and more, the relationship between mind and brain is becoming apparent. It is likely that brain research is still in its infancy—that what now is perceived to be quite advanced, complex, and sophisticated research will, within the very near future, be criticized for being overly simplistic. Because of the distinctiveness of this research area and the difficulty of drawing implications for education, this chapter differs in format from the others. The bulk of the discussion is devoted to a series of reports, some brief and others longer, of some research in the physiological area that may serve as foundations for future investigations that may have clearer potential for application in the education of adults. Note that this area of research was in such an embryonic stage that it was ignored when Brunner and his associates issued their book on adult education research in 1959.

Neurobiological research is expanding rapidly as increasingly sophisticated machinery and laboratory procedures are being developed. Advances in basic support areas such as microphotography, slide staining processes, and computer technology have contributed to the ability of the neurobiologist to collect, examine, and interpret data that were beyond reach just a decade or so ago. Ability to measure and record the electrical current generated within the brain as that organ performs its many complex tasks is an important achievement that provides an additional way for neurobiologists to pursue an ever expanding number of important research questions.

Since the measurement and interpretation of electrical patterns is one of the basic processes common to much of the current brain research, a comment on the procedure should be informative and helpful. The basic unit of measurement in many studies is referred to as evoked potential (EP). In using an electroencephalograph (EEG), the researcher connects a number of electrodes to the scalp of a subject who is purposely and selectively stimulated. Consequently, a measure of the brain's electrical response (EP) is available.

EPs evoked by the usual laboratory stimuli are of low amplitude compared with that of the alpha rhythm, which is often as large as 100 microvolts. Minicomputers and analysis of the "shape" of the electrical wave frequently reveal important information to the investigator.

Another more or less common procedure used by neurobiologists in an effort to unravel secrets of brain functions is based on brain cell analysis. The brain contains more than 20 billion neurons that are believed to generate all basic human drives. These cells are structurally interrelated by a complicated latice composed of numerous delicate axons. Through a series of electrochemical processes, messages are transmitted from distant nerve endings to these neurons, which in turn communicate among themselves. It is believed that the electrical firing of the neurons—and, hence, the messages transmitted—are susceptible to certain chemicals. Consequently, the relative abundance of selected enzymes and hormones is hypothesized to be associated with, if not the cause of, various behaviors. For example, the absence of a chemical identified as dopamine has been associated with symptoms of Parkinson's disease, and its presence in large quantities seems to be associated with some of the characteristic behaviors of schizophrenics.

Research related to the physiology and functions of the brain is on the forefront of new developments that may have significant implications for the practice of adult education. Much of the research on the topic of adult learning has heretofore addressed the psychological dimensions of learning. There are educators of adults, such as Even (1978), who believe that the significant future developments in learning theory may be in physiologically based brain research. As is the case with many other ideas and concepts, research and implications of the theories concerning brain hemispheres seem to pose a certain risk to educators. A "safe" conservative position somewhere between rejection of the area and an overenthusiastic blind embrace is called for. An extensive body of research on the topic is now available, and selected works are discussed in this chapter.

Topics that represent a dimension of learning infrequently reported by students of adult education but which are perceived to foreshadow areas of research that may soon pose new and different challenges to educators of adults are treated in the following pages. These topics include hemispheric lateralization, neurological sex differences, and chemicals and brain activity.

HEMISPHERIC LATERALIZATION

Theoretical developments and selected research in hemispheric lateralization are discussed below.

Theoretical Developments

Research and theory concerning the brain and lateralization are in a somewhat unstable state. It is not unusual for positions taken just a few years earlier to be repudiated by scholars. For example, in the process of developing this chapter, permission to quote material was in one instance refused because "of distortions that right/left hemisphere research has experienced . . . since we wrote [the article]." In confidential correspondence, one researcher in the area said, ". . . most educators have created a conceptual mountain out of a research molehill."

The concept or theory of "two" brains, i.e., the left and right hemispheres, suggests that they embody two modes of consciousness: the complementary working of the intellect and the intuition (Ornstein 1976). The physiological basis of a theoretical explanation of the integration of intellect and intuition attracts the interest of educators who are naturally concerned about ways to improve learner achievement. The importance of the recent research by neurophysiologists, psychologists, and neurologists on the brain seems to be derived from the identification of various characteristics that have been identified with one hemisphere of the brain or the other. For example, researchers believe that the left hemisphere of the brain operates on words and clearly defined symbols such as chemical and mathematical signs. It is described as being active, calculating, reasoning, and predominantly sequential and analytic in its functioning. The right hemisphere of the brain operates on pictures, is spatially oriented, perceives patterns as a whole, and operates in an intuitive, emotional, and receptive mode.

Additional information concerning the biological, physiological, and neurophysiological functions of the brain may be generated by the study of the nervous system. Kimura (1973) demonstrated that each cerebral hemisphere receives information primarily from the opposite half of the body. In vision, the eye is split in input by the sides of the brain; the auditory system, however, is less crossed in that each brain half receives input from both ears, but the crossed connections are stronger than the uncrossed ones. The tactual and motor systems are almost completely crossed, with sensations from the left half of the body and movement of the left half of the body served primarily by the right hemisphere and vice versa. The two hemispheres are themselves interconnected by nerve pathways, the largest of which is the corpus callosum. The left brain is believed to play a dominant role in speech, while the right hemisphere's functions are only now emerging, according to Kimura—but one identified function is perception of melody.

Even (1978) recommends *The Human Brain* (Wittrock et al. 1977) as a useful reference. The first part contains three new articles and a number of reprints from *UCLA Educator*. The new articles examine neuroscientific research. Teyler (1977) emphasizes the brain structures and functions, including arousal, motivation, learning, and memory as related to the interests of educators. Beatty (1977) discusses the cognitive functions and processes of the brain, specifically consciousness, perception, sleep, dreaming, and decision making. Gazzaniga (1977), a pioneer in research on split brains, summarizes the recent findings about different processes of the two hemispheres. Other chapters describe sensory data, speech production, brain processes, eye movement, and cognitive styles. Bogen (1977) deals with educational implications, mainly discussing delivery systems.

Pribram (1969) examines the neurophysiology of remembering. His research parallels the interests of Wittrock concerning the generative process of memory. Both agree that information must move from the frontal lobe to the cerebellum to be retained for discussion and application of new knowledge.

There are some who approach the topic gingerly. Roberts agrees that right/left differences do appear, but in his opinion they are small compared with the similarities. Current research thus seems to suggest that the knowledge of the hemispheric differences could help us to identify abilities that should be developed. Unfortunately, to overemphasize the hemispheric *differences* seems to be important. Some believe that both hemispheres are involved in most tasks and that dominance is a matter of degree.

A different approach to right/left brain theorizing and research seems to be gaining in prominence. This approach examines the relationship between the two hemispheres and consciousness. Roberts (1981) suggests that the left hemisphere is more often in a conscious state than is the right hemisphere and that a challenge to education is one of raising the consciousness level of the right hemisphere. He says (p. 86),

> when considering right hemisphere development and consciousness education, an important distinction must be made. Access to "right hemisphere" abilities can be in our ordinary state or can be via switching state of consciousness. In fact, fascinating research questions arise if we look at right/left hemisphere studies from a consciousness perspective. How do right/left abilities vary from state to state? Are the differences we've found so far just those of our ordinary state? Will other hemispheric differences and similarities emerge as we study other states of consciousness?

We should all be aware of the above reservations concerning right/left brain research when reading the various studies reported in the area—including the following illustrative work.

Selected Research

Kinsbourne (1979) suggests that the asymmetrical development of the human brain is associated with specific human behaviors that derive significant advantages from the phenomenon. For example, he notes that language and other sequential skills such as reading or lighting a match are usually controlled by the left hemisphere. The right hemisphere directs the process of grasping spatial relationships and material that must be dealt with simultaneously, such as sketching or reading a map. While the evidence that brain lateralization has adaptive advantages is modest, there is strong evidence that it is at least fortuitous.

Observations reveal that new babies with right-handed parents turn more or less spontaneously to the right more often than to the left, and when shown equally attractive objects from both sides, they turn to the right. Later, the same infants reach and grasp objects with their right hand, a useful specialization that seems to encourage them to practice skills and concentration that increases their learning more than if they randomly used either hand.[1] It is suggested that the localization of speech in the left hemisphere may be in some way associated with the use of the right hand for grasping objects. The association is implied by the action by which the baby simultaneously points to and names (after a certain age) an object. Consequently, it is speculated that speech specialization is given the same hemisphere control over the coordinated behavior of pointing and naming. Kinsbourne notes that while the idea of left hemispheric specialization for speech derived from the bias for right-handedness is speculation, it is a fact that speaking and orienting in space are interactive forms of behavior. Most people seem to turn their eyes and heads spontaneously to the right when they are in deep thought.

Right hand and voice coordination seems to be best when playing a piano. The right hand is perceived as a better partner to the voice, with each making fewer mistakes than when the left hand is used. Conversely, Kinsbourne observes, when the hand and voice perform separate tasks—for example, playing a melody with one hand while humming a different tune—the voice and left hand seem to be a more accurate combination. The difference is explained by what Kinsbourne calls the functional-cerebral-distance principle. According to this principle, two control centers in the brain working together on a task function best if they are closely interconnected. But if the control centers are simultaneously required to generate different, independent actions, the task is performed better if the centers involved are poorly connected.

Additional evidence of the complexity of the communication between the two brain hemispheres and the apparent specialization that characterizes each can be provided by a simple activity. Buchsbaum (1979) suggests that you place your left hand in your pocket or purse and then, without looking, make a list of what you find using your right hand. This activity requires information to be transmitted from your left hand to the right hemisphere, and since vocabulary and writing skills (for most people) are located in the left hemisphere, the information must then go to the left hemisphere for the assignment of names and listing.

Buchsbaum has used EP-based research to further examine the question of how the two hemispheres communicate with each other. Accordingly, he divided the visual field, right and left, and presented subjects with two kinds of information, words and dots. (Remember that the right visual field involves the left hemisphere—language, logic, etc.—and the left visual field involves the right hemisphere—spatial relationships, melody, etc.) Hence the three-letter words involved the left hemisphere, while the dots were grist for processing by the right.

In the study conducted by Buchsbaum, both kinds of information were presented to each visual field separately. Only the left hemisphere produced clearly different EPs for words and dots; the right hemisphere failed to indicate that it was aware of any difference between them.

In another investigation, Buchsbaum further confirmed that the right side response (left hemisphere) is faster than the left. In the study, subjects were first requested to count flashes presented to either their left or right visual fields, and then to ignore the flashes as best as they could while doing mental arithmetic problems. (EPs are larger when people are concentrating on something than when they are dividing their attention.) Once again the difference in the size of the EPs was greater when the stimuli came from the right side (to the left hemisphere).

Based on these studies, Buchsbaum seems to have confirmed some of the observations of Kinsbourne cited earlier as well as provided additional evidence of the differential processing of information according to brain hemispheres. His data may contribute further to better understanding of the communication system between the hemispheres.

Martindale (1975), focusing on alpha wave analyses in his investigation of creative people, discovered, like Buchsbaum, differential electrical activity in the two hemispheres. He notes that it is believed that the right hemisphere operates in a primary-process manner, whereas the left hemisphere is primarily responsible for logical, intellectual thought. His data on alpha wave activity during relaxation revealed that medium-creative people had more alpha (greater relaxation) and less arousal in the right hemisphere than in the left one. He interpreted the data to suggest that medium-creative people have more secondary process (left hemispheric arousal) than primary process (right arousal). Highly creative people had about the same amount of alpha in both hemispheres, a higher level than that of low-creative people. Furthermore, he believes that even though hemispheric differences may play a role in creative thought, alpha patterns count for more.

NEUROLOGICAL SEX DIFFERENCES

The suggestion that biological and physiological differences (other than the obvious physical differences) exist between males and females is subject to social/political debate. The debate frequently centers on the nature vs. nurture controversy. While we shall not resolve the issue, or even attempt to do so, here, it seems prudent to report some of the research that appears to support the premise that basic biological differences, other than those noted above, may distinctively characterize the male and female human.

Carter and Greenough (1979) believe that neuroscientists have recently discovered firm evidence that male and female brains, in lower animals and possibly in human beings, are anatomically different. They believe that the parts of the brain that control specific behavior, especially behavior related to the sexuality of the individual, are different in males and females. For example, tests on laboratory animals reveal differences in neuronal "wiring" that seem to arise, in part, from the effect of male and female hormones on the developing brain.

Sex hormones have been identified by endocrinological studies as important elements in the determination of differences in male-female sexual structures, including the external reproductive organs. Anatomical studies, complementing the endocrinological investigations, seem to provide adequate evidence that certain areas of the brain must function at a certain minimum level for an organism to produce eggs or sperm and to engage in appropriate sexual behavior. For example, damage to a small point near the base of the brain known as the preoptic-suprachiasmatic area (POA-SC) can terminate egg production in the female rat. Damage to the same region of the brain of a male rat does not prevent sperm production, but it does reduce sex drive.

Experiments thus suggest that the POA-SC area may function differently in the two sexes. Carter and Greenough speculate that sex disparities in the POA-SC region and possibly other areas may be a part of the mechanism that controls essential reproductive events.

Additional studies cited by Carter and Greenough also indicate that there may be differences in the number of certain types of synapses between nerve cells in the preoptic area of rat brains according to sex. Furthermore, it is reported that the female pattern of synapses could be altered to more closely resemble the male pattern if the female were given male sex hormones during the first few days of life. Conversely, a male rat's synapse pattern would more closely approximate a female pattern if he had been castrated early, thereby removing the source of his male sex hormones.

Carter and Greenough report that the dendrites located in the POA-SC area of hamsters are clustered in different locations according to sex. These differences indicate that the dendrites connect differently with nerve cells in other areas of the brains of males and females. The investigators believe that the growth of the cells in the hamster's brain is influenced by the release of sex hormones at a critical period early in the animal's life. They report other work to support their position such as that of an investigator who included the placement of living slices of brain tissue from young mice in a special medium. In those experiments in which the brain tissue was placed in a medium containing sex hormones, the hormones produced dramatic growth in nerve cells from the POA-SC area.

Investigations such as these have been limited to such animals as rats and hamsters. It is not yet known whether the physical differences discovered in the animals also exist in men and women. Painstaking and rigorous studies of human brain tissue are required before conclusions can be drawn. Those studies, for ethical and technical reasons, have not yet been done.

CHEMICALS AND BRAIN FUNCTIONS

Information concerning the association between certain chemical substances and brain functions as manifested in memory continues to accumulate. The potential of chemical use in learning has generated a number of popular news articles over the years—articles with such leads as "Teachers May Turn Into Pill Pushers" and "Pills May Put Things Under Hats." Other reports have also appeared outside the research journals in places like the *Phi Delta Kappan* and *Saturday Review*. In December 1979, Hansl and Hansl indicated that the "smart pill" may now be only a short testing period away.

Historically, the use of drugs in mind expansion functions is not a new concept. Drugs have been taken by many people through the years for the purposes of increased awareness. The Indians of the Southwestern United States used the popular peyote button to increase awareness during their religious ceremonies.

Drugs that have been reported as potential aids to learning and memory include the following: ribonucleic acid, pemoline and magnesium hydroxide, physostigmine, strychnine, picrotoxin, metrazol, deoxyribonucleic acid, and a compound identified as PRL-8-53. Some chemicals that seem to interfere with learning and memory include alcohol, atropine, puromycin, lead, marijuana, and scopolamine. Some of the studies of the effects of the above chemical elements and compounds have been conducted with adults, children, goldfish, and rats.

Hansl and Hansl report that after use of PRL-8-53, subjects improved their retention of nonsense syllables by 80 percent. Such intellectual functional characteristics as perception, short-term memory, long-term memory, correlation, and retrieval appeared to be chemically controlled by their particular agonist-receptor systems within the neuronal latticework. Consequently, it is logical to believe that one or more of these functions may be augmented or suppressed by chemical means through amplifying or inhibiting chemical signals that control the respective neuronal pathways. For example, retrieval of information from long-term memory seems to be mediated by acetylcholine and the cholinergic system. The system—and therefore memory—seems to be inhibited by atropine or scopolamine, while memory can be improved through increasing the cholinergic system by a drug such as physostigmine.

Hansl and Hansl offer PRL-8-53 as a substitute for physostigmine, which has been successfully used with humans suffering from Alzheimer's disease. PRL-8-53, however, does not have the negative side effects associated with physostigmine and is considered to be a safe, useful drug for boosting the cholinergic system to improve recall from a preexisting information pool.

Studies by Plotnikoff (1966) indicate that pemoline and magnesium hydroxide enhances memory in rats. His work also provides support for the consolidation theory, which is based on the proposition that a certain amount of time is required for a learned response to become "consolidated" (part of permanent memory) and that treatment with electroshock or drugs will influence the process. Plotnikoff does not establish a specific causal relationship, but it is possible that the enhancement of nucleic acid synthesis and/or protein synthesis by magnesium pemoline contributes to the consolidation of avoidance responses as noted in the experiments.

The effects of the two aforementioned drugs have been noted time and time again, but perhaps their fullest explanation and those of learning and memory extension theories is best explained by a theory that Krech (1968) has offered. His concept is that learning is a two-stage process: a short and long sequence that includes immediately after every learning trial—after every experience—a short-lived electrochemical process that is established in the brain. The process, according to the assumption, is the physiological mechanism that carries the short-term electrochemical activity that triggers a second series of events in the brain. The second process is chemical in nature and involves, primarily, the production of new proteins and the induction of higher enzymatic activity levels in the brain cells. This process is more enduring and serves as the physiological substrate of our long-term memory.

Other studies, however, provide some disturbing information concerning the potential impact of environmental insults on human beings. Fogel (1980) reports on his work with children in Philadelphia to ascertain the effect of lead upon intelligence. Using an ingenious procedure to measure accumulated lead in the dentine of deciduous teeth, Fogel and his colleagues collected the baby teeth from nearly 200 inner-city children. When the lead levels, ascertained through atomic absorption spectroscopy, were compared with intelligence scores, the researchers discovered that children with the lowest lead levels in their teeth had a mean IQ of 97, while those with the highest levels averaged a score of 80. The boys' performance was noted as being more seriously affected than the performance of the girls, but the general trend regardless of sex was toward poorer performance as lead levels increased.

Fogel's work reveals that chemicals can be absorbed into the human biological system and eventually find their way into the brain. Earlier in this section, a number of drugs that have properties that will inhibit or enhance brain activity were identified. Prior to the development of the contemporary drug culture, folklore proclaimed that certain nutrients influence the workings of the brain—for example, that carrots improve vision and that fish is "brain food." Observations of this kind are being removed from the area of mythology to reality through continuing research. Experiments demonstrate that eating certain foods can raise the levels of brain neurotransmitters—the chemicals that carry messages between the brain cells.

Experiments have produced results that indicate foods rich in lecithin, tryptophan, and tyrosine can have beneficial results. Lecithin, contained in soybeans, eggs, and liver, can raise the amount of choline in the blood and, subsequently, acetylcholine in the brain. This chemical has been identified as being involved in memory, sleep disturbance, REM sleep, and motor coordination. Tryptophan is an amino acid, occurring in small amounts in all protein foods, which can increase the amount of serotonin in the brain. Serotonin is a transmitter associated with inducing sleep, easing pain, and boosting the effect of some antidepressant drugs. Tyrosine is another amino acid found in protein foods; it can enhance the formation of dopamine and norepinephrine in the brain. Both these chemicals are associated with motor coordination, the secretion of certain hormones, and the perception of reality.

The body chemistry and the relationships between some of the chemical substances, however, are extremely complex. It is not always possible just to identify a food that contains a desirable nutrient and to eat that food to accomplish a specific goal such as improved memory. For example, since serotonin is identified with drowsiness, it may be incorrectly assumed that to go to sleep more readily one must eat foods rich in tryptophan. The assumption is incorrect because other amino acids are more abundant in protein foods; some of these can beat tryptophan to the brain's capillaries and prevent tryptophan's absorption and conversion to serotonin. In this instance, a flanking strategy is required to increase the brain's supply of serotonin. The individual should eat a high-carbohydrate, protein-poor meal, which will stimulate insulin. The insulin in turn removes the competing amino acids from the blood and allows the blood tryptophan to reach the brain to produce more serotonin.

The topic of sleep and learning will be mentioned in this section because it concerns the biological cycle and the release of hormones according to certain cycles. Research findings indicate that sleep increases the release of a hormone known as somatotrophin. Somatotrophin levels rise quickly within thirty minutes after a person falls asleep and remain high during the first half of the night. Studies (Hoddes 1977) conducted on mice indicate that the hormone seems to significantly affect learning and recall if injected five minutes before training. Translated to humans, these findings and other studies indicate that rest just prior to learning may be counterproductive and that individuals preparing for an examination should awaken at least two hours before taking the exam.

The chemistry of body cycles has received increasing attention in this day of intercontinental travel, and the importance of business and political decisions requires better understanding of the phenomena. The above illustration of the effect of somatotrophin indicates how body cycles and hormone levels are related. Additional investigations in this area, while they may have motives other than to explicate implications for learning, are likely to increase understanding that may be useful in the education of adults in the future. For example, physical and mental fatigue of adults is often cited as an obstacle to optimum participation in learning activities. How is fatigue associated with the biological clock and the absence or abundance of certain hormones that are associated with memory, concentration, problem solving, and motor skills?

GENERAL OBSERVATIONS

Much of the research reported in this chapter seems to be temporally distant from application in the traditional learning-teaching context for a number of reasons. Most of it is pursued by scholars with limited concern for immediate application in that context. The motives for the research appear to be more medical, anatomical, and theoretical. Furthermore, a large proportion of the research continues to be conducted on rats and other animals rather than humans, for obvious ethical and technical reasons. Despite these obstacles to application, the results reported here and elsewhere should stimulate the thinking of educators of adults. Even if no other results are immediately available, the data should cause teachers to reflect more carefully and intently upon the biological basis of human behavior. This cogitation may be paralleled by a search for an improved understanding of the interaction between the physiological, psychological, and sociological dimensions that characterize a multitude of teaching-learning transactions.

The research may stimulate additional insight into the problem of attention and concentration; the challenge of meeting educational needs of inner-city inhabitants whose daily lives expose them constantly to a variety of environmental insults, the magnitude of which has yet to be understood; and the possible long-term intellectual deprivation of the poor, whose diets and environments have perhaps lowered the upper limits of their mental possibilities. These studies should, therefore, challenge each educator of adults in some constructive way.

Educators and trainers should be especially encouraged by the results of the work of Krech and his associates, indicating that certain kinds of activity appear to be associated with important changes in the morphology and chemistry of the brain. This work, however, also poses an important challenge to scholars who are interested in adult learning. The results of Krech and Fogel emphasize historical environmental and nutritional problems that may affect the adult human in a cumulative fashion years, and sometimes generations, before the educator begins to interact with them.

Generally, the investigations reviewed for this chapter provide encouraging information concerning the neurobiology, morphology, and physiology of the adult human as they relate to learning. A potential negative implication is reported by Restak (1979), who indicates that EPs show a characteristic age pattern. Exactly what this means has yet to be studied. An intriguing finding comes from the work of Diamond (1978), who set out to measure brain cell loss. Using rats, for obvious reasons, she counted nerve and glial cells over the life span, at four different ages, of her rats. She concluded that for healthy, normal rats there is no significant loss of brain cells through old age. More important, she cites the potential value of enriched environments in increasing brain growth.

Increasing knowledge about biological cycles, body clocks, hormone secretion, and the effects of drugs and diet on the aging organism indicates the possibility of a brighter future for older adults and perhaps increased and improved intellectual activity by adult learners. If we can learn to use the above research areas to enhance our mental activity while simultaneously learning how to use both brain hemispheres appropriately, some obstacles in the learning performance of adults may be slightly reduced.

Educators of adults, however, are challenged by these developments. They are challenged to become better informed about them and then to seek to identify implications and to understand how to appropriately apply the findings to improve the practice of adult education.

NOTES

1. Even cautions against using terms such as right-handedness or left-handedness to refer to right/left brain concepts (personal conversation, 26 January 1982).

III · Participation of Adults in Educational Activities

4 · Reasons, Motives, and Barriers in Participation

T EACHERS, PLANNERS, AND ADMINISTRATORS of education programs for adults are all concerned about why adults do or do not engage in educational activities, making this topic one of the most popular among adult education investigators. The body of research literature concerning reasons for participation in adult education activities may be divided into two categories: (1) the census or self-report research and (2) the analytical studies. In the former, the main concern is for establishing some kind of explanatory relationship between participation and variables such as age, sex, race, and income, or in accepting the respondent's personal report of reasons for participation. The research included in the second category reflects a concern for deeper psychological motives and explanations that may not be readily apparent in the comments of the respondents in the studies. Additional statistical analysis, including factor analysis, is often used to derive clusters of reasons in orientations that help explain participation at a deeper level.

This chapter discusses a number of important areas related to the issue of reasons and motives for, and barriers to, participation of adults in education. The specific topics discussed in the following pages include a profile of the adult learner, reasons for participation as revealed through self-report and census-type surveys, motivational analysis, and barriers to participation. A general discussion of the research concludes the chapter.

A few comments about why educators of adults are so interested in participation studies are in order before we turn to the research on the above topics.

Educational opportunity for adults frequently includes activities arranged by a multitude of diverse agencies, institutions, and organizations. Because of this diversity among providers, it is often difficult to obtain inventories or census reports on numbers of participants. Even when data are available, complicating factors include inconsistent or overlapping definitions and multiple enumeration.

The enchantment of educators of adults with studies of participation is thus a normal response to a very important area of inquiry. For more than 200 years, the education of adults has proceeded in America, and more recently in some other nations, as a voluntary activity (Long 1976). The voluntary dimension of adult learning places a premium on understanding who participates, why they participate, and under what conditions participation is likely. Even in 1959, when Brunner and his associates issued their review of adult education research, more than 10 percent of their report was devoted to the topic of participation; most of that chapter, however, deals with research on social participation. The social participation data were included in *Overview of Adult Education Research* on the assumption that such studies reveal information significant to the adult educator concerned with educational participation. For example, social participation might be viewed as an actual or potential means of educating the adult participants, as a channel of communication through which to reach the adult populations as well as organizational structures for educational programs, as possible sources of competition for programs of adult education, and as appropriate objectives of adult education. The limited discussion of educational participation by Brunner and his associates reflects the stage of development of inquiries into the questions about the involvement of adults in education in 1959.

Aslanian and Brickell (1980) are of the opinion that at least five different groups are interested in information concerning participation tendencies of adults: providers of adult learning, counselors of adults, policymakers, adult learners, and scholars. Educators of adults are interested in a variety of questions concerning adult participation in education, some of which are listed below.

1. How many adults annually participate in educational activities?
2. What kind of characteristics (variables) are associated with participation?
3. Do some kinds of individuals participate more frequently than other kinds? If so, why?
4. Why do adults participate in learning activities?
5. What motivates adults to engage in education?
6. What interferes with participation?
7. How can educational opportunities be made available to every adult?
8. What can be done to enhance the possibility of participation?
9. How can educators reach the hard-to-recruit adult?

Most of the above questions have been addressed, some more often and with greater success than others. For example, numerical data are increasingly available. Cross (1979) has reviewed a number of state studies conducted during the 1970s, and the National Center for Education Statistics (NCES) reports trienniel surveys of adult participation in formal education programs. Based on the many studies of participation, one can pick either a relatively high or relatively low estimate of the number of adults engaged in learning activities. Using an adult population estimate of 160 million, the current estimates range from Tough's 1978 figure of 144 million (90 percent of all adults), to the NCES (1980) estimate of 18–19 million. Differing definitions of *learning* and *adult* account for the wide discrepancy among studies. Conservative estimates frequently indicate that approximately one-third of the adult population annually engages in a learning activity.

Differences among studies of participation are not limited to definitions. There is also variation among the research approaches reported in the literature.

Brunner noted that studies of participation conducted before 1959 were mostly descriptive. Furthermore, he described seven categories of participation studies:

1. Studies of participants in a specific institution in one community.
2. Comparative studies of students in specific programs.
3. Studies within a community concerning participation in several programs.
4. Studies comparing participation among several communities.
5. Statewide studies of specific programs or institutions.
6. National studies of a single institution, agency, or program.
7. National studies of general participation.

Burgess later (1971) provided a typology of participation research based on research approaches. Accordingly, he defines four different research approaches that have been used to determine why adults engage in educational activities:

1. Conducting an analysis of activities in which the learner participates.
2. Asking the adult learners to state in their own words why they engage in learning activities.
3. Asking learners to select from a prepared list of reasons why they participate.
4. Analyzing the adult's orientation to education.

Two additional types of participation studies can be added to Burgess's list: studies of self-directed independent learning activities and meta-research.

For purposes of simplicity, studies of participation discussed in the following sections have been placed in one of two general classes. The first category is labeled "self-report/census studies." This class includes Burgess's second, third, and fourth approaches. The second category is labeled "analytical studies." This class includes interview and/or questionnaire data that are subjected to interpretative analysis such as Houle's (1961) early work and the numerous factorial analyses and multivariate analyses of census studies as conducted by Anderson and Darkenwald (1979).

SELF-REPORT/CENSUS STUDIES

Educators of adults are fortunate to have a substantial quantity of census-type participation studies and related analyses. Investigations conducted over the past twenty years have produced findings that yield a profile of the adult learner. These data also have led to the identification of a variety of reasons for participation as well as obstacles to enrollment in educational activities. Twelve topics of related research are discussed in this section: a profile of the adult learner, ten variables often associated with participation (age, education, ethnic and racial factors, family and youthful characteristics, income, learning location, marital status, place of residence, sex, and other socioeconomic variables), and reasons for participation.

Profile of the Adult Learner

The descriptive approach that is most frequently used in self-report/census kinds of studies of participation is designed to identify relationships between participants and sociodemographic data. The variables selected for study usually include age, educational achievement level, family status, income, race, sex, and other miscellaneous items that vary among the surveys.[1]

Johnstone and Rivera (1965) described the adult participant as young, well educated, engaged in a white-collar job, and earning a moderate income. These descriptors continue to apply to participants as identified in more recent surveys reported by Cross (1981) and others.

In addition, it was noted that geographical location was also slightly associated with participation. People from the West and those living in suburbs or on the outskirts of large metropolitan centers were overrepresented among participants.

Aslanian and Brickell (1980) contrasted learners and nonlearners as follows:

1. Learners are younger than nonlearners.
2. Learners are better educated than nonlearners.
3. Adults with higher incomes are more likely to learn than those with lower incomes.
4. Learners are more likely to be employed than unemployed.
5. Learners are more likely to be engaged in professional and technical work.
6. Single and divorced adults are more likely to participate in learning than others; widowed adults are less likely to engage in learning.
7. Mothers with children under age 18 are more likely to participate than women with children over 18.
8. There are no differences in participation according to sex in the households of persons 25 years of age or older.

The association between type of employment and participation of adults in educational activities, as cited by Johnstone and Rivera and Aslanian and Brickell, has also been noted in other studies. London (1970) cited several reasons for the low rates of participation by blue-collar workers and proposed day-release for education purposes. Killeen and Bird's study (1981) of paid educational leave in England and Wales reveals that paid educational leave provisions seem to favor administrators, managers, professionals, scientific workers, and artists. They reported that where they could identify occupations, the above groups accounted for 50 percent of the places in college provisions for paid educational leave. Killeen and Bird believe, however, that their data underestimate this kind of participation. As a result, they suggest that approximately 67 percent of all places of college provision in paid educational leave were accounted for by the above groups.

Anderson and Darkenwald studied the 1975 NCES data to determine the multiple correlation between eleven independent variables, including those identified by Johnstone and Rivera, and participation of adults. Their analysis revealed that in combination all eleven variables can explain only 10 percent of the variance between participants and nonparticipants (Anderson and Darkenwald 1979). Variables such as age, educational achievement level, income, race, and sex thus independently contribute little to the explanation for participation. Anderson and Darkenwald report the following correlations between participation and the identified variable: age, $-.18$; education, $.25$; income, $.12$; race, $.04$; and sex, $-.01$ (female).

The participation data analyzed through multivariate procedures are much more helpful than those resulting from simple correlations. For example, multivariate analysis reveals that income and race, which in simple correlations are highly associated with participation, seem to derive most of their power from correlations with other variables such as age, occupational status, and educational level (Anderson and Darkenwald 1979).

The data on participation by race consistently reveal that black adults are underrepresented among participants. Various analyses, including the one by Anderson and Darkenwald, however, reveal that other sociodemographic variables associated with race are more useful in explaining the phenomenon. When education, income, and occupational status are controlled, for example, race is not a useful explanatory variable.

Variables in Participation

Ten variables that are often investigated in participation studies are discussed in the following pages: age, education, ethnic and racial factors, family and youthful characteristics, income, learning location, marital status, place of residence, sex, and other socioeconomic variables. See Table 4.1 for variables studied by twenty investigators.

Age

If all adults do not engage in sponsored educational activities at the same rate, what are some of the characteristics that might distinguish between participants and nonparticipants? Age is probably one of the first attributes to come under examination. Just as society has conditioned us to look for an association between age and learning ability, we are almost preprogrammed to raise the issue of age in any discussion or inquiry into participation data.

Young adults are consistently well represented among participants in edu-

Table 4.1

Selected Investigations of Demographic, Personal, Social, and Other Variables Associated with Adult Participation in Educational Activities

Age	Education	Family	Income	Intelligence	Learning Location	Marital Status	Occupation	Place of Residence	Race	Sex
Armstrong	CNS	Carson	Douglah and Moss	Botsman	Botsman	Aker, Jahns, and Schroeder	Douglah and Moss	CNS	CNS	CNS
Botsman	Dickinson	Dickinson	Dugger	Boyle	Hiemstra	IBHE	Dugger	Johnstone and Rivera	Froomkin and Wolfson	IBHE
CNS*	Douglah and Moss	Johnstone and Rivera	IBHE	Dugger	IBHE	Johnstone and Rivera	Johnstone and Rivera	Long	IBHE	Johnstone and Rivera
Johnstone and Rivera	Hanna†		Johnstone and Rivera		Johnstone and Rivera		Robinson	NCES	Johnstone and Rivera	NCES
IBHE**	IBHE		NCES		Long					
NCES***	Johnstone and Rivera		Robinson		NCES					
	Trenaman†									

* Commission on Non-Traditional Study
** State of Illinois Board of Higher Education
*** National Center for Education Statistics
† United Kingdom

cational activities. Definitional and data collection differences among various studies do not change this fact. The National Opinion Research Center (NORC) investigation (Johnstone and Rivera 1965), the NCES reports, and local studies all reveal that most participants are less than 45 years of age.

Longitudinal data based on comparison of the 1969–1975 NCES participation data reveal the population of older adults increased by less than 12 percent, while the rate of participation by this age group increased by 55 percent.

According to Anderson and Darkenwald, age has the second highest correlation of sociodemographic variables identified in the NCES surveys: $-.18$. Hence, age explains .03 of the variance in participation (National Center for Education Statistics 1978).

Education

Since the publication of *Volunteers for Learning* (Johnstone and Rivera 1965), there has been a general acceptance among adult educators that educational attainment is one of the best predictors of participation in sponsored educational activities. The latest NCES data (1980) on educational attainment and participation generally support the position of Cross (1979), who believes educational achievement level to be a better index to interests, motivations, and educational participation of adults than any other one variable. She reports that 89 percent of adults participating in organized learning activities are high school graduates.

The general relationship between educational attainment and participation is supported in every study reviewed for this chapter. They include a state study in Illinois (1980), two British studies in London and Oxford and Leeds (Hanna 1964; Trenaman 1957), the meta-research of Cross (1981) and Anderson and Darkenwald (1979), and the NCES data (1980).

The general association between educational level and participation of adults in learning activities is also revealed among "would-be learners" (people who indicated an interest in learning). Cross (1979) cites data generated by the Commission on Non-Traditional Study in 1972 on learners and would-be learners.

Unfortunately for those who like simple solutions, to conclude that educational attainment is the *cause* of adult participation would be fallacious. It is likely that a number of variables are associated with educational attainment, some of which may also be related to participation. There is the possibility that because of the relatively strong association (compared to other variables) between educational attainment and participation, erroneous characterizations of participants and nonparticipants may be developed. Such characterizations would describe persons with low educational attainment as probable nonparticipants and persons of high educational attainment as probable participants. Such characterizations, based on facts generated by a multitude of studies, have some value but are limited in their power to explain. An unrestrained focus on the "central tendencies" as revealed by these data takes one's eye away from individual differences—an important factor in the education of adults.

The above kinds of concerns prompted Douglah and Moss (1968) to investigate the differential participation patterns exhibited within what they described as generally assumed homogeneous groups. The purpose of this research was to determine factors associated with participation in educational activities within groups of adults of low and high educational levels. By controlling for the influence of education, the investigators believed that they could more clearly identify the influence of other factors associated with participation.

Two types of factors that may be related to an individual adult's participation were identified by Douglah and Moss (1968): positional factors and psychological factors. Positional factors refer to the positions a person occupies in the social structure, while psychological factors concern the manner in which the roles associated with the various positions are performed. The former category included variables such as sex, age, employment status, level of occupation, level of income, marital status, and place of residence. Psychological factors examined comprised four personality traits: self-reliance, withdrawing tendencies, social skills, and occupational relations.

Douglah and Moss found five factors to be associated with educational participation of persons of low education (fewer than twelve years of school). Age showed a curvilinear relationship with participation; and employment, income, and number of children were positively related with it. Withdrawing tendencies showed a negative relationship. (Note that four of the five factors are positional factors and only one is psychological.) In contrast to the findings concerning the low educational attainment group, the participation of individuals in the high educational attainment group was not accounted for to any great extent by any of the factors identified and included in the study.

Ethnic and Racial Factors

Since Johnstone and Rivera's 1965 work, it has been generally observed that disadvantaged segments of the population fail to participate in adult education as frequently as the more advantaged elements. However, as early as 1965 it was noted that when education and income were controlled, race did not appear to be a useful predictor variable.

Cross (1979) reports her analysis of NCES data for 1969 and 1975, which demonstrates numerical and percentage differences among black and white individuals in adult education. She observes that the proportion of black adults who participated over this period declined: 7.7 percent in 1969 to 6.9 percent in 1975 (compared with an increase from 10.2 to 12.1 percent for white adults in the respective years). Black adult participation did show a total net increase of 5 percent over the period, but the black adult population increased by 18 percent.

There is evidence, however, that the apparent black/white imbalance in adult education is more an artifact of social class differences such as education and income than a race difference. Froomkin and Wolfson (1977), controlling for education, show that the participation rates among white and black adults are similar: 4.1 percent. The 1978–79 study of adult education in Illinois (1980) also concludes that race does not have a pronounced effect on participation except concerning the choice between credit and noncredit activities. It was reported that white adults were more likely to engage in noncredit activities than credit activities, while the opposite was true of minorities identified in the study.

When other data, such as income, educational level, and occupational status, are reviewed, it becomes obvious that race per se is not associated with educational participation as are other factors. Consequently, educational needs and interests of nonwhites seem not to be very distinguishable from the needs and interests of individuals with low educational achievement and low income levels.

Family and Youthful Characteristics

Dickinson (1971) reports an interesting study developed to examine six representative educational variables in relation to participation to determine whether or not the use of additional educational variables would increase the power of education to predict participation compared with using only the years of school completed, as is normally done. Using a sample of married male adult learners, he concluded that only the years of school completed by the respondent and his wife remained as influences on total and vocational course participation when the effects of the six predictors—the subject's education, the subject's training, wife's education, wife's training, father's education, and father's training—were controlled simultaneously. Other research has been interpreted as suggesting that the educational level of the educational participant is the most important single factor associated with participation. Dickinson's study results suggest that in the case of male adult learners the years of education completed by the wife may also be an important factor. No similar study to determine the effect of a husband on his wife's participation has been identified.[2]

Carson's 1965 study supports the idea that the family environment may be associated with participation rates. Based on a six-year follow-up study of young men who were first studied when they were high school sophomores, Carson obtained correlations between educational, vocational, and sociopsychological factors. Full-time study was associated with high mental ability, educational achievement, high school education of parents, and professional occupational status of fathers. Part-time study was associated with lower mental ability, mother's education, educational and vocational aspirations, and achievement of the young adult male. Mental ability was singled out as a significant variable in motivation.

Boyle's and Douglah's Wisconsin-based inquiries produced data that demonstrated an association between selected youthful characteristics and later participation (Boyle 1967; Douglah 1965). Boyle reported a positive association between participation and intelligence as measured in high school, educational aspirations, and present levels of education and occupational status. Douglah also noted a positive correlation between youth leadership status and participation.

Income

The association between income and the participation of adults in educational activity is confounded by the relationship between income and other variables such as educational attainment, social class, and occupational status. Cross (1979) is of the opinion that the use of income as a factor does not add much information to the analyses by educational achievement. However, when considered independently of the other variables, the association is revealing.

Learning Location

The education of adults can be likened to the education of children and adults in colonial America in one respect: It goes on anywhere and everywhere. It takes place in the shop and the factory, in the facilities of religious groups, in libraries, and in educational institutions of several kinds. The following list illustrates the major organizations and institutions that provided adult instruction to participants involved in the Illinois (1980) study:

Illinois public and private two-year colleges	17.1%
Illinois private senior institutions	12.2%
Illinois public senior institutions	10.2%
Noncollegiate institutions	60.5%

    Business (9.6%)
    Churches (6.1%)
    High schools (3.8%)
    Professional associations (3.6%)
    Hospitals (3.3%)
    Private tutors or teachers (2.4%)
    Other—e.g., martial arts schools and military
    schools (31.7%)

According to the survey results, the great majority of adult educational activities in Illinois took place in institutions outside the traditional higher education structure. The topics reported as studied by the respondents are also diverse. The list below illustrates the point:

Business, management, and related technologies	18.9%
Health professions and related technologies	9.1%
Fine and applied arts	8.4%
Letters (literature, English, philosophy, etc.)	6.4%
Education	6.0%
Mechanics and engineering technologies	5.8%

Following a lengthy additional analysis of the survey data, the following observation was made concerning the association between the variables studied and type of institution that an adult student attends (p. 116):

> In summary, then, knowing how a student participates will not allow an observer to predict which of the four types of institutions the student attends. Put another way, none of the characteristics of participation are uniquely descriptive of participation in one type of institution as compared to all other types. The greatest distinction that does exist on the basis of such participation characteristics is primarily useful for distinguishing between the noncollegiate sector and all other sectors.

The NORC study (Johnstone and Rivera 1965), which included an analysis of provision of educational opportunities for adults in four selected cities, revealed that nine different types of institutions or organizations had provided instruction in one or more subject areas in each city.

Johnstone and Rivera believe that the NORC findings represent the most typical patterns of institutional involvements in adult education. Many of the sponsors identified in the survey provided educational programs in other subject fields as well, but over and beyond the nine mentioned above, there were only three others that offered instruction in some specific subject area in as many as three of the four cities. These were public colleges or universities in the white-collar vocational field; YMCAs in recreation, home life, and personal development; and hobby clubs. A little over half of twenty-one types of institutions, organizations, and associations contacted in the study were typically found to be involved in educating adults.

Data reported by NCES for 1968, 1976, and 1978, among other things, address noncredit adult and continuing education activities provided by higher education institutions. The total number of registrations in three classes of institutions increased from 5,643,958 to 10,154,128 participants— an increase of 80 percent over the ten-year period. At the same time the number of institutions offering noncredit adult and continuing education activities increased from 1,102 to 2,375—an increase of 115 percent. The greatest increase in number of institutions occurred among two-year colleges—an increase of 132 percent in the number of institutions (from 422 to 979). Close behind were four-year colleges: The number of four-year colleges offering noncredit adult and continuing education rose from 534 to 1,236—an increase of just over 131 percent.

Hiemstra (1972) asked a group of senior citizens who lived in a residential center or participated in center activities to identify their preferences for the location of adult education courses. They identified five locations, which along with the percentage preferring each location are noted here: residential center, 33 percent; senior citizen center, 41 percent; high school, 6 percent; elementary or junior high school, 6 percent; community college, 1 percent (14 percent, no response).

The preference for the residential center and/or senior citizen center for this sample is not surprising when the sample characteristics are considered. Furthermore, this group identified transportation and a reluctance to go out at night as important negative influences.

Botsman's 1975 report of a study of blue-collar workers in New York contains data that are not unlike those discussed above. The study results reveal that the blue-collar workers prefer the workplace as a place of study. Other preferences ranked in descending order include two-year colleges, high schools, colleges or universities, and private vocational trade or business schools.

Marital Status

Participation among Illinois (1978) survey respondents was highest among adults who were never married (59.7 percent) and lowest among widows (16.9 percent). Married adults comprised 53.0 percent of all respondents and accounted for 33.5 percent of the participants.

Participation data according to marital status are largely influenced by the age distribution of adults in each marital category. For example, 18-to-24-year-olds comprise two-thirds of all adults never married, and because participation is highest among 18-to-24-year-olds, it affects the relative participation data of never-married adults. Adults that are 18 to 24 years old and have never been married have a higher participation rate (71.9 percent) than adults in any other marital category. A similar relationship exists between the categories of adults 65 years of age and over, and widows. Of all widows, 84 percent are in the age 65-and-over category.

Two studies of participation in adult literacy classes indicated that a majority of the participants were married. One study surveyed 35 classes, and the second focused on an adult basic education program in a rural southern community, where the participants were likely to be married and over 40 years of age (Anderson and Niemi 1969; Aker, Jahns, and Schroeder 1968).

Place of Residence

There are interesting variations in the participation patterns of adults according to place of residence. Almost three-fourths of the population of participants is found in Standard Metropolitan Statistical Areas; only 1.9 percent of the participants reside in rural and farm areas (National Center for Education Statistics 1980).

Cross (1979) cites several studies, including the Commission on Non-Traditional Study (CNS) survey conducted in the early 1970s, to confirm the higher probability of participation by Westerners. Translated into another form, 1978 NCES data reveal that 83.8 percent of the adults in the West were nonparticipants, in contrast to the 89.9-percent rate of nonparticipation among individuals in the Northeast and the South. The CNS survey also revealed that nonparticipants or would-be learners among the Westerners reflected a higher interest in participation than did individuals surveyed in other parts of the country, especially Iowa.

It should be obvious that geographic location per se, like race per se, does not or cannot explain variations in participation data. As reported elsewhere in this chapter, the differences between West Milwaukee, Wisconsin, and Brevard County, Florida, concern factors other than participation in adult education. There is likely an interaction among numerous variables including personal-psychological factors such as attitudes, personal wealth, educational attainment level, and occupation, with place variables such as community wealth, population size, and characteristics that are difficult to isolate and measure.

Sex

Johnstone and Rivera (1965) reported that the participant in adult education was as likely to be male as female in the early 1960s. NCES data for 1978, however, indicate that the participant today is slightly more likely to be female. The 1978 data reveal that 57 percent of the participants were female. Analysis of the data by age groups also reveals a regular difference of about 3 percent, favoring female participation. The largest difference between males and females occurs in the 35–54 age group: 19 percent of the females in this age category are participants, compared with 14.5 percent of the males.

A comparison of NCES data on adult participation in education since 1969 suggests that women have increased their involvement in education at a rate higher than men. In 1969, the participation rate for women was 9.0 percent compared with 11.2 percent for men; in 1972, the percentages were 11.9 and 10.8, respectively. The 1975 data indicated that 11.6 percent of the adult female population were participants, whereas 11.7 percent of the male population was involved in adult education compared with 12.7 and 10.7

percent for females and males in 1978. Thus over the years between 1969 and 1978, the relationship between the sexes changed; female participation rose from 9.0 to 12.7 percent, while male participation declined from 11.2 to 10.7 percent.

Almost any explanation for the trend, if the above data constitute a trend, is open for discussion and debate. One explanation, however, concerns the changing roles of women in American society. During the period under study, significant changes in thinking by and about women were popular topics of discussion. A number of consciousness-raising and awareness-development activities were initiated for and by women during the decade. One popular topic addressed by many organizations (including higher education institutions) was women's educational programs. Additional research analysis of this phenomenon is likely to become available in the near future.

Other Socioeconomic Variables

Analysis of data concerning the association between race and ethnic groups and participation emphasizes the socioeconomic factors that appear to serve as intervening variables influencing the involvement of adults in learning activities.

Robinson (1970) noted that participation in the lower-middle-class population of the village of West Milwaukee, Wisconsin, was generally lower than that revealed in other studies. His random survey resulted in a 9.4-percent participation rate. This compares unfavorably with Johnstone and Rivera (1965), who reported a 20.2-percent participation rate, and with my 1967 study that reported a 30-percent rate in a contrasting socioeconomic community (Long 1967). Participation percentages in all age groups in Robinson's survey were lower than for similar age groups reported by Johnstone and Rivera.

A comparison of Robinson's findings and Johnstone and Rivera's national data (Johnstone and Rivera 1965) according to income also reveals important differences, except in the upper income bracket.

Nonprofessional workers in West Milwaukee reflected low participation rates. Several comparisons are available on this variable. The West Milwaukee nonprofessional worker participation rate was 5.8 percent compared with the national survey findings reported by Johnstone and Rivera (1965) for blue-collar workers of 16.4 percent. London's 1963 study of participants in California identified participation rates among nonprofessional workers as varying from 16 percent for clerical and sales personnel to 5 percent for unskilled workers. Business and professional workers in Robinson's survey had a participation rate of 14.3 percent compared with Johnstone and Rivera's 22 percent among the professional category; London noted a 22-percent rate of participation among professionals, 16 percent among managerial types, and 9 percent among small business owners.

Reasons for Participation

In addition to being concerned with questions about how many adults participate in education, many educators have practical and theoretical interest in why adults engage in study. Research into the reasons for participation is characterized by differences in procedures and thrusts. There are generally two kinds of research concerning the topic. The first (by virtue of its age and volume) has utilized relatively simple self-report inquiries wherein the respondent is asked why he or she participated or is requested to select appropriate answers from a prepared list. The second kind of investigation possibly grew out of Houle's analytical interviews that led to his small but stimulating publication *The Inquiring Mind* (1961). Following Houle, a number of investigations have been conducted with the objective of relating the data collected from participants to basic psychological motives (Douglah and Moss 1968).

The two kinds of thrusts reflected in the literature are evident in both the census-type and analytical motivation studies. For example, the census-type research has been designed to characterize reasons for participation in adult education in either specific or global language. The structural distribution of the research into reasons for participation in adult education is illustrated in Figure 4.1.

Type of Study

Kinds of Reasons	Census/Self-Report	Analytical
Global	CEEB Illinois	Boshier
Specific	Armstrong Botsman CNS Dugger NCES NORC Robinson	Boshier Houle Sheffield

Figure 4.1 Structural distribution of participation research

The specific explanations are of the type identified by Johnstone and Rivera, where the individual respondent selected from among a list of reasons such as "prepare for a new job," "help on present job," "spare-time enjoyment," and so forth. More global reasons have been identified in the State of Illinois Board of Higher Education studies. In the surveys conducted for the agency, the global reasons are "for credit" and "not for credit."

This section concerning reasons and obstacles associated with participation examines only the reasons for participation identified through the census-type studies. Analytical motivation studies are examined in the next section.

Data from eight census-type investigations concerned with reasons for participation in adult education in addition to references to other studies are discussed here. The major studies are the National Opinion Research Center (NORC) study conducted early in the 1960s and the Commission on Non-Traditional Study (CNS) survey conducted in the early 1970s. Others include a New York study conducted by Cornell University faculty in the mid 1970s; and the State of Illinois Survey of Adult Learners, and the College Entrance Examination Board survey, both conducted in the late 1970s. First, attention is directed to the global orientation of the CEEB study reported by Aslanian and Brickell and the focus on credit-noncredit distinction in the Illinois study. Then the findings of the NORC study, the CNS investigation, and the New York research are presented.

Global Reasons

Two major studies identifying "global" reasons for participation have been conducted recently. One, the Illinois Board of Higher Education survey, was conducted in an important state, and the other was a national survey conducted by the College Entrance Examination Board (CEEB) as reported by Aslanian and Brickell (1980).

According to the CEEB survey of a national probability sample of 1,519 adults 25 years of age and older, 49 percent of the respondents were identified as "learners." They were so labeled because they indicated that they had engaged in some kind of learning over the twelve months preceding the telephone interview. Eighty-three percent of the learners cited some past, current, or future change in their lives as their reasons for learning. Aslanian and Brickell indicate a fundamental distinction evident in the two groups of learners. The larger group of 83 percent was involved in learning for purposes of achieving some kind of objective; learning was the means to an end—it was instrumental. In contrast, the smaller group of 17 percent was composed of people who learned for the sake of learning; learning was the end—it was expressive.

In a less global fashion the reasons for learning were then associated with what Aslanian and Brickell refer to as "transitions." Seven kinds of transitions were noted:

1. Career   56%
2. Family   16%
3. Leisure   13%
4. Art   5%
5. Health   5%
6. Religion   4%
7. Citizenship   1%

Specific reasons for participation were identified as "triggers." The trigger events were identified by the investigators by asking the learners five questions:

1. When did you start learning?
2. Why did you start then?

3. Why not earlier?
4. Why not later?
5. What happened at that time to cause you to start then?

Based on responses to the above questions, the investigators then identified five kinds of events that they say "triggered" the learning of the respondents. All five trigger events were similar to the "transitions" noted earlier. Changes related to leisure and art were so minimal that they did not appear in the trigger events list. The five trigger events noted are as follows:

1. Career   56%
2. Family   36%
3. Health   4%
4. Religion   2%
5. Citizenship   1%

The conceptual base of the CEEB study and the interpretation of findings by Aslanian and Brickell are straightforward and defensible. Reduced to its bare elements, the logic is as follows: (1) Transitions require learning, (2) identifiable events can be associated with the transitions, and (3) the events determine the times for learning. The study, however, does not answer all our questions. For example, why did 51 percent of the respondents fail to indicate a learning activity even though *learning* is defined very broadly and a follow-up question provided an opportunity for reconsideration? If adult life is as dynamic as we now believe, "triggers" are almost continuously available, and we are faced with establishing priorities among them. Which shall we address by learning and which will we address by routine ways of adaptation? How are such decisions made to address the transition through a learning activity? What personal, social, and structural factors influence these kinds of decisions?

The research literature concerning participation clearly reveals that adults participate in educational activities for a variety of reasons. Some of the reasons have been described in self-report studies, and others have been characterized in analytical psychological investigations. Reasons range from specifics such as "to improve my occupational performance" to more psychologically defined reasons such as growth motivation. The kind of educational activities, though not always accurately revealing the motives or reasons, may be helpful in identifying major and general characteristics of participants in certain kinds of activities. For example, do participants in credit activities differ from participants in noncredit activities? If so, how? The significance of such a question becomes obvious when informed by the results of the Illinois study, which revealed that only 40.9 percent of the participants were enrolled for credit.

The research concerning participation discussed elsewhere indicates that adult education is not a monolithic concept. It is multidimensional, and consequently, just as individual differences exist concerning the preferences of adults for locations for learning, we should expect to discover individual variability concerning major kinds of educational activities such as credit and noncredit learning.

Given the pluralistic nature of adult education sources (which is the thrust of the question examined here—namely, How do the data on credit and noncredit participation compare?), most studies ignore the noninstitutional, nonsponsored education and focus primarily on educational institutions. This limitation is a significant one, but it does not lessen the value of the comparative exercise.

Differences have been noted between individuals who enroll in education for credit and their counterparts who engage in noncredit activity. For example, Froomkin and Wolfson's 1977 analysis of NCES data leads to the conclusion that nonwhites are more likely to seek certificates for their learning than are whites. A similar conclusion is called for by the 1980 Illinois Board of Higher Education study. Other differences in participation of credit and noncredit students appear when the data are analyzed by educational attainment. Those participants in adult education who have *completed* high school, college, or graduate school are more likely to engage in noncredit activities than are persons with *some* high school, college, or graduate school experience.

Demographic factors such as age, income, race, sex, and place of residence have also been analyzed to determine their association with the decision to enroll in credit and noncredit course work. Overall, the association between these demographic variables and type of credit activity was not very important. Knowledge of the above is not very helpful in predicting whether an adult will be engaged in credit or in noncredit work. Carson's 1965 work, however, indicates that there may be personal variables associated with the decision to take course work for credit. For example, he indicated that full-time students were brighter and had different family backgrounds than part-time students. Concurrently, Carson noted that full-time students also tend to be credit oriented. Additional studies of this topic are required, however, before any worthwhile conclusions can be drawn concerning differences between credit and noncredit students. The data in the studies reported here suggest that any differences that may exist may be situational and/or social as opposed to personal. For example, the tendency of nonwhites and younger full-time students to be more credit oriented in their education is logical and easy to understand. Both kinds of individuals are usually involved in career preparation where "certified learning" is desirable, if not required.

Global reasons for participating in adult learning as revealed through self-report/census-type studies are interesting and informative, but, as noted, they do not explain as much about participation as we desire. Self-report/census-type studies designed to elicit more specific reasons for participation are discussed next.

Specific Reasons

The designers of the NORC national study of adult participation identified eight popular reasons that adults engage in learning activities. The reasons identified were subsequently translated into eight statements about how courses could be helpful. The respondents, at the time of the interview, were asked directly whether any of the eight reasons had had a bearing on their most recent enrollment. Then they were asked to identify any other purposes for which the course was taken. The eight statements, along with the responses obtained, used in the national survey are as follows:

1. Become a better informed person   37%
2. Prepare for a new job or occupation   36%
3. On the job I held at that time   32%
4. Spend my spare time more enjoyably   20%
5. Meet new and interesting people   15%
6. In carrying out everyday tasks and
   duties around home   13%
7. Get away from the daily routine   10%
8. In carrying out everyday tasks and
   duties away from home   10%
9. None of these, or I don't know   7%

Six other reasons, plus a category of "other," were identified by the respondents:

1. Other work or job related reasons   3%
2. Improve skills or increase knowledge
   (general)   3%
3. Increase income   1%
4. Home or family life role   1%
5. Personality or interpersonal relations   1%
6. Other personal development   1%
7. All other   2%

"To become a better informed person" was the reason given by the largest group of respondents for participation in an educational course (Johnstone and Rivera 1965). One difficulty with this response is determining its meaning. It is possible that for some adults, becoming a better informed person is an end in itself. For others, it may be a means to a nonverbalized end. It is possible that individuals who interpreted the statement in each of the above ways believed their response to be appropriate. If such confusion does exist, how does the adult education community respond to, or interpret, the item? A second confounding factor relates to the meaning of "better informed." Is the meaning limited to cognition (i.e., the ability to cite and interpret facts), or does it include motor-skill acquisition?

The second and third most common response items provide confirming information concerning the perceived role of education in improving one's occupational status or situation. The data obtained through the survey items about reasons for participation were viewed by Johnstone and Rivera as adding little to what was already known about adult participants in educational activities. However, upon further analysis of the data, they arrived at the conclusion that one cannot always predict the reason for participation by the subject matter studied. It was discovered that regardless of the subject category identified in the survey, each of the eight reasons was selected by some participants. For example, 9 percent of those enrolled in vocational courses did so with leisure time objectives in mind, while 5 percent of the adults who studied religion said their main reason for doing so was to prepare for a new job.

Botsman's 1975 report of the study of blue-collar workers in New York also identifies additional reasons that are given for participation in adult education. His data also note differences between the reasons cited by men and women. According to Botsman, blue-collar workers stressed the importance of course utility in job-related studies. Following is a list of reasons that workers selected for wanting to study in the area of their first choice.

1. Become a better person
2. Become better informed, personal enjoyment, and enrichment
3. To earn more money
4. Be a better person, husband or wife
5. Meet the requirements of my employer, profession, or authority

It seems that although the subject areas most frequently chosen were utilitarian, workers would actually choose to participate in a program not just for economic motives but for personal satisfaction as well. A great number of reasons are clearly operative for any one individual. The mean number of reasons given for wanting to study was 10.8.

Differences in motives are observed between the sexes. Male workers cite two reasons for participation proportionately more frequently than female workers: to "work toward certification or licensing" and to "help advance in present job."

Female workers cite three reasons more often than men do: to "meet new people," to "learn more about my background and culture," and to "improve my spiritual well-being."

Different life-styles exist at different age levels; this is reflected in the decisions that workers make about free time. The older worker is less likely than the younger worker to want to take adult education courses in order to help get a new job. Table 4.2 lists reasons for participation given by younger, middle-aged, and older workers.

Table 4.2
Why Workers Want to Learn, by Age

Those under 29 (younger workers) cite

    Help get a new job
    Meet new people

more than those between 30 and 44 years. They also cite

    Help get a new job
    Work toward licensure/certification
    Work toward a degree
    Earn more money

more than the over-45 age group.

Workers between 30 and 44 cite

    Help advance in present job
    Become a more effective citizen

more than the younger workers, and they cite

    Help get a new job
    Help advance in present job
    Work toward certification/licensure
    Work toward a degree

more than workers in the 45-plus age group.

Workers in the 45-plus age group are more likely to cite

    Be better able to serve my church

than the workers under 30, and they cite

    Meet new people
    Be better able to serve my church

more than the 30–44 age group.

Source: Botsman 1975, p. 5.

Younger workers indicate more reasons for wanting to participate in adult education. This means that young workers entering the work force with a better educational background have greater expectations of continuing education.

Previous levels of education also affect the reasons that workers would participate. Workers with more education are more likely to want to work toward a degree and to learn more about their background and culture than those with less education. Those with a high school diploma or a diploma and post–high school education cite reasons for participation such as to "become better informed," "personal enjoyment and enrichment," to "escape daily routine," and "curiosity" more than the non–high school graduates (Botsman 1975).

Robinson (1965) reported the results of a British survey of adult interests that closely parallels Botsman's conclusions concerning the utilitarian nature of the educational interests of blue-collar workers. The survey data indicated that only about 1 in 10 British adults has a consistent interest in education and that the great majority of potential adult educational interests do not arise from some academic or intellectual curiosity. Instead, the wellspring of interests seems to be the personal, practical needs of everyday life. These interests are most often related to people's homes and families—home decorating, personal relationships, children's education, and practical hobbies, for example. Another source of interest is new personal and social developments, e.g., family mobility based on a new car, and increasing interest in travel abroad. A third source is people's work, including fears of retiring from work altogether.

Armstrong's 1965 study of adult education classes in the state of Washington surveyed 3,290 adult students. Two of Armstrong's conclusions concern why adults participate and differences between motives of men and women. Three reasons for participation identified by Armstrong were improving one's general education, preparing for a better job, and increasing one's occupational proficiency. He also reports that men enrolled more for "industrial" reasons and women enrolled more often for "cultural" reasons.

Dugger (1965) reports an investigation of selected factors and motives of adult learners enrolled in evening courses at Drake University. As a result of his study, he concluded that the vocational motive is very important to adults in the evening school. Most of the students were employed men aged 20–49 with above-average incomes. Furthermore, he reports that higher grade point averages were associated with a vocational orientation. He also suggests that his findings support the contention that adults' motives to participate in education vary according to age as noted by Armstrong. He described his younger participants' educational interests as "industrial" in contrast to those of older participants, which were described as commercial, academic, hobby, and avocational.

The task of identifying reasons for participation was approached from a slightly different direction in the Commission on Non-Traditional Study research. They also asked respondents to identify the area(s) they studied or would be interested in studying, from a list of 8 topics. The areas identified are vocational subjects (excluding agriculture), hobbies and recreation, general education, home and family life, personal development, public affairs, religious studies, and agriculture. There was fairly close agreement between the learners and would-be learners on the importance of the areas.

Data concerning reasons for adult participation in educational activities are collected by NCES in six categories: advance in current job, get new job, other job related, American citizenship, general education, and personal, social, or other non–job related. The first three reasons are all job associated and account for 52.7 percent of the 1978 participants; 33.9 percent engaged in learning for personal, social, or other non–job related goals (National Center for Education Statistics 1980).

According to the 1978 data reported by NCES, job-related educational activities for adults dominate the adult program schedules of the following institutions: four-year colleges or universities; vocational, trade, or business schools; business or industry; labor organizations or professional associations; and government agencies. Personal social programs are most popular in the private community organizations, among tutors or private instructors, and in the K–12 segment of the educational structure.

ANALYTICAL STUDIES

Analytical studies of adult participation in learning include those investigations that go beyond the collection of self-report data concerning reasons for engaging in study. A number of studies of this kind have been conducted in North America in the past twenty years. Several of the more significant analytical inquiries, beginning with Houle's stimulating investigation, are discussed here.

Motivational Analysis

Houle (1961) should be credited with the initiation of analytic research into participation of adults in learning activities. Based on the results of interviews with twenty-two adults, he opened the door to one of the most active areas of adult education research. It is unlikely that any other adult education book, regardless of size or methodological base, has stimulated the field of practice and study as greatly as has *The Inquiring Mind* (Houle 1961).

Houle's observations are based on an interview scale composed of nineteen questions in six major categories:

1. Do continuing learners possess any particular characteristics which make them different from other people?
2. What were the factors that led them to become continuing learners?
3. What has been the history of their continuing education in the past?
4. How much education are they now undertaking and of what kinds?
5. How do they think society views continuing education?
6. How do they themselves view it?

He was impressed by the similarity of the subjects in his sample, but he also noted differences in the major conceptions that they held about the purposes and values of continuing education. The different values and purposes appeared to Houle to cluster in three subgroups, or "learning orientations." The first of these he called the *goal-oriented*. People who are goal oriented use education as a means of accomplishing fairly clear-cut objectives. The second group, which he called *activity-oriented,* comprises individuals who take part in education because they find in the circumstances of learning a meaning that has no necessary connection, and often no connection at all, with the content or the announced purposes of the activity. The third he identified as *learning-oriented* because people in this group seek knowledge for its own sake. These are not pure types, however, and the best way to represent them practically would be by three overlapping circles.

Of the three groups that Houle identified, the goal-oriented individuals are generally the easiest to understand, because their views and behaviors are consistent with the "usual" beliefs about education (Boshier 1971). The educational activities of goal-oriented individuals are believed to be best described as occurring in episodes beginning with the awareness of a need. Consequently, the learning history of individuals in this group does not consist of a steady, even, and continuous flow. Goal-oriented learners also seem to be eclectic about their choice of institutions and methods of learning. They are moved by an interest, or a recognized need, and they respond in a matter-of-fact practical way to satisfy it. According to Houle, they read a great deal, not freely or widely, but usually along lines of well-defined interests or in connection with courses or organizational work.

The activity-oriented learners take part in learning programs primarily for reasons that are unrelated to the purposes or content of the learning activities in which they engage. Each of the people identified by Houle, in his sample, were course takers and joiners of groups. Their institutional affiliations seem to be primarily motivated by the possibilities of social contact, and their choice of activities is essentially based on the number and kind of interpersonal relationships that they would yield. According to Houle, these people do almost no reading.

Education for the learning oriented is a way of life; it might be called a constant activity instead of a continuing activity. These individuals seem to differ from the individuals in the other two subgroups more than they differ from each other. Each particular educational activity of the learning-oriented individual is an activity with a goal, but the continuity, range, and integrity of such experiences make the total pattern of participation far more than the sum of its parts. According to Houle, the learning behavior of the learning oriented has a continuity, a flow and scope, that establishes the basic fundamental nature of the participation in learning. Since childhood they have been avid readers, they frequently join groups and classes for educational reasons, and they often select the serious programs on television and radio.

Following Houle's classic study of orientations of participants in adult education, two slightly different lines of further analytical inquiry were developed. The first followed Houle's "orientation" model and is represented by the investigations of Sheffield (1964), Burgess (1971), Boshier (1971), Dickinson and Clark (1975), Grabowski (1973), Morstain and Smart (1974), and others. The second line was suggested by Knox and Videbeck (1963), who recommended that participants be viewed in terms of interacting variables, including psychological ones. Their research thrust is reflected in the literature by Dickinson (1971), Douglah and Moss (1968), London (1963), Miller (1967), and McClusky (1970), as well as by other investigators.

The following discussion of participation studies in adult education first reports selected investigations that followed Houle's learning orientations through Boshier. Boshier (1971) is considered here as a transitional investigator who followed Houle in his early work but moved over to the multivariate psychological line of inquiry.

Motivational Orientations

Houle's impact on the study of participation of adults in learning activities is not limited to *The Inquiring Mind* and the conceptual structure that he presented to the field. A number of his students developed an interest in the topic and subsequently made additional contributions to adult education. Tough (1978), whose work in the area of individual learning projects is discussed later in this chapter, is one example. The work of others is cited in the appropriate places in the following paragraphs.

Based on the transcriptions of Houle's interviews, Sheffield (1964) developed an instrument to assess learning activities vis-à-vis the learning orientations of individuals completing the instrument. The instrument was administered to 453 subjects whose responses were factor analyzed. The statistical treatment of the data yielded five meaningful learning orientations: learning, desire for sociability, personal goal, societal goal, and need fulfillment. Sheffield's findings also underscore the point made earlier concerning the multidimensional characteristic of motivation and topic or content studied. He identified four types of conferences by content, and each conference type (liberal, occupational, functional, recreational) contains individuals with each orientation, and learners of each orientation are found in each type of conference.

The conference type in which the largest percentage of learning-oriented individuals participated was the "functional" one. The smallest percentage participated in occupational conferences. Individuals with a desire-for-sociability orientation clustered in the recreational conference, with only 15.4 percent in the liberal conference. Personal-goal-oriented learners favored liberal conferences, and participated least frequently in functional conferences. Societal-goal-oriented individuals were almost evenly distributed in liberal conferences and recreational conferences. Finally, the need-fulfillment-oriented adults favored occupational conferences, while they participated least frequently in recreational conferences. The distribution of orientations according to conference type is displayed in Table 4.3.

Sheffield interpreted his findings as supportive of Houle's basic three-part typology. He suggested that the two additional orientations were in reality dimensions of two of Houle's original types. The personal-goal-oriented learner and the societal-goal-oriented individual are two subtypes of Houle's goal orientation. Likewise, Sheffield's desire-for-sociability orientation and the need-fulfillment orientation are subtypes of the activity orientation identified by Houle.

Burgess (1971) followed Sheffield and also built on Houle's conceptual base of learning orientations. He based his work on the premise that the motives of participation factor into eight groups. As a result of his survey of 1,046 respondents, Burgess concluded that motives clustered in seven factors: the

Table 4.3
Percentage of the Primary Orientations Represented by Participants
in Conference Types

Primary Orientations	Conference Types				
	Liberal	Occupational	Functional	Recreational	Total
Learning	25.0%	18.4%	32.9%	23.7%	100%
Desire for sociability	15.4%	24.6%	27.7%	32.3%	100%
Personal-goal	28.9%	26.7%	21.1%	23.3%	100%
Societal-goal	31.4%	21.4%	17.2%	30.0%	100%
Need-fulfillment	23.2%	31.7%	25.6%	19.5%	100%

Source: Sheffield 1964, p. 20. Reprinted by permission.

desire to know, the desire to reach a personal goal, the desire to reach a social goal, the desire to reach a religious goal, the desire to escape, the desire to take part in activity, and the desire to comply with formal requirements.

Burgess had hypothesized the presence of two factors that were not identified in the research. They were a desire to comply with general social pressures and the desire to study alone, or just to be alone. He believes that the latter factor clustered with the desire to know and thus was not identified as a separate factor. He found the failure of the factor on the desire to comply with social pressures to emerge difficult to explain, however. He was convinced that, like Sheffield before him, his work provided additional support for Houle's position.

While Burgess's work was under way in the United States, Boshier (1971), in New Zealand, was laying the foundations for his continuing work on the topic. Boshier, too, notes that his study "aims to develop Houle's typology further, explore its applicability in the New Zealand setting with a wide range of respondents, develop an instrument to measure motive(s) for attendance, and formulate a model of adult education participation that has cross-cultural generality."

Consequently, he developed a 48-item Educational Participation Scale (EPS), which he administered to 233 adults. The types of courses he identifies number fifty-eight and were offered by the Wellington High School Evening Institute, University Extension, and the Workers' Education Association. They include courses of 30 and 24 sessions in length and some of only 10 weeks in length and were "largely considered by adult educators to be nonvocational." When considering the validity of Boshier's results, it should be noted also that he used a sample of 233 respondents in the factor analysis solution of a 48-item scale, fewer than 5 subjects per item, whereas it is a popular convention to require at least 10 subjects per item in such analysis (see Boshier and Collins 1982).

With the above flaw in Boshier's design noted, the results of his research are reported for the reader's interpretation. Using different procedures than Burgess and Sheffield, or failing to report them, he subsequently identified 14 motivational orientations: social welfare, social contact, other-directed professional advancement, intellectual recreation, inner-directed professional advancement, social conformity, educational preparedness, cognitive interest, educational compensation, social sharing, television abhorrence, social improvement and escape, interpersonal facilitation, and education supplementation. Second-order factors were identified as interpersonal improvement/escape, inner versus other-directed advancement, social sharing, artifact, self-centeredness versus altruism, professional future orientedness, and cognitive interest.

Finally, through a third-order factor process, he obtained four independent and uncorrelated factors that are "not unlike the three-factor Houle typology." The first factor is other-directed advancement (goal orientation). Factor 2, cognitive interest, is similar to the learning orientation identified by Houle, but learning is not undertaken "as an end in itself but to prepare oneself for some future, probably educational, activity." The third and fourth factors, self- versus other-centeredness and "social contact," may be similar to Houle's activity orientation. Boshier observes that third-order factors 1 and 2 are both vocationally anchored, while factors 3 and 4 have sociopsychological origins. He concluded that the EPS is composed of 14 first-order factors, 7 second-order factors, and 4 third-order factors.

Perhaps the most challenging aspect of Boshier's investigation (for future research) was its contribution to his development of the deficiency vs. growth orientation.

Boshier later raised the question of whether Houle's typology was correct (1971). He notes that Dow (1965) concluded that the situation was more complex than Houle envisioned, particularly concerning the activity orientation. Boshier subsequently cites the work of several researchers (Burgess 1971; Sovie 1973; Flaherty 1968) who produce seven or eight factors and then suggests that their findings fail to "confirm," "sharpen," or "support" the Houle typology (1961). His major point appears to be based on an opinion that the three learning orientations suggested by Houle (goal, activity, and learning) require a one-to-one match in factor analytic studies.

Morstain and Smart (1974) added a dimension to the research concerning motivational factors in participation. Using a sample of 611 part-time credit students at Glassboro State College, they investigated two questions: how will the Educational Participation Scale factor patterns for American college students compare with New Zealand results, and how well will the EPS identify group differences according to age-sex groupings?

As a result of the study, they determined that the factors derived in their research were similar to those that emerged in New Zealand. Two of the six factors that they identified were similar to those obtained by Boshier. There are some questions concerning their conclusion, however, as Morstain and

Smart do not specifically inform us whether they compared their six factors with Boshier's 14 first-order factors, 7 second-order factors, or 4 third-order factors. For example, social welfare and cognitive interest are reported as being identical to two factors reported by Boshier. However, social welfare is a first-order factor, as are inner-directed professional advancement, interpersonal facilitation, intellectual recreation, and social contact, while cognitive interest is a label for one of Boshier's second-order factors. Furthermore, in factor analysis, to be useful, the name given to a factor should describe the factor as much as possible, yet several of the factors that emerged from the research of Morstain and Smart contained sufficiently different items to encourage them to give different titles or labels to the factors that they identified as being similar to those identified in the New Zealand investigation.

SELF-DIRECTED INDEPENDENT LEARNING ACTIVITIES

Self-directed learning has a long but vague history. My own studies of the colonial period in America reveal abundant evidence of independent learning (Long 1976). For example, there were countless self-improvement societies, a variety of instructional content in numerous newspapers, a number of bookstores in most Eastern seaport cities, and an expanding subscription library system. Benjamin Franklin is frequently identified as the quintessential adult learner. However, it is suggested here that Cotton Mather, the famed Puritan minister of Boston, set an example that Franklin later followed.

Mather, Franklin, and Abigail Adams may have been exceptional models of adult learners in the American cities of the seventeenth and eighteenth centuries, but they were not unique. Other adults such as Colden Cadwallader, a wealthy New Yorker who helped start the American Philosophical Society, and Eliza Pinckney, of South Carolina, also discovered that curiosity had its rewards, intangible as well as tangible. The rewards of learning were sufficient to encourage apprentices to study in New York, and the Salzburgers in Georgia to remain long after the Sunday sermon to learn how to plow the sandy South Georgia soil with horses.

Contemporary interest in the independent adult learner, however, seems to have received its stimulus from two sources. The national survey of adult education in the United States reported by Johnstone and Rivera (1965) served to remind students of adult education that thousands of adults prefer not to learn in school settings. These independent learners prefer other settings and procedures; 7.9 percent of those surveyed in the national survey conducted by the National Opinion Research Center (NORC) reported that they had engaged in an independent learning activity during the twelve months preceding the 1961–62 survey period (Johnstone and Rivera 1965).

Allen Tough presented the second source of stimulation of interest in the independent self-directed learner (Tough 1966). Tough's investigation of learning activities began with his doctoral dissertation, which served as a model for a number of follow-up studies by Tough and others (Tough 1971; Coolican 1973; Hiemstra 1975; Johns 1973). These studies were often cross-cultural and included subjects from diverse walks of life. Allerton (1974) studied ministers, Armstrong (1971) and Johnson (1973) studied individuals with

limited education from the lower socioeconomic levels, Coolican (1973) studied mothers, Johns (1973) queried pharmacists, and Hiemstra's 1975 sample
included other adults. Denys's 1973 research was conducted in Africa, Tough's
1966 investigation was in Canada, and Peters and Gordon (1974) selected their
sample from the Tennessee Valley of the United States. These citations serve
merely to illustrate the range and quantity of research that has been done in
the area of adult learning projects in the most recent decade.

Investigations of adult learning projects have tended to follow closely the
design and interview methodology used by Tough.[3] Basic questions include the
following:

1. How many major learning projects do people conduct in one year
   (defined as requiring a minimum of seven hours of study)?
2. What are they learning?
3. How much time do they spend?
4. Who plans and guides the learning sessions?

A number of studies of adult learning projects have been reviewed by
Tough (1978), and he believes that about 90 percent of all adults conducted at
least one major learning effort during the year before they were interviewed.
The range from one study to another is from 70 percent to 100 percent.

The typical person, according to Tough's review, engages in five distinct
learning projects in one year. Approximately 100 hours of study are devoted to
each learning project, for a total of approximately 500 hours. The range, of
course, is much greater, with some individuals devoting 1,000 hours to study
in one year.

Similar patterns are also revealed across the studies concerning the day-to-
day planning of what and how to learn. Differences may be found among
individuals in each study, but there is general agreement among the studies.
Tough (1978) reports that about 20 percent of all learning projects are planned
by someone trained, paid, or institutionally designated to facilitate the learner,
i.e., a professional. The data reveal that the professional works in a group in
about 10 percent of the projects, in a one-to-one, tutorial relationship in about
7 percent, and indirectly through preprogrammed instructional technology in
about 3 percent of the projects. In the remaining 80 percent of the learning
projects, amateurs handle the detailed day-to-day planning. Usually the amateur is the learner, but occasionally the planning is done by a friend or a group
of peers.

The most common motivation for undertaking a learning project is the
anticipation of using the skill or knowledge. The learners have tasks that they
wish to accomplish, such as a discipline task for a child, or learning to sew or
to garden. Motives based on curiosity or the desire to know something just for
the sake of knowledge and on learning for credit are seldom reported in the
studies of self-directed learning projects. Tough notes the frequency of reference to learning for credit, for a degree or a certificate, as "rare"; he says it
occurs in about 5 percent of all learning projects.

Penland (1979) has conducted the most ambitious study on this topic in
the United States. His research is based on interviews of 1,501 adults. His data
reveal a 70 percent rate of involvement among American adults, if his findings

can be generalized to the population. The mean number of learning projects reported for his sample was 4.1. Nine areas of study were ranked in the following order according to popularity: personal development, home and family, hobbies and recreation, general education, job, religion, voluntary activity, public affairs, and agriculture/technology. The learners interviewed in Penland's study most preferred to learn at home, followed by training on the job, in the outdoors, in a discussion group classroom, at a library, and at public events.

Why did the Americans studied by Penland choose to learn independently instead of enrolling in one of the thousands of adult education courses offered annually? Tough (1978) believes that the reasons cited by the learners will surprise many adult educators, as money and transportation were the least important of the ten reasons cited. Beginning with the reasons most often identified, the ten explanations offered by the respondents are listed below.

1. Desire to set my own learning pace
2. Desire to use my own style of learning
3. Desire to keep the learning style flexible and easy to change
4. Desire to put my own structure on the learning project
5. Lack of knowledge of any classes on the topic
6. Desire for immediate results
7. Lack of time to engage in a group learning program
8. Dislike for classroom situation with a teacher
9. Lack of money
10. Difficult and/or expensive transportation arrangements

BARRIERS TO PARTICIPATION

Knowledge of some of the reasons for which adults engage in educational activities, however, does not resolve all the questions about participation that are of concern to adult educators. As long as more than half the adult population fails to participate in educational activities, questions about obstacles or barriers to participation are of legitimate concern. The topic of obstacles to participation has not been as extensively addressed as has the research area concerned with explaining the reasons that adults engage in learning activities. The barriers to participation generally have been examined through the census-type survey where the respondent usually volunteers one or more reasons for nonparticipation. A distinctively different research procedure is reported by Marieneau and Klinger (1977). Even though their research procedures were different from those used in the studies reported below, findings are similar. Five barriers to educational activities identified through an anthropological approach are family responsibilities, lack of access to educational facilities, money, time, and motivation.

The voluntary nature of adult learning activities places a heavy burden upon the planner and administrator of such activities. Because adults engage in organized learning activities with limited external compulsion, educators are severely challenged to identify not only incentives for enrollment but also obstacles to voluntary participation. Just as the research literature reveals a number of variables associated with participation, it also provides an instructive list of perceived obstacles or barriers to participation.

The CNS survey of 1974 (Carp, Peterson, and Roelfs 1974) provided a lengthy list of 25 obstacles. The first five obstacles according to that survey are as follows: cost, time, don't want to go to school full-time, home responsibilities, job responsibilities. The Illinois survey identified six reasons given by nonparticipants as follows: no need, no interest; lack of time; other (too dumb, too sick); too old; distance, lack of transportation, cost; desired classes unavailable (Illinois 1980). Several of the obstacles identified are implied in the list of ten reasons for engaging in independent study as identified by Tough (1969). However, it will be recalled that lack of money and transportation were cited in ninth and tenth place as reasons for pursuing individual learning projects. This contrasts with cost's being listed first in the CNS survey and transportation, distance, and cost listed in fifth place in the Illinois survey.

Hiemstra's 1972 study of senior citizens' participation in educational activities provides eight kinds of factors that negatively influence enrollment. Listed in order of their importance, they are transportation problems, 25 percent; don't go out at night, 24.5 percent; can learn by self, 20.3 percent; courses not interesting, 7.8 percent; courses cost too much, 6.8 percent; too much time involved, 5.7 percent; and miscellaneous, 9.9 percent.

Anderson and Niemi's 1969 review of literature concerning adult education and the disadvantaged identified a number of social and psychological obstacles closely related to a lack of self-confidence, including a fear of failure, a fear of school, and a fear of change.

One of the few reported investigations of participation among blue-collar workers, conducted in five central New York counties by a research team from Cornell (Botsman 1975), reports obstacles identified by factory-employed blue-collar workers. The sample was based on 563 randomly selected workers age 18 years or older. The five most frequently perceived barriers to participation in educational activities are identified as no transportation, too much red tape in getting enrolled, cost of learning materials, cost of tuition, and past schooling difficulty.

Barriers to participation as perceived by men and women differ in the study. Females most frequently cited the following four obstacles: home responsibilities, cost of tutition, cost of child care, and takes time away from other activities. In contrast, male workers cited low grades in past, not confident of my ability, and courses I want don't seem to be available. The two sets of perceived barriers are quite different. For example, the female workers cited external constraints, whereas the males cited internal states that reflect feelings of inadequacy or anticipated failure.

It is more likely that female workers have greater responsibility for family activities than do their male counterparts in the work force. The four commonest barriers for female workers are closely related to each other and are probably a realistic reflection of the concerns of most working mothers. If a man is participating in an adult education program to learn new occupation-related skills or to update existing skills, he might be more concerned about his past ability, or lack of ability, to achieve good grades. Male workers are more likely to cite reasons such as "work toward certification or licensure" and "help advance in present job."

The barriers to participation in an adult education program are different for younger, middle-aged, and older workers. Life-styles change with age and are reflected in family and job responsibilities, personal goals, financial status, and health, and all these factors affect, in turn, a worker's willingness to begin a new course of studies. Very little overlapping of barriers exists between the younger and the older age groups in the study. For example, "afraid I'm too old to begin" is clearly a more salient barrier for 49.7 percent of the older workers than for 3.7 percent of the younger workers, while "cost of tuition" is cited as a barrier more frequently by 64.7 percent of the younger workers than by 31.1 percent of the older workers.

Younger workers who have been out of school a shorter time than those in other age groups are "tired of going to school, tired of classrooms" and have a greater concern about "cost of child care." In addition, "job responsibilities" for 29.1 percent of the younger workers, who are trying to establish themselves, seems to be more of a barrier to participation. In general, it can be seen that the younger worker, who is new to the job market, who may work more hours weekly, who may be starting a home and family with all the initial expenses of becoming established, perceives quite different barriers.

The factors that motivate older workers to participate are more likely to be related to personal enrichment or growth than to occupational considerations. Thus, "courses don't lead anywhere" is cited as a significant barrier for only 1.9 percent of the older workers but for 13.5 percent of the younger, who are motivated for more specific purposes.

Level of occupational skill also plays an important part in influencing perceived barriers to participation. Six major barriers were categorized by level of skill. The study shows that unskilled workers cite "job responsibilities" as a barrier more frequently than skilled or semiskilled workers. This may be because the unskilled group works six to eight hours a week more, on the average, than the better-trained workers.

Two other factors cited by the unskilled group are a substantial lack of familiarity with the procedures of enrollment and concern about inadequate preparation for an adult education program.

The perceived barriers to participation in adult education were also studied by level of previous education. Again, it is seen that "cost of tutition" is one of the most frequently cited factors that workers of all occupational skill levels say is a significant barrier. Other perceived barriers are not shared by nearly as many workers. Workers who have gone on with their education beyond high school are less apt to cite personal inadequacies (lack of confidence, age, inadequate preparation) than the non–high school graduates; this parallels the situation when workers are categorized by level of occupational skill. Better-educated workers perceive more difficulties with the system than with themselves, according to Botsman (1975).

There is considerable agreement among the studies by the Commission on Non-Traditional Study, the Illinois State Board of Higher Education, Hiemstra, and Botsman. Transportation and cost factors are cited as important perceived barriers in each study. The New York–based study of blue-collar workers surfaced two new factors that may be unreported factors among the other samples: enrollment red tape and prior academic performance.

Table 4.4 displays the various obstacles to adult participation identified by

Table 4.4
Obstacles to Adult Participation in Education as Identified in Six Studies

	CNS	IBEH	Hiemstra	Anderson and Niemi	Botsman	Marieneau and Klinger
1.	cost	no need, no interest	transportation	lack of self-confidence (fear of failure, fear of school, fear of change)	transportation	access to educational facilities
2.	time	time	don't go out at night		red tape (enrollment)	family responsibilities
3.	don't want to go to school full time	too dumb, too sick	can learn by self		cost of learning materials	finances
4.	home responsibilities	too old	courses not interesting		cost of tuition	time
5.	job responsibilities	distance, lack of transportation, cost	courses cost too much		past schooling difficulty	motivation
6.		desired classes not available	time			
7.		miscellaneous				

the six investigations discussed here. Cost is cited as a factor in five of the six studies, time in four, and transportation in three of them.

Cross (1981), Darkenwald and Merriam (1982), and I have arrived at similar generalizations concerning obstacles to participation. Marieneau and Klinger (1977) have also suggested a related explanation. Cross and I both use three explanatory categories, while Darkenwald and Merriam use four. According to Cross, the reasons for failure to participate can be subsumed under one of the following categories: dispositional, situational, and institutional. I labeled the types of barriers as institutional, personal, and social. Marieneau and Klinger's two-part classification specifies the reasons as situational or value oriented. Darkenwald and Merriam describe the barriers as situational, institutional, informational, and psychosocial.

The four conceptual typologies designed to identify general barriers to participation are all very similar. Each recognizes the importance of the situations in which people live (I included this concept in the larger idea of social barriers). Each recognizes the importance of personal variables through the use of labels such as dispositional, personal, value orientation, and psychosocial. Darkenwald and Merriam believe it necessary to separate informational barriers from larger classifications used by Cross and me.

The development of these typologies of barriers to participation is encouraging because it removes the emphasis on nonparticipation from personal and/or social explanations only. It signals a recognition of the interaction of personal, social, and institutional variables. Further clarification and understanding of barriers and obstacles to participation may also contribute to a refinement of understanding concerning motives and reasons for participation.

GENERAL OBSERVATIONS

Studies of adult participation in learning activities are of direct interest to a large number of educators of adults in various agency and organizational contexts. These studies fall into two general types according to research procedures: self-report/census-type studies and analytical inquiries. As a result of the research concerning adult learner activity, we have a good profile of adult learners and have a fairly reliable understanding of how they differ from non-learners.

We have information on self-directed learners who learn independently or with limited assistance or direction from others. They plan and conduct a majority of their learning themselves. Topics studied, however, in self-directed learning appear to differ from those studied more frequently in institutionally sponsored learning activities. We do not know why this is so. Several speculations could be offered, but there is no good empirical base on which such an explanation rests.

Reasons for learning independently do not closely coincide with obstacles to learning such as cost and transportation. While these explanations are high among the reasons that nonparticipants give for not engaging in institutionally sponsored learning, they are ranked lowest among the reasons given by independent learners for preferring self-directed activity.

It can be observed that the phenomenon of adult self-directed learning presents a special challenge to educators of adults. The peculiar aspects of the challenge lie in the fact that most educators of adults are located within a particular institutional or organizational structure, while self-directed learning is "a-institutional" (Hiemstra and Penland 1981).

Study of self-directed learning is generally recognized as a legitimate area of inquiry for educators of adults. It is believed that through knowledge gained by studying self-directed independent learning activity we may improve our ability to facilitate the learning of the learner engaged in sponsored learning activity. Nevertheless, the greater interest in participation studies remains in sponsored educational activity.

Studies of participation in sponsored activities are numerous. Generally, the studies are designed to identify and estimate numbers and important personal-social characteristics of learners, and the reasons, motives, and obstacles connected with participation. We have observed that these studies are mostly descriptive or analytical. They reflect research approaches identified by Burgess about 15 year ago. Two additional research approaches are now evident, however. They include the study of independent self-directed learning activity and meta-research. Meta-research on participation is significant for several reasons. First, its emergence would not have been possible without a sufficient volume of participation studies to support it. Second, cross-study comparisons provide additional insights and are mutually confirming. Third, longitudinal comparisons allow scholars and administrators to identify trends and make reasonable projections about the future. Fourth, different analyses and interpretations are possible.

The variety of studies and range of variables included in the research into participation are apparent in Table 4.5. For the purpose of this book, studies completed since Verner and Davis (1964) reported their work have been combined for interpretive purposes. Variables identified as having some association with participation as well as those that were not reported as having a relationship are noted in the right-hand columns of the table.

Despite the great progress that is apparent in the research in participation, a number of challenges remain. Inconsistent definitions continue to plague the topic. Consequently, an advocate of a particular position can make almost any estimate of the number of participants and find support in the literature. For example, the person who wishes to accentuate the negative can cite the NCES data and say that almost 90 percent of all adults do not participate in a learning activity. Conversely, an advocate who wishes to emphasize the positive can cite Tough and say that approximately 90 percent of all adults engage in at least one learning activity annually.

Broad definitions of learning are as threatening as extremely narrow ones. To be useful, a definition must discriminate among phenomena. If it is so broad that all phenomena are included, we have only one class that includes everything. Such a situation is not productive. In contrast, an extremely severe and restrictive definition may limit eligible phenomena so drastically as to make the class so narrow that it has no value.

Studies designed to inform us of reasons, motives, and obstacles in participation have not produced the desired definitive answers we seek. This is not to observe that these studies are useless; they are, in fact, informative and helpful, up to a point. It is obvious to those who have examined this literature that

Reported by Verner and Davis (1964) and Long

Factor	Number of Studies VERNER AND DAVIS			Number of Studies LONG			Number of Studies TOTAL		
	Total	Some Relationship	No Relationship	Total	Some Relationship	No Relationship	Total	Some Relationship	No Relationship
Personal Factors									
Socioeconomic									
Age	11 (4)*	6 (3)	5 (1)	3 (3)	3 (3)		14 (7)	9 (6)	5 (1)
Sex	6 (2)	3 (1)	3 (1)	1 (1)		1 (1)	7 (3)	3 (1)	4 (2)
Education									
Level Completed	10 (3)	8 (2)	2 (1)	2 (2)	1 (1)	1 (1)	12 (5)	9 (3)	3 (2)
Dislike of School	1	1					1	1	
Prior Failure	5 (2)	1	4 (2)	1 (1)	1 (1)		6 (3)	2 (1)	4 (2)
Time Since Attendance	1	1					1	1	
Kind of Diploma	2 (1)	1 (1)	1				2 (1)	1 (1)	1
Prior Exper. in Adult Ed.	6 (3)	5 (2)	1 (1)	2 (2)	2 (2)		8 (5)	7 (4)	1 (1)
H. S. Course				1 (1)	1 (1)		1 (1)	1 (1)	
Language Spoken				1 (1)	1 (1)		1 (1)	1 (1)	
Reading Speed & Accuracy				1 (1)	1 (1)		1 (1)	1 (1)	
Vocabulary				1 (1)	1 (1)		1 (1)	1 (1)	
Reading Comprehension				1 (1)	1 (1)		1 (1)	1 (1)	
Marital Status	4 (2)	4 (2)		2 (2)	1 (1)	1 (1)	6 (4)	5 (3)	1 (1)
Head of Family				1 (1)		1 (1)	1 (1)		1 (1)
Dependents	3 (1)	2 (1)	1	1 (1)	1 (1)		4 (2)	3 (2)	1
Occupation	7 (2)	3 (2)	4	2 (2)	2 (2)		9 (4)	5 (4)	4
Father's Occupation				1 (1)	1 (1)		1 (1)	1 (1)	
Race	3	3					3	3	
Income	2 (1)	2 (1)		2 (2)	2 (2)		4 (3)	4 (3)	
Social Position				1 (1)	1 (1)		1 (1)	1 (1)	
Change in Social Position				1 (1)	1 (1)		1 (1)	1 (1)	
Change in Occupational Class				1 (1)	1 (1)		1 (1)	1 (1)	
Changes in Employment				1 (1)	1 (1)		1 (1)	1 (1)	

* All figures in parentheses indicate the number of studies that tested the statistical significance of their data.

Table 4.5 (cont'd.)

Factor	Number of Studies VERNER AND DAVIS			Number of Studies LONG			Number of Studies TOTAL		
	Total	Some Relationship	No Relationship	Total	Some Relationship	No Relationship	Total	Some Relationship	No Relationship
Psycho-social									
Intelligence	2 (1)	1 (1)	1	1 (1)	1 (1)		3 (2)	2 (2)	
Motivation									
Reasons for Enrolling	4 (2)	2 (2)	2				4 (2)	2 (2)	2
Job Advancement	5 (2)	3 (2)					5 (2)	3 (2)	
Social Participation	3 (2)	2 (2)	1				3 (2)	2 (2)	
Registration to Vote	1 (1)		1 (1)				1 (1)		1 (1)
Miscellaneous									
Anxiety Test Scores	1		1				1		1
Liked Taking Tests	1	1					1	1	
Liked Assignments	1	1					1	1	
Veteran Status	1 (1)	1 (1)					1 (1)	1 (1)	
Home Ownership	2 (2)	2 (2)					2 (2)	2 (2)	
Length of Residence	1 (1)	1 (1)		1 (1)		1 (1)	2 (2)	1 (1)	1 (1)
TV Ownership	1 (1)		1 (1)				1 (1)		1 (1)
Time Owned TV	1 (1)	1 (1)					1 (1)	1 (1)	
Student Grades	1	1					1	1	
Personality Traits	1			5 (5)	4 (4)	1 (1)	5 (5)	4 (4)	1 (1)
Situational Factors									
Distance from School	3 (2)		2 (2)				3 (2)		2 (2)
Mode of Transportation	2 (1)	2 (1)					2 (1)	2 (1)	
Travel Time				1 (1)		1 (1)	1 (1)		1 (1)

Institutional Factors

Administrative

Time of Day	3 (1)	1	2 (1)			3 (1)	1		2 (1)
Season of Year	5	5				5	5		
Day of Week	2 (2)	2 (2)				2 (2)	2 (2)		
Frequency of Meeting	3 (2)	2 (2)	1	1 (1)		3 (2)	2 (2)		1
Length of Course	4 (1)	2 (1)	2			5 (2)	3 (2)		2
Length of Session	1 (1)	2	1 (1)			1 (1)			1 (1)
Tuition Charged	3	2				3	2	2	1
Size of Group	3 (2)	1 (1)	2 (1)			3 (2)	1 (1)	1 (1)	2 (1)
Counseling	6 (1)	6 (1)				6 (1)	6 (1)	6 (1)	
Student Load	3 (2)	2 (1)				3 (2)	2 (1)	2 (1)	
Kind of Courses	5 (1)	5 (1)	1 (1)	1 (1)		6 (2)	6 (2)	6 (2)	1 (1)

Instruction

Teacher Training	2 (1)	2 (1)				2 (1)	3 (1)	2 (1)	2 (1)
Teaching Experience	3 (1)		2 (1)			3 (1)			2 (1)
Teacher Rating	2 (1)	2 (1)				2 (1)	2 (1)	1	2 (1)
Changing Teachers	1	1				1	1		
Student Satisfaction	3 (1)	2	1 (1)			3 (1)	3 (1)	2	1 (1)
Teacher Performance	1† (1)†	1 (1)	1 (1)			1† (1)	2	1 (1)	1 (1)
Discussion Activity	2 (2)	1 (1)	1 (1)			2 (2)	2 (2)	1 (1)	1 (1)

Reasons for Discontinuing

14 | | | | | | 14

Attendance Factors‡

Course Preparation				1 (1)	1 (1)	1 (1)	1 (1)		1 (1)
Course Meets Needs			1 (1)			1 (1)	1 (1)		
Course Understanding			1 (1)			1 (1)	1 (1)		
Teaching Methods				1 (1)	1 (1)	1 (1)	1 (1)		1 (1)
Median of Instruction				1 (1)	1 (1)	1 (1)	1 (1)		1 (1)
Formal Instruction			1 (1)			1 (1)	1 (1)		
Approachability of Instructor			1 (1)			1 (1)	1 (1)		
Informal Interaction			1 (1)			1 (1)	1 (1)		
Sociability of Classmates			1 (1)			1 (1)	1 (1)		
Satisfaction			1 (1)			1 (1)	1 (1)		

† This study found one instructor's behavior related and nine not related to dropout rates.
‡ This study focused on attendance rather than attrition as defined by dropping out.

motivation and obstacles are likely multifaceted. At the least, they are broad inclusive constructs rather than narrow exclusive constructs. It is also likely that there are a number of forces at work that "push" and "pull" the adult toward and away from participation. Aslanian and Brickell's transitions and triggers concept seems to address only the factors "pushing" an individual into the learning context. The factors that "pull" against participation are not identifiable in their scheme. We have identified a number of factors through factor analysis that may be sufficient cause for participation, but we have not been successful in isolating and describing what is necessary for participation.

The entire corpus of factor analytic studies is based on a rational concept. There is an underlying assumption that an instrument such as the Educational Participation Scale provides a valid means of identifying motives. A different position, which has not been identified in the literature, is the possibility that motives cannot be discerned with a standardized paper-and-pencil instrument. This position suggests that motives operate at a subconscious level and, as such, are best ascertained by projective techniques.

NOTES

1. Despite the age of the NORC study, the findings and conclusions continue to be confirmed by more recent work. Because of its historical significance, the NORC inquiry is cited heavily in this chapter. Anderson and Darkenwald (1979) suggest that the low correlations between participation and the identified sociodemographic data justify a continuing search for better explanatory variables.

2. Rice (1979) and Dooley and White (1968) report related findings that indicate that adult individuals are influenced to participate in education by the opposite sex. Rice studied spouse support as a variable in the participation of mature women, and Dooley and White studied psychological variables, including one identified as reflecting the Mating Erg, based on the Motivation Analysis Test developed by Cattell. The Mating Erg was significantly associated with participation at the .01 level.

3. Spear and Mocker (1981) have added another dimension to self-directed learning inquiries by their attention to what they call the organizing circumstance or environmental determinants in approaches to self-directed learning.

5 · Models of Adult Participation

THE PARTICIPATION STUDIES discussed in Chapter 4 reveal an extensive and complicated array of variables that seem to be related to participation of adults in learning activities. Consequently, the scholar and practitioner are challenged to bring some kind of order to the mass of findings. One way to do this is through the development of explanatory models that abstract and synthesize the critical substance of the findings into a manageable conceptual structure.

Over the years, a number of efforts have been made by educators of adults to develop models of participation that would explain or predict participation. Lorge provided one of the earliest concepts in modern adult education literature. He used what is identified as a needs satisfaction approach. Accordingly, he speculated that people have "wants" in four areas. They want to (1) gain something, (2) be something, (3) do something, or (4) save something. He provides examples in each of the four categories (Lorge 1947).

Douglah and Moss (1968) suggested some components of a model, while Douglah later (1970) summarized the characteristics of models then in use. Douglah and Moss indicated that participation is related to two general kinds of factors: positional and psychological. These are discussed in greater detail in Chapter 4. Four variables are included among the positional factors (age, employment status, income, and number of children), and one variable (withdrawing tendencies) is identified as a psychological factor.

Characteristics of models in use as identified by Douglah (1970) were based on five motivational concepts: (1) a basic needs satisfaction model, (2) Maslow's hierarchy of needs, (3) Miller's application of Maslow's hierarchy to social structures and forces in society, (4) Havighurst's concept of developmental tasks, and (5) Houle's learning orientations. Furthermore, Douglah suggested that these models collectively have the following implications for adult educators who plan programs: (1) adult education must serve purposes that address the needs of the learners, (2) the purposes must be highly valued by the learner, (3) benefits must be competitive, and (4) structures and procedures must not be barriers to participation.

In the years since Lorge and Douglah shared their thoughts with the field, additional models have emerged. Five such models (including Miller's model, which existed prior to Douglah's work) are selected for discussion here. A sixth model, the transitions and triggers model of Aslanian and Brickell, is discussed in Chapter 4.

FIVE MODELS OF ADULT PARTICIPATION

The five models discussed in this chapter are as follows:

1. Miller's Force-Field Model
2. Boshier's Congruence Model
3. McClusky's Margin Model
4. Expectancy-Valence Model
5. Cross's Chain-of-Response (COR) Model

The models are presented in terms of their general historical development and/or appearance in the literature. When possible, appropriate research concerning the models is also noted. (Some other models are briefly noted following the presentation of five major ones.)

Miller's Force-Field Analysis

Harry Miller's concept of force-field analysis of participation in adult education, unlike most of the literature reported here, is not research; it is a theoretical position or model by which participation may be studied. However, it is included in this discussion of research for several reasons. First, inclusion does not violate the purpose of the book but is actually consistent with the goals set for it. Second, since the idea is derived from Kurt Lewin's research, it has a research base. Third, it seems to have directly influenced the thinking and research of Boshier.

Two necessary tasks common to many educators of adults are difficult, if not impossible, to perform with any degree of confidence without some valid idea about participation. These tasks, as identified by Miller (1967), are (1) to make tentative predictions about future trends in participation and (2) to develop plans for increasing participation in desirable educational activities. Accordingly, Miller shares a plan to improve our ability to deal with these tasks. The plan he offers is drawn from Lewin and other psychologists interested in motivation. However, Miller does not introduce his concept without observing the difficulties encountered by those who have specialized in the study of motivation, human or animal. It is recognized as a complex and frequently contradictory area of study.

Participation in most adult educational activities is voluntary; thus, Miller indicates that involvement represents a person's commitment of time and energy in competition with desires and options to be engaged in a number of other activities. This assumption is strengthened by Haldane (1962), who reports that the majority of past students did not reenroll at the London Working Man's College not because of disappointment with their experiences there but because they developed other interests which appealed more than evening classes. These interests, acccording to Haldane, were often related to their course of study at the Working Man's College, and so, in a way, they had achieved their goals. Thus, two important factors for model builders are introduced here: (1) the attraction of other activities relative to participation in education and (2) the subjective assessment by the learner of goal achievement.

Two additional assumptions of Miller's are as follows:

1. The learner's willingness to undertake an educational activity demonstrates some personal need.
2. Personal needs do not operate in a vacuum. They are shaped, conditioned, and directed by the social structures and forces of the society in which the individual lives and to which he or she has become acculturated.

Miller (1967) opted to use Maslow's 1954 hierarchy of needs as the framework for establishing the origins and nature of human needs that have a bearing on his model. A similar framework has also been adopted in Boshier's 1973 speculations about fundamental psychological foundations of participation. At the time of Miller's 1967 work, Maslow's hierarchy consisted of five levels of need. From lowest to highest they are survival, safety, belonging, recognition (status), and achievement and self-realization.

Within the framework provided by the two basic assumptions about human need and social forces, Miller's third assumption emerged. That assumption posits an expectation of patterns of interaction between the variables represented in his first two assumptions and "that any particular pattern will generally result in the same level of participation" (Miller 1967, p. 4). The four patterns of participation predicted by Miller are as follows:

1. When strong social forces *and* strong personal needs move people toward a particular educational objective, the congruence should result in a high level of participation in programs relevant to that objective.
2. When strong personal needs among a particular group of people move them toward an educational objective, but there are no supporting or facilitating social factors, the participation level will be low generally, but erratically and spottily high.
3. When personal needs in a particular group are weak but social forces are strong, participation originally will be fairly high but may drop sharply after an initial period.
4. When personal needs and social forces conflict, the participation level will depend on the strength of the social force in the given

situation, but there will be a considerable amount of tension within the program itself.

It is assumed that weak personal needs in combination with weak social forces will result in extremely low participation.

Maslow's hierarchy of needs has a long history of use among adult educators. It is limited, however, in its ability to accurately reflect reality. Many exceptions can be cited to illustrate that the hierarchy does not always operate. Particularly threatening its veracity is the expectation that needs at each lower level be satisfied before the individual addresses needs at the next level. Thus, Miller's model is weakened by the assumptions associated with Maslow's hierarchy.

A second weakness of the elegant concept concerns the concept of social forces. Miller limits his discussions to Gans's 1962 useful descriptive sociological work. Additional conceptualization and treatment of the concept of social forces is desirable. For example, there is little question that we live in a complex social order with variable cross-currents among the social forces. What happens when these forces conflict? Miller shared a speculative prediction about participation when personal needs and social forces conflict, but he failed to speculate about conflicts within each category, i.e., conflicting personal needs and conflicting social forces. For example, the middle-class individual was represented as having recognition (status) needs and Western society as generally strongly supporting efforts to meet those needs. But today, many middle-class individuals also have a safety need at the lowest level of that concept (i.e., personal safety) and survival needs at a high abstract level (i.e., economic survival in a "stag-flation" economic condition). It does not appear that Miller's model predicts participation outcomes in such complex situations.

Drawing heavily on Gans, Miller seems to join a host of sociologists who appear to believe that the identified social rankings within a society are stable and immutable. Part of the problem is caused by the fact that a particular social ranking is often influenced by the array of power in a society. London (1970) observes that social class studies thus often serve to maintain the status quo rather than indicate the evidence of other groups and segments of the population who may reflect different characteristics. Furthermore, according to London, there can be no question that the dominant views of society are greatly influenced by the ruling class or establishment, and sociologists often indicate that the prevailing view is the "true" view. Scholars are cautioned to be aware of contending views that are sometimes in conflict with the dominant perspectives. Furthermore, there is a danger of identifying the dominant views within each social class as the only set of values and beliefs that are represented in each class. In reality, each class is heterogeneous and may reflect as many significant within-class differences as between-class differences. Failure to consider within-class differences results in a caricature of the class rather than a description of individual members of it.

In conclusion, Miller's model based on Lewin's 1947 field theory seems to offer a provocative concept for further development. Miller's model has value to adult educators even though it contains two basic weaknesses: it is too simplistic, and it is founded on a questionable conceptual base in Maslow's hierarchy of needs. On the other hand, it has been a productive concept even though no research in participation has been identified that specifically and directly employed the model.

Boshier's Congruence Model

Boshier's 1973 congruence model of participation is derived from a number of sources in the fields of social psychology and organizational psychology and from the work of third-force psychologist A. H. Maslow. Based on work in the above fields, Boshier theorizes that dropout and nonparticipation are of similar origins and that "congruence" versus dissonance can be developed as an explanatory concept for both phenomena. Accordingly, he suggests that research should seek to identify the congruence/dissonance of critical environmental/psychological variables. For example, theoretically it would be beneficial to know how different institutions, adult education teachers, and so on, are perceived by students or potential learners. He bases his congruence model heavily upon dropout studies that he conducted in New Zealand, where he discovered that students who dropped out had higher measures of incongruence on a psychological inquiry into four concepts: Other Adult Education Students; My Adult Education Lecturer; Myself; and Myself, Where I Would Like To Be. The basic premise of the congruence model seems to have sufficient support in the larger body of social psychological literature; however, the connection between motivation variables related to the dropping of a course by a student and motivation variables associated with nonparticipation require additional research.

The results of a number of participation studies in the United States and in Great Britain are equivocal.

London (1970) reports a study of participation among a sample of working-class males, and some of his findings are supportive of the congruence theory while others are not. For example, he discovered that having liked school during one's youth and having had a desire to continue schooling are positively associated with participation. In contrast, past scholastic performance was not associated with participation in his sample. A "felt lack" of education did not seem to be a strong motivation to continue formal learning. London discussed the possibility of incongruence between the planners of adult education who approach the process from a middle-class bias and the attitudes, life-styles, and values of potential lower-class participants.

London also identified some other areas of possible incongruence between the professionals in administrative and teaching positions. He identified these as myths about the nature of blue-collar life, particularly concerning the manual worker's interests, capacity, ability, and potential for learning. Some of the myths that he identified are that workers are not capable of sustained intellectual effort, and therefore are not able to benefit from continuing education; that blue-collar workers do not value education; that intellectual ability is demonstrated early in life and if not manifested then, will not later appear.

An explanation for the frequency with which "cost" is identified as a barrier to participation is provided by London. He noted that the individuals in his sample often cited cost as an obstacle. But he also discovered that individuals in the sample were not well informed about adult education. Therefore, the reference to cost as a barrier when educational activities are generally inexpensive may not be a factor of financial resources but associated rather with an information shortage.

Cost is perceived here as one environmental factor that may be controlled in studies of "congruence." Since working-class samples in New York and Great Britain indicate that costs are important factors in nonparticipation, efforts to reduce such costs may indeed improve congruence on one factor. Boshier and Baker (1979) studied the effect of fees on participation among a Canadian sample. Another study where a financial variable was analyzed is reported by Londoner (1974). His study also tends to support Miller's, Boshier's, and McClusky's (1970) models. Londoner reports a significantly higher preference for educational goals among a sample of paid adult students who had returned to high school with the assistance of public agencies. Londoner's findings provide some influential support for the concepts of participation that seek to explain educational involvement in terms of support systems or resources.

The idea that a person's educative behavior may be related to his or her attitudes was also the subject of an inquiry by Seaman and Schroeder (1970). While the results indicated a significant positive correlation (.05 level) between the level of education and extent of educative behavior, no significant relationship was noted between attitudes toward continuing education and extent of educative behavior.

Robson (1966) conducted a study in the English city of Sunderland to examine the relationship between social neighborhood and parents' attitudes toward education. Questionnaires were completed by 188 parents of boys scheduled to sit for the 11+ examination in 1964. Robson found a significant correlation between social class and educational aspiration, whether the parents are ordered by class of the father, class of the mother (as judged by her premarital work), or a combined score of both mother and father. However, areal forces (neighborhood analysis) increased the favorableness of attitudes toward education in four of seven areas. The largest deviation from the pattern of scores that would be expected if social class alone determined the attitudes developed occurred in a skilled working-class area. Thus, the neighborhood in which the individual lives seems to have some relationship to his or her attitudes toward education *over and above* the general pattern associated with class membership.

Robson suggests that neighborhood characteristics may be an index to an individual's self-image and that the neighborhood itself might be a factor in the kinds of pressures that are brought to bear on the individual to participate in any formal educational associations.

London (1970) proposes some actions that adult educators may undertake to stimulate the interest of adults in participation. The prospects, however, may not be very great, as Trenaman's 1957 British study reported that one's attitude toward education appears to be quite stable and persistent throughout life. Trenaman believes that educational attitudes are formed early and persist throughout adulthood. However, he observed that attitudes are accompanied by *some acceptance* of educational values: even the most hostile individuals usually accept some educational values. Unfortunately, the resistance to education seems to be strongest at the lower social levels, perhaps because educational attitudes are compounded by deeper social attitudes.

Sprouse (1981), following the work of Boshier and Riddell (1978), studied participation motivations of older adult learners in two different kinds of educational settings in Wisconsin: individuals in three community-based learning centers, and auditors at the University of Wisconsin–Madison. Even though there were some differences between the two groups on variables such as educational levels, preretirement occupation, and income, the motivations did not differ. The learners from the University of Wisconsin campus reported more education, higher-status occupations, and greater incomes, but the primary motive for the older learners in both settings was cognitive interest—to learn for the sake of learning. A total of four "motivational orientations," identical to those identified by Boshier and Riddell, were observed: cognitive interest, social welfare, social contact, and escape/stimulation.

An investigation into motives of participation among a sample of 843 nurses engaged in continuing education (O'Connor 1980) identified seven "motivational orientations": compliance with authority, improvement in social relations, improvement in social welfare skills, professional advancement, professional knowledge, relief from routine, and acquisition of credentials. The motive labeled professional knowledge was considered to be the strongest motive, and improvement in social relations, the weakest. Further analysis conducted to determine the relationship between the motivational orientations and three different degrees of legal requirements for the continuing education of nurses—mandatory, proposed, and voluntary—revealed no relationship except on the acquisition of credentials factor.

Certain social-demographic variables also revealed limited relationships. Age, number of children, and full-time employment were positively associated with the improvement in social relations factor.

Two of Boshier's major propositions, however, appear to be in conflict. His first implied proposition relates to congruence, i.e., the individual's participation or nonparticipation is a function of the amount of agreement between the individual's attitudes, beliefs, and values, and the degree of discrepancy between them and the attitudes of teachers and other learners and/or the beliefs and values manifested or transmitted through activities in the learning environment. Environment seems to be broadly defined by Boshier to include economic, sociological, and psychological dimensions as well as physical aspects. Hence, he cites his work with Baker (Boshier and Baker 1979) concerning the effects of fees on attendance. His work to this point does not include any experimental investigation on other variables.

The second proposition concerns the concept of motive. His implied postulate is generally at odds with the major schools in psychology and social psychology. He suggests that instead of motives arising out of a state of disequilibrium, which "drives" a person to seek homeostasis, at least for some people the drive arises from a need for heterostasis.

The apparent conflict between these two basic theoretical propositions has not been mentioned by Boshier. According to a vast body of psychological research, some of which is used in support of the first proposition, people seek congruence between their behavior and the behavior of others; congruence between their attitudes, beliefs, and values and the attitudes, beliefs, and values of others with whom they interact on a regular and continuing basis; and, finally, congruence within their own system of attitudes, beliefs, and values. Failure to achieve the congruence results in a state of disequilibrium, which people seek to reduce by a number of strategies, for example, modifying or misinterpreting information or cues to make them congruent, rejecting the information, or ignoring threatening data. The basic explanation for this behavior, however, rests upon the construct of homeostasis. According to the proposition reflected in the general literature of dissonance, people prefer a balanced state (internal congruence), and when a state of imbalance arises, steps (behavior) will be taken to reestablish homeostasis. Commander (1971) believes that a deviation from optimum congruity induces pressure on the individual to shift behavior toward equilibrium. Osgood, Suci, and Tannenbaum (1957) indicate that the congruity principle seems to be a general process in cognitive events.

In his study of attitudes, Osgood (Osgood, Suci, and Tannenbaum 1957) identifies three elements: (1) source, (2) process (evaluation), and (3) the object of the concept. Applying this model to situations in participation, we arrive at the following examples.

	Source Valued	Process-Evaluation	Object	
1.	A. Friends →	favor →	education	Congruence
	B. Subject →	favors →	education	
2.	A. Spouse →	objects →	education	Incongruence
	B. Subject →	favors →	education	
3.	A. Teacher →	encourages →	group discussion	Incongruence
	B. Learner →	dislikes →	group discussion	
4.	A. Institution →	favors →	day classes	Incongruence
	B. Learner →	dislikes →	day classes	
5.	A. Teacher →	likes →	middle-class values	Incongruence
	B. Learner →	dislikes →	middle-class values	

Figure 5.1 Osgood's model applied to participation

Source: Based on Osgood, Suci, and Tannenbaum 1957.

Applying Boshier's idea to Osgood's model, Boshier's concept of congruence is revealed in practical terms. Others such as Heider (1946), Newcomb (1961), Cartwright and Harary (1956), and Festinger (1957) have written extensively on this topic. Thus, the idea of cognitive balance, or congruence, has a strong empirical and theoretical base. Boshier's first implied foundation proposition then seems to be on a sound theoretical foundation. Unfortunately, the apparent conflict between the idea that congruence is actively sought as a means to maintain or to reestablish homeostasis and the second implied proposition, which indicates that heterostasis is the goal state, is not explained. The paradox is as follows: If heterostasis is the goal state, why will an individual seek homeostasis through the means of congruence?

These findings do not directly invalidate Boshier's congruence theory, but they do indicate that research in the area must proceed with vigor and with precisely defined parameters and terminology.

McClusky's Margin Theory

McClusky (1970) has described his margin theory as one that may be applied to involvement in community development and to participation and dropout in adult education. Like Miller, as a psychologist, McClusky draws his idea from the field of psychology. His source, however, is more directly related to Thorndike, Guthrie, and Hull than to Lewin, with a mixture of gestalt psychology of perception. The model derives from the traditional S–O–R (stimulus→organism→response) psychology with an emphasis on the "O," or individual.

McClusky represents the learning situation as requiring the expenditure of resources. Each individual possesses a finite supply of resources, and the supply varies among individuals. Each individual also has a number of responsibilities. The responsibilities are identified as "load" in McClusky's scheme, whereas the resources are referred to as "power." Succinctly put, "margin" is what is left over after one subtracts load from power (Power – Load = Margin). McClusky says that margin can be thought of as surplus power. It is the power available to a person over and beyond that required to handle his load. By load, we mean the demands made on a person by self and society. By power, we mean the resources that a person can command in coping with load (i.e., abilities, possessions, position, allies, etc.). Margin may be increased by reducing load or increasing power; it may be decreased by increasing load and/or reducing power. We can control both by modifying either power or load. When load continually matches or exceeds power, especially if both are fixed, out of control, or irreversible, the situation becomes highly susceptible to breakdown. If, however, load and power can be controlled—or better yet, if a person has access to a reserve (margin)—he or she is better equipped to meet unforeseen emergencies, is better positioned to take risks, can engage in exploratory, creative activities, is more likely to learn, and so forth—i.e., to do those things that enable him or her to live above a plateau of mere self-subsistence.

McClusky is of the opinion that there is a rough similarity between the ideas of load and power and certain other concepts. For example, stress may from one viewpoint be considered a kind of load. Load is also quite similar to the idea of input in communications theory; that is, input is a load delivered to a system of transmission. If input is too ambiguous, or if its volume and rate become excessive, a condition of "overload" arises, resistance sets in, and breakdown may occur.

The ideas of power and margin also have their analogues. For example, resilience may be regarded as a kind of latent power. It is the capacity to recover after expenditure, depletion, or exhaustion. Margin may be related to the notion of capital in economics. Here, net profit may be considered a surplus for distribution, reinvestment for expansion, or increased productivity. Also, in engineering the factor of safety is a direct application of the idea of margin. In this case, after estimating the greatest stress to which a building, bridge, or machine may be subjected, additional units of strength are built into the construction as an assurance that liberal margins of safety will be available to the client, according to McClusky.

But the key to the meaning of margin lies not in the subconcepts of load and power but in the relationship between them. For example, the amount of power that a person possesses will obviously have a strong bearing on the level and range of his or her performance. But the strategic factor for a person's selfhood is the surplus, revealed by the load-power ratio, that he or she can apply to the achievement of a preferential development. In the light of the theory, therefore, a necessary condition for participation is access to, and/or the activation of, a margin of power that may be available for application to the processes that the learning situation requires.

In the preceding discussion of the S–O–R formula and the margin theory, it will be noted that except for a few instances the reader has been left largely on his or her own to relate these concepts explicitly to the psychology of adults as a special field of inquiry. That they are relevant is quite clear. In the processes of behavioral development, the elements of S, O, and R become woven together in complex patterns of acquisitions, and as the years advance, the O, as indicated above, becomes increasingly a uniquely dominant factor in the transactions involved. Likewise, in the realm of margin, the adjustments of load to power become matters of overarching concern as a person accumulates and later relinquishes adult responsibilities and modifies the varying roles that the successive stages of the life cycle require. But a full recital of the relevance of S–O–R and margin requires more attention than this occasion permits.

Like the force-field model of Miller, McClusky's theory of margin has not been applied frequently in research activities. Main (1979) reports one of the few recent studies employing the power-load-margin concepts. His study, however, is concerned with the teaching-learning transaction rather than with participation and is discussed elsewhere.

Expectancy-Valence Theory

Bergsten reports the continuing work of the Department of Educational Research of the Stockholm Institute of Education designed to explain why some people participate in adult education and some do not. His report indicates that after a study of theories of motivation, the project was based on cognitive rather than behavioral theories. Like Miller, Bergsten (1980) based his concept on the work of Lewin (1947) and others who use the concepts of expectancy and valence. *Expectancy* is defined as a belief in the probability that particular actions will lead to certain outcomes. *Valence* is defined in terms of the anticipated satisfaction that may be derived from an outcome and value attributed to the actual satisfaction that it gives. The expectancy-valence theory proposes that a person's behavior is a result of a field of forces with direction and magnitude. The strength of a force is a product of valence and expectancy. The theoretical position is that people who view participation in adult education as a means of satisfying certain needs and believe that they have a possibility of completing the study will participate, while those who do not have positive beliefs will not participate.

The theoretical position of Bergsten also includes work and leisure as sectors of life that fill most of an individual's lifespace. Hence, due to the significance of work and leisure, they should be incorporated into the expectancy-valence model to better explain differential participation rates among adults.

The model is ahistorical in nature. Accordingly, behavior is perceived to result more from changes in beliefs about the current environment than from changes in the strength of past habits. Events that have occurred previously are of interest only to the extent that they can modify current conditions. These events have left marks in the current lifespace as a preparedness for action set, which is considered as a hypothetical variable reflecting such variables as the individual's personality, ability, and beliefs. Conceptually, the rest of the model is embedded in the current environment.

The model is based on the proposition that participation in adult education is associated with the actual life situation of the individual. This element is heavily informed by current work and leisure roles. However, one cannot, according to cognitive theory, explain a person's behavior directly from knowledge of the actual life situation. Personal needs as experienced by an individual are perceived to be dependent upon the actual life situation and will clearly influence a person's perception and interpretation of his or her life situation. Consequently, the level of expectancy that participation will result in desirable effects is determined by the readiness for action within the individual and his or her perception and interpretation of the actual life situation. According to this theory, the needs that a person experiences determine the valence of a given course or program. If adult education is consequently seen as a means of satisfying these needs, a positive value will be placed on participation. Thus, valence is tied not only to participation itself but to what it can lead to in the future.

Based on the expectancy-valence theory and an extensive review of related literature, Bergsten developed a number of hypotheses concerning participation in adult education. He subsequently drew a sample of 1,080 persons equally divided between the sexes, from six Swedish municipalities and from three age groups (28–32 years, 42–46 years, and 56–60 years). An interview instrument including 109 items was used to collect data in seven areas: previous and present family situation, work, leisure, previous participation in adult education, attitudes toward and preferences concerning adult education, obstacles to recruitment, and knowledge about adult education. No differences were noted in the response rate according to age or sex.

Bergsten's findings concerning participation in adult education are summarized here. Fully 79 percent of the sample indicated that they were interested in adult education of some type. Types or areas of adult education identified in order of frequency of preference are leisure, present job, citizenship, parenting, personal development, new job, and other. Usually, respondents identified more than one area or type of education. Interest, it should be noted, did not require commitment or obligation; therefore, the relatively high percentage of individuals responding favorably must be considered with caution. On the other hand, Bergsten believes that the high interest in educational activities is directly related to the fact that the interest areas are based on central adult life roles.

Considerable differences among the areas of interest are associated with differences in age. The oldest group, 56–60, showed the lowest interest for all kinds of education. The other two age groups did not differ significantly according to educational areas except for education focusing on the parent role; the greatest interest in this topic was among the youngest group, 28–32 years. Bergsten was satisfied that the data showed that interest in adult education does not decrease until late in life, even within a group of people with limited formal education.

Interest in more expressive types of education varied less from group to group than interest in more instrumental forms of adult education. Accordingly, it was concluded that there are relatively large groups of potential adult students with respect to the occupational sector among people with limited previous formal education.

It was hypothesized that the interest in adult education for the present job and in nonwork-related adult education is positively related to previous participation in adult education. The results indicated that for all areas of interest except "new job," those who had previously participated in adult education were more interested in doing so again. One possible explanation for this finding is that a pervasive positive attitude toward adult education has steered the behavior in both cases. Another speculation offered by Bergsten implies the reverse—that previous participation may have affected the attitudes toward adult education in a positive way. In both cases, it appears that the model explains the behavior, as the value placed on adult education (valence) and the belief in certain outcomes resulting from participation (expectancy) are crucial factors for actual participation.

Other findings in this area also tend to support the position taken earlier concerning attitudes toward education based on the work of Trenaman (1957) and London (1963). In this instance, since both previous participation and current interest in adult education are weakly associated with previous school experience, they cannot explain the strong relationship between previous participation and interest in adult education. First-time recruitment is thus an important activity in adult education and should not be overlooked. An interesting sidelight to this finding concerns the degree of similarity in the desired educational content reported by both previous participants and nonparticipants.

Bergsten also noted that the relationship between work satisfaction and interest in adult education suggests an integrated relationship with respect to education for one's present job, a compensatory relationship concerning education for a new job, and a neutral relationship with respect to nonwork-related adult education. Furthermore, the study produced findings that suggest that respondents who used their leisure for involvement in "cultural" activities such as reading books and visiting exhibitions; attending concerts, the theater, and museums; and using libraries were especially interested in adult education for the present job, for the leisure role, for the role of citizen, and for personal development. In addition, actual participation in organizations was positively associated with interest in adult education for all content areas except for education for a new job, where the greatest interest was noted among individuals who were not organization members.

Bergsten's study also confirmed a suspicion harbored by many. Those with little leisure time manifested greater interest in adult education than those with much leisure time. Bergsten indicates that the last finding implies that basic values and attitudes are of more importance in the choice of leisure-time activities than is the amount of leisure time. Thus, an increase in the amount of leisure time will not automatically result in large numbers of additional participants in adult education.

Cross's COR Model

Cross (1981) recently shared what she terms "the rough beginning" of a conceptual structure designed to identify relevant variables and hypothesize their interrelationships. She refers to her concept as a chain-of-response (COR) model. Seven key elements are identified:

1. Self-evaluation
2. Attitudes about education
3. Importance of goals and expectations that participation will meet goals
4. Life transitions
5. Opportunities and barriers
6. Information
7. Participation

The model is based on the premise that participation in adult education is the result of several related responses. According to Cross, this concept is consistent with contemporary theoretical revision in motivation theory, which describes motivation more as a constantly flowing stream than a series of discrete events. It is noteworthy that she indicates that forces for participation begin with the individual and move toward external conditions in the order noted above, though she cautions that it should be understood that forces flow in both directions. The major structural elements in Cross's model are discussed individually in the following paragraphs.

Self-evaluation as defined by Cross seems to concentrate upon personal confidence and achievement motivation.

Attitudes about education are the direct consequences of an individual's own past and arise indirectly from attitudes and experiences of significance to others.

The above two elements of the model are linked by Cross's assumption of a relatively stable characteristic stance toward learning, which may be positive or negative. Consequently, she proposes a consistent reinforcing interaction between self-evaluation and attitudes about education.

Importance of goals and expectations that participation will meet goals is based on the expectancy-valence theory identified with Lewin, Vroom, Bergsten, and Rubenson. This structural element consists of two major units: (1) valence, which is the importance of the goal, and (2) the individual's judgment that the successful attainment of the goal will bring about the desired reward. An interaction between expectancy and self-evaluation emerges. Specifically, it is suggested that people with high self-esteem expect success.

Life transitions as an element in the model reflects a concern for adjustments to new phases of the life cycle. Cross identifies this component closely with Havighurst's idea of "the teachable moment." At this point in her discussion of the model, Cross indicates that motivation to participate will interact with the next element.

Opportunities and barriers are believed to play an important role in the eventual learning behavior of the individual. Cross indicates that if the prospective adult learner gets to this point in the model with a strong desire to participate, he or she is expected to overcome minor barriers. In contrast, moderate barriers may exclude the weakly motivated.

Information concerns accurate information about adult learning activities. It is a critical element in the model, according to Cross, because in its absence, opportunities are not discovered and barriers may appear to be exaggerated.

Cross provides two illustrative scenarios to demonstrate how the variables interact to result in participation in one case and in nonparticipation in another. Her model is useful in diagnosing some particular trouble spots that traditionally seem to beset program planners. For example, it is suggested that most efforts of recruitment to learning begin at the fifth step of her model (opportunities and barriers). According to Cross, this is much too late to be very effective. Elimination of barriers will not be extremely effective for the highly motivated and may be too little, too late for the weakly motivated. Based on this line of reasoning, then, adult educators and their programs should be extremely sensitive to what goes on in steps 1, 2, and 3, which are psychosocial and developmental in nature.

The potential significance of these elements of the model is indicated by the studies by Boyle, Carson, Dickinson, Douglah, and Marieneau and Klinger cited in Chapter 4. As Marieneau and Klinger noted in their study, external barriers generally are easier to change than internal ones.

Cross's model is too recent to have been tested. It is, according to Cross, the result of research, but she also indicates a need for testing it and revising it as necessary. The model, however, seems to be weakened by the very strong assertion that self-esteem and personal confidence as described by Cross are universally and consistently correlated in a positive fashion.[1] While this view may have support in some circles, there is the possibility that individuals with external locus of control, who tend to attribute success to other sources than themselves, may have high self-esteem. How do these people fit into the model? Furthermore, it is implied that individuals with a high self-esteem will always have positive attitudes about education. Such an assumption can be questioned. Because these criticisms concern fundamental properties of the COR model, it is important that Cross or others address them.

OTHER MODELS

At least five other models in varying stages of development and use can be found in the literature. Like those discussed in detail above, they require further testing and refinement. There are few major differences between the theoretical and conceptual bases of the five minor models and those of the models just discussed other than prominence in the literature, with the possible exception of the one attributed to Tough below.

Other models of motivational analysis include Boyd's 1965 physiological-psychological-social/cultural model, Berry's 1971 Multi-Phasic Motivational Paradigm for Adult Education, and a developmental task concept based on the work of Havighurst (1952; Havighurst and Orr 1965). Grotelueschen and Caulley (1977) have also suggested a model of professional education based on beliefs, attitudes, and intentions. According to this idea, it is proposed that beliefs, attitudes, and intentions interact in such a way as to cause participation or to prevent it. Darkenwald and Merriam (1982) provide the latest model. Their psychosocial model of participation is a probability model that is based on Darkenwald's previous research concerning participation. It seems to be a good descriptive model that lacks power to reflect relative weights of the identified variables. It contains many of the characteristics of the other models analyzed by Cross (1981).

Tough (1979) has shared what appears to be the beginnings of an emerging model to explain participation in self-directed learning. His model is very reminiscent of Lorge's incentives to adult learning cited at the beginning of this chapter. Tough and his colleagues place a heavy emphasis on conscious anticipation of benefits resulting from self-directed learning. Four stages noted in the model include (1) engaging in the learning activity, (2) retaining the knowledge or skill, (3) applying the knowledge or skill, and (4) gaining a tangible or intangible reward.

Each of the above models requires additional testing. They are, however, not very unlike the five major models discussed in detail in this chapter except in being somewhat less prominent in the literature.

OBSERVATIONS AND SPECULATIONS

Studies of adult education participation constitute an important and sizable segment of the literature of adult education. Even though the topic has been examined at least since the Gallup Poll of adult education participation in 1945, this review suggests that additional studies are required. As was noted previously, reliable and valid data and explanatory concepts concerning participation are vital to the efficient planning and provision of adult education programs.

Even after almost 40 years of enumerating participants in adult education activities, it is obvious, from estimates that vary by almost 50 million, that our ability to accurately inventory or simply count the participants in adult education programs is suspect and our results lacking in credibility.

A variety of definitions and inconsistent terminology, after decades of discussion, continue to be used by adult educators conducting participation investigations. Difficulty in agreeing upon the definition of *adult* and *adult education* is at the root of some of the differences noted in numerous estimates. Other complications are created by the pluralistic nature of the field. Adult education is not limited to one social institution. It permeates society sufficiently to be found among hundreds of agencies, institutions, and organizations, many of which may not be aware that they are engaged in adult education.

In spite of these difficulties, however, there is a much firmer information base concerning participation than existed when Brunner and his associates included ten pages on the topic in their highly useful book. Whether we agree with Aslanian and Brickell's 1980 estimate of more than 60 million people or the National Center for Education Statistics' 1980 estimate of less than 20 million, there is a general acceptance that at least 18 million adults were engaged in an educational activity in 1978. Or, if we prefer to look at rates of participation, we can elect to use one in five or one in three. We have assurance that the rate of participation is fairly high.

These numbers, however, fail to communicate much within themselves. It is when they are examined according to demographic, social, and other personal characteristics that the numbers become useful in informing the program planning process. These data are helpful in identifying participants according to age, educational attainment, income, race, and sex. Through analysis of this information, adult educators know that educational attainment is most strongly associated with participation and that combinations of age, education, and income account for most of the identified variance in adult education participation. Similarly, the educator is informed that while individuals of minority, racial, or ethnic origins are underrepresented among participants, that phenomenon seems to be more a factor of social class than of race or ethnic origin per se.

It is also instructive for those engaged in the adult education enterprise to study the data on locations of learning activities. These data reveal that different social classes and age groups seem to have their own preferences for where they participate in adult education. These data do much to inform planners about the dispersal of programmatic adult education in American society. They also reveal or suggest some of the realities faced by certain segments of society, such as the elderly, who prefer to participate in places that are easily accessible and available during daylight hours. The surveys also indicate that the workplace may be a more attractive place for learning than an educational institution for blue-collar workers and other working-class individuals.

Houle (1961) provided an additional tool for the analysis of personal motives for engaging in educational activities. He offered a three-part typology that classified adult learners according to "orientations": activity-oriented, goal-oriented, and learning-oriented. Houle's typology became popular as the NORC survey data were being analyzed (Johnstone and Rivera 1965). Shortly thereafter, Boshier (1971), Burgess (1971), Douglah and Moss (1968), Knox and Videbeck (1963), Miller (1967), and Sheffield (1964) introduced other elements such as additional factors and concern for social and other psychological variables to account for participation.

The social scientists Lewin (1947) and Maslow (1968) strongly influenced the direction of research into adult participation. At least two of the five models reviewed here are based on Lewin's force-field concept: Miller's model and the expectancy-valence model. Miller's and Boshier's models also rely heavily upon Maslow's hierarchy of needs.

Maslow's hierarchy is attractive, but it is also the subject of some significant criticism. [See comments in Chapter 8 by Diggins and Huber (1976).]

Additional critical observations concerning the concept are available in the work of Korman, Greenhaus, and Badin (1977). The theoretical framework suffers from several weaknesses, including inability to meet the scientific canon of disproof and being analytically limited.[2] Furthermore, there is evidence that, conceptually, the stages may be inconsistently described, thus lacking in explicit specification. Examples of this criticism are available in Miller's 1967 discussion of survival and safety needs and in Berry's 1971 discussion of the same concepts. Miller relates the needs to the sociotechnological culture of Western industrialized economies, while Berry limits them to more primitive social levels.

The force-field concept of Lewin is also attractive. It enables the investigator to clearly conceptualize a variety of variables as positive or negative forces. The two models discussed in this chapter that are based on expectancy seem to derive much of their strength from Lewin's work.

Boshier's model, based on the need for personal-social congruence and its ultimate relationship to two deep-seated psychological syndromes, has some attractive elements. It does not, however, have the appeal of the Swedish expectancy-valence model. The expectancy-valence model is not without some methodological challenges, such as how to determine valence accurately.

Cross's analysis of Miller's, Boshier's, and the expectancy-valence models led to the identification of similarities among them. Summarized and paraphrased, Cross's conclusions are noted below.

1. All provide for an analysis from an interaction point of view.
2. All include some reference to or recognition of Lewin's field theory.
3. All are cognitive rationalist in perspective.
4. Personality is prominent in varying degrees, with the greatest emphasis noted in the congruence and expectancy models.
5. All include social learning theory and reference group theory.
6. All make use of concepts associated with incongruence or dissonance.
7. Maslow's concept of a needs hierarchy is identifiable in each model.
8. Expectation of reward is common to each model, with greater emphasis noted in the expectancy model.

It appears that the same general characteristics are identifiable in the other models discussed here, though McClusky's margin theory is perhaps more S–O–R oriented than the others. There are also a few differences readily apparent among the models. The expectancy-valence model has been described by Bergsten as being ahistorical, whereas most of the other models provide for some historical dimension, such as the development of personality and attitudes, family backgrounds, and socioeconomic status.

NOTES

1. The reader is cautioned against assuming that self-esteem is causally related to participation in adult learning activities. There is evidence that participation in learning may not be an index to mental health or psychological development (Boyd 1961). There is also evidence that undereducated or disadvantaged persons (in terms

of education) may have a very high self-esteem (Gill 1982; Hopper and Osborn 1973). Also, we should be careful in attributing the origin of low self-esteem solely to one's previous educational experience. Other social relationships outside the educational framework may have greater impact on one's self-esteem than the educational experience of childhood. Self-esteem is perceived to be a useful concept. However, its usefulness as a universal explanation for very complex behaviors such as participation in learning is likely to be limited.

2. Madsen (1974) said that he was first inclined to feel justified in calling Maslow's theory *"rather speculative"* [italics Madsen's]. He indicated some doubts about his early opinion after he reconstructed Maslow's theory of motivation. Based on Madsen's reconstruction of the motivation theory, he obtained findings that he interpreted as indicating that the motivation theory is more empirical than he had previously believed. Readers who have an interest in meta-research and motivation theory should refer to Madsen for further information.

6 · Attrition and Persistence

A S A VOLUNTARY ACTIVITY, adult learning is subject to many pressures. Adults engaged in learning often do so at the expense of other pleasant activities or through a shift in role behavior. Douglah (1970), as noted in Chapter 5, indicated that participation in educational activities often competes with alternative activities and that educators of adults should strive to ensure that the benefits of participation in learning are at least equal to those that might be derived from some other kind of behavior. The absence of coercion to participate in most learning activities means that the adult is unusually free to decide upon continuing in a learning activity when confronted with some competing phenomenon. Consequently, educators of adults are often concerned with the problems associated with attrition in learning activities—especially institutionally sponsored activities.

This chapter examines the state of knowledge as developed through appropriate research activity concerning attrition (dropout or wastage) and persistence in adult learning activities. It consists of three major divisions: (1) scope and significance of the problem, (2) review of related research, and (3) implications of the research reviewed.

SCOPE AND SIGNIFICANCE OF THE PROBLEM

Questions concerning the attrition rate among adult students rate in importance with those concerned with participation. The frequency with which adults fail to formally complete educational programs is of longstanding concern in many countries. Research into the phenomenon referred to as wastage in the United Kingdom and dropout in North America has been concerned with a set of questions similar to those raised by investigators concerned with participation.

The data generated thus far by the research reviewed reveals a remarkable similarity between dropouts and nonparticipants and between persisters and participants. The participant and the persister in adult education appear to be described by similar socioeconomic characteristics. The elements common to both participation and persistence and nonparticipation and dropout suggest that these phenomena may emerge from the same psychological syndrome. If so, the more we learn about dropouts, the better we may understand nonparticipants and vice versa.

A recent study in the United States (Mezirow, Darkenwald, and Knox 1975) reports that 40 percent of the adult education teachers surveyed reported a student attrition rate of 10 to 24 percent during the first five weeks of class; another 17 percent of teachers surveyed reported attrition rates of from 25 to 49 percent. One adult educator (Niemi 1976) has said that attrition is among the most severe problems confronting adult education. Boshier (1972) reported average attendance in New Zealand departments of university extension to be only 50 to 60 percent; Lam and Wong (1974) estimated the attendance rate among participants in noncredit extramural university courses offered by the Chinese University of Hong Kong to be about 50 percent.

Reasons given for withdrawing from adult education programs seem to be similar across varied cultures. For example, reasons for dropping out of adult literacy classes in Saudi Arabia are reported, in order of decreasing frequency, below (Hamidi 1978).

1. "Students low calibre"
2. Travel and household changes
3. Work
4. Seasonal work
5. Shortage of materials
6. Personnel shortage
7. Organizational problems
8. Household responsibilities
9. "Shyness or psychological reasons"
10. Illness

A list of reasons not unlike those reported elsewhere is also available from Kuwait (Al-Adasany 1972). The most commonly reported reasons for dropping out were family problems, transportation, affronts to personal dignity, interference with work, teacher attitude, fatigue, and classroom setting.

The severity of attrition in adult education programs has been adequately documented. But why is attrition important? The significance of the problem lies in two areas: practical and theoretical. The practical implications of the problem are related to the group nature of many of the sponsored educational activities designed and offered by institutions for adults. The system devised for the purpose is one that is based on the assumption that individuals who participate in sponsored group learning activities will collect together under the direction of a teacher for learning. All kinds of resources—human, physical, and material—are obtained and allocated based on the assumption. Thus, failure of a large number of participants to regularly take part in the group learning activity has implications for the use of resources and the productivity of the group learning experience. The problem is especially critical when learning activities are financed on the basis of average attendance data.

The problem of attrition also has practical implications related to teaching and learning activities. These implications are derived from at least seven variables in the learning context: structure, ambience, location, length, frequency, content, and interpersonal relationships.

The theoretical implications of the attrition problem address the area of learner motivation. Motives to learn are critical features of the adult education enterprise. Knowledge of dropouts and of how they compare with individuals who complete course work has theoretical implications that are related to other topics of interest to adult educators. These other areas that are believed to be related to learning behaviors include instructional procedures, motives for learning, and participation, to name a few.

REVIEW OF RESEARCH

Status and Methodological Concerns

The status of research concerning attrition in adult education has changed significantly since the work of Brunner and his associates (1959). In 1959, Brunner cited Spence and Evans (1956), who described the situation as follows:

> The matter of dropouts was considered to be "one of the foremost problems facing adult educators" by the AEA Research Committee in 1955. However, the Committee noted that:
>
> 1. There has been almost no comprehensive research on adult education dropouts.
> 2. There have been some related studies in other areas.
> 3. There have been suggestions from several adult educators regarding the handling of dropouts. Most of these, however, are not based on experimental evidence.

The absence of a substantial body of research literature on dropout was revealed by Verner and Davis, who in 1964 reviewed thirty studies on the topic conducted between 1928 and 1963. Some of the investigators identified by Verner and Davis did not seem to be aware of previous studies, and consequently, the research sometimes proceeded without the benefit of knowledge generated by earlier work. Even today, those interested in the problem of attrition should find Verner and Davis's review informative.

Brunner suggested that one of the main reasons for the neglect of research concerned with dropouts from adult education activities was methodological. He correctly observed that dropouts more or less become unavailable after discontinuing their study, and hence are also inaccessible to investigators. However, in the years since 1959, a number of studies of the attrition question have been conducted. Many of these have collected important and useful data, as suggested by Brunner, at enrollment time. These data may be helpful in determining possible differences between those who continue in adult education courses and those who do not.

At least three general questions concerning attrition in educational programs for adults are of interest to educators of adults:

1. Are individuals who fail to complete (drop out of) educational activities different from those who complete educational activities? If so, how do they differ?
2. Why do people drop out of educational activities before the activities formally end?
3. Can the dropout phenomenon and nonparticipation be explained by the same model?

A review of a number of studies of attrition in adult education conducted in three countries and the Crown Colony of Hong Kong will reveal how well we can answer the above questions.

There are three principal sources of data for studies of attrition: the participant, institutional records, and institutional personnel.

The participant serves as the primary source in a number of studies reported. Of the thirty studies reviewed by Verner and Davis, fifteen were based on data obtained from all enrollees. In each of the eleven studies discussed in the following pages, the participants completed a variety of questionnaires, scales, and other forms.

Institutional records were used to provide data for nine of the studies reviewed by Verner and Davis. None of the ten reviewed here used institutional records other than attendance records.

Six of the studies reviewed by Verner and Davis were based on information from institutional personnel. None of the eleven most recently reviewed studies discussed here used such information.

Psychological Variables

Londoner's 1972 study was cast in a motivational framework based on the work of Talcott Parsons, a sociologist whose proposition is based on the possibility of classifying personal actions or activities according to the timing of the gratification obtained when an individual participates in an activity (Parsons 1951). Accordingly, it is suggested that some activities are pursued in order to obtain immediate gratification, while others are expected to yield a delayed gratification that occurs at the conclusion of the activity. The former type is identified as an expressive-consummatory orientation and the latter as an instrumental orientation. In social system terminology, instrumental activity orientation is equated with *means,* and an expressive orientation is analogous to *end.*

According to the concept, the instrumental action system has two basic future-oriented functions: (1) to orient the system to the external (beyond the individual, i.e., the internal) environment according to the delayed future gratifications and (2) to maintain and integrate the system within itself in terms of delayed future gratifications. Although the concept refers to the organizational structure and actions of social systems, Londoner believes that the action-oriented model may prove useful for the purpose of examining the behaviors of adult students concerning perseverance in educational activities. He assumes that perseverers are oriented toward the external function, i.e., that they participate in adult education to obtain future tangible goals related to their external orientations to work and the social environment. He believes that nonperseverers are also future oriented, but in terms of the internal dimension of the concept, i.e., that they enroll in adult education to satisfy personal inner-directed needs that are designed to result in a more integrated, stable, and self-assured person in the vocational and social environments.

Londoner's research based on the ranking of eleven education goals drawn from the literature indicates that perseverers generally rate external goals as a more important reason for enrolling in an educational activity. He notes that the internal-nonperseverance association was partly confirmed. Furthermore, he suggests that the importance of external goals increases with age, marriage, employment, and increases in income. He notes a decided shift to specific tangible goals achievable through education among adult perseverers. Age and marital status are interpreted by Londoner as pivotal linkages that are associated with a shift from an internal to an external reference.

Londoner's interest in gratification as an explanatory concept for persistence versus dropout among adult voluntary students is shared by Cochran (1967). According to his study of individuals enrolled in a Manpower Training and Development Program in aircraft assembly, individuals who completed the program were high in their delayed gratification orientation. He reports a significant difference in delayed gratification patterns of those who completed the program and those who dropped out without good cause.

A study of 104 adult males engaged in a vocational training program in Calgary, Alberta, was conducted by Sainty (1971) to identify variables useful in predicting attrition or persistence. His research was based on a model similar to those used by admission officers. His design included 22 major continuous predictor variables and 21 major noncontinuous predictor variables. He obtained 17 significant correlations. The four predictor variables most strongly associated with the dependent variable (dropout or completion) were age, .514; number of grades repeated, .449; occupational status, .462; and number of jobs held in the past year, .409.

The profile of the dropout compared with the completer as identified by Sainty's investigation is reported below. When the seventeen significant variables identified by Sainty were combined, the dropout differed from the completer in that the former

1. was less intelligent.
2. had a lower speed and accuracy score on the Gates Reading Survey.
3. had a lower vocabulary score on the Gates Reading Survey.
4. had a lower comprehension score on the Gates Reading Survey.
5. was younger.
6. had completed fewer grades at school.
7. had repeated more grades in school.
8. had either not attended high school or else was not likely to have taken an academic course in high school.

9. was more likely to have failed to complete any further education that he had undertaken.
10. was from a lower social position (Hollingshead scale).
11. was from a lower occupational class (Blishen scale).
12. had a father who was from a lower occupational class.
13. was more likely to be downwardly mobile in social position.
14. was more likely to be downwardly mobile in occupational class.
15. changed jobs more often than his counterpart in his previous twelve months.
16. had a lower rate of pay in his last steady job.
17. was less likely to speak a second language, French included.

Sainty summarizes the results as constituting a "non-success" syndrome. He observes a correlation between dropping out of an adult education activity and previous failure in a number of areas. Furthermore, the data as presented indicate that those who drop out have not, as a rule, been as successful as the perseverers in their previous school or work experience.

Boshier (1973) is of the opinion that dropout is an extension of nonparticipation, i.e., that there are variables commonly associated with both phenomena. He exhorts researchers to recognize that both dropout and participation are derived from an interaction of internal psychological and external environmental variables. His theoretical position is based on the need for personal and personal-other congruence derived from the self-concept theory of Carl Rogers. Accordingly, a basic proposition in his thinking is that self-acceptance and acceptance of others are linearly related; hence, the magnitude of self-other ratings is associated with dropout/persistence behavior.

Based on the results of his New Zealand study, Boshier is of the opinion that dropout occurs as a function of the interaction between the adult student and his or her educational environment. Specifically, he believes that the degree of congruence between the student's self-concept and the two most important aspects of the adult education environment—other students and the professor—are associated with the decision to drop out or to persist.

He reports two New Zealand–based inquiries. The first of the studies is based on 2,436 participants enrolled in continuing liberal noncredit courses at Wellington Evening Institute, the Department of University Extension of Victoria University of Wellington, and the Wellington Workers' Educational Association. The second study included 1,274 adults described as being from Wellington and 98 Auckland University Extension participants. In the first of the reported studies, he discusses the use of a new instrument that he labeled the Dropout Prediction Scale. In that study, he concludes that individuals who persist differ from those that drop out in terms of their concept of the individual who completes an educational activity. The perseverers consider those individuals who continue throughout a course to be more worthy. In contrast, those who dropped out view individuals who fail to complete courses and those who persist with equal favor.

In the second study, Boshier used his original instrument, the Personality and Educational Environment Scale, to examine the concept of self-other congruence in greater detail. The results of the second study are more extensive than those reported for the former. He concluded that "deficiency" motivated students dropped out more frequently than "growth" motivated ones.[1] He also noted an association between attrition and the following variables: age, marital status, transportation, prior experience in education, source of information about the learning activity, educational achievement level, occupation, place of birth, religious affiliation, course content, and class size.

Boshier was impressed that the interaction of the above variables failed to be as important as correlations between scores on his Personality and Educational Environment Scale and dropout. He concludes that 30 percent of the variance explaining dropout is revealed by discrepancy scores derived from the total of self-other, self-lecturer, and self-ideal dimensions on his instrument. Accordingly, he observes that reasons for nonparticipation and dropout are not to be found exclusively within the individual.

The idea of congruence as posed by Boshier is addressed by the studies of Lam and Wong (1974) (who did not focus specifically on dropout but on the broad question of attendance) and Davis (1963). Both these inquiries produced results that can be interpreted as being supportive of the important role of instructors and classmates. However, the findings reported by Lam and Wong indicate that self-other congruence may not be as simple as it sounds. More will be said about these two important studies later in the chapter.

Wilson (1980), like Londoner, Sainty, and Boshier, seeks to explain the dropout phenomenon in terms of personality variables. Using the Gough Adjective Check List, he obtained results on eight of the twenty-four scales that he used that were interpreted as being significantly different for persisters and individuals who discontinued their study.

Individuals who were identified as completers are described as being more obliging, tactful, diligent, practical, and compliant. They are believed to be more interested in stability and reducing risk. In relationships, they are pictured as being more concerned about the needs of others, more supportive, more persevering, and more able to yield to the reasonable requests of others.

In contrast, individuals who were described as dropouts are presented as being more rebellious and hostile. They are represented as less socialized, more impulsive, headstrong, and irresponsible. They are believed to be less able to maintain prolonged effort, are more impatient, and are more comfortable with disorder and change than are the completers. People who drop out are perceived as being indifferent to the feelings and needs of others. They are described as being less willing to subordinate self and more desirous of attention and authority. They seek succorance and appear to have a greater need for supportive and dependent relationships than do perseverers.

Scharles (1966) selected students enrolled in the Hillsborough County, Florida, Adult Evening School as his subjects. Data were collected through the use of the Edwards Personal Preference Schedule. He noted significant differences between male dropouts and male completers on two personality characteristics. The persisters scored higher on the affiliation need scale and lower on the autonomy need for achievement scale.

Hurkamp (1969) also studied the dropout question from a perspective similar to Sainty's. She developed a questionnaire composed of 39 attitudinal items and 27 personal data elements. She obtained the data from 595 students enrolled in a Wellesley College adult education program in order to conduct a comparative analysis between the 178 dropouts and the completers. She reports significant differences between the two groups on seven items: course success/failure, time spent away from home and family, participation in "open house" activities, quality of instruction, previous school experience, amount of education desired, and course difficulty.

Social-Demographic Variables

Dickinson and Verner (1967) examined eleven social and demographic characteristics of students who dropped out of 98 public adult night school courses in Canada. The dropout rate was 27.8 percent of the original enrollment of 2,075; 577 students who dropped out of educational courses before the course officially ended were identified for the analysis. The analysis revealed statistically significant differences between the persisters and the nonpersisters. Age, marital status, dependents, occupation, and previous participation in adult education activities provided significant discrimination between the two groups of students. Failure to continue was most prevalent in the youngest age group, as 20 percent of the original enrollment compared with 28 percent of the dropouts were between the ages of 15 and 24. With 23 percent of the participants between 35 and 44, and an additional 14 percent in the 44-to-54 age category, the noncompletors accounted for 20 percent and 10 percent respectively for these two older age groups. A larger percentage of single students in relationship to the total single population in the original enrollment dropped out. Thus, single students dropped out at a higher rate than did married students.

Generally, the number of children of the students was positively associated with withdrawal. The data are not strictly linear, however; adults with four children persisted at a higher rate than students with three or five children. Dropouts were also characterized as having had no previous adult education experience. Finally, there were significant differences according to occupation. Housewives tended to persist better than any other occupational group. Clerical workers and laborers had disproportionately high numbers of dropouts. Furthermore, withdrawal by occupation was related to both subject matter and course length. In their conclusions, Dickinson and Verner also noted that the association of course length with persistence is obvious, but the specific attributes of subject matter need more detailed analysis.

Instructional Environment Variables

Two investigations that focus on instructional interaction as an explanation for attendance problems were mentioned earlier. Davis (1963) examined eight classroom activities occurring during the first class session and students' attitudes toward the first session for some clues to the dropout phenomenon. Accordingly, he determined that instructor activities at the first class session could possibly reduce the dropout rate. He concluded that it is important that the instructor talk to the students as equals. Activities that were not significantly correlated with attitudes or persistence include an explanation of the course by the instructor; the opportunity for students to introduce themselves; encouragement by the instructor to engage in discussion of class content; the use of movies, slides, or drawings; an instructor emphasis on the importance of the next class; arrangements for personal comfort; and personal greetings from the instructor at the beginning of the class.

Lam and Wong (1974) studied the association between content and attendance and the association between structure and attendance among participants in noncredit extramural university courses sponsored by the University of Hong Kong. *Content* is defined as those sensory impressions that learners receive and cognitively organize in their learning experience. *Structure* is the patterning of content within the learning activity by sociopsychological forces that affect how learners perceive and organize the stimuli in the situation. More specifically, structure is the dynamic component of experience, and it is assessed by interpersonal and intrapersonal processes. The investigators concluded that degree of course understanding, need fulfillment, approachability of the instructor, and amount of informal and formal interaction were all positively and significantly related to attendance rates, whereas sociability of classmates and attendance rates were negatively and significantly related.

The studies of attrition of adult learners reviewed here reveal three different approaches used by adult educators to provide an explanation for attrition in adult and continuing education programs: (1) psychological characteristics, (2) sociological characteristics, and (3) instructional variables. The distribution of studies clusters in the first two areas, psychological and sociological characteristics. Verner and Dickinson, Boshier, Davis, and Lam and Wong identify some instructional variables that may either encourage attendance or at best fail to address special needs of the individual who is likely to withdraw from a learning activity before it is completed. Other than with these investigations, however, there seems to be a general tendency to search for explanations exclusively within or around the individual, for example, in personality characteristics that militate against perseverence (such as an inability to delay gratification) or in factors in the work or home environment that might keep the individual away from the learning activity (such as a need for two jobs, household responsibilities, and so forth).

A review of the studies reported here also indicates that researchers have tended to restrict their investigations to one set of possible explanations. For example, even though Sainty and Hurkamp examined two different kinds of data and engaged in multivariate analysis, they did not examine the association between either of these kinds of variables and instructional variables. For example, what kinds of instructional variables seem to have the highest association with perseverence of individuals with the kinds of negative personality and social status variables that characterize noncompleters? Lam and Wong, for instance, indicated that sociability of classmates was negatively related to attendance; likewise, Wilson indicated that dropouts were less socialized, and Scharles's data suggested differences in affiliation need among noncompleters. Assuming that the adult educator is faced with a group in which from 20 to 60 percent of the members can be described as above, what can that teacher do at the first and subsequent sessions to provide the succorance, gratification, and autonomy needs suggested by the research?

No consistent definition of attrition or dropout is used in the literature. Hence, a number of individuals in varying circumstances are reported as dropouts. There is even the possibility that some definitions label as dropouts some participants who have better attendance than those labeled as persisters.

Greater precision in defining the dropout should strengthen conclusions in this area of research.

Near the beginning of the discussion of attrition in education, it was indicated that adult educators are concerned with at least three questions:

1. Are individuals who drop out different from those who persist in educational activities? If so, how do they differ?
2. Why do people drop out of educational activities before the activities formally end?
3. Can the dropout phenomenon and nonparticipation be explained by the same model?

How well have the above questions been answered by the research reviewed here? Some insight into the first two questions is now available as a result of the numerous investigations conducted in this area over the past twenty years. However, our confidence in responses to the three questions decreases as we progress from the first question to the last.

Studies of attrition in adult education and among college students reveal similar findings. Both kinds of studies have identified personal demographic and social factors that are associated with persistence and attrition in differing degrees. Therefore, there is some evidence to support an affirmative answer to the first question listed above. Table 6.1 provides a summary of eleven studies concerned with characteristics related to attrition and persistence among adult learners.

The same data also give some insight into how the two groups differ. For example, there is rather firm evidence that generally those who continue are older, are married, have a different delayed gratification pattern, and different affiliation and achievement needs. Those who withdraw appear to have usually been less successful in previous schooling activities, may have academic weaknesses such as reading problems, and may be less successful occupationally. There is also some evidence that dropout may be triggered by certain activities or components of the school setting.

The other two questions concerning attrition that are of interest to adult educators remain to be answered. Boshier's work addresses both questions. However, answers based on his research are at best highly tentative. His congruence-based theoretical position is attractive. Succinctly, dropout can be explained in terms of an inadequate match between (1) the student's self-concept and his idealized self-concept, (2) self/others (students), or (3) self/instructor. Unfortunately, the parsimonious dimension of this theory is complicated by the addition of the growth/deficiency concepts. Furthermore, it is not clear how other motivations are considered in the theory. For example, how strong does another interest or need have to be to negate the influence of congruence, and under what circumstances will this occur? Suppose, for instance, that we have a student who is marginally interested in learning a foreign language and whose congruence score is just above adequate (whatever that may be). Halfway through the course this student has an opportunity to engage in a competitive activity in which he or she has great interest. Is one able to explain the student's withdrawal from the language course in terms of congruence? A second issue concerns the necessary and sufficient relationship among the three dimensions of congruence. Can the congruence theory explain dropout if congruence is high on one of the dimensions and low on the other two? Is congruence on a particular dimension more important than that on another? Is the cumulative congruence measure more important than minimum scores on each dimension?

The possibility of explaining nonparticipation and attrition by the same theory is an extremely attractive one. The congruence and force-field theories and other models of participation seem to contain elements that may apply to both phenomena. On the other hand, it seems that two different sets of forces may be at work. For example, nonparticipation may be viewed as a stable state that requires dynamic movement toward participation. In contrast, dropping out of a course might be considered movement from an active mode to another active mode or to a stable state.

FUTURE DIRECTIONS AND IMPLICATIONS

This review indicates that considerable progress has been made in attrition research since Brunner's review of 1959. It appears that the research has moved through a series of orderly descriptive steps from demographic descriptions to personal/social descriptions into psychological descriptions. During the same period, the research moved from univariate to multivariate analysis. However, the tendency has been to remain at the descriptive level of analysis. Explanatory research is now needed. This research must also move beyond the descriptive focus on the learner to an explanatory approach that includes broader social and institutional factors, as suggested by Davis and others.

Some of the questions raised by Boshier's congruence theory need to be examined by carefully designed studies. Some questions should be raised concerning the variety of instruments used to collect data for analysis. For example, Scharles (1966) used the Edwards Personal Preference Schedule, which has been questioned on some points. Thorndike and Hagen (1977) observe that the representativeness of the adult sample used for normative purposes is questionable and that consistent validity data are meager.

Boshier's use of semantic differential scales seems to be a movement in the right direction as long as certain limitations are observed. First, the semantic differential scale was designed to measure attitudes, not motives. Second, it is a verbal response instrument, and Thorndike and Hagen (1977) note that a person's actions may not correspond to verbally endorsed beliefs and feelings.

Generally, procedures currently used in dropout studies fail to meet criteria recommended by McClelland (1958) for studying motives. He has identified four criteria that should guide investigations of motives:

1. The measure of a motive should sensitively reflect the presence or absence of a motive or its variations in strength.
2. The measure of a motive should reflect variations in only that motive.
3. The measure of a motive should give the same reading for an individual or a group under the same or nearly the same conditions.
4. The measure of a motive should have relational fertility.

Table 6.1
A Summary of Eleven Studies of Adult Participation in Education, 1964–1980

Investigator	Population/Sample	Data Collection Instrument	Personal Characteristics Associated with Withdrawal	Instructional Characteristics Associated with Withdrawal
Davis 1963	34 Personal Survival in Disaster classes, Florida	Kropp-Verner Attitude Scale, Class records		Instructor behavior at first class meeting
Cochran 1967	594 unemployed trainees, mostly 18–26	Delayed Gratification Pattern Index	Different delayed gratification pattern	
Scharles 1966	600 Hillsborough County, Florida, Adult Evening School students; 140 randomly selected subjects	Edwards Personal Preference Schedule	Persisters scored higher on affiliation need and lower on autonomy need for achievement.	
Dickinson/Verner 1967	2,075 adult night school students, Canada; 577 dropouts	Key sort registration cards	Younger/single, number of children higher, no previous participation in adult education, clerical workers, and laborers.	
Hurkamp 1969	595 Wellesley College Adult Education Program participants; 178 dropouts	Questionnaire: 39 attitude, 27 personal data items	Course success/failure, time spent away from home and family, participation in open house activities, quality of instruction, previous school experience, amount of education desired, course difficulty	
Sainty 1971	104 males, vocational center, Canada; 57 dropouts	Questionnaire	Less intelligent, lower reading speed/accuracy, lower vocabulary, lower reading comprehension, younger, less education, repeated more grades in school, lower social position, lower occupational class	

Study	Sample	Instrument	Findings	
Londoner 1972	134 participants, summer adult high school, Midwestern city	Questionnaire and Parsons's External-Internal Scale	Internal goals, younger/single	
Boshier 1972	1,000 Wellington High School Evening Institute; Dept. of Univ. Extension of Victoria University; Wellington Workers' Educational Association	Semantic differential scales, Dropout Prediction Scale	Regard dropouts in the same or more positive light than persisters	
Boshier 1973	2,436 noncredit course participants in the Wellington High School Evening Institute; Dept. of Univ. Extension of Victoria University; and Wellington Workers' Educational Association classes. 233 randomly selected individuals; 948 Wellington persisters; 326 Wellington dropouts; 98 Auckland University participants	Semantic differential scales: Educational Participation Scale, Personality and Educational Environmental Scale	Deficiency motivated, young, single, users of public transportation, no prior experience in adult education, lower educational attainment, self/ideal-self discrepancy	Course content, class size, self/other–self/ lecturer discrepancies
Lam and Wong 1974	70 adults enrolled in two noncredit summer courses, Extramural Dept., Univ. of Hong Kong	Mailed questionnaire		Compatability of course content with learner needs, approachability of instructor, amount of formal and informal interaction, negative relationship with sociability of classmates
Wilson 1980	142 high school completion students, Midwestern city community college; 29 dropouts	Gough's Adjective Check List	More rebellious and hostile; less socialized; more impulsive, headstrong and irresponsible; more impatient; more comfortable with disorder and change; indifferent to the feelings and needs of others; assertive; less willing to subordinate self; more desirous of attention and authority; seek succorance	

Assuming that McClelland's criticisms of self-report instruments for purposes of identifying motives are valid, there is obviously a need for adult educators to turn to the use of projective techniques.

Thus, advancement of research concerning attrition in adult education can be encouraged by two developments: (1) improved explanatory research designs using multivariate analysis techniques and (2) new and strengthened instrumentation or use of projective techniques and procedures currently available.

The reported research concerning attrition of adults engaged in educational programs has provided a suggestive descriptive profile of the individual who may manifest a tendency to discontinue an educational activity prior to its formal conclusion. The results of several studies confirm the possibility that attrition is related to both student elements and institutional elements. While the adult educator's freedom and capability to address many of the student elements are limited, there may be a little more that can be done to reduce the negative impacts, and possibly generate additional positive impacts, of the institutional elements.

Based on the research that indicates that young, single adults without a previous history of participation in adult education are dropout candidates, teachers of adults should determine which individuals fall into this high-risk group at the earliest possible time. Such data may be obtained in registration information and be made available to the teacher before the first session meets or can be obtained directly or indirectly during the "get acquainted" session of the first class meeting.

The data suggest that many individuals who drop out are not accustomed to success. Such individuals may be taking a great psychological risk to even enroll in an educational activity and are likely to be very insecure and lacking in confidence. As first-time participants in adult education, knowledge of what is expected of the learner is probably very limited. Information on the activity is likely in short supply. So we have failure-oriented, impulsive, and insecure individuals who enter the learning environment along with others for whom the environment is not only not alien but totally comfortable. It is clear that the potential dropout as described is in need of some kind of support. The fear and insecurity must be translated into safety and confidence at an early stage of the learning process. A number of procedures are available to achieve the goal. Learners should obtain some information on what kinds of demands should be expected from the learning group, family, friends, employer, and others. How can they address the conflicting demands?

The teacher is also challenged to provide an early opportunity for success with the learning experience. Learners should be able to believe that what is being taught is important. They must be able to see how it relates to other important parts of their life. During this process, the teacher is challenged to provide experiences that confirm the worth and dignity of each learner. All these things can be addressed by the sensitive teacher. More serious problems of personality and social adjustment may be addressed by attractively provided adult counseling services.

Teachers of adults should be sensitive to the range of educational goals that may be represented among even a small group of adult learners. The dilemma of teachers who are able to correctly identify some goals while failing to assess the importance of others is documented by Londoner, who followed up his study of dropouts in a midwestern American city adult evening school with a study of teacher perceptions of identified goals of individuals who completed a course and of those who quit. His study was based firmly on the literature that emphasizes the importance of teacher sensitivity to learner goals. While the teachers and the adult learners in both categories generally agreed on the rank order of the eleven goals identified by Londoner, there were some significant differences between the teachers and students in each category on certain goals (Londoner 1972).

Londoner interpreted the differences in importance attributed to selected goals as an indication that the teachers were not aware of the significance of a goal such as participation "for one's self improvement," "to gain prestige with one's friend," "to stand on one's own feet," and "to help others later on." The teachers generally ranked these goals as being of lower importance than noted by the students. In contrast, the teachers identified the goal "to pass the GED test" much higher for completers and lower for those who dropped out than did the students. An alternative possibility that should be mentioned is that due to the nature of the data collection instrument, the students provided self-report goals that failed to accurately reflect their true motives. A second alternative that applies to the teacher ranking in importance of educational goals of the dropouts is the possibility of a bias that reflects a stereotypic view of students who drop out. The possibility of an alternative explanation is enhanced by another finding reported by Londoner. He divided the teachers into two groups—those with less than one year of experience and those with one to ten years of experience—for additional analysis of the data. The more experienced teachers failed to agree with the rank order of goals, whereas the inexperienced teachers and the students did agree. These findings suggest at least two possibilities: (1) that the experienced teachers were sufficiently sensitive to select hidden and nonreported motives, or (2) that the experienced teachers were sufficiently insensitive, compared with the inexperienced teachers, to recognize the real motives of the students as reflected in their self-report rankings.

Regardless of the correct explanation, Londoner's research serves a useful purpose. It indicates that, overall, teacher identification of stated goals is possible. It also confirms the reality that even experienced teachers may fail to accurately perceive the importance of all educational goals even from a relatively short list—hence, the importance of teacher sensitivity to the variety of motives that may bring the adult back into the classroom.

Administrators can be of assistance to teachers in devising institutional responses that may reduce the attrition rate. Two variables of importance include length of the course and frequency of class meetings. Dickinson and Verner's 1967 Canadian study identified course length as being associated with dropout rates. Ulmer and Verner (1965) indicated that attrition rates were lower among students whose class met once a week in comparison with students whose classes met more often. These findings tend to indicate that one class meeting weekly built into 8-to-10-week modules may have greater holding power, other things being equal, than longer courses or more frequent meetings.

The studies reviewed here illustrate the range of educational activities and geographic locations represented in the literature of attrition in adult education. Even though each investigation occurred within a culture generally classified as a capitalistic, democratic, industrialized economy, there is a notable range within the classification in geographic location as well as kinds of educational institutions and educational programs providing the context for the inquiries.

NOTES

1. Boshier's theory of congruence was explained to include concepts of deficiency motivation and growth motivation based on the work of Abraham Maslow. Motives are determined by factor analysis of the Educational Participation Scale. More is said on this topic in Chapter 4.

IV · Program Development

7 · Aspects of Program Building

PROGRAM BUILDING is one of the fundamental activities in which the educator of adults commonly engages. It appears to be a skill based on a combination of art and science—with the emphasis on art. The research literature on the topic is extensive. It is, however, difficult to organize and report in a meaningful way because of the diversity of research designs, methods, and topics.

The research on several of the basic program development procedures, such as needs assessment, promotion and marketing, and instructional decisions, is sufficiently extensive to warrant individual chapter treatment. Other procedures, however—for example, selection of instructional personnel— have not received enough research attention to discuss here. This chapter reports some of the conceptual and research foundations for program design and production, learner involvement in planning, and choice of physical facilities.

The first part of the chapter discusses program elements and conceptual bases of program building, concepts of program building as reflected by five models, and research concerning selected program development procedures. A brief review of the limited research available concerning the efficacy of learner involvement in the planning and operation of the learning activity follows. The third section notes the state of research in the important area of appropriate facilities for the education of adults. Some general observations concerning the research on program development and some comments on implications for the practice of adult education conclude the chapter.

PROGRAM DEVELOPMENT

Approximately a third of the research in adult and continuing education is concerned with aspects of program development, which includes both planning and conducting educational activities for adults. The research emphasis on program development concerns should not be surprising because the tasks related to location, needs, objectives, activities, and evaluation are crucial to the success of the program. Despite the high visibility of research concerning some aspects of program development for adults, the consequences of the inquiries are limited by two factors. Much of the research is limited to case studies and is written primarily from an advocacy point of view. Furthermore, investigators tend to emphasize selected phases or procedures such as needs assessment and evaluation. Consequently, other major dimensions of the process remain relatively unexplored. Investigations have tended to focus on selected program planning and evaluation procedures, instructional methods and materials, and the special needs of target client groups, including ways to adapt educational programs to their situation.

Program Elements

As suggested above, program development includes an extremely broad range of concerns and procedures. Those activities that have become topics of study include target or client groups, sponsoring organizations, and procedures used by planners to develop and provide the desired resources in the appropriate sequence. Agencies engaged in the planning and provision of educational programs for adults include universities, voluntary organizations, labor unions, business and industry, libraries, public schools, government agencies, the military, and other assorted entities. Among the various purveyors of educational programs for adults, activities are frequently planned at three levels. Community-wide programming theoretically focuses on the educational needs of the (geographic) community, institutional-level programming centers upon the goals and mission of specific institutions as they offer activities for a targeted group, and activity programming focuses upon the implementation of selected, usually highly specific, educational provisions by agencies.

Organizations that plan and provide educational programs for adults at any of the above levels relate to the participants through methods or formats that may emphasize the individual learner, small or large groups, or the larger community. These three formats may be illustrated by correspondence study, class instruction, and community forums, respectively. In addition to the variety of program levels and instructional methods, an equally diverse range of program planning processes are used by the purveyors of educational activities. The processes employed in programming activity include the sequence or order of activities undertaken by the planners to design, implement, and evaluate educational programs.

According to Rusnell (1974), the program-planning literature within different interest areas of adult education can be classified according to its approach to the design of planning models. These design approaches may be organized around conceptual functions or flow charts. Planning models based upon conceptual functions consist of a list of major functions that are considered to be essential in the planning process; planning models based upon flow charts consist of specific planning activities represented within a series of flow-chart lines suggesting in detail the order of activities to be followed. Although a model based upon one approach might be transformed to the other, major differences between the approaches are evident with respect to their specificity of tasks and systematic ordering of activities.

Planning models that list conceptual functions are not specific in terms of activities to be performed, and no prescribed order of events is indicated (other than a normal sequence of events as suggested by progress in the planning process). An example of a conceptual function planning model is provided by Boone, Dolan, and Shearon (1971). That model is focused at the institutional programming level and contains four major planning functions: (1) developing the institution and maintaining its renewal process, (2) linking the institution to its publics through need analysis and leader involvement, (3) program design and implementation, and (4) program evaluation and accountability. Within each function, a number of constituent elements and tasks are identified as factors to be considered in operationalizing the function.

Planning models based upon the flow-chart approach are specific in terms of activities to be performed. Detailed sequences of phases and feedback loops between activities are customarily represented by the flow-chart lines. A systems approach to planning, including the usual kinds of diagrams, is characteristic in the flow-chart planning models. LaForest (1973) provides an example of that approach in a model for program planning in adult basic education. The model consists of nine major subsystems that he considers important in planning an adult education program: (1) develop ABE program, (2) quantify operating parameters, (3) identify program needs, (4) promote program, (5) apply enrollment procedures, (6) plan and conduct program, (7) recruit and select faculty, (8) train faculty, and (9) conduct terminal evaluation. Through a procedure of expansion in detail, the model is outlined in flow-chart format; 210 subsystems and 172 relationships between the subsystems are delineated by signal paths as used in the systems approach to planning.

In addition to models based on the two fundamental approaches to the design of planning models, a number of other program planning models contain elements of each approach. For example, models presented by Houle (1972) and Knowles (1970) are combinations of the two approaches identified by Rusnell. They are discussed in detail in another part of this chapter.

Many programming agencies in adult education agree upon the effectiveness of a general sequence of planning functions, and each agency ordinarily adapts the sequence to its own purposes. For example, Rusnell's review of the literature relating to training in business and industry reveals one such adaptation of functions that is often mentioned as a basis for effective program planning. Although the terminology used by different authors varies for the suggested planning activities, a sequence of four functions is often included in the literature as an integral sequence among more extensive planning models. The four most often cited functions are (1) determine the training needs, (2) design the program, (3) provide the instruction, and (4) evaluate the program.

Conceptual Bases

Program building in adult and continuing education appears to be based on a kind of amalgamation of four different approaches. The historically oldest set of procedures seems to be informed by theoretical formulations borrowed from Tylerian curriculum development and is called the classical rational model. In contrast, a somewhat more recent process is referred to as the naturalistic model. The latter is attributed to Walker (1971), who describes it as a series of decision points at the explicit and implicit levels. At the explicit level, the program planner must make decisions based on an advanced consideration of alternatives; at the implicit level, the decisions may be habitual or based on precedent. According to Mazmanian (1980), Walker's approach to explicit design decisions is somewhat analagous to Dewey's model of decision making: (1) pressures on the decision maker, (2) analysis of the problem, (3) a search for alternative solutions, (4) consideration of the consequences, and (5) a decision. The concept of implicit design decisions is similar to the idea of bounded rationality that includes simplifying the process of choosing among alternatives. Instead of a goal of maximizing a decision, the planner is concerned with a course of action that is "good," but not necessarily the best.

The naturalistic model is constrained by temporal considerations: it has a beginning (the platform), an end (the design), and a process (deliberation) to enable the beginning to progress to the end. In contrast, the classical rational model derived from Tyler is a means-end model: it states a desired end (the objective), a means for attaining the end (the learning experience), and a process (evaluation) for determining whether the means achieves the end.

The concept of learner needs and the emphasis on needs assessment by educators of adults are consistent with the conceptual requirements of both planning models. The models, however, differ in the roles that they assign to objectives. In the classical model, objectives determine the learning experiences. Objectives are necessary for the naturalistic model; they are, however, only one of many means for guiding the search for better educational programs.

Pennington and Green (1976) suggest that, at least in continuing professional education, program planning is a blend of the two approaches to program development. They are of the opinion that planners use the language of the classical model to discuss program building. As they describe their planning actions, however, it seems that personal values, environmental constraints, resource alternatives, and other factors influence the process.

Research into the different complex processes that constitute program development reported in this chapter is related directly or indirectly to the classical and naturalistic models as explicated by Mazmanian and by Pennington and Green.

A third approach to program development that is occasionally reported in the literature in the United States (and which has a wide following in other nations) is based on the work of Paulo Freire in South America. Freire's politically inspired concept of educational program activity includes two major elements: (1) thematic research and (2) the educational program. The combination of the two major components constitutes the overall education program— research and the curriculum of the future program; methodology or process and content are to be perceived as a unified concept.

The processes utilized in Freire's approach differ from the models discussed above in a number of respects. First, the research procedure, which may be partially analogous to the needs assessment phase of other models, is in reality a part of the learning process in which the learners actively engage.

Thematic research is represented as a process through which the participants begin to grasp their particular social reality as expressed in a series of interrelated themes or topics. Typical themes might include work, unemployment, and wealth (Apps 1979).

Learning objectives thus emerge as a result of the thematic research and are elaborated, refined, and modified in the "circles of culture," where the themes drawn from the research are posed as questions or problems. Resources employed in the discussions that characterize the circle of culture include a variety of materials—newspaper articles, stories, poems, drama—that suggest and reinforce the identified themes. Recently reported research concerning the Freirian approach includes that of DeVries (1978), Coggins (1973), and Spencer (1980).

Apps (1979) identifies the liberal education approach to programming as providing a fourth type of programming process. If the liberal education approach indeed qualifies as a fourth type, it is one that includes a range of procedural elements or structures. For example, the procedures do not usually include any efforts to define needs as indicated by the Tylerian model. Nor does this type seem to reflect the temporal quality or the explicit/implicit dimensions of the naturalistic model. The structure of the learning experience can, perhaps, be said to have its genesis in the content of liberal education.

Concepts of Program Building

The literature reports several different, but frequently related, concepts for the creation of specific educational programs for adults. Four of the more popular models and an additional new one have been selected for brief discussion here.

The conceptual schemata identified for varying degrees of discussion include the Indiana Plan (or participation training), Houle's fundamental system for the design of education, Knowles's andragogical model, Boyle's principles of program planning, and Schroeder's typology of learning systems. The Indiana Plan is discussed in greater detail because of the supportive research available. Other proposals for program planning procedures are discussed only briefly because of the lack of research in some areas.

The Indiana Plan

Paul Bergevin and John McKinley developed a procedure for developing educational programs for adults known as the Indiana Plan or participation training (PT). In the twenty-year period between 1955 and 1975, more than 8,000 participants were involved in more than 300 institutes offered by Bergevin, McKinley, and their associates to instruct participants in how to use the plan. In addition to the more than 300 institutes conducted in the United States, others were conducted in Canada, Denmark, Japan, and Australia (McKenzie 1975). Table 7.1 illustrates the variety of participants and purposes served by the institutes.

The Indiana Plan, or PT system, has been the subject of a number of studies. McKenzie's 1975 analysis of the plan from a systems perspective is instructive, as his work identifies the several elements of the system in terms of their internal relationships. The major elements of the system include teambuilding, program planning, implementation, and evaluation. According to McKenzie, objectives and outcomes are perceived to be related to the system but are in a sense extrinsic to it.

McKenzie's analysis of the component elements of the PT system is useful for application and study of the program planning technique. For example, the first phase of the procedure—teambuilding—can stand alone as an educational process, or it can be instrumental in assisting a planning group to accomplish the planning and implementation phase of the plan. Because of inexperience in "planning" educational programs, in contrast to "taking" educational programs, adults usually need the experience of teambuilding before they engage in the planning and implementation stages. It is this phase that addresses the content concerns of the learner. According to McKenzie, the

Table 7.1
Participants in the Participation Training System at Indiana University

Institutions or Client Systems	Participants	Purposes
General hospital	Professional and para-professional staff	Staff development and training
Mental hospitals	Patients	Continuing education Milieu change
	Staff	Staff development
Church	Members of church	Continuing education Problem solving
School district	Counselors	Problem diagnosis
Military installation	Officers	Staff development Professional education
School administration office	Administrators	Staff development and problem solving
University	Nurse supervisors	Continuing education
University	Agriculture extension agents	Problem solving
Elementary school	Students	Participative learning
School district	Administrators Faculty/parents Pupil personnel staff	Problem solving Problem solving Staff development
Prison	Inmates Administrators	Continuing education Staff development and problem solving

Source: Leon R. McKenzie, "Participation Training: Introduction and Analysis." *Viewpoints*, 1975, *51* (4), 4. Used by permission of the publisher, School of Education, Indiana University.

second stage includes the six-step procedure recommended by Bergevin, Morris, and Smith (1963, pp. 14–21):

1. Identifying a common need or interest
2. Developing topics
3. Setting goals
4. Selecting appropriate resources
5. Selecting appropriate techniques and subtechniques
6. Outlining each activity and the responsibilities to be carried out

To this a seventh step, evaluation, is added.

A small body of research literature exists on the Indiana Plan. At least a dozen dissertations and additional studies have been reported in the literature. The general thrust of the investigations reported indicate that the Plan is useful for a variety of purposes. For example, Miller (1963) reports that following experience with the PT system, a group of older adults reported greater willingness and more ability to communicate their feelings, opinions, and attitudes. Shay's 1963 work with alcoholic patients also reported that the experience contributed to greater integration and adjustive changes in self-concept. Castle (1965) and Gordon (1965) also report research concerning the Indiana Plan; their findings support the conclusions of others that the experience can be therapeutic and successful in changing attitudes.

Drane (1967) and Frye (1963) investigated other educational aspects of the plan. Frye was concerned with the underlying theory of the process, including the role of the trainer. Accordingly, he concluded that the educational conditions in the plan are an embodiment of principles of learning in a democratic context, principles of method for collaboration among adult learners in the process of growth, and tasks to be performed in training adults how to learn. Drane's study focused on the relationship between achievement and the use of the process. He concluded that when the participation training replaced literacy instruction for four weeks during a fourteen-week series of classes, improvement in reading among the experimental subjects was equal to that of the control subjects who received the additional four weeks of literacy instruction.

At least two studies of the Indiana Plan have generated negative findings. Imbler's 1967 study of the effect of participation training on closed-mindedness, anxiety, and self-concept of a group of male union members revealed that no significant differences were noted between control and experimental groups following treatment. Partin (1967) studied the impact of the system on changing acceptance of self and others among two groups of adult attendants at a state mental hospital; one group used the PT system and the other another procedure. He reports that no differences at the .20 level of significance were observed between the two groups.

Stubblefield (1975) notes that there are aspects of the PT system that cause some participants to experience difficulty. For example, he is of the opinion that since the Plan differs in some respects from other learning/training models in which individuals have participated, expectations derived from earlier experience with the other models contribute to frustration. Additional difficulty is encountered when the participant responds to the PT system in a way that is acceptable for another model but unacceptable in the PT system.

Stubblefield identifies two kinds of difficulties encountered by participants in the early sessions: (1) they have difficulty mastering the skills of writing topics, goals, and outlines, and (2) they have trouble recognizing that structural elements are means to an educational end and that their properties can enhance the group's effectiveness. The difficulty in accepting the structure is perceived by Stubblefield to, in effect, result from participant resistance to acknowledging needs and problems, to changing behavior, and to disciplined participation. Other difficulties are encountered with free, voluntary expression, consensus decision making, placing content in proper perspective, and accepting the need for personal growth, and with the reinforcement model of learning used in the Plan.

Houle's Fundamental System

In 1972, Houle, one of the most respected leaders in the field of adult education, published his fundamental system of program design. A review of Houle's design as presented below reveals its similarity to and differences from the structure of the Indiana Plan. His system is based on seven assumptions and seven decision points. The assumptions are these (pp. 32–33):

1. Any episode of learning occurs in a specific situation and is profoundly influenced by that fact.
2. The analysis or planning of educational activities must be based on the realities of human experience and upon their constant change.
3. Education is a practical art.
4. Education is a cooperative rather than an operative art.
5. The planning or analysis of an educational activity is usually undertaken in terms of some period which the mind abstracts for analytical purposes from complicated reality.
6. The planning or analysis of an educational activity may be undertaken by an educator, a learner, or an independent analyst, or some combination of the three.
7. Any design of education can best be understood as a complex of interacting elements, not as a sequence of events.

Decision points and components of an adult educational framework compose the design of an activity. The components are to be understood as a complex of interacting elements, and not as a logical sequence of steps. In applying Houle's model to a learning situation, one may begin with a component and proceed to the others in any order. The seven decision points are shown, with various components, in Figure 7.1.

Knowles's Andragogical Model

Knowles's 1970 andragogical model contains some of the same elements as those identified in the Indiana Plan and Houle's system, and in a similar sequence. The steps in Knowles's system are these:

1. Setting a climate for learning.
2. Establishing a structure for mutual planning.

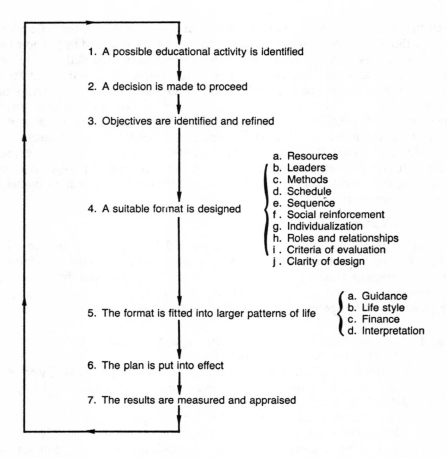

Figure 7.1   Decision points and components of an adult educational framework

Source: C. O. Houle, *The Design of Education*. San Francisco: Jossey-Bass, 1972, p. 47. Reprinted
      with permission.

3. Diagnosing needs for learning.
4. Formulating directions (objectives) for learning.
5. Designing a pattern of learning experiences.
6. Managing the learning experience.
7. Evaluating results and rediagnosing learning needs.

No research has been identified that has been specifically designed to test
the application of this model.

Boyle's Program Planning Principles

Boyle (1965) has identified what he calls eleven program planning principles that he recommends for program planning groups in the Cooperative Extension Service:

1. Over-all objectives of the agency should be considered.
2. Educational needs of the potential program participants should be
   considered.

3. Interests of the entire community should be considered.
4. A wide range of resources should be given consideration.
5. The planning group should include local citizens who are potential participants in the program.
6. Democratic processes should be used wherever possible in planning the program.
7. Various methods which might be used in reaching the objectives should be explored in the planning.
8. The program planning process should be continuous.
9. Program planning processes should allow for flexibility.
10. Provisions should be made for appraisal and evaluation of the program.
11. The planning group should coordinate its planned activities with those of other adult education agencies.

Boyle has recently (1981) elaborated on the 1965 model outlined above. Boyle's new position suggests a more complex procedure than noted in the earlier model. For example, the latest comment on the topic has distinguished among three types of programs: developmental, institutional, and informational. Space does not permit a full description of these different types according to purpose and design. The developmental model is the most complex of the three and the informational type is the simplest. Each type of program should be informed by fifteen concepts that in turn are reflected in broader, more inclusive, action phases. Developmental programs are built through eight action phases compared with five for institutional programs and three for informational programs.

Schroeder's Typology of Adult Learning Systems

Schroeder's 1980 typology is not limited to program processes in the same sense that the previous conceptions are. Schroeder defines the purpose of his approach as a search for order in adult education and as a means to analyze agent systems, client systems, and program planning processes. The payoff for his concept is perceived in terms of how helpful it proves to be in assisting practitioners to become more discriminating in the use of knowledge and to researchers in becoming more realistic and generative in their search for knowledge. Of specific interest to this chapter are his concepts concerning decision points. In contrast to several of the models discussed thus far, this model provides for an analysis of decision points at both macro and micro levels. Three decision points are identified at each level. At the macro level, the program planner is concerned with decisions concerning educative needs, program objectives, and program procedures. The micro level decisions are related to learning needs, learning objectives, and learning experiences.

The analytical structure proposed by Schroeder provides the practitioner and researcher with a scheme for determining the nature of control in decision making concerning programs for the education of adults. His concept contains two major systems—agent systems and client systems. Analysis of the program-planning process may include either or both the systems at either of two levels: the micro level or the macro level. Basically, it appears that agent systems tend to include the more institutionalized and traditional social organizations that are usually task directed, whereas the client systems are composed of the more flexible, transitory, and person-centered groups. The degree of control exerted by the respective systems will be reflected by the nature of judgments concerning decisions about educative needs, program objectives, program procedures, learning needs, learning objectives, and learning experiences.

Only Boyle's principles of program planning, among the concepts discussed here, address the macro concerns explicated in Schroeder's system; each of the other programming procedures is restricted to processes identified at the micro level. Schroeder's macro decision points are concerned with educative needs, program objectives, and program procedures, while those at the micro level concern learning needs, objectives, and experiences.

Fourteen propositions concerning potential relationships between the three hypothetical program types—agent centered, client centered, and eclectic—are offered by Schroeder as guides to action and topics of research.

Research

Research concerning programming for the education of adults appears to be of two kinds. One kind is concerned with the analysis of the entire programming process, and the other focuses on one step or component. Examples of investigations into two or more of the process components include the work of Brady and Long (1972), Everitt (1974), Pennington and Green (1976), and Rusnell (1974).

Brady and I were concerned with the question of differences between perceptions held by adult educators and urban planners about the importance of adult education program planning procedures. A review of the literature yielded thirteen program planning procedures, each with five implementation steps. Based on the assumption that educational preparations of the two groups being studied were different, the research was conducted to determine whether the two groups would identify different procedures as being more important. Subsequently, we arrived at the following conclusions:

1. Major differences exist between perceptions of the two groups; adult educators ranked almost half the procedures as more important than the urban planners did.
2. Major differences in the perceptions of the two groups concerning the importance of implementing actions exist.
3. A low correlation between the ranked data exists for the two groups.

Everitt (1974) conducted an investigation very similar to that reported by Brady and me. He compared perceptions of program planning procedures of adult educators and governmental trainers. Specific differences between his groups were not the same as those identified by us. Everitt found that adult educators perceived studying the city's comprehensive plan, establishing an advisory committee, and determining the suitability of facilities to be the important first steps in program planning, while governmental trainers saw them as determining the adequacy of classroom lighting, temperature, and acoustics, and providing opportunities for participants to practice the desired program.

A comparison of these two studies reveals an interesting similarity in action steps perceived to be less important by the urban planners and governmental trainers. The adult educators perceived the use of advisory committees, provision for relaxation, and evaluation to be more important. Furthermore, both the urban planners and governmental trainers seemed to have a greater interest in physical elements.

Another study of program planning processes is reported by Pennington and Green (1976), who used the grounded theory approach to investigate the planning process used in continuing professional education units in selected midwestern universities. Based on their research, they identify a general planning model consisting of six clusters of tasks and decisions: originating the idea, developing the idea, making a commitment, developing the program, teaching the course, and evaluating the impact. A variety of subelements were generated for each of the above topics, with the exception of teaching the course. The twenty-nine subelements identified by Pennington and Green include many of the steps suggested by others such as Boyle, Brady and Long, and Houle—for example, needs assessment, identification of resources, setting objectives, and evaluation. Some distinctive elements noted in their planning concept include awareness of legislative mandates, market analysis, and literature review.

The study of program development processes in continuing professional education revealed four areas where practice was different from that recommended in the literature. It is indicated by Pennington and Green that insufficient attention was devoted to analysis of client needs, determination of objectives, designing instruction, and evaluation. Furthermore, the data generated by the study concerned *successful* programs; program planning processes for unsuccessful programs, if different, were not identified.

LEARNER PARTICIPATION IN PLANNING

The desirability of including the learner in the planning and management of educational programs for adults is one of the pervasive characteristics of adult education as reflected by the literature. The importance of the procedure is noted by Bagnall (1978), who identifies ten authors who have supported the practice of learner involvement in planning and another three who have also indicated that it is desirable to involve the learner in the planning and management of the learning activity. Most of the sources cited by Bagnall, however, are more philosophically than empirically based. The literature noted is hortatory, and the authors are engaged in sharing opinions or assumptions concerning the importance or desirability of involving the learner in the program planning and management.

Progress in developing a firm research foundation for this topical area has been slow. Brunner and his associates (1959) devoted approximately four pages to the topic of lay participation in program planning and cited eleven studies on the topic conducted between 1937 and 1955. The majority of these studies were related to program planning in the Cooperative Extension Service. The primary thrust of the work that they reviewed concerned the question of the relationship between attendance and lay involvement in planning programs. The research reported was generally in agreement that attendance is frequently greater in programs that are developed through the involvement of the learners or their representatives.

While the practice of involving adult learners in planning the educational activity and in involving them in managing it appears to be based on a common philosophical concept, the research and practice related to the two components are naturally distinct. Participation in planning the adult learning activity seems to provide for two different kinds of involvement. One kind of involvement is through an advisory committee that includes one or more representatives for the learners who will enroll in the program. The other kind of involvement is based on the participation of the learners themselves in the planning of the program.

Participation in management of the learning experiences is more extensive than involvement in the planning. Conceivably, the planning responsibilities can be limited to goal setting, identification of resources, and general advance scheduling of activities. In contrast, management of the learning experience may include planning, continuing active decision making, and functional responsibilities during the total learning experience through the final evaluation. Planning models cited early in this chapter that provide for the involvement of *learners* in the planning of educational activities include the Indiana Plan and the model based on Freire's work. The importance of such learner participation was also perceived more favorably by adult educators than planners or governmental trainers in studies reported earlier.

Two possible sources may be identified for the practice of involving adults in planning and/or managing the learning activity. The first of these is the progressive school movement or philosophy, which emphasizes relevance and action learning. These elements place a premium on learner-centered teaching procedures, and it is logical that such procedures should relate directly or indirectly to the concept and practice of engaging the learner in a process that obtains input and intrinsic involvement of the learner with the instructional activity.

A second source is the work of social psychologists interested in production and management tasks in business and industry. The literature of that field could be translated conceptually to some of the interests and concerns of educators of adults. Unfortunately, the emphasis on the beneficial aspects of learner involvement from an enrollment number point of view has not stimulated research in other areas of perhaps greater importance to the educator of adults. Professionals and amateurs engaged in program development are naturally interested in developing programs that will be attractive and well attended. Beyond that concern, however, the planners want to know whether learner participation in the planning and management of the learning activity results in more or improved learning. Learner retention rates and enjoyment or satisfaction with the learning activity are important concerns, but the primary interest seems to be related to the question of learning efficacy.

Research on the topic generally addresses the association of total attendance, satisfaction, achievement, relevance of course content, and/or cognitive retention with the involvement of the learner or representatives of the target group in planning and management of the program.

The volume of related research reported in reputable places is very limited. There is the research concerned with the practice of obtaining learner participation indirectly through advisory committees composed of representatives who can theoretically speak for the potential learners. These studies generally are concerned with the impact of such involvement on attendance. The research reported by Brunner and his associates on this point confirmed the utility of the practice, and no new studies that should cause us to reconsider the conclusions reported in 1959 have been identified; therefore, those kinds of investigations will not be discussed further here. A second kind of research concerning the topic is research into the practice of student planning, and a third focus of the research concerns learner participation in managing the learning activity. Only a few studies in the former area have been identified. A larger volume of work that indirectly touches on the questions of learner involvement in managing the learning activity is provided by those individuals who have followed Tough's 1966 and 1978 studies of self-directed learning projects. These latter studies (see, for example, Allerton 1974; Coolican 1973; Denys 1973; Hiemstra 1975; Johns 1973; Penland 1979) do not directly address some of the concerns that are appropriate to the sponsored group-learning programs that characterize the more formal adult education activities, but they seem to be sufficiently related to be useful in arriving at some improved understanding of the processes and benefits of learner-managed activities.

FACILITIES

The selection, arrangement, and use of physical facilities are tasks that confront planners of educational programs for adults. Unfortunately, research concerning the topic is limited or unreported. Personal experience indicates that much of the programming for adult learning uses physical facilities that are not specifically designed for the education of mature learners. Facilities generally fall into one of the following classes: (1) traditional education settings designed for children or young adults, (2) facilities designed for other activities such as those provided by community rooms in banks or hotels, (3) educational facilities of religious organizations, and (4) residential adult learning facilities or similar locations devoted to day use without the residential component.

Because of the limited availability of research specifically concerned with facilities designed for use in the education of adults, a heavy dependence is placed here upon related research. The related research, which may be useful in deriving some implications for adult educational practices, includes a varied mix of inquiries. Some of the work cited is based on school facilities for children and young adults; other inquiries were conducted in nonschool settings such as offices and counseling facilities. Other related research examines issues related to physical proximity and other relational factors in a number of settings. Unfortunately, just a few of the investigations reviewed are directly concerned with the adult learner in an educational context.

Physical Environment

Traditionally, adult educators, along with other teachers, have been burdened with a dependency on their own common sense regarding the effect of the physical-environment factors on the learning processes of the learner. In the minds of educators, the physical environment or architectural design may not appear to be as active a determinant in human development as the influence of an instructor or peer group; however, Myrick and Marx (1968) believe that the physical environment is a valid factor for examination because of its capacity to withstand changes associated with time, human beings, or shifts of user groups.

The neglect of the physical environment as a topic of educational inquiry is explained by several authors. Friedman and Juhasz (1974) believe that the explanation is found in the background of the large majority of psychologists, who come from a more traditional viewpoint and are accustomed to explaining behavior in terms of "relationships *between* persons or states that were thought to exist *within* persons." According to this belief, people administer rewards or punishments, and the milieu, man-made or natural, does not have any influence on behavior. According to Wohlwill (1966), psychologists never fail to point out the importance of stimulus factors as a determinant of behavior, and the role of environmental influences in behavior. Yet as a group they have had relatively little to say about the importance of the environment.

Propst (1975) believes that the neglect of the physical environment's involvement in affecting human behavior or needs is due to three factors, namely, (1) overfamiliarity with its overt characteristics, (2) a tendency of physical arrangements to static formality, and (3) the widespread assumption that physical setting has little impact on organizational functioning.

Passing from a neglect or complete absence of thought concerning the role of the physical environment, authors have begun to include the environment as a factor in behavior. Hall (1969) is given credit for coining the term *proxemics* to describe the effect that the environment has on an individual's behavior. Usually the individual is defined as the primary "actor" and the environment as the "surround." David and Wright (1975) defined "surround" as lying outside boundaries of a social system and having only marginal influences on its ongoing activities.

Brodey (1967) indicated that a more active role is played by the environment. He noted that persons must be continuously taught by their environment, both human and unhuman, and that they require the novelty that they metabolize through their learning as much as they need oxygen. Brodey further provided an alternative to the person-environment concept. He offered that the surroundings could be considered the "object" and the person the "environment." For Brodey, the design of rooms, wall space in a home, or other physical setting actively controls the actions within the setting.

David and Wright described the continuing interaction between the environment and the individual by using Piaget's assimilation and accommodation theory. According to this view, environmental learning is not limited only to assimilation of information from the environment into the learner's behavior repertoire but also involves an appropriate change within the learner—an accommodation to the requirements of the environment. For example, to learn to open a door, a child has to manipulate the handle and find out whether the door needs pushing or pulling and what the weight of the door is (assimilation). He or she must also do the right things—turn the handle the right way, push or pull with appropriate force, and then accommodate himself or herself to the experience of "door opening."

Architectural Design for Facility

Fixed-feature space and flexible-feature space are only two productive research concepts in the investigation of space arrangement. The architectural design of the classroom or conference room is another important area of study.

Getzels (1974) has written that different architectural arrangements of classrooms imply different images of the students. The rectangular classroom in which students' chairs are bolted to the floor in straight rows with a teacher's desk front and center is equal to an "empty organism" that learns only from the teacher. The square classroom in which chairs are movable and a teacher's desk is located in a corner is congruent with the image of an "active organism," or participation in the learning process. Circular-arranged classrooms with no teacher's desk project the "social organism" image, or learning from peers. The final design in modern classroom arrangements is that of the "stimulus-seeking organism," illustrated by an open classroom with no desks and featuring resource tables and activity areas. Open classrooms suggest a search for novel and challenging approaches to learning. Getzels summarized by saying that the physical organization of the classroom is shaped by values about the learning process and that, in turn, the physical design shapes the way students learn.

Broadwell (1976), who comes from a business training background, proposes a slightly different psychology of design by offering two different categories: the "learner-centered" and "teacher-centered" arrangements. He labels the design configuration based on participation limits. In other words, if a particular design arrangement limits the learner's participation, it is essentially a teacher-centered design. The instructor controls the training, the communication flows, and the learning patterns. Thus, the high visibility of the instructor forced by a specific physical plan causes the student to constantly seek instruction from one source—the teacher. The "face-the-front" classroom seating plan is a prime example.

On the other end of the psychology-of-design spectrum, the learners are placed in arrangements that facilitate participation and interaction with group members. Considerable reduction of instructor visibility is realized in terms of controlling the "step-by-step" process toward learning. In this scheme, the flow from activity to activity is perceived to be more natural. The learners are generally less aware of the change, and the instructor has not surrendered real control but only some of the visibility in exercising control.

The U-shape arrangement is offered as an illustration of Broadwell's point, since the teacher can at any time reclaim control by positioning himself or herself in the U-shape design. The circular pattern creates a stronger learner-centered design, and greater difficulty is incurred by the teacher in regaining control or reentering the group, especially when group members are in the process of sharing equally with peers and instructor.

While physical arrangements can imply different images of the students, students also have perceptions about the open-space classroom arrangement as noted by Gauvin (1977). One major finding revealed that 45 percent of the students believed that the open-space environment provides for more opinions to be formed by students and teachers than the self-contained classroom. This finding was interpreted to suggest that even though the teachers allowed for greater variety of activities in an open classroom, there were many more constraints placed on student behavior. Students also indicated an increased work-load for the open-facility design. This phenomenon was explained by teachers who wanted to minimize student restlessness by overloading students to keep them quiet. One implication drawn by Gauvin was that there is a need for periodic assessment of the perceptions of those who use an educational environment concerning the use of that environment.

Cocking's 1958 position, though taken twenty years before, was similar to that of Gauvin. He urged that adult educators consider the learners and utilize their talents and abilities in facility planning. Cocking perceived adult education planners to be the "servants" of the enterprise and felt that the best way to serve is to put the people who are most concerned—the learners—into the vantage position.

People often are overly passive and not willing to reshape environments. Altman (1975) documents the opinion that adults adapt too readily; he cites the failure of conference participants to protest table and chair arrangements that are not conducive to group discussion. As evidence, participants will willingly stretch their necks to see one another, speak to people sitting behind them by twisting around, fidget in uncomfortable chairs, and so on.

Amenities

Environmental variables more subtle than spatial and furniture layout can also affect behavior. The color of the walls in a room, perception of the room as "beautiful" or "ugly," and whether it is provided with such amenities as comfortable chairs or carpeting may all be important to the conferee learning. Maslow and Mintz (1965) asked college students to rate the "energy" and "well-being" of several individuals from a series of photographs of their faces. The seating sessions were conducted in a "beautiful" room, an "ugly" room, and an "average" room. The subjects in the beautiful room rated the photographs as higher on energy and well-being than did the subjects in either the average or ugly rooms. The effect of the ugly room was decidedly more negative than that of the average room.

Three environmental conditions were varied in the experimental rooms in another study. Tognoli (1973) studied the variations of three environmental conditions in order to understand how different settings can alter behaviors in terms of attitudes. Each subject was taken into one of two experimental rooms of identical size, one with a window and the other without. The subject was asked to sit in a padded or wooden chair. The room was either carpeted and had pictures on the wall or was unembellished.

The subjects found the embellished room more interesting than the unembellished room. If the room was embellished and/or had a window, it was rated as more pleasant. A soft, padded chair combined with a windowless and unembellished room was rated as uncomfortable, but a wooden chair in an embellished room was rated as comfortable. So the effect of the furniture seems to depend on the context in which it appears. The comfortable ratings for the wooden chair and the soft chair can be understood only in relation to the other two architectural conditions. Apparently, a wooden chair located in an otherwise pleasant room may be rated as more comfortable than a soft chair located in an unpleasant, windowless room.

Yet another study focusing on effects of a windowless environment was conducted by Karmel (1965), who examined the effects of a windowless classroom environment on high school student drawings. The results showed that subjects in a windowless classroom had negative feelings toward their school and as a group tended to express themselves in a more maladjusted and unhappy way than children in a windowed environment. Another study (Sommer 1969) was designed to examine a college classroom and found several problems due to a windowless environment, one of which was greater absenteeism, along with evidence of other escape behaviors.

Interestingly these results are in complete disagreement with at least one adult conference center designer. Kobler (1974) indicates that windows are bad for meetings; they are distracting and introduce a fatigue factor.

Other subtle physical environmental factors that have been studied primarily with children are illumination and color.

Gilliland (1969) is of the opinion that the proper visual environment cannot be overestimated. The importance of the visual environment is emphasized by his estimate that 25 percent of the body's energy is consumed in the seeing process. With this amount of energy being expended, it should be difficult to ignore the visual environment in the learning process.

Birren (1969) noted that past thought concerning an ideal environment was one in which the light levels are ample for the task at hand and of uniform brightness. That level of illumination that would hold the eye to a steady level of adjustment was recommended. More recent research, however, indicates that all functions of the body are in constant flux, according to Birren. To support this idea, Birren cited M. D. Vernon, a British psychologist, as indicating that normal consciousness, perception, and thought can be maintained only in a constantly changing environment. A state of sensory deprivation occurs where there is no change, and the capacity of adults to concentrate deteriorates, attention fluctuates and lapses, and normal perception fades.

Sharpe (1974) supported Birren by writing that bright lights dull wits at all levels and that mental activity in problem solving, decision making, and social conversation are affected. Smith (1978a) developed Sharpe's ideas further and observes that any light source or light-blocking device such as a window or eyeglasses can lead to headaches, fatigue, or general ill effects. He also indicates that the human endocrine system will not function properly under artificial light. Trainers can prevent this light-related phenomenon from interfering with trainees' ability to concentrate, says Smith, by having training sessions outside or in areas illuminated by sunlight streaming through full-spectrum windowpanes. The difference between Smith's opinion and Kobler's position points out the necessity for appropriate scientific investigations into the effect of physical elements on adult behavior. Lighting environment influences posture and balance, according to Gilliland (1969), and serious physical handicaps may result from improper lighting.

Color is a most important factor in the visual environment for both children and adults. Gilliland believes that color generates psychophysical effects on human beings. These psychophysical effects include overt acts, feelings of warmth and coolness, alteration of judgment, variable appetites, apparent camouflages, variable fatigue, difficulty in focusing the eyes, and illusions of change in size, weight, and distance.

Smith (1978b) cites the Hygiea Studies completed in Gloucestershire, England, whose results are similar to Gilliland's but are more explicit as to what colors affect individuals in various ways. For example, red causes a subject's pulse rate, blood pressure, and respiration to show a marked increase. Blue decreases the vital signs and is a good color for hospitals. Green should be incorporated inside ambulances due to its seeming ability to settle shock victims. Yellow appears to alleviate migraines and asthma.

Psychophysical responses to color have been attributed to the phenomenon known as chromatic aberration. Birren (1958) believes that this phenomenon is the physiological basis for psychological effects of colors, i.e., for perception of colors as warm and stimulating or cool and relaxing. Accordingly, he recommends that rooms scheduled to be action oriented be decorated in warm colors (yellow, red, and orange), while rooms planned for quieter activities be decorated in cooler colors (blue and green).

Finkel (1975) refers to a study conducted in Germany in the early seventies regarding the impact of environment on mental health. Using children as subjects, the psychologists found, according to Finkel, that colors have a decisive influence on a child's mental performance. Children in the study categorized colors as beautiful (hues of blue, yellow, green, and orange) and ugly (white, black, and brown). The German study reported an average improvement of 15 IQ points for those in beautiful environments accompanied by positive social reactions such as friendly words, cooperation, and smiles.

Smith (1978b) seems to disagree with Birren (1958) on the effects of yellow colors. Smith notes that yellow is considered to be a detached color and should therefore assist in creating a quiet mood within a testing room; it also could promote insecurity. Because of the latter possibility, Smith advised not to use a role play technique in such a yellow room. The consoling impact of yellow as perceived by Smith does not match Birren's recommendation of using yellow as a stimulant.

Environmental Factors and Social Interactions

Since the field of adult education is concerned with people who, in most instances, will be collected in groups, adult education appears to operate in the social environment. Adult learning can be influenced by its social surroundings and, thus, possibly affected by limitations imposed by social circumstances. However, if adult educators can have knowledge of the circumstances existing in a social environment, they may be aware of present or future opportunities to turn the social environment to the best learning advantage.

Perhaps one way to gain knowledge of the social milieu is through the investigation of social interactions. London (1964) and Bligh (1977) believe that the different relationships between people develop and change as a result of interaction processes taking place. These interactions and their processes have more influence upon behavior, motivational drives, and personality development than do norms, environment, and a person's inner drives.

Mead (1934) describes human beings as able to engage in social interactions due to their ability to take one another's viewpoints. Interaction helps people have common expectations of each other. For Mead, the foundations of a group rest in the abilities of people to develop and assume their roles, to understand their relationship to others and their roles, and to organize their behavior to fit into behavior that others may possess.

Fisher (1980) reports one of the few recent studies of the association of environmental factors with the behavior of adult learners. His study was designed to provide information concerning the relationships between the physical environment of a residential conference center and social interaction of adults. The study design was based on the premise that social interactions are an important factor in the education of adults and that environmental factors may be in some way associated with human feelings and social interactions of adults. Accordingly, he requested his subjects to provide a systematic appraisal of the relationship of physical surroundings in the University of Georgia Center for Continuing Education with feelings and interaction frequency.

As a result of his study, Fisher arrived at the following conclusions:

1. Different physical locations are perceived to be associated with varying frequencies of social interactions.
2. Environmental elements such as colors, windows, and ceiling height are associated with social interaction frequency.
3. Some environmental elements are associated with positive feelings.
4. Some specific physical locations are related to positive feelings.
5. A significant relationship exists between positive feelings and social interaction frequency in some physical locations of a residential continuing education center.
6. Environmental elements associated with social interaction frequency also are associated with positive feelings.
7. Environmental elements identified by descriptors as Bright, Warm, Open, and Windowed are identified with greater feelings of security, sociability, and freedom and with greater frequencies of social interactions.

Sally White's 1973 review of available literature led to the observation that information about how adult learning environments should be organized to facilitate learning efficiency is sparse, scattered, and relatively superficial. This observation remains current even though it has been speculated that the physical environment can affect or account for as much as 25 percent of learning. As a result of her review, White concluded that there is general agreement that facilities for adults should have an aura of adulthood to contribute to adults' feelings of ease, confidence, and capabilities; be flexible in room configuration; reflect the capability to change the environment; and provide for availability of multi-purpose equipment. Furthermore, social and psychological implications of seating arrangements should be considered. Specific items of concern include space, fixtures, and furniture; the use of colors and lighting; other visual and auditory factors (such as the disruptive quality of clutter and decrements in hearing ability among adults); and recommended temperature, humidity, and air motion.

OBSERVATIONS

Programming skills and knowledge are among the crucial competencies of educators of adults. A distinctive characteristic shared by many educational programs for adults is the need to be self-supporting. There are some major exceptions, including Defense Department programs, Cooperative Extension, business and industry, some religious programs, and some social service programs supported by public schools and other public agencies. A greater variety of educational activities for adults, however, depend directly upon their ability to attract paying customers who defray the expenses associated with the activity.

The problems associated with the requirement that adult education programs be financially self-supporting are not unknown to administrators and researchers. However, limited study of topics appropriate to this area of inquiry is reflected in the research literature. Windham, Kurland, and Levinsohn (1978) edited an interesting issue of *School Review* that focused on the topic "Financing the Learning Society." Related studies of social policy decisions that have implications for the provision of governmental support for adult education are also limited. Examples of some of the work available include Fox (1982), Griffith (1976), Griffith and Dhanidina (1975), and Stewart (1981).

The profit or self-support requirement thus adds another dimension to the program planning process that is not critical in other educational programs. Even among some of the institutions and organizations that provide educational opportunities as a service, such as the Cooperative Extension Service, satisfaction and voluntary participation are critical factors that are closely related to the concerns of planners in agencies that must develop money-making programs. Therefore, satisfaction as measured by the diverse subjective criteria of the learners is a critical factor that must be seriously considered by the planner of adult educational activities.

From the inception of a program idea, whether it is an inspiration of the educator or a recommendation of a potential learner, the planner is concerned with a number of interacting variables. These variables have been studied by several educators and have been systematically organized to provide different program-planning models. In 1972, Brady and I identified at least sixty-five action steps in the process, and LaForest (1973) noted more than 200.

The potential variance and interactions among the multitude of variables easily explain why program planning or program development is one of the major research interests among adult educators. However, research models that will clearly explicate the nuances of the various relationships among the diverse variables are needed. For example, as is noted in Chapter 8, it is obvious that organizations offer educational programs for different reasons. Specific mission objectives and other incentives may justify the adoption of distinctive programming concepts. If this is the case, how are these distinctive concepts applied and how do the outcomes differ from those of other organizations? For example, if a county political party, the League of Women Voters, and an institution of higher education all sought to develop a program on "practical politics," how would the nature of the three organizations influence the program planning process?

Somewhat analogous to the problem discussed above is the question concerning philosophical and educational backgrounds of the program planners. Brady and I (1972) and Everitt (1974) have reported findings that indicate that professionally trained educators of adults subscribe to procedures that are more person centered than those of urban planners and governmental training directors, who seem to demonstrate a person-versus-task orientation. If these differences are evident in some of the program-planning action steps, how might they affect other variables in the process?

Studies of the role and effect of physical surroundings, ranging from architecture to furniture and wall coverings, in educational settings for adults are woefully inadequate. Even though there is a recognition that educational locations for adults should have an "adult aura," research designed to identify associations among important variables is extremely limited.

Despite the needed research and the desirability of improved designs of additional investigations, the literature on the various procedures of program development is encouraging. The rudiments of several pragmatic planning models are available. Satisfaction seems to be associated with learner involvement in the planning and operation of learning activities. Evaluation is a regular topic of discussion, and a few studies have identified some potentially productive variables for studying the association between physical facilities and learner behaviors.

Ultimately, the pragmatism of adult education indicates that educators of adults are challenged to develop programs that accomplish several objectives. The programs must be financially self-supporting in many instances. Programs must be perceived to have some social/personal value. They must be satisfying to the learner. And the learner is expected to achieve something. Evaluation studies may identify some of the processes associated with the above outcomes as well as measure the impact of educational programs. Finally, there is reason to suspect that physical surroundings may influence feelings and social environments that also are associated with important outcomes—satisfaction and achievement.

Given the amount of hortatory literature concerning the topic of participation of learners in goal setting, program development, and program management, however, the research base for the practice remains unseemly limited. Even two of the three studies that have directly addressed the fundamental matter of learner achievement are seriously flawed because of sample size and/or research procedures. The conflicting data concerning achievement is not unlike the data that fed the debate about achievement of students in lecture courses versus students enrolled in discussion courses.

Because of the implications derived from the philosophical emphasis on learner participation in planning and operating the learning activities in adult education, this topic is perceived to be among the more important ones that require additional research activity.

8 • Needs Assessment

SUCCESSFUL CREATION AND OPERATION of educational programs for adults involve coordination of complex interacting processes. The specific identities of the many processes and the relationships among them are not yet fully agreed upon. Even concurrence upon the agreed-upon processes awaits additional work of scholars and practitioners. One of the key elements in successful programming, upon which there is some agreement and an extensive body of literature, is needs assessment. The significance of the activity is indicated by its inclusion in most of the general program planning models reported in the literature. The general program model begins with the concept of need. Even though it is variously phrased, the exhortation to plan the educational programs based on knowledge of the potential participants is clear.

Despite widespread agreement in the program planning literature concerning the desirability and necessity of needs assessment as an initial activity, the concept is not without problems. The difficulties identified in the literature scatter across an expanse of concerns, theoretical and practical. The existing sources of guidance to performing needs assessment are inadequate, and some of the more commonly known available resources can be described as limited in both quantity and utility (Beatty 1976). There is also evidence that the identification of educational needs as an initial program planning activity is often neglected completely, is superficial, or is post-hoc (Griffith 1978). For example, even though the objectives of some agencies, organizations, or institutional missions encourage the provision of an educational activity, an assessment of the needs of a specific target group may not be conducted prior to the initiation of the program. According to Griffith, this kind of situation explains what he believes to be an inconsistency between the ideal program planning process and the real. Whereas the ideal process begins with an assessment of the educational needs of a specific group, he says that the practice of conducting a cursory assessment is often one of the last steps in the planning process.

Investigations related to the concept of need as a structural element in program development appear to be more a reflection of a principle of practice based on an assumption rather than one based on empirical grounds. Discussions of the importance of needs assessment in program planning seem to have their genesis in several separate but related dimensions of adult education, including the voluntary nature of educational activities of adults, the issue of participation, and concepts of motivation. Drawing from these three characteristics, adult educators seem to have reasoned as follows:

1. Educational participation for adults is voluntary.
2. Therefore, to *attract* adults to educational activities, the activities should be based on the needs and interests of the learners.
3. A favorable relationship between identified educational needs and educational activities should thus be an important planning objective.
4. Successfully achieving a relationship between needs and activities will result in an individual's active commitment (greater effort and persistence) to the learning activity.

There is also a possible ethical dimension to the issue as well as the pragmatic one mentioned above. The ethical aspect concerns the responsibility of the planner of educational programs for adults to ultimately provide a learning experience that actually addresses a real need of the learner. Failure in this activity results in the provision of an unwanted or unneeded educational activity, which would be tantamount to defrauding the learner.

The assumption that needs assessment is important, if not critical, in planning educational activities for adults has many reputable supporters. The list of proponents of needs assessment is too lengthy to list here; examples include Lindeman, Bryson, Bergevin, Houle, and Knowles, to name just a few. Additional evidence is provided by the references in this chapter.

As early as 1936, Bryson noted that "it is part of our basic theory of adult education that men and women take part in it [adult education] because of their own felt needs" (p. 119). The problem of identifying the critical factor of need, however, was also noted by Bryson. He agreed that it is easy to observe that adult education is always a response to the felt need and declared purpose of a mature student, but the adult educator cannot always safely rest in the belief that the adults in a given community will demand the kinds of educational activities that will meet their desires. He said, "It is complicated by the fact that people do not know what they are interested in, except in terms of what is available to them" (p. 122).

A similar observation was noted in 1959 by Brunner and his associates, who cited Fryer's 1931 observation that a limitation of "stated interests tests" concerns the validity of an individual's comments about interests in things that he or she knows little or nothing about.

The challenge presented by one principle that would define the adult educator's mission as one of enlightenment and another that urges needs assessment is not necessarily a paradox, but it can be. A paradox exists when needs assessment is limited to what the literature refers to as "expressed interest." An expressed interest is fundamentally something that the adult says that he or she wishes to study. Bounded rationality naturally limits individuals in identifying interests according to experience. Defining need in terms of desire is also a source of philosophical conflict, as we shall see later.

Bryson's comments also reveal a characteristic of more recent writing. He, like some contemporary scholars, made no distinction between needs and interests. Brunner et al. included the discussion of educational needs in their chapter on adult interests, in which twenty-five pages are devoted to "interests" and two pages to needs.

Bergevin (1967) declares that an effective program of adult education should consider the needs and interests of the learner. Furthermore, he believes that it is important for program planners to attempt to discover and meet the "real" needs of the learner as well as the needs of the social order. Bergevin's emphasis on what he highlights as real needs is his way of distinguishing between what he labels a symptomatic need, a felt need, and a real need. Even though Bergevin failed to explicate the terms, they will become clearer as this chapter unfolds.

Apparently influenced by the psychological literature, Houle (1972) indicates that needs may be related to emotions. While he does not reveal his personal position, he notes that some theories of adult education have employed concepts of needs or interests that imply the existence of tension or pleasure. This reference quite likely is to the issue of "homeostasis," a basic psychological concept that generally represents humans as seeking to maintain relative equilibrium. Consequently, a need causes tension; fulfillment of the need reduces tension and thereby results in pleasure.

Up to this point in the discussion of the concept of need in adult education, we have noted a number of terms such as *needs* and/or *interests, expressed interest, real needs, felt needs,* and *symptomatic need.* The many terms used to refer to what is often a common construct within such a short space reflect one of the problems that educators of adults have in their struggle to consistently conceptualize and investigate needs assessment. The research literature on the topic generally falls into three general areas. The first of the three areas discussed here includes research into the conceptual or definitional aspects of need. The second area includes studies designed to demonstrate how needs assessment may be carried out. Research literature available in the second area includes those studies that describe a *procedure* for conducting needs assessment. The third thrust of the research is represented by those investigations into the needs of adults in specific groups or communities. Selected research in each area is discussed in the following pages.

CONCEPTS AND DEFINITIONS

As demonstrated by the previous list of terms, educators have used a number of labels to define and describe a common phenomenon referred to as need.

Unfortunately, we shall not be able to resolve the problem caused by the lack of precision in defining the construct here; our purpose is to reveal the variety of definitions and concepts that have arisen out of efforts to arrive at some understanding of, and explanation for, the role and nature of needs, wants, interests, and related concepts. While there is substantial comment available on interests and wants, the primary thrust here is upon the need concept. There seem to be four conceptual foundations on which the literature is based: the biological, the psychological, a combination of the biological and psychological, and the educational. (The biological and the psychological concepts will here be considered together, after which the educational concepts will be discussed.)

Needs are often compared or contrasted in each of the four categories with wants or interests. Frequently, needs are distinguished from wants by the power or depth of the construct as reflected by motive, drive, or the consequences of failure to satisfy the need or want. Accordingly, it is theorized that a person may want something yet not need it. Within this framework, the existence of a need is perceived to be indicative of a situation in which deprivation is psychologically or physically harmful. In contrast, failure to satisfy an interest is not perceived as having any significant long-term effects.

Biological and Psychological Concepts

As derived from the discipline of psychology, the concept of need has two different dimensions. To some, need is a biological construct; to others it is a psychological construct. Additionally, need may be used for either biological or psychological properties, or both. Selected theoretical positions concerning need as discussed in the literature of psychology are discussed in the following paragraphs.

The biological dimension of needs as revealed in the psychological literature is most vividly portrayed in the theoretical work of Clark Hull. He represents needs as operating both in the formation of habits and in their subsequent functioning—primary motivation. Because of the energizing action of needs in the latter role, he refers to them as drives. According to Hull's 1964 review of the research, particularly that related to hunger, thirst, injury, sex, and the action of certain substances such as caffeine, he was led to conclude that all primary drives (needs) produce their effects by the action of various chemicals in the blood. He proposed that drive substances, such as various endocrine secretions, are released into the blood by certain kinds of strong stimulation or themselves initiate stimulation of receptors through their evocation of action by selected parts of the body such as the intestinal tract and genitalia.

In contrast to Hull's concept of primary motivation, wherein needs are biologically based and are consequently thought of as being innate, the psychological dimension of needs provides for the possibility that they may be learned. (It is useful to pause here and remind ourselves that *need* is a label for an abstract construct. For example, it is not absolutely correct to say that food is a need; when such statements are offered, we really mean that food is the object that is required to satisfy a need, which may be a biological imbalance in the human organism.)

Rotter (Sahakian 1970) conceives of needs and goals as having the same ultimate referents but different appropriate uses, to distinguish between environmental conditions determining the direction of a person's interaction with the environment (goals) and the focus on personal determination of direction (needs). In other words, goals are environmental reinforcements for satisfaction of personally directed behaviors identified as needs. Furthermore, Rotter hypothesizes that an individual's behaviors, needs, and goals are not independent but are a part of a functionally related system. He also uses *need* interchangeably with *motive*.

Needs, according to Rotter, have three essential components. One of these is the set of behaviors directed toward the same goal or to similar related goals. He calls these behaviors *need potentials*. The term is used to refer to the potential strength of such behaviors; that is, the probability that they will emerge in given situations. The second major component is made up of the *expectancies* that certain behaviors will lead to outcomes that the individual values. The third major component of needs is the value attached to the goals themselves—the degree to which an individual prefers one set of satisfactions to another. The term *need value* is used to define this component.

Rotter's concept seems to underlie the model of participation developed by Bergsten discussed in Chapter 5. Need potentials may be weak or strong according to the two other components, expectancy and need value. Either or both of the latter components will change the strength of the need. For example, a high expectancy of obtaining a highly valued goal enhances the need potential and the appropriate behaviors. In contrast, a low expectancy of a low-valued goal will result in a weak need potential, and behaviors that may be half-hearted and inconsistent. A more complex situation exists when an individual has medium expectations concerning a highly valued goal; ambivalence may characterize the behaviors.

A major aspect of Rotter's social learning theory is the importance that it gives to the psychological situation of individuals, both in understanding and predicting behavior. In contrast to any approach that places the stress on internal states, this view, because of its basic learning-theory assumptions, emphasizes that an individual learns through past experiences that some satisfactions are more likely in some situations than in others. Thus, differences exist not only in the strength of different needs but in the way in which the same situation is perceived by individuals.

Reactions to different situations depend on one's past experience, which therefore constitutes an important aspect of individual differences. The psychological situation, then, provides the cues for individual expectancies that behaviors will lead to desired results.

Rotter's social-learning model (Sahakian 1970), which emphasizes needs and goals, is based on very broad needs that are designed to include most learned psychological behavior: recognition-status, dominance, independence, protection-dependency, love and affection, and physical comfort. Rotter's typology of potential, expectancy, and value is a useful conceptualization and will be suggested by a typology later reported by Scissons. Scissons (1980) does not indicate that his typology is derived from the work of Rotter; the concepts, however, are not unlike. Scissons reports three types of needs—competence, relevance, and motivation—that greatly resemble the interactive aspects of Rotter's conceptualization.

Diggins and Huber (1976) provide a list of eight terms that are often used to refer to inner states, urges, or impulses that cause a person to behave in specific ways. They are *drive, need, motive, goal, wish, desire, purpose,* and *intention.* It is suggested that drives and motives are frequently used to refer to phenomena of different origins. Physiological drives are believed to originate from deprivation of something that the individual needs for physical survival, such as food and water. In contrast, most psychological motives are believed to be learned, not innate, and frequently represent those things we want but that are not necessary for physical survival. Thus, a need is usually interpreted as something required for survival, while wish, want, and desire refer to things that may make people happier but are not required for survival.

Sullivan (Diggins and Huber 1976) theorized that all people have two basic motives reflecting their physical and psychological needs. They are the desire for satisfaction and the desire for security.

Maslow (1970) has offered what has been described as an attempt to formulate a list of universal motives.[1] His hierarchy of needs is as follows:

1. Physiological
2. Safety
3. Belongingness and love
4. Self-esteem
5. Self-actualization
6. To know and to understand
7. Aesthetic

The basic thesis of Maslow's hierarchy of needs is similar to that of stage development: An individual must progress from each level to the next, and the lower level must be basically satisfied before movement to the higher level is possible. He further classified his scheme into two kinds of general needs: deficit needs and growth needs. The former include the first four basic or lower-order needs of physiological, safety, belongingness and love, and self-esteem. The latter include the three higher-order needs of self-actualization, the need to know and understand, and aesthetic needs. Diggins and Huber are of the opinion that Maslow's division of the hierarchy was accomplished for the purpose of relegating those things needed for existence into the deficit category.

The idea of a hierarchy of needs has received partial support from research studies. People are believed to display relatively little interest in "higher" activities when their physiological and safety needs are not satisfied—when they are cold, hungry, thirsty, or fearful. One demonstration of this idea is provided by Keys and his co-workers, who subjected voluntary subjects to semistarvation for a number of weeks (Keys et al. 1950). Eventually, these men thought of little but food, and many of their normal activities and interests succumbed to the constant hunger.

Reports from concentration camps and places where severe catastrophe or other stress has occurred indicate that people's normal values, interests, and social behavior often disintegrate when they are subjected to prolonged physiological deprivation and severe insecurity. Davis (Diggins and Huber 1976) discovered that workers from underprivileged backgrounds lacked ambition and interest in what their work was about. These workers were presumably still attempting to satisfy physiological and safety needs and could not worry themselves about the higher aspects of their work, such as pride in doing their job well.

It is important to note that these research findings provide no evidence about the needs above the physiological and safety needs. According to Diggins and Huber, psychologists generally agree that little support has been found for the hierarchic relationships among the higher needs on Maslow's list.

Other psychologists who have defined needs in terms of both biological and psychological dimensions include Murphy (1958) and Fromm (1955). Murphy has provided a list of four "inborn needs": visceral needs, activity needs, sensory needs, and escape or avoidance needs. Fromm identifies five needs that arise from the conditions of the human's existence: relatedness versus narcissism, transcendence-creativeness versus destructiveness, rooted-ness-brotherliness versus incest, sense of identity-individuality versus herd conformity, and the need for a frame of orientation and devotion versus irrationality.

To briefly summarize this section, the psychological literature reflects concern for "needs" of two kinds: physiological and psychological. The physiological needs are considered innate, and the psychological ones are learned. *Drive* is a psychological term used in some instances to distinguish the innate physiological needs from the learned psychological ones, which are sometimes referred to as motives. Hence, the concept has emerged as illustrated in Figure 8.1.

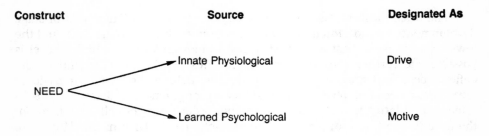

Construct	Source	Designated As
	Innate Physiological	Drive
NEED		
	Learned Psychological	Motive

Figure 8.1   The need construct as represented by the literature of psychology

Educational Concepts

The preceeding review of needs as described and defined in psychology and a similar review of needs in adult education are not necessarily the same. However, it is generally accepted that the basic biological and psychological needs have relevance to education and that they provide an explanatory basis for adult learning.

Even though the concept of needs as a basis for planning educational experiences has a respectable pedigree that includes such luminaries as Berge-vin, Bryson, Dewey, Lindeman, and Tyler, it has been described by Monette

(1979) as "rather fuzzy." Monette's review of the adult education literature concerned with need reveals a number of difficulties with the term. He identified four major categories into which the implicit and explicit definitions of need fall—basic human needs, felt and expressed needs, normative needs, comparative needs—and variant uses of the term.

Basic Human Needs

Knowles (1970) is of the opinion that knowledge of basic needs will be helpful in prescribing certain conditions that should be considered by the planner of educational activities for adults. Here, according to the context of Knowles's comments, it is assumed that *basic needs* is used to refer to certain innate *and* learned needs similar to the lower-level needs in Maslow's hierarchy. Elsewhere, he defines an educational need as something a person ought to learn for his or her own benefit, for the good of an organization, or for the welfare of society. It can be objectively defined as the gap between one's present level of competence and a higher level as required for effective performance as defined by learners, their organization, or society. The idea of educational need is further developed along psychological lines as the distance between an aspiration and a reality. Furthermore, according to Knowles, one can define educational needs narrowly or broadly. Broadly defined, they encompass the totality of one's aspirations concerning an idealized self. Narrowly defined, they may be limited to one specific area of desired competence, such as being able to make a straight cut of lumber with a handsaw or to play a musical instrument.

Knowles's scheme concerning educational needs and interests reflects the psychologist's classification of needs and wants as he attempts to distinguish between them. The analogy is weak, however, because in Knowles's scheme, needs parallel the psychologists' wants, which include interests or preferences.

Felt and Expressed Needs

The most commonly used term is *felt need*. *Felt need* and *expressed need* are used more or less interchangeably, and they also seem to represent the same dimensions included in the term *symptomatic need.*

Normative Needs

A need is considered to be normative when it defines a deficiency between a standard to be achieved and conditions that actually exist. For example, if first-year typing students are expected to achieve a typing speed of fifty words per minute, and the learner's speed is forty words per minute, the standard is not met, and there is a normative need for the student to increase typing speed by ten words per minute.

Comparative Needs

A comparative need is identified by comparing two groups or individuals according to selected characteristics. If one group, usually those not receiving an identified service, fails to compare favorably with those who receive such service, a need is identified comparatively.

Based on the philosophical position that the general purpose of adult education is the development of individuals who fulfill themselves and freely serve the society, which values individuals, Sheasha (1961) offered a definition of needs and wants. According to Sheasha, needs and wants have the same root: they are feelings that require satisfaction. Beyond this common origin, they are perceived to differ.

Needs are accordingly conceived of as "feelings" that require satisfaction as long as an increase in an individual's satisfaction does not decrease the *total* amount of satisfaction for all people within a community. Needs are classified within two types: (1) felt needs and (2) unfelt needs. Both are represented as being similar, except that one is recognized by the individual and the other is not.

In comparison, Sheasha conceived of wants also as feelings that require satisfaction, but in this case it is not necessary that the increase of one individual's satisfaction increase the *total* amount of satisfaction of all individuals in the community. According to Sheasha, needs are always good, but not all wants are good. In this conceptualization, the ideal society is represented by a manifestation of felt needs 100 percent of the time and of unfelt needs and undesirable wants none of the time. Ultimately, it seems as if Sheasha equates wants as always bad and thus undesirable.

Philosophical Issues

Monette's (1977, 1979) philosophical discussion of needs assessment in adult education reveals what he believes to be an overly technical preoccupation of adult education theory. Accordingly, he represents the general literature on needs assessment, including the Tylerian model of curriculum development, as reflecting an industrial model that is concerned with input (student), processes (learning experiences), and output (behavioral objectives). He argues persuasively that needs assessment is not restricted to empirically determinable facts; the process also includes complex value judgments.

The failure of adult educators to consider the philosophical implications of need definition and need assessment has contributed to a schism between practice and prescription. Prescription in adult education program development, as noted at the beginning of this chapter, extols the importance of initiating the process with needs assessment, i.e., identifying the educational needs to be met by the learning experience. In practice, it appears that the adult educator is placed in one of the following positions:

1. Accepting the learner's "felt needs" as a basis for planning the learning experience
2. Accepting the learner's "felt needs" as a basis for planning the learning experience, but choosing from among the expressed needs and establishing a priority order among them
3. Rejecting the "felt needs" as inappropriate according to some set of values and thus providing a different kind of educational experience
4. Using a process similar to the one used by Freire, whereby the "felt needs" are used as a departure point within a fairly well-articulated philosophical framework
5. Following some possible combination of the above—or possibly none of the above, but making some other yet unidentified response

Drawing from the earlier work of Archambault (1957), Atwood and Ellis (1971) supplement Bryson's 1936 and Leagans's 1948 observations concerning "real" educational needs. The central thrust in the effort to distinguish between real and felt needs seems to be twofold: First, there is the indication that a felt need may be highly transitory and may not accurately represent a real need (one that is relatively persistent and negatively affects the individual); and second, it is implied that the professional status and responsibility of the educator requires him or her to do more than "merely serve the people."

The responsibility of adult educators to march to a tune different from that played by felt needs was pointed up by Blakely (1952) thirty years ago. He regretted the tendency of adult educators to idolize adult learners so far as their expressions of wants are concerned, and called for the practice to be seriously reconsidered. The adult educator should not be defensive about refusing to be merely a waiter serving in a cafeteria line. Accordingly, Blakely shared his philosophical position concerning the mission of adult education as including the education of adults for self-improvement and for the improvement of their citizenship.

Following his review of the literature on the concept of needs in adult education, Monette (1979) arrived at eight conclusions (here paraphrased):

1. There appears to be consensus in the literature on need that felt needs or wants per se are inadequate for defining educational objectives.
2. Prescriptive needs ("real needs") per se are also inadequate.
3. Various needs approaches to educational planning (felt needs, prescriptive needs, basic human needs, and combinations of these) are by no means value free; that is, they do not obviate the educator's responsibility for making judgments of value.
4. While need language is used in practice both as slogan and as articulation of an approach to program development, it is important to distinguish one use from the other.
5. Need might best be defined from the educator's perspective, that is to say, as prescription. Because of its stress on intentionality, the term *want* might best replace *need* as motive.
6. The term *need* (except perhaps in slogan form) always implies, more or less directly, some standard or valued state of affairs or certain social norms against which need is measured.
7. Discussion of needs revolves around technological or scientific questions; rarely does it involve relevant philosophical questions in the realms of ontology, epistemology, or axiology.
8. Needs must be sifted through the "philosophical screen" of the sponsoring institution for the defining of objectives.

Need as a Multidimensional Concept

Robbins's 1981 review of the concept of need as reflected in the literature of fields such as psychology, sociology, marketing, and education encouraged him to describe three aspects of the concept. The three aspects are the conditions of need, the dynamics of need, and the dimensions of need.

The aspect of conditions of need represents human needs as internal driving forces that influence behavior. They are characterized in a number of ways, such as deficiencies to be overcome, as inner motivating forces to be fulfilled, and as goals or expectancies to be attained. On the second aspect, dynamics of need, the process of ameliorating needs is explained as a cycle of energy arising from tension, motivation, goals, satisfaction, and new energy. The energy obtained through the fulfillment of needs is perceived as making growth and the meeting of other needs possible. According to Robbins, both these aspects are addressed by learning, which plays an integral part in each person's understanding of life's circumstances, alternatives, and values.

The third characteristic of need is the multidimensional aspect of the concept. Robbins identified four distinct manifestations of human need that illustrate the multidimensional aspect: source, type, intensity, and social scope. The source of need may be either internal, as in the case of physiological needs, or external, as in the case of cultural or economic needs. Five types of human needs occur in the literature: physiological, psychological, social, personal, and ontological. Intensity of need ranges from basic drives arising from extreme deprivation such as near starvation to incidental needs for satisfaction of only general interest or curiosity. The social scope of need includes individual, group, institutional, local community, and large societal need.

Scissons (1980) also offers a multidimensional definition of educational need. Educational need is conceived in terms of three fundamental need components—competence, relevance, and motivation—and two categories of higher-order definition based on the basic components—wants and complex needs. The three fundamental need components, singularly or in some combination, subsume many, if not all, of the varying definitions existing in the literature. Competence refers, in a general manner, to a person's ability to perform a range of skills. Relevance refers to the usefulness of those skills to an individual. Motivation refers to the predisposition of the individual to improve his or her competence.

Wants are characterized as involving a combination of motivation and one of the remaining two need components. For example, a person may be an incompetent musician and not be interested in remedying the situation; hence, there is little or no motivation to meet that need. Ultimately, according to this model, it is a person's wants that become instructive to the educator. The model provides a relevance-weighted want and a competence-weighted want as constructs. The relevance-weighted want is based on an individual motivation to learn about something that is important; skill or competence is not a factor. In contrast, a competence-weighted want is a manifestation of an individual's motivation to learn about something because he or she is aware of his incompetence in the area.

Finally, the concept includes two categories of complex needs: discrepancy needs and derived needs. A discrepancy need includes the need components of relevance and competence but excludes motivation. A derived need includes all three need components: competence, relevance, and motivation.

Misanchuk (1981), a colleague of Scissons', has developed a procedure for statistically examining the competence-relevance-motivation model of needs assessment. Following earlier work with Scissons, he determined that the procedures in use did not provide adequate information for decision making. It is agreed that the most powerful educational need exists when there is a high job relevance and low perceived competence. Conversely, a weak educational need is believed to exist when there is low job relevance coupled with high competence. Unfortunately, previous statistical treatments did not adequately address multivariate data dimensions. Accordingly, Misanchuk has recommended a proportionate-reduction-in-error approach for this purpose.

The work of Misanchuk and Scissons in the area of needs analysis in business and industry remains in the conceptual and formative stages. Their work, however, appears to be promising—especially in those occupational settings where job analysis permits the identification and measurement of required competencies.

TYPOLOGY OF PROCEDURES

Needs assessment procedures as reported in the literature reflect a variety of purposes and designs. Needs assessment activities range from broad populations to individual learning groups. They include geographic communities and communities of interest. How can such a complex assortment of investigations be conceptually ordered for improved understanding and communication?

One scheme of diagnostic models includes three families of needs. The first two relate to individuals, and the third concerns systems such as societies, communities, and institutions, and subsystems of these (McKinley 1973). The three models of assessment or identification of needs are (1) mass approaches, (2) individual appraisal models, and (3) system-discrepancy models.

Adult educators who have an interest in needs assessment are most likely to be acquainted with either the mass approaches or the individual approaches such as recommended by Knowles. A few representative investigations have been selected from recent literature to illustrate the different types of approaches as identified by McKinley.

Mass Approaches

A statewide study conducted in New York and a study of American Indians are included in four illustrative studies of needs based on mass-survey approaches. One is concerned with needs in political jurisdictions. Another focuses on a particular segment of the population, while the remaining two deal with two different kinds of special populations in selected geographic areas.

Individual Self-Fulfillment

Individual self-fulfillment orientations are embodied in mass approaches using interviews, questionnaires, and other similar means of collecting data. Four significant conclusions emerged from a statewide survey in New York (Veres and Carmichael 1980). Data were collected in personal interviews with 28,615 adults in ten regions of the state. The sample (aged 16 or older and not full-time students at the time) provided information about their past participation in continuing education, present learning interests, perceived obstacles to participation, preferred conditions for participation, and need for information and counseling services.

The findings were interpreted as indicating that most adults are interested in learning, though they differ on how, where, when, and why they wish to pursue their interests. Specifically, the choices and reasons cited for the selection of a person's main learning interest differ according to his or her life situation or particular characteristics as a potential learner. Five of the differences that seem to be important in decisions concerning the development of any means to meet educational needs of adults are these:

1. Most adults with an annual family income of $7,000 or less indicate that their primary interest is job related.
2. Adults without a high school diploma ranked attainment of high school equivalency highest.
3. Members of minority groups seem to have common learning interests that cut across various ethnic or racial group memberships and appear to reflect previous education, family income level, employment status, and place of residence.
4. Learning interests differ according to age level, with younger people having the greatest desire for credit, diplomas, or other forms of credentials and older and retired adults indicating a greater interest in learning for personal or avocational reasons.
5. Men and women report differences in learning interests, even though half the women interviewed gave job-related reasons for learning choices.

Selected Appeal

Another type of mass approach is focused on presumed needs of a known segment of the population based on research data, packaged materials, and program formats already tested with special populations.

Kovach (1980) has reported a needs assessment survey of adult Indians in the United States, under way at this writing. The procedures include the use of three survey instruments: (1) a field interview administered to more than 4,100 adults, (2) a survey of state education association directors, and (3) a survey of Indian Education Act, Title IV, part C, program directors. The field survey, which is the main element in the process, is administered by Indian data collectors to gain community support, trust, rapport, and more productive individual content. The survey is described by Kovach as an advance over other educational needs assessment activities because it includes test questions designed to measure competency in areas of math computation, reading, consumer skills, and legal knowledge. He is of the opinion that these procedures provide an accurate quantitative measure of actual needs.

Dobbs's 1966 investigation of self-perceived educational needs of adults in two different neighborhoods in Indianapolis, Indiana, illustrates the use of the interview method to identify educational needs. According to his study, Dobbs was able to identify the aims, hopes, and problems of individuals interviewed. Accordingly, he noted areas in which additional educational services might be helpful to the people in the two neighborhoods. Education was perceived as a solution to many of the economic and occupational problems of the community or as a means to reach other goals.

Sheridan and Shannon (1979) report a useful needs assessment model that they employed to identify training needs of governmental staff members of the city of Spokane, Washington. They developed a conceptual framework based in part on the work of Bradshaw (1974). Accordingly, they designed procedures to assess the following kinds of needs (Sheridan and Shannon 1979, pp. 221-222):

1. Normative Need: This, the expert or professional administrator or social scientist identifies as need in any given situation. A "desirable" standard is laid down and is compared with the standard that actually exists—if an individual or group falls short of the desirable standard then they are identified as being in need. . . .
2. Felt Need: Here need is equated with want. When assessing need for a service, people are asked whether they feel they need it. . . . Felt need is, by itself, an inadequate measure of the "real need." It is limited by the perceptions of the individual. . . .
3. Expressed Need: . . . is felt need turned into action. . . . One does not demand a service unless one feels a need but, on the other hand, it is common for felt need not to be expressed by demand. . . .
4. Comparative Need: By this definition, a measure of need is found by studying the characteristics of those in receipt of a service. If people with similar characteristics are not in receipt of a service, then they are in need.
5. Client Need: This is what the client or user of professional services defines as needed from the professional. It does not assume a uniform perception of need, as need varies among client groups depending on the situation.

Three general conclusions were reported as a consequence of the needs assessment. They include the identification of three major skill areas in which training was needed. It was also observed that the design for training assessment must reflect not only the participants' perceptions of their training needs but also the perceptions of experts and people served by the employees. The third conclusion notes that staff needs vary across departments, agencies, and locations; hence, skill areas should be emphasized to reflect those differences.

The investigators report that the five need concepts identified above proved to be useful in three ways. First, the procedure was a systematic way of identifying the educational needs of the city employees. Second, the model allowed the investigators to prioritize the identified needs to more effectively use available resources. Third, the procedure yielded needs that would not have been identified if the program planners had relied only on the self-reports of the target group. The model contains three major elements:

1. Identification of sources of data on each kind of need noted above
2. Identification of the appropriate data collection techniques
3. Determination of proper sequence of data collection activity

One of the most interesting findings reported by Sheridan and Shannon relates to conflicts in identified needs. They reported that the employees did not see a critical need in communication training, whereas their consumers perceived the staff members as being ineffective in certain communication skills. Three questions were raised by this contradictory finding (Sheridan and Shannon 1979, p. 228):

1. Whose perceptions of needs should have the greater weight: the learners, the consumers whom they serve, or the experts? Also, what weight should be given to the perceptions of agency administrators and of professional organizations?
2. In developing a training design, should educators try to convince adult learners to include subject areas that they do not think they need?
3. If developing the training design is perceived as a negotiation process between the educator and the learner, what are the most effective ways of negotiating this issue?

Community Needs

Community needs-assessment activities have a range of characteristics. For example, they may focus on individual needs, broader community needs, or some combination of the two. They may be extremely complex and highly sophisticated surveys that include thousands of respondents, or they may be very simple conversations with a few community leaders. Some of the characteristics of specific procedures have been identified by McMahon (1970). They include community surveys, community study, advisory committees, consultation with members of the power structure, interviews with a target audience, problem solving groups, and informal conversations.

Community studies are distinguished from community surveys. Community studies have been defined as a search for facts and figures. List (1969) says that a study is often an outgrowth of a survey. Community studies as identified by Hand (1960) may be conducted through four distinctive approaches: (1) the social welfare approach, which includes the analysis of agencies, institutions, and services, (2) the social unit approach, which examines the community as a social unit, (3) the ecological approach, which examines spatial and temporal relationships, and (4) the use of the study process as an educational process leading to social action.

One popular proposal for community analysis in the literature of adult education was offered by Blackwell (1967), who challenged evening college administrators to become familiar with seven features of their communities:

1. Population base
2. Institutional structure
3. Value systems
4. Social stratification
5. Informal social relationships
6. Power structure
7. Community ecology

The University of Missouri has been a leader in the recent development and use of community surveys. In a recent pamphlet, List (1969) provides basic instruction concerning appropriate survey procedures. He points out that one purpose of a survey is to avoid what he says Lippitt calls "the collusion of ignorance." Tips on timing, sponsorship, and procedures to use in conducting, tabulating, and reporting a survey are provided.

The literature of community development, rural sociology, and related fields of practice that touch on this topic is too extensive to cite in detail here. The reader is referred to McClusky, McMahon, and other sources for detailed descriptions of community surveys. Diverse approaches are reported in the abundant literature, but there are few comparative data to confirm the relative effectiveness of the different approaches (Long, Anderson, and Blubaugh 1973).

Individual Appraisal Models

One of the better-known models for individual learner assessment is that reported by Knowles (1970). Because of its high visibility and availability, discussion of that model here is limited. Basically, the procedures call for the learner to develop a profile of competence based on selected topics. This profile is interpreted as revealing the areas in which the learner is proficient and the areas in which the learner perceives himself or herself to be below a desired level of competence. Two other quite different models are reflected by the work of Scissons and Spencer, as reported in the following paragraphs.

Scissons (1980) is working with a procedure that he refers to as psychometric needs assessment (PNA). This procedure is distinct from the classical model of self-perceived deficiencies, interest finders, and so forth, in that the PNA procedure involves the use of standardized psychological test instruments for determination of target-group personological characteristics. Thus, PNA focuses on appraised levels of personal functioning. Scissons represents this procedure as one conducted by others (as opposed to learner self-diagnosis) for the purpose of decision making concerning ways to meet the identified needs. The procedure seems to be best suited to use in certain situations in which (1) specific skills/knowledge criteria exist and (2) a comparative sample that reflects the desirable levels of competencies is available. Thus, the procedure is likely to be of greatest value in business and industry, government and military organizations.

Drawing upon Freire's concepts concerning the importance of relating education to the broader personal concerns and needs of learners, Spencer (1980) conducted a series of open-ended interviews with older adults in ten New Jersey communities. The interview process was designed as an indirect and projective method of obtaining insights into personal attitudes, values, and perceptions that may be difficult to obtain using more direct methods.

Spencer conducted group interviews of ten to fifteen older adults at local community or senior citizen centers. Visual stimuli designed to elicit information on tax issues were used. Pictures were thus selected according to their ability to symbolize specific problems or policies and their ability to evoke a response.

The interview discussion provided the educator with two responsibilities: first, to elicit responses from all participants to achieve the broadest possible range of opinions and experiences; and second, to move the discussion from specific and immediate reactions to the pictures toward a discussion of the largest issues and concerns symbolized by the pictures. Thus, the participants were encouraged to express their attitudes and perceptions while also revealing areas of knowledge and uncertainty.

As a result of the content analysis of the interviews, which yielded important themes and topics, Spencer concludes that as a needs assessment method, the nondirective group interview has important implications for program planning designed to serve the needs of older adults. With its emphasis on the affective as well as congnitive levels, it enables planners to center educational experiences on the real concerns, values, and attitudes of the potential population. Educational programming that reflects this orientation has the potential to foster self-awareness and promote commitment to action.

System-Discrepancy Models

Beatty (1976) has offered one of the more recently conceptualized models in this area. Her model is primarily designed for use by individuals involved in needs assessment at the geographic community level. According to Beatty, existing models are of such skeletal dimensions that they are inadequate, and if the planner obtained all the information indicated, he or she would be confronted with the task of gathering and processing an encyclopedic array of information. Key elements of her model are represented by the following questions: (1) What information should be collected? (2) Where is the information stored in the community? and (3) How can the information be retrieved from the community? Accordingly, her model is composed of three parts: (1) a classification scheme for human needs, (2) an indicator component, which will determine what information should be collected within the constraints of the classification system, and (3) an information collection component, which will elaborate sources of, and retrieval strategies for, the indicators selected.

SOURCES FOR INFERRING NEEDS

In addition to some lack of clarity concerning the definition of an educational need, practitioners also encounter some difficulty in determining the sources of information that may be helpful in determining the needs of a group or individuals. Kempfer (1965) was concerned with this question in a survey of 530 adult education administrators concerning ways of identifying educational needs and interests of adults. As a result of the study, he identified eleven sources of information concerning educational needs.

The three most important sources of information concerning educational needs available to administrators of educational programs for adults as identified by Kempfer were local directors of adult education or their counterparts, advisory groups for specific fields or areas of study, and ad hoc advisory committees set up to consider a definite problem, need, course, or subfield. The three least useful sources were individuals from the community, individual faculty members, and a general administrator (such as the superintendent of instruction).

On a broader level, Knowles (1957) identified five sources of educational objectives for adults: self-perceived needs and interests of learners, society, local community, the sponsoring organization, and a body of knowledge and wisdom. He suggested that problems arise in the conduct of adult education when only one or two of these sources are considered. Instead of focusing on only one of the sources at the expense of the others, educators of adults are encouraged to consider all the sources collectively.

Despite Knowles's exhortation to include data from each of the five sources, he acknowledges that most of the literature—research and hortatory—indicates that it is not customary for educational planners to formally collect information from each source. Educational needs within a geographically defined community, a socially defined community, or among individuals are usually inferred from data formally obtained from one or more of the following sources:

1. Advisory committees
2. Clinical assessment
3. Knowledge of social developments
4. Professional experts
5. Surveys
6. Theoretical constructs supplemented by demographic and other data

Regardless of the sources of information concerning needs, the process of assessment requires that someone make decisions about what the data actually mean. The decision about a need may be made by the individual learner or by the educational planner. Furthermore, the interpretation of the data may lead to classifying the need according to any one of the need concepts (basic, felt, normative, and so forth).

OBSERVATIONS

This review of the literature concerning the need concept in adult education supports Monette's contention that the concept is indeed a "fuzzy" one. Many of the writers referred to here have attempted in some fashion to communicate their special use of the idea to their readers. For example, Bergevin wrote about felt needs, symptomatic needs, and real needs. Sheasha tried to distinguish between the "feelings" labeled needs and wants. Knowles described needs conceptually as a "gap" between an ideal and reality. Robbins and Monette reviewed the literature and ended up with quite different conceptualizations. Monette identified four labels used to distinguish among four need constructs: basic human need, normative need, comparative need, and expressed need. Robbins identified three major classes for discussing and examining need: condition, dynamics, and dimension. Finally, Scissons provided a typology of needs according to relevance, competence, and motivation that contributes to wants and higher complex needs.

Interests, needs, and wants are not used consistently among the articles reviewed. Extreme differences exist among the physiological, psychological, and educational concepts. For example, the physiological aspect of need places an emphasis on the harm that an organism is subject to as a result of an unmet need such as hunger or thirst, and considers such a need as innate. In this literature, need is equivalent to motive or drive. The innate concept is in contrast to the psychological concept, where the need construct is learned; the consequences of failing to satisfy a need may be limited to temporal disappointment, sadness, or some other undesirable but not necessarily harmful state. It has been suggested that learned needs focus on security and satisfaction—what the scientists who conceptualize need as a physiological/biological construct describe as wants.

My own impression of the literature suggests that one explanation for the extreme divergence and absence of agreement among those who have attempted unsuccessfully to overcome problems with the concept lies in faulty analysis and disregard for popular semantics. For example, Sheasha and Houle seem to focus on the essence of need; the construct is defined as a feeling of tension or pleasure. Scissons defines the construct by function. Knowles conceptually describes need, and others such as Bergevin and Monette use description as the basis for definition. Robbins mixes functional and descriptive attributes.

It would seem that the most productive future research would be concerned with the functional characteristics of need. Promising work along these lines would likely be based on Rotter's and Scissons' typologies. Better resolution of the debate concerning the definition and character of needs would be helpful in facilitating means by which the construct of needs could be assessed. McMahon, however, argues against efforts to arrive at what he calls a fixed and restrictive definition of need. He is correct when he suggests that clarification of the educator's own thinking is essential and that the differences between need and desire must be clear. But it is difficult to understand how significant advances may occur in the process of needs assessment if educators of adults have difficulty in communicating their basic concepts.

Needs assessment is without question one of the basic elements in the philosophy of adult education. However, we will continue to encounter difficulty in practicing that aspect of program development as long as we cannot communicate what we do to assess needs and, more important, what it is that we are assessing.

NOTES

1. It is customary to identify only five classifications of needs in Maslow's motivation theory. Seven have been reported here based on Diggins and Huber (1976) and Madsen's 1974 comments concerning this issue. Madsen says that the needs for knowledge and understanding and aesthetic needs, as identified by Maslow, are either included in self-actualization needs or are closely connected with that class of needs. According to Madsen's analysis of Maslow's work, he concludes that Maslow is not clear on this point.

9 · Promoting, Marketing, and Recruiting

THE LITERATURE OF ADULT EDUCATION was for years nearly silent on the topic of enlistment for learning, yet there is an apparent historical dimension to the educator's concern for attracting adult students. The colonial newspapers cited in my 1976 book indicate that educators of the seventeenth century were aware of the need to inform potential students of the availability of learning activities. The more recent twentieth-century concept of needs assessment is also an indirect reflection of an awareness among educators of adults for some kind of mechanism, strategy, or procedure that would improve the prospects of a program's succeeding. Kempfer (1965) notes that the procedure of involving community members on advisory committees seemed to increase the participation in educational programs conducted in the communities.

Educators and trainers in various settings are concerned with several dimensions of enlisting adults in educational programs. The approaches used to accomplish the objective are subsumed under three general headings: promotion, marketing, and recruitment. While each of the three kinds of activities is ultimately concerned with increasing the number of adults engaged in educational activities sponsored by a given institution or in general, each reflects different philosophical and procedural frameworks. None of the terms are new. Marketing as a concept is perhaps more current in its application to educational programs. Promotion is discussed in limited terms in previous educational literature, and recruitment of students has long been an important activity. The application of these concepts to educational programs for adults and the research on which the practices are based are topics of increasing interest.

Program promotion has received an increasing share of attention in the research activities of scholars and practitioners interested in the educational activities and pursuits of adults. In the United States, the research thrust has focused on concepts derived from business under the label of marketing. Emphases on increasing adult participation in educational programs in the Nordic countries have been identified as recruitment activities. The two concepts are as distinctive as the labels indicate. Representative investigations from the United States and the Nordic countries are reported in the following pages.

MARKETING EDUCATION

Prior to the most recent decade, educators were unlikely to use the term *marketing*. Neither *marketing* nor *promotion*, previously the more commonly used term, appears in Brunner's 1959 index. Less than two pages is devoted to promotion in the 1960 *Handbook of Adult Education in the United States* (Knowles 1960). Even then, promotion and advertising were studied not for the purpose of obtaining students but for the purpose of creating public understanding of adult education. The 1970 handbook (Smith, Aker, and Kidd 1970) devoted seventeen lines to the topic of promotion. The relative inattention to the study of promotion and marketing issues in the education of adults in the last twenty years is emphasized by the information provided on the topic in the three important publications cited above.

Promotion Activities

McGee (1959) indicated that a survey of "merchandising" practices in adult education conducted in the early 1950s caused many respondents to object to the thought of "selling" adult education. He suggested that the strong opposition to the idea was based on two reasons. First, the matter of professional commitment and professional preoccupations had caused professional educators of adults to believe that they were somewhat above the commercial arena. Accordingly, the professional was perceived as dealing in values with no monetary equivalent. Second, the opposition to the concept of adult education merchandising may have arisen from pressures exerted by internal pressure groups identified by McGee as the detached, the romantics, and the opportunists. The detached pressure group is composed of those who believe that educational institutions should stand apart from the larger democratic audience and the values of the contemporary culture. The romanticists were described by McGee as those who believe that there is a huge democratic audience wildly beating bruised hands against the doors of educational facilities, hungering and thirsting—even lusting—in their demands for participation. Finally, the third group, the opportunists, is represented by those educators who provide courses that they don't believe in, who do not practice lifelong learning, who believe that people should take their courses because they know what people need.

Another earlier reference to promotion of adult education and the recruitment of students is provided by Stern (1965). Stern's logical analysis of program promotion clearly indicates an association between promotional activities and the quality of other elements in the programming process.

Youse (1973) provides an interesting and thoughtful discussion of promotion and recruitment activities. He identifies and examines several of the activities commonly associated with the promotion of education programs for adults. In addition, he indicates, in a manner consistent with Stern's observations, that programs are promoted by activities not usually identified in the literature. For example, he urges educators to examine registration procedures and the use of the telephone. Youse believes that the registration experience of part-time students is critical in the formation of attitudes toward the educational institution. Every possible effort should be expended at that point to demonstrate interest in potential students and assist them as much as possible.

The telephone is identified as a frequently abused promotional tool. The abuse indicated by Youse, however, is one of insensitivity. In a number of instances, a telephone call from a prospective student is the result of other expensive publicity efforts. It is unfortunate if all that work is undone by an insensitive response to a telephone inquiry.

Other promotional tools identified by Youse include faculty, direct mail, newspaper and radio advertising, and telephone solicitation.

Faculty

The role of the faculty and administrative personnel in promotion and recruitment is one of those areas about which little information is available. It is readily recognized that some administrative personnel have specific tasks related to the promotion and recruitment activities. In some instances, there are staff members with specialized training in marketing and promoting programs. In others, the tasks associated with promotion and recruitment are assumed by staff members with little experience in such activities other than that gained through on-the-job activity. The role of faculty is even less clearly identified in discussions concerning promotion and recruitment. Youse limits his comments to suggesting that faculty should be available at registration to discuss student concerns.

Direct Mail

Few studies are reported in the literature concerning the use of direct mail. Youse, Schact (1971), and Wuerger (1971), however, all agree that bulk mail is not generally a bargain. The regulations that must be met and delays in delivery often add sufficiently to the cost of bulk mail to encourage the use of first class mail. On the other hand, Schact indicates that bulk mail is not accorded the degree of unfavorable treatment that might be expected. His survey of alumni of the University of Wisconsin revealed that only 1 percent of the respondents indicated that they open *only* first class mail. Furthermore, 85 percent of the respondents remembered receiving a brochure mailed at bulk mail rates. Therefore, it appears that the main considerations for educators in deciding upon the appropriateness of bulk mail focus on the points of timeliness and the effect of postal regulations.

Wuerger provides one of the most detailed analyses of direct mail campaigns identified in the literature. Basing his report on the activities of the

Engineering Extension program at the University of Wisconsin, he provides useful experiential data. For example, he reports that the highest average attendance produced by the most effective mailing list was 3 persons per thousand. A combination of three mailing lists raised the rate of response to 3.8 persons per thousand attending engineering institutes and 0.8 per thousand attending short courses.

Newspaper and Radio Advertising

The rising costs of postage and printing serve to stimulate further consideration of newspaper and radio advertisements of educational programs for adults. Youse suggests that program administrators need to engage in some careful studies of the relative productivity of these media compared with each other and with direct mail campaigns. When brochure printing costs are added to the other costs associated with mail campaigns, radio and newspaper advertising may be very competitive. Furthermore, it is suggested that certain audiences may best be reached by selected newspapers and radio stations—for example, community newspapers versus regional newspapers and classical music radio stations versus popular music stations.

Telephone Solicitation

No studies reporting costs and benefits of telephone solicitation efforts as part of educational program promotion were located. However, Youse provides some useful advice on this topic. For example, he indicates that telephone solicitation will be more successful when it is aimed at individuals who have previously participated in a program and when the telephone call follows, within a reasonable time, mailed information. In other words, telephone solicitation, according to Youse, is primarily a supplement to a direct mail campaign. To illustrate this point, he cites an example in which ten applicants have been secured through direct mail and the educator uses the telephone to complete the course registration of fifteen students.

A secondary procedure includes using the telephone at the time of an inquiry stimulated by other media. In this instance, a prospective student may call to inquire about a learning activity and indicate indecision. Rather than just permitting the prospect to make a decision without additional support, a staff member may encourage the individual to register for the course and to sit in on the first class. For example, "Miss Smith, why don't you register for the French Art course and sit in on the first class? You will then be able to determine if the course meets your needs. If it does, you can enroll as a regular student. If it doesn't, it will be our pleasure to have had you as our guest."

Marketing

In contrast with the earlier period, recent activities in continuing education and extension circles reveal an interest in the use of marketing tools in university extension. A marketing conference for adult educators was held at the University of Chicago in 1973, and there were two sessions on marketing extension services during the same year at the National University Extension Association (NUEA), Region III, annual meeting. The 1974 NUEA annual meeting focused on the theme "Marketing Continuing Education." At each of these meetings, educators stressed the need for adult and continuing education professionals either to seek the help of professional marketers or to develop marketing skills within their own staffs (Buchanan and Barksdale 1974). In 1969, Kotler and Levy introduced the idea of marketing as a valid function of nonbusiness organizations such as schools and hospitals.

Though many academic marketers failed to quickly support the concept, a number of educators, including Buchanan and Barksdale, recommended marketing strategies to educators of adults. Their research is presented in some detail in this chapter. Kotler (1979) has recently reported a number of examples of marketing activities of educational institutions. He is also quick to observe that it is dangerous to equate marketing with intensified promotion. For example, he believes that aggressive promotion produces strong negative reactions among institutional constituencies (such as faculty) and that such promotion may alienate as many as it attracts.

According to Kotler, a genuine marketing program has been undertaken by relatively few colleges. He describes the approach used by these select institutions as market-oriented institutional planning. The procedure emphasizes the multidimensional aspects of marketing in contrast to mere promotion. The approach includes research into more fundamental questions such as market, resources, and mission. The University of Houston is cited as an institution that has employed market-oriented institutional planning. Others include New York University, Northwestern University, and Kent State University.

Marketing is distinguished from promotion and advertising. Marketing consists of four major conceptual categories: product, place, price, and promotion. Hence, marketing includes promotional activities and advertising efforts, but the process extends well beyond those traditional activities. The issues or questions to be addressed in market-oriented institutional planning clearly place marketing on a different level. This does not mean that educators of adults have neglected all the issues connected with marketing, such as those associated with broad social trends, how the institution should define its primary market, and so forth. Many administrators of educational programs for adults have been sensitive to the issues identified. The most obvious one is needs assessment. The important distinction, however, is in the total process, which seems to be normally neglected by educational administrators.

Marketing Studies in Adult Education

Since Kotler and Levy's 1969 article, administrators of educational programs for adults have demonstrated increasing interest in marketing as an element in program development. The increasing awareness of the concept and acceptance of the procedures are revealed by the numbers of dissertations and other published research concerned with the topic. Several selected research reports on the topic of marketing in adult and continuing education are discussed in varying degrees of detail in the following pages. Hertling's article is first because it was one of the early published articles on the topic; Buchanan and Barksdale's work is discussed in detail because it makes the point that some institutions of higher education are engaged in marketing activities and apparently have been for a number of years. Other investigations are reported in varying degrees of detail as they are used to illustrate trends and directions of the marketing concept in the education of adults.

Market Analysis

Hertling (1973) is of the opinion that many administrators concerned with the education of adults are currently involved in some form of market research. For example, they survey present or former program participants, solicit opinions of community leaders, conduct general surveys, consider the advice of various kinds of advisory committees, and secure and analyze personal data to develop profiles of program participants. The approach to market analysis, however, is often informal, irregular, and unsystematic. Consequently, he notes that a decision to offer a course, program, or conference for an adult audience generally involves market decisions in addition to educational and financial considerations. Marketing research is perceived as the best way to provide the information needed to make sound decisions; it does not guarantee success, but it minimizes failure.

Resource and Mission Analysis

Seeking an opportunity for interdisciplinary research between the marketing and adult education professions, Buchanan and Barksdale (1974) conducted an investigation to determine whether marketing techniques, tools, and concepts are used by state universities and land-grant colleges in conducting the service function and, if so, how widely they are used. University service was chosen for several reasons, according to the investigators. First, the service function of the institutions is the principal extension activity of the university or college; therefore, if any segment of the university or college employs marketing techniques and tools, it would be expected to be this division. Second, the service sector in the institutions is experiencing internal and external pressures for resources and increased services. Internal pressures are generated by teaching and research segments of the university as they compete for appropriations, which in many instances are being reduced. Simultaneously, pressure associated with wider acceptance of lifelong learning is increasing and creating for higher education a new environment at a time when regular student enrollments are declining. The new environment presents a challenging opportunity since increasing numbers of businesses and consulting firms now offer courses using innovative educational methods to anyone with the money to take advantage of the service.

Buchanan and Barksdale designed their study to obtain data on specific extension activities and practices from a selected population of extension educators. The member institutions of the National Association of State Universities and Land-Grant Colleges (NASULGC) constituted the population studied. A total of 93 returns (94 percent) were received from a membership of 99 institutions—90 usable questionnaires, two refusals, and one with no extension program.

The investigators are convinced that there is no doubt that service units of the responding institutions are engaged in marketing. The respondents unanimously indicated that they offer a variety of services to the general public such as conferences, workshops, seminars, noncredit classes, cultural programs, and area studies.

Respondents expressed an awareness in the pricing of these services. The pricing policies varied by institution and type of offering. A clear majority have established fees and/or price structures for noncredit classes, conferences, workshops, seminars, and cultural offerings.

A variety of communication methods—direct mail, magazines, newspapers, personal visitation, radio, television, posters, and word of mouth—are used by the institutions to inform the public of service offerings. The returns indicated that all institutions used at least one method; newspaper advertisements are the most prevalent.

Results indicated that most institutions follow similar procedures in the delivery-of-service channels. Noncredit classes, conferences, institutes, and workshops are provided on campus by most responding institutions. A majority of the respondents also offer the same programs off campus in an apparent effort to expand their markets.

Thus, requirements commonly included in the definition of a marketing function—two parties interested in exchange, communicating this interest to each other, and each possessing something of value desired by the other—are met by the majority of the responding schools.

According to Buchanan and Barksdale, continuing higher education has often emphasized the importance of needs assessment to help in the determination of needs. Since this is one of the two main factors comprising the marketing concept studied, it was not surprising that the investigators concluded that most respondents practice the marketing concept philosophy, at least in some measure, in their service units. Clearly, a majority of the schools were revealed to be client-need oriented in their effort to respond favorably to requests from their constituency for unoffered services: they design specific service programs or delivery systems to appeal to a particular group; they use some form of organized, client-need research activity; and they use evaluation instruments to obtain performance data from their clients.

However, the institutions fail in the total implementation of the marketing concept because of the failure to require everyone in the organization to become customer oriented. Marketers suggest internal training programs to instill this notion in all employees. The majority of respondents do not conduct internal training to instill customer orientation in their people. Of those offering such courses, most use on-the-job training, with only a few providing some sort of formal training, according to Buchanan and Barksdale.

The second factor most frequently noted by marketers in stating the marketing concept is the idea of profile and not volume when looking at potential marketing strategies or plans. Taking this notion into the nonprofit world of continuing higher education, the university should base its programming or offerings on some cost/benefit factor rather than on popularity of courses or volume of enrollment. The researchers observe that a majority of the responding institutions use some evaluative system to select their service offerings and thus accomplish stated goals. The data reveal that almost 70 percent of the schools have specific goals or objectives for their service units; of these, more than 90 percent are able to evaluate their programs using defined goals.

Buchanan and Barksdale believe that the respondents have adopted the marketing concept and are trying to implement the philosophy in a manner not too different from that of profit-making organizations. The difficulty that they encounter in implementation seems to be caused by a lack of planning for the concept to be communicated to all employees in the service units and by an absence of a priority ranking system based on some objective evaluation process. The latter problem seems to be the more serious of the two and probably will be more difficult to overcome. Profit-making organizations can base their selection of products on the bottom line of the balance sheet, but educational institutions must consider many intangible factors in their attempts to quantify some objective priority ranking or selection process.

Marketing's Four P's

Business organizations commonly attempt to increase their share of the market by altering and improving the marketing variables under their control. These are usually summarized as the four P's of marketing—product, price, promotion, and place. Service units of educational institutions possess a similar opportunity, and a majority of the respondents are perceived by Buchanan and Barksdale as using three of marketing's four P's—product, promotion, and place. Less than half, however, use price as a marketing tool.

A majority of the institutions indicated at least three ways in which they alter their "product line" in responding to the varying wants of different groups. Approximately 90 percent periodically change their service programs to meet changing needs and requests of the public. Almost as many accommodate change by adding new programs to their existing offerings; 68 percent stated that they had eliminated services to comply with current needs.

Promotion is an element of extension service that has been discussed from the beginning of the movement. A majority of the respondents use several communication methods to increase the public's awareness of their services and to inform them of program content. As mentioned earlier, newspaper advertisements are the most frequently used method of promotion.

The concept of place is important in university extension. In fact, the need to move out from the campus to the populace was the prime reason for beginning an extension movement. It was not surprising, therefore, to find that more than 90 percent of the respondents attempt to increase attendance or the utilization of some of their service programs by offering them off campus. Delivery systems vary from the direct selling of programs by service units in outlying towns to the wholesaling of programs through community groups and chambers of commerce, according to Buchanan and Barksdale.

Pricing seems to be a common problem for the institutions responding. Less than half indicate that they change the price of their services to increase public utilization. This is a surprising finding, as extension units usually are faced with the requirement to provide from 50 to 90 percent of their income. Most seemed to believe that programs should be priced high enough to recover costs (in most cases) but not too high for participants. Extension leaders seem to avoid prestige pricing completely.

In addition to the information on the four P's, the data indicate that respondents regularly employ other marketing management concepts such as generic product, target groups, differential advantage, integrated marketing planning, market intelligence, and marketing audit. The concepts have been highly developed in the business community, and it appears that extension leaders have adopted them to a lesser degree. It is not apparent that extension educators are making optimum use of them, however. Responses indicate a substantial lack of appreciation for marketing techniques as a desirable means of accomplishing educational goals. Many of the respondents are perceived by the investigators as equating marketing with selling.

Shipp and McKenzie (1978) provide an extensive discussion on the use of market research techniques for educators. The 41-page document contains basic information that might be useful to the educator seeking to develop a marketing research thrust. They recommend a research program that includes six elements: program research, price analysis, promotional investigations, studies of distribution (time and place), marketing performance evaluation, and client research not related to any area of marketing decision.

Marketing segmentation, the definition and description of the primary market, is illustrated by the work of Goodnow (1982). Building upon previous participation studies, she investigated the usefulness of psychographic variables in segmenting adult learners at one community college. Her research was based on the use of two instruments: one was designed to determine why adults participate in educational activities, and the other to identify program preferences. The results of Goodnow's investigation indicate that marketing segmentation for adult education programs is possible.

Analyses of the orientations of the learners studied by Goodnow, along with other data, contributed to recommendations that might be adopted to increase enrollment at the institution studied. Furthermore, the data were interpreted as providing affirmative evidence for the following:

1. Market segments can be differentiated by learning orientations.
2. Market segments can be differentiated by program offering preferences.
3. Market segments can be differentiated by demographic characteristics.
4. Membership in each market segment can be predicted with at least 70-percent accuracy by demographic characteristics.

Goodnow suggests that the use and application of marketing concepts as identified above contributed to an increase in enrollment at the institution studied.

Shipp and McKenzie (1981) report marketing strategies developed subsequent to the identification of seven distinctive patterns associated with nonparticipation in parish adult education. The seven patterns, or market segments, identified are resistence to change/education, alienation, marginality, social nonaffiliation, confusion, program nonrelevance, and activity. The investigators note that a balanced marketing strategy takes into account three major elements: (1) the educational needs assessment procedure in the parish, (2) program planning and all that this entails beyond the selection of topics, and (3) promotional activities. No information is provided concerning the actual application of the recommendations or results that may have been observed.

A recent example that illustrates the increasing responsiveness of educators of adults to the marketing concept is provided by Bock (1980). She devotes approximately eight pages of a chapter to a discussion of marketing adult education and indicates that marketing can yield two specific benefits to educators of adults. The first is increased satisfaction of learners as a result of increased attention to the expectations of potential participants. The second perceived benefit is improved efficiency in the institution's student recruitment activities. The interested reader should find Bock's discussion of the topic useful.

Shipp (1981) equates dependence on "selling" (as contrasted with marketing) with a heavy reliance on promotion designed to induce the consumer to buy. According to this practice, producers are limited to producing what they want to, and they ignore the needs of the purchaser in the process. They depend on their ability to coerce or persuade, through ethical or unethical means, the consumer into buying the product. This approach is perceived to be at the root of many questionable activities that are sometimes incorrectly referred to as marketing in education today. Such undesirable practices include the development of information pieces that promise more than an educational activity can produce and the practices of recruiters who convince prospective students that more education automatically changes one's social and economic situation. This concept, however, is not to be confused with marketing, according to Shipp.

RECRUITMENT FOR EDUCATION

It could be suggested that at least two perceptions concerning responses to educational opportunities are held by educators of adults. Some may be inclined to view the potential participant as someone who is best attracted by the use of sophisticated techniques ranging from market analysis to skillfully packaged programs as discussed in the first section of this chapter. Another view seems to indicate that adults are believed to be prevented from participating in educational activities by a variety of structural, psychological, and informational variables, and that the best way of involving adults in education is through some kind of procedure that reduces the influence of the obstacles and increases the power of educational opportunity to attract. Recruitment programs are not unknown in most countries today. As North American adult educators seem to have invested more heavily in marketing activities during the most recent decade, Nordic educators appear to have contributed significantly to the development and study of recruitment activities.

During the last ten years, several important and interesting investigations designed to improve recruitment of adults for education have been conducted in the Nordic countries. These research programs are quite different in thrust and concept from the marketing studies conducted in the United States. Nevertheless, both kinds of research are informative and address a major element of the program-planning model identified early in Chapter 7. Rubenson (1979) reports the recruitment research in the Nordic countries as being similar to the research conducted in North America concerning participation. He identifies three categories of the reported research:

1. Studies aimed at describing the participants in selected types of adult education
2. Studies designed to compare participants and nonparticipants with respect to selected characteristics

3. Studies that concentrate on a target group such as the underprivileged

Rubenson suggests that the research on the topic followed a developmental pattern from research in the first category to more recent investigations in the third one. Comparative studies, at the intermediate level, are perceived as being less dynamic than the recent third-level research that focuses on the total living situations of the target groups and where adult education fits into the life situation.

The research reviewed indicates that the classic relationships identified in North American studies between participation and age, education, and social status also hold in the Nordic cases. Similarly, expanded educational opportunities in that region of the world have served to increase the educational differences within as well as between generations. As a result of the phenomenon, Denmark, Finland, Norway, and Sweden have all initiated studies of recruitment strategies and design. The development of the research is uneven among the four countries; most of the current research appears to have been conducted in Sweden. Figure 9.1 is the result of a paradigm developed as a starting point for the analysis and interpretation of previous research on recruitment. This structure of recruitment for education is designed to facilitate the consideration of micro- and macro-level data such as structural social conditions, the individual's psychological conceptual apparatus, and the link between these levels.

Social Structures and Active Preparedness

As the North American models of participation draw heavily upon the work of Lewin, the Swedish model does also. This is the expectancy-valence theory reported in Chapter 5. However, Rubenson observes that knowledge about how an individual interprets the psychological field, the central thesis of the theory, cannot by itself yield an understanding of recruitment. It is necessary to include the social structural factors and to analyze the interaction between them and the individual's conceptual system in order to obtain a valid interpretation for recruitment. Thus, the paradigm represents participation as a function of the individual's interpretation of the psychological field that has developed through interaction with structural factors in society. According to this concept, through the socialization that has occurred within the family, the school, and occupational life, individuals have developed attitudes and approaches to, among other things, different forms of adult education. This process is viewed, within the concept represented by the paradigm in Figure 9.1, as a hypothetical variable that is associated with the individual's degree of preparation to participate in adult education.

Concurrently, the focus of structural factors is directed toward elements in the current environment that may be positively or negatively associated with participation. These include the degree of hierarchic structure in the environment; values of member and reference groups; possibilities for study such as determined by admission policies, financial aid, and course offerings; information; physical accessibility; and other variables. The other main element of the paradigm is the current needs of the individual. This element, among other things, represents his or her material situation and the develop-

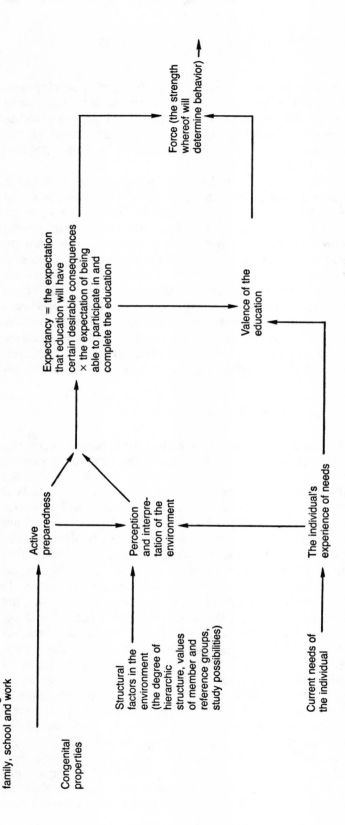

Figure 9.1   Paradigm of recruitment in adult education

Source: Rubenson 1979. Reproduced by permission.

mental tasks confronting the individual at particular stages of the life cycle.

Rubenson observes that recruitment may not always be explained directly on the basis of the actual situation without taking into consideration how the situation is interpreted. The paradigm represents this by two levels of intermediate variables. The first level comprises active preparedness, perception, and interpretation of the structural factors and experienced needs. Figure 9.1 illustrates how these three elements determine valence and expectancy, which subsequently result in a force whose strength determines behavior. Recent research is cited in the following paragraphs to illustrate why adult education up to now has increased rather than decreased the educational variance between and within generations.

The fact that educational level consistently shows the highest correlation with participation in adult education has been adequately documented by the research discussed in Chapter 4. But how is the phenomenon explained? To some extent, it may be explained by the observation that the highly educated are often in occupational positions that offer opportunities for participation in different forms of education. Rubenson cites the Nordic material (SCB 1978), however, as revealing that the differences in participation are very large even when noncompetence-giving adult education is concerned. One explanation for the phenomenon lies in the concept of socialization. As a consequence of socialization, it is argued, adult education has become a part of the value system of some groups but not of others. Thus, participation in noncompetence-giving education has been shown to be a part of the leisure style consisting of cultural activities that are most commonly found in the middle and upper classes—social classes that also represent a large proportion of those individuals with higher educational achievement levels.

The school, an agent of socialization, is often pointed to in public debate as a major villain in accounting for the association between educational level and participation in adult education. This scenario says that the school is guilty of creating among some the value orientation that encourages further learning and is equally guilty of creating among others a negative attitude toward all school-related activities throughout life. Rubenson, however, warns that it is not very fruitful to concentrate on the school's contribution to one's experience of comfort-discomfort as an explanation for subsequent participation in adult education. Instead, researchers are encouraged to study existing trends in educational sociology, where the purpose is to clarify the functions of the school in society and to analyze how the curriculum and teaching process transfer value systems to individuals. Unfortunately, analyses of the educational system and its functions in society have not, in fact, taken any serious interest in the adult education sector (Karabel and Halsey 1977). Rubenson observes that where the Scandinavian countries are concerned it is probably impossible to analyze correctly the role of education regarding the division of power in society without looking, at the same time, at what part popular education has played. Ultimately, it seems that active preparedness does not decide participation deterministically but interacts with the structural conditions in the environment.

Structural Factors

Norwegian material cited by Rubenson indicates that structural factors tend to strengthen previously established inequalities in education. Accord-

ingly, the paradigm illustrates how those who have a high degree of preparedness and who are in environments in which they have a range of possibilities
for influencing their situation often have positive attitudes toward adult education and also usually have the best access to education. This conclusion has
encouraged the research concerned with recruitment to focus on investigations
concerning social structures such as working life and residential areas.

Working Life

Material cited by Rubenson supports the thesis that a direct correlation
exists between job design and the individual's life outside work. For example,
when the range of personal initiative on the job is limited by factors in the
work process, the individual employee's ability to participate during leisure
time in activities that make such demands seems to decrease. Additional evidence of the impact of work processes is revealed by other studies cited by
Rubenson. For example, when employees are given increased responsibility
over their own work, they demonstrate a greater interest in participating in
decision-making processes. Such changes also influence their leisure-time activities and lead to more active leisure. Direct evidence to support this line of
reasoning is provided by the work of Knudsen and Skaalvik (1979), who report
a strong association between an individual's ability to control his or her situation and participation in adult education.

Pantzar's 1977 Finnish-based study of shift workers and how they use
their leisure time also provides strong evidence of the impact of job elements
on other life dimensions. He reported that workers employed in a three-shift
job structure had no more leisure-time pursuits than workers who regularly
work days. Furthermore, shift workers participated in leisure-time studying
less than day workers. Pantzar further demonstrates how the organization of
educational institutions and their schedules are often incompatible with the
leisure schedules of shift workers.

Recruiting Activities

A variety of major outreaching activities have been conducted in the Nordic countries, both in housing areas and at workplaces.

FÖVUX and SAMVUX

Few, if any, Nordic adult educational experiments have stimulated as
much interest internationally as the experimental program FÖVUX pursued
with outreaching activity. Using personal contact to interest people in adult
education is, of course, not new; on the contrary, it has a long history in adult
education in most countries. The distinctive characteristic of FÖVUX is that
the outreaching activity is given a more established form and organization on
the basis of earmarked state funds to act as a recruitment model. Three factors
are identified by Rubenson as accounting for the success of FÖVUX:

1. Selectivity concerning those who were approached
2. Advantageous study conditions resulting from financial aid provided
   by the government
3. The process used in the project

Recruitment for education through FÖVUX occurred in workplace and housing areas. Prospective participants in education activity were personally contacted by an agent who left a printed brochure with the contact. In some housing area visits, the time available for each contact was seven minutes. The project is cited as being successful, and the data seem to confirm the conclusion. For example, 64 percent of those recruited during the first year had never participated in any form of studies after comprehensive school. Because of the special supportive measures provided by governmental assistance, it is difficult to distinguish clearly the significance of outreaching activity. However, interviews with those affected show that many probably would not have participated had they not been contacted in the way they were. In connection with the outreaching activities, the following factors are identified by Rubenson as worthy of examination:

1. Level of ambition
2. Where the activity is carried out and by whom
3. The coordination between different study agents

In the following, these aspects are dealt with from a more general angle.

The fundamental dividing line is between outreaching activity as a short-term tool for recruitment and as a long-term instrument for giving the individual as fair a chance as possible of judging whether he or she should commence some form of studies. In the earlier experiments in housing areas, the principal interest was to inform about a particular provision with the aim of recruiting people. Moreover, the time available was so short that the procedure could be regarded as "a verbalized brochure method." Those who can profit from this kind of approach are people who already have high study inclinations—many of whom would register anyway.

In the SAMVUX project, outreaching activity has been analyzed from a redistributive policy perspective. The authors stress that the fundamental idea should not be to recruit as many as possible in the short term. Instead the study organizer should, apart from giving a comprehensive picture of adult education, also start a contact that could be regarded as the first step in a process that may eventually lead to recruitment. This means a departure from the short-term recruitment campaigns that have dominated the activity.

Rubenson says that it has become popular to agree with the ideas of SAMVUX. However, he is unaware that the "long-term model" has ever been tried. To a great extent, the experiments still proceed more according to the campaign model. The explanation is not in insufficient will but in the fact that the funds for the activity are allocated in such a way that long-term experiments are made difficult or completely impossible.

Work in recent years is characterized as a transition from informative to communicative outreaching activities. More current experiments have given considerably more time to the personal contact than previous ones. Reports from the study organizers also show that they are now faced with new and difficult situations in the role of "therapist." The data indicate—according to expectations—that with the longer time it has been possible to get more people in the target group interested. The FÖVUX success is, apart from the favorable study conditions, a consequence of the high level of ambition, abundant time, and well-educated study organizers.

Different Forms of Outreaching Activities

It is usual in the Nordic studies to distinguish between outreaching activity in housing areas and at workplaces. In the Kronoberg Project, as well as in FÖVUX, the main part of the activity has been conducted at workplaces. Judging from the number recruited, it is obvious that the greatest successes have been achieved at workplaces. Several interacting factors are believed to have contributed to this.

In housing areas, the study organizers are not able to get hold of everyone. Another reason is that the groups who are outside the labor market are often the extremely disadvantaged and hard-to-recruit groups. Particularly exposed groups are people on early retirement pensions and the long-term unemployed. Other groups are immigrants, the handicapped, and those working in the home.

A fundamental difference is that the contact within housing areas is directed at individuals, while contact at the workplace is collective. Substantial literature on the impact of member and reference groups on individuals is available. According to Newcomb (1950), the former type is a group of which the person is an acknowledged member, e.g., the family, or political or religious groups. The individual shares the norms of the group not only because he or she is acknowledged but also because he or she has learned to satisfy personal needs on the basis of the commonly accepted norms. Often, however, one learns to utilize norms from groups of which one is not an acknowledged member. Brunner (1959) touches on the relation between participation in adult education and the norms of member groups where he refers to a study by Houle (1957) that showed that education programs based on the interests of individuals reached smaller numbers of people than those that were based on the pattern of values in the group. Thus, it was found that the course preferences of the persons consulted were determined more by the values of the group than by individual interests.

The work group, regarded as a member group, has traditionally exerted a strong pressure among manual workers. It has been shown that adult education as it has developed is a part of the upper and middle classes' value systems that conflicts with the values of the working class. Rubenson believes that the success of FÖVUX is explained partly by the fact that the outreaching activity has included the overwhelming majority of the work group, thus affecting not only the individual but also one of that individual's most significant member groups.

In contrast to the situation with the work group, it is more difficult to build on the target group's member and reference groups where outreaching activity in housing areas is concerned. However, this is possible to a limited degree. Thus the government's terms of reference for the experimental program in housing areas contain a point about the outreaching activity's having to take place in cooperation with organizations and about special attention's having to be paid to those working in the home, immigrants, and the handicapped. It is difficult to determine what effects this has had. However, in the cases where cooperation has taken place, it is stressed that housing, immigrant, and handicap organizations have played an important role. This has been particularly true of the immigrant organizations, without whose cooperation it would have been very difficult to reach out.

Finnish Activities

Kekkonen (1980) has provided a summary report on similar recruiting experiments conducted in Finland. She notes that the Finnish experience generally has not been as successful as the Swedish activities. The relative differential in the success of the programs in the two countries is explained, in part, by the absence of governmental support in Finland. According to Kekkonen, financial aid for the experimental recruitment activities in Finland was provided on a sporadic and occasional basis.

The first experiment of outreaching work in Finland was conducted under the guidance of the Institute of Adult Education at the University of Tampere as a research project of eighteen adult education students who were already working as adult educators. The stimulus of the investigation was a Finnish research report that indicated that about 20 percent of the adult population of Finland participates in adult education; the majority of the Finnish adult participants are people with good primary education. The lower the primary education, the fewer participants.

OBSERVATIONS

This chapter addresses a major concern to educators of adults in most areas of the world: the task of interesting adults in participating in educational activities. The two primary content divisions of the chapter, however, are quite distinctive. The first concerns a market orientation adopted to some degree by a number of agencies, institutions, and organizations in the United States, and the second, the "service" orientation of the Nordic countries.

The marketing approach discussed in the chapter appears to reflect a basic concern for the institution. To grow, even to survive, the institution must pay its bills; and to pay its bills, it must have student fees unless funds are provided from another source. Hence, marketing focuses to a large degree on meeting a fundamental requirement in many American organizations. The service orientation is philosophically different from the marketing view. According to this perspective, educational opportunities are socially desirable and individuals are recruited into educational programs for the purpose of personal and social development.

The two orientations are not likely to be present in pure form in either of the geographic regions examined, however. It would be a great disservice to the philosophical nature of many American educators of adults to flatly conclude that they are uninterested in the personal and social aspects of adult education programs, and it may be gratuitous to infer that all Nordic educators have no interest in the survival and expansion of their programs. Nevertheless, the two concepts are different in origin and primary function.

The American research in marketing is expanding rapidly. It, however, seems to suffer from a highly repetitious character. Three of the four P's (product, promotion, and place) are frequently examined with limited variation in design. The issue of price and the role that it plays in marketing educational programs for adults has not been clearly explicated. Increasing costs associated with the travel of extension personnel represent a potential change in practices formerly used in a number of situations. Complementary improvements in telecommunications suggest the possibility that new conceptualizations concerning place in the four P's of marketing may be in order.

The Nordic studies in recruitment to adult education indicate the creative use of government support for the education of adults. The studies reported here also reflect insightful combinations of social psychological theory to explain some of the factors in nonparticipation and to design programmatic activities to mitigate the negative strength of some of the variables. Recruitment activities demonstrate a comprehensive concept that identifies factors in educational participation at several levels—the learner level, the institutional level, and the broader social level. The potential interaction of forces at each level is considered and is therefore offered as the basis for a more enlightened approach than studies or projects that focus exclusively on personal variables, institutional variables, or broader social variables.

V · The Teaching–Learning Transaction

10 · Personal Variables and the Learning Process

THERE ARE AT LEAST FOUR WAYS of conceptualizing learning activities in which adults engage. They are institutionally (other) planned learning, personally planned learning, randomly acquired learning, and serendipitous nonplanned learning. This chapter and the one that follows are concerned with the first of the above kinds of learning—learning that occurs as a consequence of having activities *primarily* planned and structured by others. More specifically, these two chapters emphasize research findings concerning ways and means of what is traditionally referred to as teaching or instructing adults.[1]

In 1959, Brunner and his associates discussed in two chapters some of the same kinds of research examined here. One chapter focused on methods and techniques in adult education; the other explored the use of the discussion technique. It is, of course, possible to devote an entire volume to research concerning one or more educational methods and another to instructional techniques. Consistent with the general objective of this book, two chapters are devoted to the general topic of learning and instruction. The content of Chapters 10 and 11, however, is different from the content of Brunner's work. This chapter is concerned with some of the more significant research concerning models of learning and personal variables. Chapter 11 reviews and discusses research that focuses on social and activity variables.

THE LEARNING PROCESS

The learning process has been conceptualized in several ways. Appropriate theories of teaching-learning have evolved in relationship to the various models of learning. Siegel (1967) identifies five general kinds of theoretical orientations that include most of the major instructional theories:

1. Psychotherapeutic theory (Rogers)
2. Cognitive theory (Woodruff)
3. Social-interaction theory (Biddle, Adams)
4. Learning theory (Jahnke, Ausubel)
5. Teacher-learner behavior theory (Siegel, Gagné)

The first three of these orientations emphasize teacher behavior, the fourth is informed by learning theory, and the fifth places equal importance on the behavior of the teacher and of the learner. There is thus no grand theory of instruction for adults or children. The numerous concepts derive support from a variety of theoretical conjectures and research results. Choice of an instructional theory is preferably made through a rational and deliberate process. The basis of selection includes the propositions and parameters of the theory most closely related to the instructor's philosophy concerning the nature of humanity, the nature of reality, and the purpose of learning.

The distribution of the five classifications of instructional theories reflects the generalized distinctions observed in attitudes and beliefs about human beings: they are either active or passive in the process of change. According to the extreme positions, an individual is conceived of either as an actor who spontaneously initiates his or her own actions or as an object whose behavior is merely a response to external agents. The concept of the human as a passive being is reflected in the behavioristic view. Theorists of this persuasion are concerned with antecedent conditions that explain the learner's behavior. This model includes two major components: (1) the initial antecedent conditions (for example, the motive forces—stimuli or needs) that initiate or inhibit the learner's behavior and (2) the secondary determinants of behavior (such as rewards and punishments) that strengthen and shape responses once they have been initiated.

Those who subscribe to the view of humans as active beings conceive of the individual as one who develops by personal actions. Theorists who take this position are concerned with the processes that underlie psychological action and with how that activity generates development. Two schools of thought dominate this theoretical area. One sees development as an ontogenetic process, and the other conceptualizes development as an equilibration process. In the former, the process is directed toward increasing differentiation, centralization, and hierarchic integration of mental organization. In the latter, development proceeds from relative disequilibrium to increasing equilibrium (Langer 1969).

A number of scholars have devised models of learning to indicate conceptually how they believe learning occurs. Models such as these are helpful to the teacher of adults and to instructional theorists who seek to relate teaching activities to theoretical learning processes. Most learning models are generic paradigms; no effort has been made to distinguish between concepts according to the age of the learner.

Dubin's Analysis

Dubin and Okun (1973) identify eight learning models for explication. They identify a proponent for each model and indicate the key concepts, role of instructor, amount of structure, and theoretical conceptual level. See Table 10.1 for an illustration of some of the selected components.

Based on their analysis of the representative learning theories, Dubin and Okun identify from three to eight instructional implications. For example, instructional applications derived from Skinner's behavioristic theory include the following teacher behaviors:

1. Do not use aversive stimuli.
2. Do not reinforce undesired behavior.
3. In the early stages of learning, reinforce every desired response; once learning is proceeding as expected, switch to "variable reinforcement schedule."
4. Reinforce immediately, especially in early phases.
5. Establish convenient secondary reinforcers that are easy to employ.
6. Extinguish undesired responses by withholding reinforcement.
7. When shaping the behavior of individuals, develop very carefully the hierarchical arrangement of responses.

Selected Learning Models

The three models of learning discussed in the following pages are from the adult education literature.

Verduin's Instructional Model

Verduin (Verduin, Miller, and Greer 1977) has provided one of the few models for adult instruction. According to Verduin, Miller, and Greer, the process of adult instruction should begin with two important procedures: "(1) assessing the entering behavior of the adult student, and (2) defining student and class goals to be achieved in the learning effort." It is suggested that these two operations occur in combination for the purpose of establishing learning and instructional goals that are attainable. Subsequent to the setting of goals, the teacher identifies the content designed to achieve the goals, and instructional procedures are identified, materials selected, and learning activities developed and organized for effective learning. Assessing entering behavior, establishing objectives, and defining learning procedures are represented as the "planning" phase of the instructional process.

The classroom phase includes direct interaction among learners, content, and teacher. The climate or learning environment should be positive and supportive, and teachers are singularly cautioned to take steps to provide such a social atmosphere. Verduin's model is illustrated in Figure 10.1.

Table 10.1
A Comparative Analysis of Selected Learning Theories

Learning Theory	Distinctive Concept	Proponent	Critical Activities	Role of Instructor	Amount of Structure*	Level of Learners' Abstraction
Behaviorist	Operant conditioning	B. F. Skinner	Reinforcement, shaping	Behavior modifier	9–10	Concrete operations
Neobehaviorist	Learning systems	Robert Gagné	Task analysis, hierarchical categories of learning	Manager of conditions of learning	7–10	Concrete operations, formal operations
Cognitivist	Reception learning	David Ausubel	Advanced organizers, subsumers, cognitive structure	Disseminator of information	5–8	Concrete operations, formal operations
Cognitivist	Discovery learning	Jerome Bruner	Classification, coding systems	Stimulator	4–7	Formal operations
Humanist	Nondirective teaching	Carl Rogers	Self-actualization, phenomenological field	Facilitator	1–3	Formal operations

*10 = greatest structure

Source: Adapted from Dubin and Okun 1973.

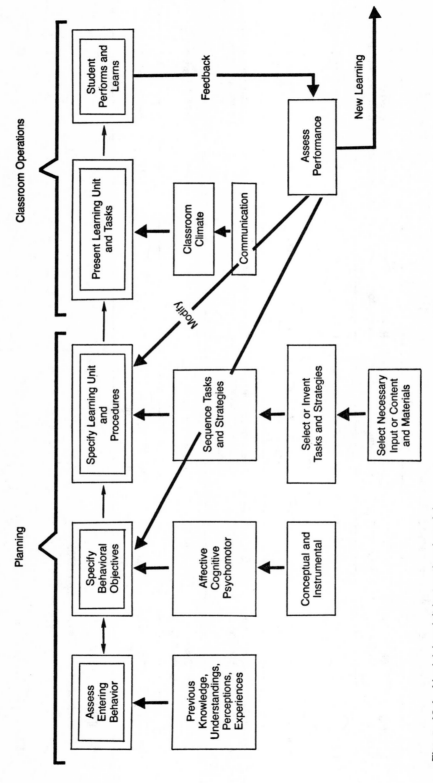

Figure 10.1 Verduin's adult instructional model

Source: Verduin, Miller, and Greer. *Adults Teaching Adults*. Austin, Texas: Learning Concepts, 1977, p. 51. Reproduced by permission.

Even and Boyd

Based on the work of Robert Boyd (1969), Even (1981) has offered a model of the adult learning process based on three dimensions of time: past, present, and future. Each time dimension is influenced by a variety of variables. For example, the past time dimension includes variables associated with memory. The future time dimension concerns variables of probability and assumptions. The present time dimension includes those activities generally associated with cognition as noted below.

The first step in the process, according to Even, is *attention* provided to a perceived new idea. The attention is elusive, and if not held, the learning ends. If attention is held, it is due to selective interest by the learner, which is related to and and bound by related thoughts from the learner's retention system (memory) regardless of the form in which the idea comes packaged.

The next step is a shift from initial attention to the *differentiation* by which the new idea is related (by memory) to what the learner already knows about the topic. Since selective interest is based upon prior interest or ideas, there is a comparison of the new idea with prior interests or ideas. If the teacher cannot help the learner analyze the relationship of the new idea to prior interests or ideas, the learning ends. However, if the learner can associate the new idea with prior ideas, he or she will continue to maintain selective interest in the new idea.

Maintaining selective interest through the differentiation stage is essential to the willingness of the learner to remain open to *structuring*. Structuring entails finding a place for the new idea in the memory of prior experiences once it has been differentiated in the previous stage according to its uniqueness or similarity to other ideas. If a "fit," or place for the idea, cannot be found by the learner, with or without the teacher's help, learning ends. Learners often keep asking questions to derive their own individual structuring of an idea. Whole new ideas have to be tentatively attached to similar but not-same ideas for a short time, while more is learned upon which to build a new structure in the memory or retention system.

If a place is found for the new idea in the memory (either temporary or permanent), then the learner remains open to begin the next stage of *analyzing* the idea more closely to determine what the idea is really all about. If upon further scrutiny the idea loses its luster, learning ends. If upon analyzing the idea, there is promise and reward, then an attempt is made to truly question the potential other uses or reasons to know the idea. Analyzing is a problem-solving process.

If the learner determines that the idea has real promise or if it is perceived as being helpful, permanent *integration* with the memory takes place. However, if, after closer examination and many attempts to find out why and how to use the idea, the new idea is burdensome (harder to fit into a previous experience than originally thought) and integration cannot take place easily, the learning ends.

After "fitting and integration" occurs, the learner begins to abstract on the potential other—both immediate and future—uses of the idea. The uses of the idea become the probability or possibilities of future memory needs and the idea becomes a part of the retention system to be acted upon or used again. This stage is called *generalization*.

PLM Teaching-Learning Model

Based on McClusky's power-load-margin theory, Main (1979) has developed his PLM model of teaching and learning. His concept of the teaching-learning process contains six major elements evenly divided in two kinds of value systems: nurturant and instructional. The three components of the nurturant value system are interpersonal warmth and affiliation, ability to cope with change, and respect for the dignity of the person. Components of the instructional value system are the concept of power-load-margin, learning options based on self-evaluation, and self-enhancement and goal achievement. Main represents the model as one that encourages mutual respect and shared responsibility between the teacher and the learner. The social system upon which the model is based is one of moderate structure. Finally, the concept identifies margin and motivation for learning as prerequisites.

Main defines *load* as the demands that are made on an individual by self and society. It consists of two kinds of interacting variables: external and internal. *Power* refers to the resources that are available to cope with the load. It also consists of two sets of interacting variables: external and internal. *Margin* is a function of the relationship between power and load. It is surplus power, or power (resources) available over and beyond that required to handle load. Margin is perceived as a necessary condition for learning because without the surplus power, the learner has no resources to apply to the learning process. It is thus power to choose from a range of alternatives while maintaining one's life space.

The three models reported in the previous pages have identified some common elements in the learning process that should be addressed by instructional procedures. They include personal variables, self-other variables, and environmental variables. Research concerning some important personal variables in the teaching-learning transaction is discussed in the following part of this chapter. Similar research relating to self-other and environmental variables is reviewed in Chapter 11.

COMMON PERSONAL VARIABLES

Research related to several subcategories of this class of variables is discussed in Chapter 2. Three are examined here: intelligence, experience, and cognitive/learning style. Each of these three topics is related specifically to research appropriate to the learning-teaching transaction in adult education.

Intelligence

The literature indicates the possibility of at least two different positions concerning the association between intelligence test scores and learning ability. The arguments of proponents of both positions seem to have some logical basis. Pressey (1956), for example, expressed the opinion that the content of adult intelligence tests is not a valid measure of adult learning abilities because the tests' content is school oriented and, consequently, of little interest to adults. Others, such as Knox, Grotelueschen, and Sjogren (1968), have conducted research that indicates a high correlation between intelligence and learning ability as measured on achievement in a variety of learning tasks.

If intelligence is given another definition—for example, knowledge of a particular topic, the same conclusion seems to hold. Even though he was not examining the same issue discussed above, Grotelueschen (1979) provides supporting evidence for the conjecture that prior knowledge is associated with successful learning. Thus, even though educators of adults can forcefully argue the merits of motivation and the importance of maturity in the learning-teaching transaction, all other things being equal, the intelligence of the learner remains an important variable.

The continuing advantage of intelligence at a younger stage of life has been demonstrated to persist in performance tests administered across the life span. Cross-sectional studies provide evidence of an increasing range of individual differences in learning abilities (as measured by intelligence tests) at least through the sixth decade of life. It is believed that the most intellectually able people increase their learning ability during childhood and adolescence, obtain a higher plateau in young adulthood, and either gradually increase or maintain their learning ability during adulthood. In contrast, the less intellectually able seem to increase their learning ability more slowly (Knox 1977a).

Experience

The concept of the adult learner as an experienced person engaged in learning is among the most popular in adult education. This is not to say that all learners are experienced in learning a given content; it is to say that all adult learners have experienced some learning and that all adults have some experiences that may be related to their learning. We are concerned here with the latter idea.

A number of reputable leaders in the field of adult education have emphasized experience as a distinguishing feature that characterizes adult learners. Schwertman (1960) attributed the following conceptualization of adult (compared with nonadult) experience to Houle:

1. Adults have more experiences.
2. Adults have different kinds of experiences.
3. The life experiences of adults are organized differently.

It is Stern (1960), however, who has best synthesized the implications of experience for the education of adults. The experience of living involves changes of direction and challenge over a long period of time, which has resulted in purposive personal growth and development—in essence, adults have already been partly educated by life.

Diekhoff (1960) provides additional elaboration to Stern's observations concerning the role of experience in the adult learner's learning activity. Accordingly, he explains how the differently organized experience of adults is reflected in the choices of themes that they write or in the interpretation that they place on the books that they read. Diekhoff indicates that other important techniques in adult learning-teaching are to be understood by the instructor of adults only after he or she adequately understands the role of experience in the adult learner's learning activity.

Quantitative empirical research on the role of experience in the education of adults is, unfortunately, missing. One cannot object strenuously to the observations of scholars, philosophers, and practitioners such as Diekhoff, Houle, Stern, and Schwertman. Other adult educators of the stature of Kidd (1975), Knowles (1970), and Rogers (1973) have also admonished us to keep in mind the significance of the experience of adults when planning educational activities for them.

Cognitive/Learning Style

Cognitive and learning styles have spawned a productive area of research. Conceptually, the distinction between cognitive style and learning style remains muddled, and further precision is required in the basic dimensions of the two constructs. Cross (1976) has limited cognitive style to the theoretical laboratory investigations; thus, by implication, learning style is concerned with the applied practical dimensions of the construct. No such restriction is placed on the term here. Both learning style and cognitive style as used here refer to the distinctive cognitive approaches that some individuals manifest in learning behavior. Research reported in the following paragraphs includes the work of investigators who use both terms. Some use the two terms interchangeably. The appellation used in the following pages is, in each case, the one selected by the investigator.

Recent research using adult samples provides a considerable body of evidence to support the hypothesis that there are different learning styles (Elliott 1975). Some studies, however, indicate that while some learners may reflect sufficiently distinctive learning behaviors to permit definite identification of a dominant learning style, others may not (Bennett 1978). Furthermore, the research indicates possible associations between certain cognitive/learning styles and other variables such as age, aptitudes as reflected in courses of study and occupations, achievement, and preference for certain educational techniques.

Age

Educators of adults are interested in the possibility that age may be associated with learning styles. A demonstrated relationship wouuld provide some useful clue to the planning of learning activities. Therefore, it is important to note that age has been suggested by some investigators as being associated with learning styles. Hunter (1977) has indicated that there is sufficient difference between younger and older learners concerning learning style to refer to the phenomenon as another generation gap. According to his research, younger learners (less than 24 years of age) prefer peer associations, work with inanimate devices, listening, iconics, and direct experience. In comparison, older learners (24 years of age and older, mean age 34) prefer traditional class organization, including detail and interpersonal competition, qualitative emphasis, and listening and reading activities. Hunter's conclusions are supported by the findings of DeCosmo (1977) and Wegner (1980).

Hunter's investigation indicates that while older learners reflect traditional educational values, there is a need to develop new instructional strategies for younger adults. The new instructional strategies will likely include increased technological application and individual learning activity.

Aptitudes

The cognitive characteristics associated with a field-dependent or field-independent style and the personal attributes related to each have been identified with choice of student electives, majors, and early vocational preferences as well as later vocational choices. The different characteristics are also related to performance in different subject matter areas in school and to changes in academic majors (DeCosmo 1977; Wegner 1980; Witkin 1973).

Cognitive organization associated with cognitive/learning styles is believed to be associated also with independent variables such as occupation and other environmental elements. Evidence of such relationships has been reported by Bennett (1978), DeCosmo (1977), and Pigg, Busch, and Lacy (1980).

Many educators of adults are interested in the findings of Witkin, Dyk, et al. (1962) concerning cognitive/learning styles because of the implications of the research for the teaching-learning transaction. If it can be assumed that learners have distinctive cognitive styles, it can also be proposed that teachers have preferred styles. Furthermore, if learning style affects the way a learner learns, it is also possible that the teacher's style affects the design of learning activities. Witkin (1973) reports that the construct of cognitive/learning style has been found to be associated with both learning and teaching behavior. Teachers and learners matched in cognitive style have shown mutual positive evaluation, whereas teachers and students who are mismatched tend to evaluate each other negatively.

Achievement

Different cognitive organization as inferred from activities designed to explicate cognitive or learning styles seems to be associated with learning outcomes. There is some evidence to indicate that field-dependent persons do less well in mathematics and also experience some difficulty in reading comprehension (Czarnecki 1980). Furthermore, achievement on the GED and in other learning activities has been demonstrated to be associated with cognitive styles (Donnarumma, Cox, and Beder 1980; Andrulus and Bush 1977).

Techniques

The evidence for an association between cognitive/learning styles and preference for, or achievement with, selected educational techniques and devices is ambiguous. Some studies (Bertinot 1979; Wallace 1980) indicate that there is no relationship between different cognitive approaches to learning and achievement or choice of techniques and devices. Others (Cawley, Miller, and Milligan 1976) report that there is an association between learning styles and preferred teaching techniques. Kolb's (n.d.) contention that preferences for certain educational techniques are correlated with specific learning styles has not been universally supported; however, additional study in this area seems to be justified on the basis of Bertinot's and Wallace's findings.

OTHER PERSONAL VARIABLES

The previously discussed three classes of personal variables—intelligence, experience, and congnitive/learning style—do not exhaust the inventory of variables associated with the teaching-learning transaction. Other variables of longstanding interest to educators of adults include anxiety, curiosity, and motivation.

Anxiety

Adult learners may be even more susceptible to some influences of anxiety than younger learners (Kalus and Patchner 1982). One reason for such an opinion resides in the part-time occasional nature of formal learning for adults. Another is related to the possibility that a return to the formal learning setting for some adults may be associated psychologically with previous failure. Anxiety as a topic of study, however, is not a simple one. Questions arise concerning the phenomenon as a situation-specific trait and as a general characteristic. The conclusions of numerous studies also have proved to be equivocal.

The phenomenon of anxiety and its relationship to learning are discussed in the following paragraphs. Specifically, the discussion focuses upon an examination of research devoted to anxiety and test performance. Because of the limitations of space and the great numbers of related investigations in this area, selected representative studies are reviewed. The selected studies tend to reveal relationships between the two components of anxiety and learning, and the relationships between anxiety and performance on tests. A review of the literature devoted to anxiety and performance reveals a scarcity of investigations involving an adult population. However, the implications of the investigations reviewed present a challenge to those concerned with adult learners and the effect of anxiety upon learning and achievement.

Anxiety has been conceptualized as being of two types: state and trait. The former is believed to exist only under certain conditions, such as when an individual is taking a test. The latter is a more generalized form of anxiety as a personality characteristic. Individuals who score high on certain anxiety measures may not be anxious at all times. State anxiety is believed to be most often associated with personally threatening situations such as tests. In a testing situation, anxiety responses include heightened physiological activities and self-effacing statements. Such responses are identified with reductions in performance level (Sarason 1961).

Spielberger, Gorsuch, and Lushene (1968) have argued for the importance of this distinction between anxiety as a permanent aspect of personality and as a transitory reaction to stressful situations. For purposes of definition, state anxiety (A-state) is conceptualized as a condition of the organism characterized by subjective feelings and heightened autonomic nervous system activity.[2] Trait anxiety (A-trait) denotes individual differences in anxiety proneness, that is, the disposition to respond with A-state to situations that are perceived as threatening. Spielberger and his associates have distinguished between anxiety as a state and as a disposition. They view both A-state and A-trait as unitary conditions on which persons may differ only in intensity.

Studies designed to investigate the relationship of anxiety to performance indicate that highly anxious subjects differ from subjects low in anxiety in that the performance is lowered under conditions of personal threat or stress.

Mandler and Sarason (1952) investigated the influence of anxiety, as evoked by a testing situation, on the performance of typical intelligence test items. Two groups of subjects (a high-anxiety group and a low-anxiety group), all sophomore and junior college students, were selected on the basis of an anxiety questionnaire. The results of the study indicated that the optimal performance conditions for a high-anxiety group are those in which no reference to previous performance is made between testing situations, and that the optimal conditions for a low-anxiety group are those in which the subjects are given a failure report after the first test.

Spielberger, Gorsuch, and Lushene (1968) have hypothesized that high A-trait subjects tend to perceive situations involving ego threat as more threatening than do low A-trait subjects. Other kinds of threats, such as physical pain or danger, are perceived as equally threatening by the two groups. Hodges (1967), in a major test of this viewpoint, found that subjects placed in a situation involving the threat of failure reported a significant increase in state anxiety and that these increases were greater for high A-trait than for low A-trait subjects. Hodges found no relationship between A-trait level and state anxiety increases in a situation involving threat of electric shock.

The results of a 1970 study by Morris and Liebert appear to contradict Hodges' findings. The Morris and Liebert study was designed to examine the possibilities of (1) the presence of a fear-of-failure element in the A-trait scale of the State-Trait Anxiety Inventory, (2) the presence of a fear-of-failure element in the worry scale, as opposed to the emotionality scale, and (3) a predictive relationship between A-trait and worry. The first hypothesis, that high A-trait subjects would show higher A-trait scores than their low A-trait counterparts only under conditions of failure threat, was not supported. The study further indicated that subjects who differ in trait anxiety experience corresponding levels of A-state in a variety of situations and, in addition, may experience differential elevations of A-state in ego-threat situations.

Research undertaken by Kight and Sassenrath (1966) and Walsh, Engbretson, and O'Brien (1968) has demonstrated no clear relationship among anxiety level, knowledge of test results, and performance. Although no relationship was demonstrated by these studies, they did show that all these variables and their intercorrelations must be recognized.

The studies surveyed here indicate that in spite of much research and theorizing on the topic of anxiety as a personality variable and as a factor related to academic achievement, a body of consistent findings has failed to emerge.

The majority of studies of anxiety have been directed toward undergraduate college students. In most cases, the subjects were psychology and sociology students. From a research viewpoint, an adult population has rarely been involved in anxiety-achievement studies.

Curiosity

How important is curiosity in adult learning behavior? The literature of adult education is ambivalent on the question. Curiosity seems to be particularly important in individually guided adult learning projects. Tough (1969) found that satisfaction of curiosity was the second most common reason for engaging in adult learning projects among thirty-five adults that he interviewed. Others (Carp, Peterson, and Roelfs 1974) have reported that many adults cite curiosity as a reason for engaging in adult learning activities. A different position has been taken by those such as Miller (1964), who contends that pure intellectual curiosity is a weak and rare form of motivation for adult learning. Robinson (1965) arrived at a similar conclusion after analyzing data from a survey of adult learning interests.

For adults, relevance or perceived value has a marked bearing on the desire to learn, and this factor often outweighs any influence of curiosity. Comparison of the results of studies of curiosity in motivating learning suggests that the importance of curiosity in motivating learning may decline after adolescence. However, generally positive findings concerning the influence of curiosity on motivation merits further study of the nature of the relationship of situational curiosity with adult learners.

Motivation

Motivation as an important hypothetical construct in explaining numerous behaviors is variously conceptualized. In addition to having concerns about what motivation really is, or how best to define and describe it, we are aware of its perceived importance in various settings that include the workplace and educational institutions. While we are specifically concerned here with motivation for learning, reference will be made to models and theories that have been developed and used by industrial psychologists. It is believed that motivation concepts as applied to the workplace may be helpful in the refinement of motivation models for group learning activities. This discussion of motivation as a personal variable in learning provides a general overview of several diverse concepts.

Space does not permit a summary of the diverse theories of motivation that are recognized by educators of adults and others. Some prominent theoretical positions are identified in the following list for additional consideration by the reader.

1. E. L. Thorndike
2. Clark Hull
3. B. F. Skinner
4. Sigmund Freud
5. Carl Jung
6. Erich Fromm
7. Kurt Lewin
8. Abraham Maslow
9. Carl Rogers
10. Robert Havighurst
11. V. H. Vroom

The above list represents a wide range of scholars from a variety of philosophical and disciplinary orientations. It includes S–R theorists, third-force psychologists, and industrial psychologists.

Motivational Theory and Adult Education

While many motivational theories have implications for adult education research, theory, and practice, a review of some representative applications of motivational theory to adult educational situations generally reveals a distinct preference for theories that take into account the dynamic and social aspects of motivation as applied to learning.

It often has been reported in psychological and sociological literature that childhood and adolescence present a series of new problems and situations to be dealt with by the individual. An extension of this idea has been reported by Havighurst (1952), who deals with adulthood as a developmental period with its own transition points and crises. According to Havighurst, the developmental tasks of adulthood are those things that constitute healthy and satisfactory growth in our society. They are the things that a person must learn if he or she is to be judged—by others and self—a reasonably successful person. Through an intensive study of adults (mainly 40–70 years old) in Kansas City, Havighurst arrived at a set of "developmental directions" in which a middle-aged person should grow. Directions discussed are mental flexibility versus rigidity, emotional expansion versus constriction, expansion of interests beyond the work role, valuing wisdom versus valuing physical power, and body transcendence versus body preoccupation. Within this framework, a list of developmental tasks of middle age was developed. Since the tasks of middle age are set for the individual both by the expectations of society and by individual motivation and aspirations, Havighurst attempted to measure the degree of motivation or desire for achievement of individuals to accomplish various tasks as classified by social roles. The results indicated great differences among individuals within age and social class groupings as well as large differences between social classes concerning the priority of certain tasks or groups of tasks.

Havighurst also generated a supplementary theory relevant to adult education from his research. His theory is expressed in the term "teachable moment." A teachable moment occurs with great urgency over a relatively short period of time as a developmental task becomes important to the individual. At this time, the individual's motivation to learn is greatly intensified and education is "extremely effective." As an example of this teachable moment, Havighurst cites the motivation of a young couple to learn about child-rearing at about the time of the birth of their first child.

Boyd (1961) attempted to observe "basic motives" of adults participating in a noncredit collegiate-sponsored evening class program. His research was designed according to the ego developmental crisis theory of the neo-Freudian psychoanalyst Erik Erikson. Erikson (1943) had theorized that the adult ego faces three major sequential crises: in young adulthood, intimacy versus isolation; in adulthood, generativity versus stagnation; and in maturity, integrity versus disgust and despair. Boyd used an interview technique to determine how the ego handled these crises in selected individuals. Basic motives were defined as "the desire to overcome a crisis arising in the interaction of the psychic-social fields within an organism." Boyd came to tentative conclusions that adults in noncredit programs appear to be "retarded in their growth of a healthy personality" as defined by Erikson's stages and that groups of courses (for example, humanities or language) rather than age groupings appeared to indicate more homogeniety of ego profiles. Boyd (1965) stated that research such as his implies that adult educators shed light on and raise questions as to how the adult can be helped to move along and through these ego development stages.

Tough's detailed study (1971) of the adult's learning projects includes interviews indicating that the anticipated benefits of a learning project are a significant factor in a person's motivation for learning. His approach to why a person begins a learning project is based primarily on the growth-expansion theory of motivation. The reasons for undertaking a learning project as rated by the learners, and the benefits flowing from each reason, are illustrated by his diagram of the "relationships among the benefits that a learner may expect from a learning project" (Figure 10.2).

Tough uses three words for describing a large cluster of benefits that the learner may obtain from a learning activity: pleasure, self-esteem, and others. *Pleasure* is used to include a large cluster of benefits that are related to "feeling good," happiness, delight, or other positive emotions, including avoiding or reducing unpleasant feelings. *Self-esteem* is used to refer to those feelings about one's self. Finally, the term *others* relates to how others feel when they become aware of the learner's accomplishments; it can represent the regard that others have for the learner or the learner's avoidance of displeasing others or reducing their regard.

An overview of major influences on adult motivation to learn may be of some value in obtaining a knowledge of the adult's motivational structure as a whole. While this is not intended to be an all-inclusive list of influences, some of the major factors identified in the literature are treated.

Physiological Change and Decline

Although physiological pressures are generally thought to be of much less importance in the motivational makeup of the adult than in that of the child and adolescent (Pressey and Kuhlen 1957), physical change and decline often act as limiting circumstances influencing motivation at different adult stages. The general decline in strength, speed of reaction, endocrine function, and general body tone generally associated with aging and especially with old age often has a marked effect upon behavior and motivation (Kuhlen 1963). In late middle-age (about 45–65), for example, the individual, while social expectations continue to press upon him or her for achievement, may have to allow for a slight decline in energy and/or abilities. In older age (65 and up), as many studies illustrate, the large majority of adults are motivated strongly to preserve and guard their energies and health. In this period of life, many adults have been observed to develop "strategies" to avoid "inappropriate tasks or situations," which might reveal their inability to perform in relation to those younger (Boyd and Oakes 1969).

Social and Cultural Factors

The effect of social influences on adult learning and motivation was recognized and noted early, as was illustrated by Thorndike's (1928, p. 124) remark that adults quite often learn much less than they might 'in part due to a sensitiveness to ridicule, adverse comment, and undesired attention, so that if

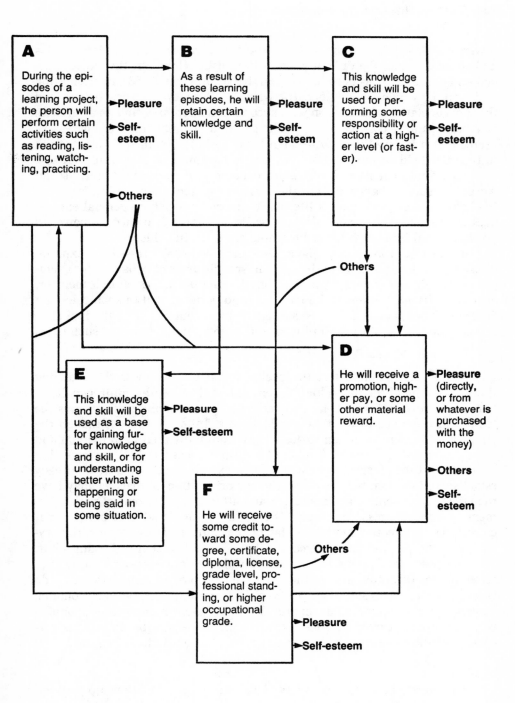

Figure 10.2 The relationships among the benefits that a learner may expect from a learning project

Source: Allen Tough, *The Adult's Learning Projects: A Fresh Approach to Theory and Practice in Adult Learning.* (2nd ed.). Toronto: OISE, 252 Bloor St. West, 1971, p. 47. Reproduced by permission.

it were customary for mature and old people to learn to swim and ride bicycles and speak German, the difficulty might diminish." However, the effect of social and cultural forces need not be negative. R. A. Love (1953), in attempting to determine why many adults participate in college-level studies, determined that an association of education with success and happiness, and an awareness of education as a positive value in the solution of problems, were necessary prerequisites to enrollment. Although these socially obtained values are not universally held in our society, they are often powerful motivating factors.

According to Jensen (1964), adult concern with expanding their "social worth and success" appears to be the "primary source of motivation for learning" over a large part of adult life. Since American society in general encourages competence (i.e., knowledge and skills) as the road to success, powerful positive social influences toward learning are often in evidence.

Havighurst (1952, 1964; Havighurst and Orr 1965) stressed the expectations of society pressing upon the adult in specific areas of behavior, for example, the adult as a parent, as a child of an aging parent, as church member, citizen, or friend. Although the motivation to perform well in such roles is a function not only of social expectations and ideals but also of individual aspirations, Havighurst's research illustrates the motivational power of such roles.

Time and Money Perceptions

One of the major factors in developmental psychology is the changing time perception of the individual. According to this view, the adult, usually in his or her thirties, becomes aware that goals, progress, and so forth must be viewed in reference to the time available in a finite life span. Although the effect of this time perception varies widely from individual to individual and among various age groups, Kuhlen (1963) and Jensen (1964) indicate that sublimits in time perspectives may heighten existing motivation in an already established direction, may be crucial in the orientation of goals, or may have the effect of concentrating frustration and attendant symptoms of maladjustment of certain ages. This factor is relevant to adult education in that it constitutes an effective motivating factor that differentiates between the psychology of the old and middle-aged and that of the adolescent and young adult.

The possession or lack of money can also be an important motivating force. Money can often dictate the "relative freedom" of an individual to do what he or she chooses. Kuhlen (1963) cites, for example, the strong economic demands on the individual during the 30–40 decade, which, he feels, coupled with a desire for career advancement, probably is responsible for a large percentage of the enrollment of young adults in adult education programs.

Interests

Psychologists and educators have long recognized a relationship between interests and the quality and quantity of learning. The interests of adults take on an especially important character because of the operation of "differentiation." This concept refers to a "diversification of abilities, skills, attitudes, interests, etc." within the individual as he or she moves through the adult years. In other words, adult interests are liable to be specific, while youth interests are more "global" (McClusky 1964).

Adult interests, according to Thorndike (Thorndike et al. 1935), show only a slight decrease in their total volume with age from the twenties to the sixties. This slight decrease is largely due to a decline in interest in physical activities; the kinds of interests that would generally support adult learning (e.g., reading and writing) show no decrease. Other factors liable to affect adult interests include occupation, abilities, age, and curiosity.

The Need for Achievement

The psychologist David C. McClelland has put forth a theory of achievement motives that develop out of growing expectations (McClelland et al. 1953). Adult education in America, which most often involves middle-class participants, is especially influenced by this type of individual motivation. Middle-class American society generally places a high premium on a strong achievement orientation, and thus many individuals are forced into an achievement situation to which they might respond behaviorally in a variety of ways, including remaining static, striving to achieve success, or striving to avoid failure (Teevan and Smith 1967).

A number of investigators have recognized that the need for achievement is an important factor among young adults, especially for men. A study of Veroff et al., drawn from a nationwide sample of adults, illustrates this need for achievement as operating especially in young adulthood and middle age (Kuhlen 1963). Following the lead of McClelland's research, Rees and Paisley (1967) studied the relation of the need for achievement motive among adults to media use and information seeking. Rees and Paisley obtained achievement scores from selected responses to questions, which they then used with other factors (e.g., age, education, perceptions of the media) to establish "predictors" of certain behavior. Although other predictors often were stronger than achievement motivation when analysis was done, the factor revealed a certain strength—perhaps one to be investigated further. The achievement motivation revealed a predictor strength at the .02 level of confidence or better on such adult behavior as adult education through self-study, readership of nonfiction books and newsmagazines, use of the public library, and viewing of serious television programs.

Frustration

Behavior changes are recognized as having been motivated by frustration by such theorists as Freud and McClelland. Kuhlen (1963) suggests certain age-related factors that may prove frustrating to adults (some of which are discussed elsewhere in this book), including limitations of time and money, physical change, degree of status, skill deficits in occupations, and/or inability to change some disturbing circumstance or source of unhappiness.

SUMMARY

This chapter has reported selected research concerning models related to the teaching-learning transaction. Three models were discussed. They are the work of Verduin (Verduin, Miller, and Greer 1977), Even and Boyd (Even 1981), and Main (1979). Variables common to the models discussed can be placed in three categories: personal variables, self-other variables, and environmental variables.

Research concerning personal variables in adult teaching and learning was also reported here, while research concerning self-other variables and environmental variables is discussed in Chapter 11. Topics in the personal variable category, as examined in this chapter, include the following: intelligence, experience, cognitive/learning style, anxiety, curiosity, and motivation.

While much of the research reviewed in Chapters 10 and 11 tends to reflect a possible overemphasis on "psychological" explanations for teacher-learner interactions (see Rubenson 1982), there is evidence that educators of adults are becoming more interested in social, structural, and environmental variables. Several of the studies reported and discussed in the three chapters on participation and persistence in adult education address variables outside the "psychological" arena. Schroeder (1980) has provided a concept for macro-analysis for program planning, and Cross (1981) has joined with Bergsten (1980) and others (Marieneau and Klinger 1977) in the study of participation.

NOTES

1. *Teacher* is a term that is not always preferred among educators of adults. Euphemisms such as *mentor* and *facilitator* have been adopted as substitutes to reflect the philosophy of andragogy and self-directed learning. The role of the "teacher" has a long and honorable history that includes such luminaries as Jesus, Plato, and Socrates. *Teaching* may be variously defined to include those behaviors that some find objectionable as well as those that they find acceptable. As used in this chapter, teaching includes a range of behaviors from those traditionally identified with highly structured authoritarian settings to those associated with more permissive learner-dominated contexts. Darkenwald and Merriam (1982) also recently struggled with this term and said, "teacher is used here because it is familiar, but it is defined in its broader sense to denote anyone who directly facilitates learning" (p. 17).

2. Physiological changes associated with a heightened arousal state have been documented by Eisdorfer, Nowlin, and Wilkie (1970).

11 • Self-Other Relations and Self–Learning Activity Interactions

THE PRECEDING CHAPTER examines important personal variables that are believed to be associated with the teaching-learning transaction. The topics discussed in that chapter include learning models, common variables and some personal variables such as experience, cognitive/learning style, anxiety, curiosity, and motivation. Topics in this chapter include self-other variables, such as relations with other learners and instructors, and self–learning activity variables, which include the techniques and format of instruction.

SELF-OTHER RELATIONS

Educators of adults may be more sensitive to the potential influence of numerous noncognitive variables on the teaching-learning transaction than are teachers of younger people. Educators of adults have ample reason for believing that the range of noncognitive differences among adults may be even greater than that of the cognitive differences. The great variety of social experiences that adults encounter across the life span significantly expands the opportunities for differences to develop. The concept of individual differences thus constitutes an important consideration in analysis and design of the teaching-learning transaction. Learners are said to have important relationships with three elements in a learning activity: the instructor, other learners, and the content. Studies of the teaching-learning transaction have addressed at some time, to some degree, each of these kinds of relationships. Relationships between learners and content, however, are seldom examined independently of other variables. Therefore, references to content relationships are included in the generalizations about relationships of learners with instructors and other learners.

Relationship with Instructor

Boshier's 1972 congruence theory (discussed in some detail in Chapter 5) seeks to explain the dropout behavior of adult learners within a framework of incompatibility between the learner and instructor. Likewise, others have cited the importance of learner-teacher relationships as a variable to be considered when offering an explanation for failure of learners to complete a sequence of class meetings.

Bligh (1977) has emphasized the importance of the social dimension in the education of adults. He is of the opinion that the recent advances in telecommunications and related educational innovations are generally irrelevant because of the neglect of the social variable. According to Bligh's view, education too often has been perceived as a presentation and communication process rather than a social process of elicitation. This view posits that the former process can only present information for the learner to acquire. Thus, changes in learner disposition, thought, motive, and feeling are not addressed by the inactive mode of information reception but require active methods of learning, such as discussion. Bligh's conjectures, however, are not supported by several studies reported later in this chapter. The studies indicate that achievement through electronic broadcast formats may be equivalent to that through face-to-face instruction. The findings in this area are equivocal, and inferences from existing evidence are tenuous.

The concept that social climate is an important variable in the education of adults is a popular one. The instructor is usually represented as the key figure responsible for the development and maintenance of the appropriate social relationships within the adult learning program. Stock, Murgatroyd, Bohman, and others have commented on this instructional role.

Stock (1974) identifies four teaching behaviors identified with success; three of the four directly affect learner-teacher relationships. He indicates that teachers of adults should strive to develop warmth, indirectness, cognitive organization, and enthusiasm. The importance of certain teacher competencies that influence or establish the climate for interpersonal relations is further indicated by Murgatroyd (1977), who offers an observational checklist for rating teacher characteristics. Of the fifteen items, at least eight are concerned with factors associated with interpersonal relationships, for example, rapport, individual relationships, demeanor, warmth, degree of formality, flexibility, and confidence.

Adult learners prefer teachers with whom they can identify and who are competent in both subject matter and interpersonal skills; several studies support this observation. Competence in both content and interpersonal skills is perceived as important. In other words, an individual who is incompetent in his or her field of study cannot overcome that deficit by being a "jolly good fellow." Achievement is also related to the degree with which learners identify with the instructor (Bohman 1968). This latter association is further strengthened by a study conducted in two adult high schools in DeKalb County, Georgia. Roberson (1980) reports that students are quite perceptive in their awareness of teacher concern. His research indicates that students' assessment of teacher concern is associated with teachers' self-acceptance scores, students' self-acceptance scores, and students' acceptance of others. In contrast, one study (Castillo 1976) indicates that while learners prefer a teacher who displays an interest in them, some teachers are unaware of this significant factor.

A small group of additional studies provides further support for the premise that the personal relationship between learner and teacher is an important variable in the teaching-learning transaction. Studies cited in Chapter 6, conducted by Davis (1963) and Lam and Wong (1974), reported the association between certain instructor behaviors and learner perseverance. Apps (1981) has identified a list of nine exemplary teaching principles, at least six of which directly include learner-teacher relations: (1) know your students, (2) use students' experiences as class content, (3) provide a climate conducive to learning, (4) provide students feedback on their progress, (5) help students acquire resources, and (6) be available to students for out-of-class contacts.

Satisfaction, an important goal in the education of adults, has been identified as being associated with students' perceptions of teachers' conformity with adult education principles. Berg (1969) identified a list of eight principles of adult education and surveyed more than 1,500 students in 100 University of Colorado extension classes to determine the relationship between the teacher's demonstration of the principles in the classroom and student satisfaction. The principle of satisfactory personal and social relationships was among the five principles that were identified by the students as being associated with satisfaction.

By inference, it can be assumed that other important teaching principles such as the use of appropriate instructional techniques may be necessary but not sufficient to account for learning achievement. The importance of the nature and quality of interpersonal relations between learner and teacher (Lam and Wong 1974) is one of the basic concepts of the education of adults as noted by Knowles (1973). Kidd (1975) also addresses the need for an emotional and physical environment that stimulates and supports learning.

Relationship with Other Learners

A basic principle of adult education is that learning activities are free of coercion from the teacher and other learners. Jenkins (1960) has described the situation as follows (p. 57):

> We have discussed the needs of the student for acceptance. . . . Inasmuch as these needs are emotional ones which exist in the relationships between people, they can also be met in large measure by the other students. . . . As students find it possible to accept each other and reaffirm each others' value

and worth, and as they find it less necessary to compete with and attack each other, each of them will find greater personal security. . . . And, as they are open to communication, they are then open to new stimulation and to learning.

While the act of learning may be a very personal and individual matter, learning activities designed for adults frequently occur in social settings that involve two or more people. London (1964) observed that the field of adult education works with people, who in most instances, will be collected in groups; consequently, adult educators operate in the social environment. Some believe that the social interactions and their processes among learners are more influential upon behavior, motivational drives, and personality development than are norms, environment, and a person's inner drive. Hence, educators of adults have often turned to social psychological and group dynamics literature for instruction concerning the teaching-learning transaction.

Many educators of adults are aware of the need to consider and make use of the needs and experiences of each individual adult learner in program design. They also recognize that many of the designs of learning experiences, for which they are responsible, include bringing individual learners together in groups. The fact that individual learners operate in groups challenges educators to reanalyze the processes, methods, techniques, and educational devices that they use with groups of learners, as well as how they plan goals for programs, diagnose needs of learners for programs, identify measurable objectives, develop content, and carry out and evaluate programs for groups of adult learners, based on the implications of known knowledge of group phenomena.

Despite the apparent significance of the social environment as defined by the interpersonal relationships that exist, or which may be created, among a group of learners, the topic has not been sufficiently and systematically examined to permit easy application. Many variables and situations associated with the diversity of adult learners and learning contexts complicate research and application in this area, which is characterized more by awareness that social conditions are important than by knowledge of how to best develop optimal social climates.

Achievement and Satisfaction

Many studies concerning social interaction among adult learners have focused on questions about achievement or satisfaction. The research findings reach near unanimity on the issue of satisfaction. The studies identified and reviewed all indicate that adult learners prefer group learning techniques and formats. Similarly, the studies designed to determine achievement differences or acquisition of information seem to generate findings that group learning techniques are no more effective—and in some instances less efficient—than the lecture technique (Willsey 1962; Orme 1978). Olmstead (1970) points out that discussion when used with a lecture may increase the depth of understanding of knowledge gained by the lecture technique.

Group Techniques

How do group techniques contribute to the achievement of desirable goals related to satisfaction? Several investigators (Brieger 1980; McKinley 1960) indicate that group techniques contribute to the following:

1. Enhancing motivation for learning
2. Developing positive attitudes concerning the later use of course materials
3. Improving problem-solving skills
4. Increasing feelings of self-worth
5. Increasing willingness and ability to accept and help others
6. Increasing willingness and ability to communicate verbally and nonverbally with others
7. Increasing independence from the instructor

Butler's 1965 study of lecture and conference techniques generated conclusive results that favored the conference activity. He reported that subjects taught human relations by the conference method learned more and retained more than subjects taught human relations by the lecture method.

Some differences among learners concerning their preferences for group activities exist. Blackburn and Douglah (1968) indicate that a majority of their study sample preferred group techniques and formats such as classes, discussion groups, short courses and lecture series, and workshop institutes. Adults in their sample who were most likely to prefer individual formats such as correspondence courses, books, consulting with experts, newspapers, magazines, and television were likely to be older women with low educational levels and low incomes.

Personality in Self-Other Relationships

Personality is one of the noncognitive factors that is believed to be significantly associated with teaching-learning behaviors. The importance of personality in learning, particularly in social settings, has contributed to interest in social learning theory. One explanation of social learning theory is provided here.

Social Learning Theory

Major assumptions of the theory, which determine which concepts are considered most useful in explaining human behavior, are as follows (Phares 1976):

1. The unit of investigation for the study of personality is the interaction of the individual and his or her meaningful environment.
2. The emphasis of the theory is on learned social behavior.
3. There is unity to personality; as individuals grow older, change is possible through proper selection of new learning experiences, but behavior and personality take on increasing consistency.
4. Social learning theory emphasizes both general and specific determinants of behavior; it regards behavior as determined both by situation-specific factors and by dispositional elements.
5. There is a purposeful quality to human behavior; behavior may be said to be goal directed in the sense that people strive to attain or to avoid certain aspects of their environment.

6. The occurrence of a behavior of a person is determined not only by the nature of importance of goals or reinforcements but also by the person's anticipation or expectancy that these goals will occur.

Expectancies are regarded by social learning theories as prime determinants of behavior. Behavior is determined by the degree to which people *expect* that their behavior will lead to goals.

One theoretical construct for explaining learning behavior, locus of control, evolved out of the above set of assumptions following experimental testing. According to tests of hypotheses based on the identified assumptions, it was found that the predicted changes in the probability of a behavior occurred only when the outcome was perceived by the person to have been contingent on his or her behavior. If an outcome was perceived to be the result of luck, chance, or the influence of others, the person tended to discount that particular outcome as having no relation to behavior.

Locus of Control

Adult education literature attributes characteristics to the self-directed learner that are similar to the characteristics of the internally oriented individual described by the findings of studies on locus of control. The self-directed learner is described as an adult who voluntarily participates in learning activities, who is autonomous and possesses the organization, knowledge, and skills essential to learning effectively. If a relation can be established between self-directed learning and internal locus of control orientation, the accumulated research on locus of control would provide a vast resource for planning and practice in adult education.

The literature contains a relatively select number of research studies concerned with locus of control theory that should be useful to educators of adults.

Individuals identified as "internals" are information seekers; they are inquisitive and usually better informed about their status than are "externals." For example, tuberculosis patients described as having internal locus of control have been characterized as knowing more than externals about their condition and as being more inquisitive and less satisfied with the information concerning their health available from the hospital (Seeman and Evans 1962). Inmates in a reformatory school identified as internals were more knowledgeable about the way the institution operated, more informed about parole regulations, and more aware of long-range economic factors that could affect their future (Seeman 1963).

The individual's perception of the situation will affect the amount of time and attention given to a task. Three different studies indicate that internals devote more attention to decisions about skill-related matters than do externals. The results of one, conducted by Rotter and Mulry (1965), showed that internals spent more time deliberating about their decisions than did externals when the task was thought to demand skill.

In two later studies, these results were replicated with some variation. Julian and Katz (1968) found that internals took more time to make decisions as the difficulty of the decision-making increased. Externals did not differ in the amount of time they took to make decisions to the same degree. They behaved as if there were no differences between simple and difficult choices.

DuCette and Wolk (1973) felt that several questions were left unanswered by these and similar studies. They felt that it was not clear whether the superior ability at "cognitive processing" of internals is found in all situations or only in those that allow some degree of control. They also questioned the degree of difference between internals and externals and whether the differences extend to all types of environmental cues. They developed a series of tasks that allowed the subjects to extract information from their environment. The tasks were both experimental (allowing varying degrees of control) and nonlaboratory. The hypothesis tested was that internal subjects, in situations where information can be obtained that will lead to solution of a problem, demonstrate a greater ability to extract information from their environment and then use this information to solve a problem.

The data were clear in supporting the contention that internal subjects were more sensitive to environmental stimuli. Internals demonstrated the ability to use experience with a task to improve their perception of performance, they were more accurate in remembering successes when feedback was provided, and they were quicker to devise an invariant rule from an ambiguous situation and use it to solve a problem. It was argued that the various behaviors examined in the study—the extraction of a rule, recall, and the use of information—represented three different cognitive processes. It was felt that the major strength of the data lay in making it clear that internal subjects differed from the externals on all three processes.

Several studies on the effect of feedback on student behavior according to locus of control are of interest in determining the degree to which extrinsic reward affects the behavior of internal and external students.

Hammer (1972) studied the effects of different kinds of written teacher comments on student performance according to the students' locus of control. Exam papers of 87 CCNY undergraduates were handed back with either no comment, a designated comment for each grade level (an A received the comment "Excellent"; a B received the comment "Good," etc.), or a specified comment that took into consideration the students' usual level of work (a student who normally got A's but received a C would receive the comment "O.K., but I know you can do better"). The students' locus of control was determined by their scores on the Rotter I–E scale. Treatment effects were determined by the students' grades on the next exam.

The most important finding of the study was the correlation between control of reinforcement orientation and the no comment and specified comment by past performance groups. Internal students who did not receive comments tended to do better on the next exam than external students who received no comment. External students who received the comments directing their attention to their usual level of work did better on the next exam than did the external students who received no comments. No significant difference was found between the internal students who received no comment and those who received the specified comment. Hammer suggests that for external students, teacher comments can have a motivating effect, not only because they are positive reinforcement, but also because they encourage the student to reflect on the possibility of controlling the grade.

The question of why the internal students did not increase their performance on the second test under the specified comment condition remains. Hammer suggests that the internals may have felt that they were being deprived of some of their control of the environment by having the teacher label their exam grades.

Baron, Cowan, Ganz, and McDonald (1974) sought to determine whether white elementary students and college students would respond under conditions of self-discovery of success (intrinsic feedback) vs. verbal praise (extrinsic feedback) in the same way in which lower class black students had in a previous study (Baron and Ganz 1972).

In all three of the studies, there was a consistent pattern of effects. The interaction between locus of control and feedback was significant, showing that internals performed better than externals when intrinsic feedback was used, while externals performed better than internals when interpersonally mediated (extrinsic) feedback was used.

The implications of locus of control are not limited to learning performance. There is some reason to believe that the construct may also be helpful in explaining participation and perhaps even the choice of learning activities. Peters (1969) reports findings that indicate that adult participation in some learning activities may be associated with an individual's locus of control orientation. Zahn (1969) also reports the work of Adams (1961) to support the conjecture that control relevance may be a factor in an adult's choice of learning activities.

Attitude Change

In a study on the effect of communicator status on attitude change, Ritchie and Phares (1969) predicted that externals would exhibit greater attitude change when receiving information from a high-prestige source than when receiving information from a low-prestige source. In addition, it was predicted that externals would show more attitude change than internals when both received communications attributed to a high-prestige source. No differences were expected between internals and externals when both received low-prestige communications, and no differences were expected between internals who received high-prestige communications and those who received low-prestige communications. All three of the original hypotheses were supported. The authors concluded that externals appear to be influenced according to the prestige of the source, regardless of previously held opinions or communication content, while internals seem to be more responsive to the content of a communication than to the prestige of the communicator.

Other studies on attitude change should be mentioned here. McGinnies and Ward (1974) studied attitude change as a function of source of credibility and locus of control. They observed, as did Ritchie and Phares (1969), that externals reacted more to a highly credible source than to a source of less credibility and that internals were not differentially affected by source credibility.

Cognitive Style and Locus of Control

While cognitive style and locus of control are two theoretically distinctive properties, the research literature reports fairly consistent findings with regard to the relationship between field dependence and responses to social influence and locus of control. Cawley, Miller, and Milligan (1976) identify five major theoretical propositions concerning field-independent and field-dependent cognitive styles:

1. Individual differences in cognitive behavior are stable.
2. There is consistency in cognitive styles across different learning situations.
3. Cognitive style is not associated with intelligence.
4. Adults have an identifiable preference for certain stimulus attributes to which they attend and, consequently, for the way they process information.
5. An analytic approach is associated with the notion of field independence, and a global-relational attitude is associated with the idea of field dependence.

Cognitive style concerns the ways in which individuals select, organize, and process the learning experiences in the environment. The characteristics of the analytic learner have been described as including longer attention span, greater reflectivity, and deeper concentration. The analytic learner tends to be more sedentary, prefers formal learning situations, sees a teacher as a source of information, prefers complexity, is achievement oriented and competitive, and prefers social distance. A global orientation, on the other hand, does not require a long or concentrated attention span, and relational learning is characterized by a short attention span and distractedness. The relational learner has been found to prefer informal learning situations, to see the teacher as another individual, to be less oriented to achievement and competition, and to prefer simplicity and social integration. Learning must have relevancy to one's life, feelings, and experiences; learning is a social experience.

Studies reported earlier support the hypothesis that there is a differential predilection to respond positively to social reinforcement. It has been found that internals performed more competently on a learning task when there were no social reinforcements proffered, whether praise or censure; that externals were more positively affected by anticipated social evaluation than were internals (with internals attending more to information-bearing cues that were intrinsic to the task); and that the presence of an observing audience was associated with improved retention of verbal material for externals but not for internals. It seems reasonable to assume that externals are both more attentive and more positively responsive, as well as facilitated in their performance of various tasks by the presence of social cues. Internals, on the other hand, seem more resistant to social influence and, at the least, distracted by social cues in attempting to cope with various tasks.

Furthermore, it seems plausible that field dependence and locus of control offer complementary predictions of the response to certain social events, though these variables are themselves empirically independent. It appears that internals and/or field-independent subjects would seem to be more comfortable and efficient when engaged in tasks without salient social cues. External and/or field-dependent subjects, on the other hand, appear to be facilitated by social cues and, if anything, to decline in performance when social reinforcements or feedback is not readily forthcoming during given tasks.

Implications for Adult Education

Herem (1978) has synthesized a list of conditions of learning that are applicable to adult education:

1. Learning requires motivation to change.
2. Active involvement of the learner promotes effective learning.
3. Learning depends on past experiences.
4. Learning effectiveness depends on feedback.
5. An informal atmosphere aids the learning process.

The research on locus of control orientation and its relationship to social influence creates some question concerning the differential requirements of each of the above. Whereas students with external locus of control may do well with active involvement and feedback, and in informal atmospheres, the internally controlled student may not respond as readily.

Kidd (1975) says that "it is interesting to note that the preferences or prejudices in favor of one practice or another rarely have much to do with the relative effectiveness for learning of each form" (p. 242). In discussing group processes in adult education, he adds, "there is a place for individual effort, and a primary object of all education is the unfolding, the expansion of an individual, not his contraction or smothering in any kind of group or mass" (p. 247).

Knox (1978–79) notes that the motives that cause adults to devote their time and attention to learning episodes are and should be a major determinant of learning outcomes. He points out that motives are multiple and varied in their specificity and in the extent to which the learner is aware of them.

Unfortunately, as Cawley et al. (1976) pointed out, the research on motivation in adult education has dealt largely with investigations of Houle's typology or expansions thereof, with meeting role-change needs, or with Maslow's hierarchial need theory. The locus of control construct offers adult educators an alternative route of investigation into adult learning.

The differential approaches to learning found between individuals with internal locus of control expectations and those with external control expectations should serve as guides for planning alternatives for instruction that could appeal to people reflecting the different kinds of orientations.

Knowles (1973) discusses the assumptions on which he bases his model of lifelong learning. One of his assumptions that is of particular interest here concerns skills of learning. According to Knowles, for effective lifelong learners the desired skills include (1) the ability to identify the data required to answer the various kinds of questions, (2) the ability to locate relevant and reliable sources of the data, (3) the ability to select and use the data efficiently, (4) the ability to organize, analyze, and evaluate data to get valid answers to questions, and (5) the ability to generalize, apply, and communicate what has been learned. It is obvious that adult educators should not use the same techniques with adults who are still in need of the above skills as they would use with adults who possess them. From the research on locus of control orientation, it appears that adults with an internal locus of control are more likely to possess the above traits. Such adults could be given greater flexibility in the acquisition of knowledge and the choice of learning experiences.

It appears that individuals who have a predominantly external locus of control orientation perform better in a social setting where an informal atmosphere, positive feedback, support of their peers, and social reinforcement are present. It also appears that for the external to perform best, there needs to be some structure and guidance. The teacher (mentor, facilitator, or whatever) should appear as a highly credible source of information with high prestige, while at the same time maintaining a warm, positive psychological environment. Research indicates that the lower socioeconomic levels have a greater percentage of external individuals, while the middle and upper-middle levels have a greater percentage of internals (Joe 1971; Lefcourt 1972; Phares 1973).

Internal students appear to perform best in situations where they are autonomous and in control of the situation and in which they can rely on their own judgment and definition of the situation. The internal student is more likely to be influenced by content than by status, prefers intrinsic feedback to praise or comments offered, and does not show improved performance in social settings.

One important question at this point is "How can the adult educator provide the atmosphere and direction needed for both types of individuals within one program, classroom, or workshop?" Another question that has not been answered concerns the attitude with which the internal student enters a learning environment. Much of the research done on internal-external locus of control has been done in an experimental setting other than the regular adult education settings. If the person with an internal orientation approaches the learning activity with the intention of delegating to the instructor some of the student's own autonomy, the problem posed by the first question would be easier to solve. If the internal *expects* structure and guidance from the teacher, then the task of designing the social atmosphere becomes one of compromise—providing enough positive feedback and social interaction to facilitate the externals but not to the extent that the internals react negatively. This appears to be a fruitful area for research.

Another possibility for providing the internals with learning activities more in keeping with their approach to learning would be to provide alternatives. Nontraditional kinds of learning activities where the individual with an internal locus of control serves as his or her own mentor might prove very appealing to such individuals. One argument against televised courses for college credit has been that there is a need (on the student's part) for social interaction and feedback. This need is apparently very attenuated in the individual with an internal locus of control, and for such individuals independent study or televised instruction might be a rewarding experience. If the locus of control construct is a valid one in regard to adult learning, then adult educators should investigate alternative, nontraditional approaches to learning that would take into consideration the characteristics of the internal student.

SELF-LEARNING ACTIVITY INTERACTIONS

Research and generalizations based on selected findings discussed to this point continue to reaffirm an important principle in the education of adults: Adult learners constitute a highly heterogeneous population. Teachers of adults are confronted with important decisions about designing optimal teaching-learning activities. The choices in strategy, timing, and specific learning activities are not made any easier by the possibility of countless combinations of learning activities (techniques, subtechniques, formats, and devices) for diverse learners with varied cognitive and personality characteristics and quite different learning objectives.

Research in this area is constantly expanding despite the complexity of the task facing the investigator who seeks, through empirical research and other means, to provide instructive findings. In fact, the scope of research that could be discussed here is sufficiently extensive to effectively limit the possibility of such a discussion. Therefore, the topics treated in this section are highly selective and have been included because of their general application to broad questions of high interest to educators of adults. Three major questions of adult educators concerning learning activities that are being addressed with some frequency and skill are these:

1. What does research say on the issue of learner involvement in the planning of the learning activity?
2. What does the research say about structure?
3. What is known about the efficacy of selected formats/devices?

Learner Involvement

The field of adult education responds with a surprising amount of agreement to certain principles such as (1) begin where the learner is, (2) identify and address learner needs, and (3) involve the learner in planning and conducting the learning activity. Havighurst (1964; Havighurst and Orr 1965) has written extensively of the importance of the readiness of the learner to learn, which covers elements of the first two of the above principles. The third principle, which concerns the involvement of the learner in planning and conducting the learning activity, remains to be adequately addressed at two levels: through a review of appropriate research and by means of additional well-designed investigations. The limited amount of research on this critical position concerning practice in the education of adults is surprising when one considers how many are recommending it.

Despite the popularity of the concept of learner participation in designing and conducting educational experiences, only eight research projects dealing with the efficacy of the practice were identified in the thousands of abstracts, articles, publications, and reports reviewed for this volume. The identified investigations were dated between 1966 and 1981; six were reported in the last five of those years. The most recently reported of these (Kerwin 1981) includes a challenge to adult educators to examine the practice to determine whether student involvement in program design and operation is the most effective way of facilitating learning in adults. Kerwin's study, however, was not designed to determine the association between learner participation and achievement or satisfaction. Each of the remaining seven investigations was designed to examine the association between achievement or satisfaction and learner involvement in the planning and operation of educational programs.

Five of the seven identified studies have contained data that are interpreted as being supportive of the practice. Cole and Glass (1977) and Pine (1980) reported that involvement had a significant positive effect on achievement and favorable attitudes; McLoughlin (1971) reported no difference on achievement but a significant difference on attitude; Vedros and Pankowski (1980) reported a significant difference in achievement among learners involved in planning but no difference in attitude. Finally, Welden (1966) noted that greater satisfaction was reported by learners who engaged in the planning of programs.

Coates (1980) reported that learners in sessions described as traditionally designed and guided by instructors were more satisfied with their learning experience than learners who had an opportunity to more actively determine program content and operations. Moorehead (1977) reported no difference between his control and experimental groups.

Unanimity is lacking among the findings of the different studies concerning the relationship between achievement and student involvement in planning and operating the learning activity. The findings, however, are weighted in favor of learner participation in goal-setting and learning activities. The findings concerning satisfaction are more consistent. Each of the studies that examined satisfaction as a dependent variable reported a positive relationship between participation (involvement) and satisfaction.

The principle of learner participation in planning and operating the learning program has a rich philosophical history. Many of the prominent contemporary leaders in adult education have praised the practice. Knox (1977a), for example, has asserted that up to one fourth of the available time can be devoted to the process of diagnosis, needs appraisal, and objective setting; if the process is well done, the learning achievement can be greater than if the entire time were devoted to learning activities. The specification "if the process is well done" is a criterion that may not be easily met (nor even readily agreed upon).

The visibility of the principle as a characteristic of the adult education process requires that the question be submitted to further examination. It is also recommended that other investigators devote more time and effort to specification of learner participation with operational criteria that allow for appropriate replication.

Structure

The role of the learner in planning and conducting the learning program is closely related to another issue in adult learning-teaching activities: level of program structure.

How much structure is desirable in educational activities for adults? Or, under what kind of learning activities—structured or nonstructured—do adults perform best? Or, what is meant by structured and nonstructured learning activities? Even though there is some discussion in the literature of adult education concerning the role of, and preference for, unstructured activities, the concept has not been clearly developed. Following Bergevin, McKinley, and Smith (1964), it is suggested that all learning activities are structured. They derive their structure from a number of sources—institution, instructor, and other interpersonal and intrapersonal processes. It appears that references to nonstructured programs concern those learning activities that reflect limited advance planning, unclear roles, ambiguous goals, unspecified tasks, undefined resources, and great flexibility. In contrast, structured programs are perceived to be those that reflect advance planning, clear specification of instructor and learner roles, established learning goals, a specified body of content, a specific sequence and pace of activities, clear task responsibilities, resources, techniques, procedures, and evaluation procedures and that are reasonably committed to the conceived teaching-learning plan.

It is possible that some programs will reflect varying degrees of "structure" on each of the above elements. Perhaps there are few instances outside academic-courses-for-credit learning experiences in which all the elements identified in the high-structure mode are present.

Research

The research literature concerning the general topic of structured vs. nonstructured educational activities for adults is not overly abundant. There are, however, some general outlines emerging from the available findings.

Two recent studies of the relationship between achievement and level of structure in educational programs (Davison 1972; McGrane 1979) reveal no significant correlation. On the other hand, Taylor's 1970 study using air force trainees reports differential performance in structured learning activities according to aptitude:

1. High-ability trainees performed better in unstructured training programs.
2. Middle-ability trainees performed well when permitted to work at their own speed.
3. Low-ability trainees required a completely structured program with small step sequences.

One study (Wientge, Dubois, and Gaffney 1970) has been identified that compared the achievement of learners in a conventional college class with that of students in a more permissively organized course. Learners in the experimental course had greater freedom of participation and class attendance. The report noted that achievement was positively associated with the permissive conditions.

Lyne (1981) concluded that adults at lower stages of cognitive development prefer highly structured directions for course assignments and activities. Individuals at higher stages of cognitive development prefer more flexibility and diversity. Lyne and also Roelfs (1975) report that preference for structure is associated with age: older subjects tend to prefer more structure in learning activities.

The few studies available concerning relationships between level of structure in learning and such selected variables as ability, achievement, and age provide stimulating but inconclusive results. Because of the popularity of such educational techniques as discussion and discovery learning procedures in adult education, additional research concerning concepts, definitions, perceptions, and philosophy of structure in learning activities deserves—yes, requires—more careful systematic attention. One of the first steps that should be taken to improve understanding in this area is to improve the conceptualization of "structure." Then it should be possible to examine the relative relationships of different structural elements as noted at the beginning of this section.

Advance Organizers as Structural Elements

The value of learning would be substantially reduced if every new bit of information or skill was erased from memory within a short time period. Models of learning include retention as an act in the process as well as a future resource. Therefore, models of instruction seek to ensure provision of activities designed to improve retention. Advance organizers are an object of increasing research in the area of retention.

An advance organizer is a concise body of information introduced prior to study. Typically, the information that comprises the advance organizer is at a higher level of abstraction, generality, and inclusiveness than the information embodied within a text. Ausubel (1977) explains: "The principal function of the organizer is to bridge the gap between what the learner already knows and what he needs to know before he can successfully learn the task at hand" (p. 168). Further, the advance organizer is intended to provide "ideational scaffolding," which can be used to categorize, store, and recall the new information extracted from the text. Educators who wish to design their own advance organizers are encouraged first to examine some excellent examples collected by Weil and Joyce (1978).

Advance organizers are procedures that help the learner focus on specific learning objectives or content. Limited research findings (Howe 1977; Taylor 1977; Walker 1978) affirm the value of advance organizers. When provided, they appear to improve learner achievement. They are recommended by the conceptualization of learning and retention as a creative search for meaning as opposed to a reproduction of facts and events. Within this framework, it becomes important for the learner to become aware of the "new learning" and relate it to existing knowledge. This view of learning extends beyond the recall of specific isolated memory traces. Comprehension is the result of a combination of information (both newly acquired and established) to arrive at new constructions (Glynn and DiVesta 1977).

Advance organizers may be used in continuous discourse (lectures and conversations) or in written material. The majority of the work cited here concerns advance organizers in written material. Howe (1977) also reports on limited experience with continuous discourse.

Outlines of textual material constitute an advance organizer that may be presented to adult learners prior to beginning a reading assignment. The outline depicts the topics in a text, the sequence of presentation, and relationships among the topics. As a structural mirror of the organization of the text, it alerts the reader to the inherent organization of content as well as to the important topics within the material. Similar outlines also have been demonstrated to be effective in assisting the recall of information.

The value of statements of explicit learning goals presented to learners prior to initiating a learning activity has also been studied (Blaney and McKie 1969). A number of studies with young adults (for example, Glynn and Muth 1979) indicate that when instructional objectives are provided in advance of text study, information related to the objectives is recalled much better than information unrelated to the objectives, and the increment in the recall of objective-related information is secured at the expense of objective-unrelated information.

Several educators of adults recommend that elderly learners be provided with Ausubelian organizers in advance of text study. Bolton (1978) maintains that "advance organizers are especially helpful to older learners in conceptualizing the new material to be learned. . . . outlines or abstracts of the information to be learned or demonstrations of the skills to be acquired help older learners incorporate the new learning into their existing cognitive structures" (p. 331). Unfortunately, she cites no empirical evidence to support her claims.

Comparison of Selected Techniques

Perhaps the most extensive body of research concerning adult instruction is the one that includes comparisons of educational techniques. Unfortunately, it also may be the least definitive. The continuing debate concerning the relative effectiveness of discussion and lecture techniques illustrates the point. Dietrich (1966) reviewed 185 studies on this topic and Verner and Dickinson (1967) reviewed at least 132 sources to arrive at the general conclusion that each technique seems to have optimal application for specific learning-teaching objectives.

Lecture

Verner and Dickinson arrived at fourteen conclusions concerning the appropriate and inappropriate uses of the lecture technique. They noted six conditions for which the lecture is a suitable technique and eight conditions for which it is unsuitable. The six conditions that favor the use of lecture are all information or content based. For example, the lecture is suitable when information dissemination is the basic goal. Other conditions are related to the availability of the information, the desirability of organizing and presenting information in a specific way, and so forth. In contrast, the lecture is not suitable, according to Verner and Dickinson, when other educational goals are more important than acquisition of information. Two learner-centered criteria for determining the suitability of the lecture technique are also identified. It is suggested that when learner participation is crucial to achievement of the objective, the lecture is not the best technique. Furthermore, the lecture is not recommended by Verner and Dickinson when the intelligence and educational attainment level of the learners are average or below average.

It is recommended that the lecture technique also meet certain structural or organizational criteria. The eight criteria identified are keeping major points to a minimum, providing introductory and concluding summations, presenting the material in a meaningful way, selecting illustrations that are appropriate to the learners, keeping the presentation within thirty minutes, maintaining a simple language and style, relating speed of delivery to the complexity of the material and the experience of the learner, and providing some supporting instructional technique to involve the learner.

Lecture, Discussion, and Lecture-Discussion

Palmer and Verner (1959) conducted an informative comparative study of lecture, discussion, and lecture-discussion. Their study was designed to investigate possible differences in achievement and student satisfaction among the three educational techniques. Two aspects of satisfaction were examined: quality of the instruction, and morale. No difference in achievement among the three groups was noted. The lecture-discussion group, however, was significantly more satisfied with the experience. The preference for the lecture-discussion technique was explained as follows:

1. Students wanted a lecture for at least part of the class period to be certain of having covered everything important.
2. They wanted an opportunity to participate, but if they had to choose between full participation (discussion) and minimal participation (lecture), they would prefer the latter.
3. They preferred a change of pace to break the monotony of lecture or discussion only.
4. They frankly admitted that the discussion technique required too much extra work in preparation.

Other Comparisons

Numerous studies of the relative efficacy of diverse instructional techniques are available for review. Summary presentations of the variety of investigations here are not perceived to be appropriate. Generally, the researchers reporting findings and conclusions on the topic are concerned with at least three of the following four major questions:

1. Did the students learn?
2. Comparatively, how well did they learn?
3. Comparatively, how well did the experience satisfy the learners?
4. Which techniques were most effective in attitude changes?

Most studies report that some learning occurred under each of the experimental conditions investigated. The studies include a variety of techniques such as computer-assisted instruction, correspondence, discussion, field-based instruction, individualized techniques, lecture, modular instruction, readings, and simulation (with and without discussion). Generally, the studies tend to indicate a preference for some kind of discussion technique. Discussion independent of some organizing or structuring technique, however, does not seem to be preferred. Barnett (1973) reports "discussion only" to be the least preferred of three techniques for knowledge gain, but structured presentations with group discussion were ranked first on behavioral change. Villaniel (1979) also reports that achievement and retention were higher with the modular instruction technique than with discussion. Strayer (1979) ranked simulation with discussion and required reading groups as the two lowest among five different techniques used in her study on tests of achievement; learners in the two groups taught by simulation with discussion and by lecture techniques reported more favorable attitudes.

These findings, along with Butler's 1965 study cited earlier, strongly suggest that adults prefer some interactive learning activity to a lengthy lecture. Furthermore, the findings appear to imply that the learner desires some kind of guidance or control of the activity to keep discussion focused.

Scanland (1970) reported that attitudes were changed significantly in a computer-assisted instruction group, whereas they were not changed in a lecture/discussion group. The efficacy of computer-assisted instruction compared with discussion in accomplishing attitude change is at variance with the long history of the association between discussion and attitude change. A number of earlier studies have demonstrated the relative efficacy of discussion in contributing to attitude change. The lecture and discussion methods were found to be approximately the same in effecting attitude changes by Guetzkow, Kelly, and McKeachie (1954) as well as Johnson and Smith (1953). However, other studies on attitude change indicate that the discussion method is more effective. It has been suggested by Maier (1953) that peer group pressures exert greater attitudinal influences than those which arise in situations dominated by the traditional instructor. This position has been confirmed by classroom experiments conducted by Ruja (1954). In addition, Preston and Heintz (1956) as well as Hare (1952) have demonstrated that participatory leadership is more effective than supervisory leadership as a method of producing changes in attitude in small groups.

The literature indicates that the most important contributions favoring the greater effectiveness of the discussion method as a means of changing attitudes have resulted from the work of Lewin and his associates. These investigations demonstrate that in the majority of situations the group-decision technique was more effective than the lecture technique in changing behavior patterns.

One of the classical experiments in the field was performed by Lewin when he compared the relative effectiveness of discussion groups and formal lectures in influencing a group of women to alter an attitude that they had toward certain foods (Lewin 1943). His findings indicated that the discussion method was a more effective tool than the lecture method in changing this attitude.

Scanland's research should be replicated, and if consistent findings are generated, then additional investigation into explanations is required. Lewin's basic work noted earlier, and the social-psychological literature generally, supports the notion of peer influence as a strong variable in attitude and behavior change. What variables can be identified to explain the greater impact of computer-assisted instruction on attitude change?

Comments

Without question, the mixed bag of findings outlined above does not easily simplify the search for a solution to questions about preferred instructional techniques. For at least a century, the literature of education has included studies comparing the efficiency and effectiveness of instructional techniques. Over the same period, there have been conflicting findings that suggest that research questions have sometimes been inadequately phrased. Too often researchers have been concerned with comparing techniques without first considering the purpose of the instruction. The importance of that point is revealed in the preceding report of recent comparative research. Some of the findings reported by Verner, Palmer, and Dickinson concerning lecture and discussion have been in the literature for at least thirty years. By now, it should be obvious that some techniques are more effective with some people for some purposes than others. However, many educational activities have multiple objectives; for example, knowledge gain, improving skill, changing attitudes, and satisfaction with the learning experience. Furthermore, many educational activities include a large variety of learners with differing goals, intelligence, prior specific knowledge, cognitive styles, learning styles, and personalities.

Palmer and Verner (1959) addressed the issue in one way when they discussed their findings. Based on the research concerning the lecture-discussion issue, it should be remembered that in comparing the lecture with other educational techniques, the majority of the studies have shown that the lecture is equal to or better than other techniques in terms of immediate recall; however, when measuring delayed recall, other techniques prove to be superior to the lecture in most cases. It is clear, then, that the purpose of the educational activity should exercise some influence on the selection of the technique to be used. Palmer and Verner suggest that in most adult education activities immediate recall is of less importance than sustained learning; therefore, the use of the lecture is less desirable. In those cases where passing an examination is the immediate objective (for example, content review courses), the use of the lecture is indicated because of its superiority in immediate recall.

Spence (1928) has stated that the question of comparative efficacy among techniques is of less importance than determining the situations under which a particular technique is the more efficient. Others have suggested that superiority in learning associated with one technique over another is more a factor of the relationship of the learner to the technique than a factor inherent in the technique itself—a point which has some current support in the research into cognitive/learning styles.

It is obviously not a simple matter to select the appropriate technique. The educator of adults should consider more than the efficacy of the technique itself or the nature of the subject matter. As he or she seeks to establish a functional relationship for learning between the student and the content, the educator of adults needs to have a perception of the nature and previous educational experiences of the learner so that the choice of technique will be acceptable to that learner and develop his or her security in the learning process. Furthermore, according to Palmer and Verner, the technique should not make greater demands upon the learner's time and interest than he or she is willing to meet, and it must be continuously challenging.

Educational Technologies

Recent developments in telecommunications and rising costs associated with transportation are exerting increasing pressure upon planners of adult educational activities to discover new ways of programming. The development is even more challenging because the status of research concerning traditional programming remains limited. Educators of adults, however, are aware of some of the implications of new technology for the field. Research on a variety of problems is thus beginning to accumulate.

There are six major educational telecommunications methodologies currently available to educators (Curtis 1979):

1. Public Broadcasting (radio and TV)
2. Instructional Television Fixed Service (ITFS)
3. Teleconferencing-Telewriting (via standard telephone circuits)
4. FM-Broadcasting Station Multiplexing
5. Community Antenna Television (CATV)
6. Satellite Circuitry

Most of these six methodologies were initiated to meet differing student body needs and delivery requirements. Each is therefore likely to have its own group of proponents. These methodologies have yet to be integrated into a coherent, coordinated educational delivery system, even on a local operating level, let alone on a statewide, regional, or national level.

In addition to the telecommunications revolution, which has tremendous implications for the delivery of instructional services to adult learners, a number of related technological advances have been noted in associated electronic and other media. These include the video disc, the universality of cassette tape recorders and players, videotaping capability at nominal expense, home computers, and advances in programmed instruction (including computer-assisted instruction).

One of the basic concerns, according to the nature of the research questions examined, is the relative effectiveness of technology as a "method" of extending institutional outreach. Some of the research in this area is not unlike that which is concerned with educational techniques. It is comparative. The comparisons are often between a traditional method or format such as a campus class and a class at an off-campus site using telecommunications or other technological advances such as computer applications to instruction.

As noted in the discussion of research findings concerning specific techniques, there are also some general trends in the results of investigations of technological applications. For example, seven studies identified on this topic all report either no difference in achievement or attitude changes when technology is the independent variable, or greater achievement and attitude change. No study reviewed reported results that favored face-to-face techniques over televised instruction, or traditional teacher-based instruction over computer-assisted instruction.

Computer-Assisted Instruction (CAI)

Simutis (1979) studied military instruction in language arts and math using two modes of instruction: traditional and traditional plus computer-assisted instruction (CAI). Scanland (1970) composed three groups: those who received instruction using CAI, those taught by lecture-discussion, and those receiving no instruction.

Both researchers report findings favorable to the use of CAI. Simutis reported greater achievement when traditional instruction was supplemented by CAI, and Scanland found significant changes in attitude among those taught with CAI. Sherman and Glore (1970) examined a different problem with their research, and reported findings that should be encouraging to teachers. They were concerned about attitudes toward CAI and indicated that students familiar with CAI hold more positive attitudes toward the use of computers in instruction. However, both those experienced with CAI and novices expressed a need for a teacher.

The few studies available on the effectiveness of CAI in the education of adults have thus generated results that tend to be in agreement with Bligh's 1977 observations. He describes CAI as a "disappointment." The absence of firm evaluative data on the effectiveness of CAI in the education of adults continues to contribute to questions concerning CAI's potential and relevance. Disappointment with CAI is not because it has been demonstrated, in some instances, to be equal to performance using traditional teaching procedures, but because it has not demonstrated how the instructor's role can be extended so as to accomplish improved learning on the part of the learner.

Television

After some thirty years with television as a common cultural element, issues concerning its role and function in education remain. Research questions in recent investigations seemingly have been posed so as to demonstrate that television is as good as traditional methods and techniques. Negative criticism concerning the use of television centers on the passivity normally associated with its use. Bligh (1977) informs us of findings that indicate that television is not noted for stimulating thought. The device has been identified with "teletyposis" which is associated with the absorption of information at a superficial level with little understanding of the more significant aspects of that information.

The task of proving that television can be more effective than traditional teaching methods and techniques has not been successfully accomplished. Of 202 studies of televised instructors at the college level, 152 report no significant difference in effectiveness compared with traditional methods. Traditional instruction was superior in twenty-eight cases and less effective in twenty-two (Chu and Schramm 1967). Educational television has been most successful when the televised instructor has been complemented by techniques that emphasize the social aspect of the learning activity (Bligh 1977).

Buckley (1962) concluded that television can be used as effectively as face-to-face instruction for teaching reading to adults. Conlin et al. (1973) found that there was no difference in achievement between students taught by telelecture and others taught by regular lecture. Neidt and Baldwin (1970) also reported that the achievement of graduate engineering students taught by the use of videotaped instruction was no different from the achievement of a traditional on-campus group.

Brown et al. (1973) concluded that adult learners reacted positively to mediated instructional programs but that both subject matter and personal characteristics influenced achievement and acceptance. These investigations recommend that program planners consider the subject matter and the interests and backgrounds of the target population.

In the absence of proof that television can be more effective in instruction than traditional approaches, other justifications for its use must be provided. These justifications may include economic and political reasons. Some of these reasons may not necessarily require evidence that television is better; it is sufficient to note that television is equal to other methods that may be more expensive, more restricted in outreach and so forth. These issues have philosophical dimensions that also must be addressed by educators of adults.

The research available for review here seems to emphasize that while televised instruction is not better, there is no difference in outcomes.

Programmed Instruction (PI)

Programmed instruction is included in the discussion of educational technology rather than in the section on instructional techniques because the broader definition of technology includes "software" concepts. Research concerning programmed instruction (PI) is not unlike that found in other areas of instructional investigations. Early on, attention was focused on comparative studies designed to identify relative differences, if any, in different approaches to PI and between PI and conventional instruction. Hartley and Davies (1977) pooled the results of some 110 studies to see if any generalizations could be noted. They found the PI group significantly superior in 41 cases, not significantly superior in 54, and significantly worse in 15.

These findings require little comment. It is obvious that programmed instruction can be as effective as conventional instruction in many cases. But perhaps of equal or greater interest are the studies that compare a program plus an instructor with an instructor alone or a program alone. Of twelve studies identified and reported by Hartley and Davies, eleven are cited as evidence that an instructor plus a program is the best system.

Results of studies of PI for adults of all ages suggest that there is no simple method of programmed instruction that is universally appropriate for everyone doing a given task. Two tentative conclusions indicated by the literature, however, are that older learners probably prefer to work with programs longer than do younger ones, and that the more activity included in the program, the better.

The absence of useful conclusive findings in the comparative studies of programmed instruction is not new. Twenty years ago, Krumboltz (1963) labeled such efforts as futile, giving five reasons:

1. Classroom teachers vary so widely in "conventional" instruction that no basis for comparison exists.
2. Programs themselves vary so widely in their scope and quality of writing.
3. The criterion test may have been designed to measure only a limited objective.
4. Results will not lead to abandonment of either teachers or programmed instruction.
5. There is an absence of useful information as to how either programmed instruction or conventional instruction can be improved.

Lumsden (1975), based on his perception of the futility of comparative studies of programmed instruction and conventional instruction, directed his attention to an analysis of selected programs. He points out that few of the materials for programmed instruction available in the early 1970s had been properly validated before they were marketed. Accordingly, he reports three validation studies that examined the effectiveness of the instructional programs. Following McGuigan and Peters (1965), he reports a G ratio for each experiment. G equals actual achievement (posttest minus pretest) divided by possible achievement (maximum possible score minus pretest score). In addition to obtaining a G ratio for each program, he also devised procedures for testing the significance of other variables, such as verbal reinforcement and audiovisually presented redundant information. The results of the experiments indicated that each program was validated as effective (a G ratio of .50 or better). One program was revised to obtain the minimum level. The other experimental questions were also answered in the affirmative.

OBSERVATIONS

Research designed to demonstrate the efficacy of selected teaching techniques has generally indicated that the identified teaching variables make little difference (Gage 1977). Preinstructional variables such as intelligence, pretested achievement, and social class background have accounted for more of the variance in learner achievement than has the instructional variable. The findings, which are more disappointing to some than others, are associated with a number of factors. First, "teaching" at the time of observations constitutes such a small slice of time and effort in the total learning of the adult that any difference is likely to be influenced and reduced by the cumulative effect of other variables. Second, the complexity of the teaching-learning transaction is such that many variables are potentially important; many of these may be unintentionally neglected. Inclusion of a large number of variables increases the size of the sample required for testing. Thus, many studies of the effectiveness of selected teaching techniques are compromised at the very beginning through uncontrolled variables and small samples.

Lumsden (1975) comments on this point by observing that research in teaching methods should have made one thing perfectly clear: There is no single technique or format best suited to the needs of all students. Some variables that have been shown to discriminate between students exposed to different instructional methods include intellectual ability (Eigen 1962), degree of anxiety (Cronback 1967), underachievement-overachievement (Strolurow 1966), and ascendency (Snow, Tiflin, and Seibert 1969).

A further criticism of research concerning teaching techniques and methods in the education of adults is associated with the general research paradigm in use. The general research paradigm for studying the efficacy of instructional techniques is the process-product paradigm (Gage 1977). According to this framework, investigators search for processes, instructor characteristics, and behaviors in the form of teaching styles, techniques, models, or strategies that predict and possibly cause "products" such as student achievement and attitudes.

The process-product paradigm appeals directly and naturally to the predilection of educators at all levels. It is an almost automatic response to desire to improve education through improving the teachers and other educational functionaries who come into contact with learners, directly or indirectly. Even though the paradigm has enlisted the allegiance of most investigators of teaching over the past several decades, it is not without its flaws as currently conceived (Doyle 1978). Two areas often overlooked by the process-product paradigm include mediating processes and classroom ecology.

The traditional paradigm and its revision to accommodate the inclusion of mediating variables and classroom ecology variables are illustrated in Figure 11.1.

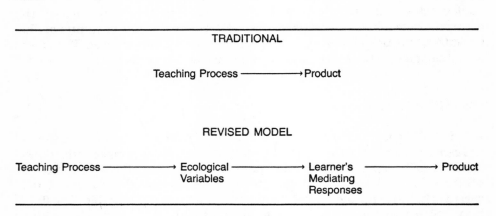

TRADITIONAL

Teaching Process ⟶ Product

REVISED MODEL

Teaching Process ⟶ Ecological ⟶ Learner's ⟶ Product
                    Variables   Mediating
                                     Responses

Figure 11.1   A comparison of the traditional process-product research paradigm and a revised model based on Gage (1977) and Doyle (1978)

Adoption of the revised process-product paradigm would generate additional research that focuses more directly on learner behavior. Investigators of educational processes in the education of adults may learn from the researchers in programmed instruction, who for years focused on the device and techniques with limited results only to turn more recently to studying the learner. There are, of course, some examples of this kind of focus in adult education research. Tough (1966) and those who follow his model have produced volumes of findings concerning the individual's behavior in self-directed learning. However, more work along the lines of that reported by Taylor (1977) and Howe (1977) is recommended.

Most studies concerned with the efficacy of different instructional techniques and methods are overly simple. Multivariate analysis is required to identify the possible influence of several variables. Howe (1977) shares the results of an investigation designed to determine differences among six learning conditions. He reports that in all conditions subjects were exposed to identical information for an identical total amount of time. Yet retention scores differed by as much as two to one.

Even though educators of adults have demonstrated a continuing interest in the social dimensions of the learning activity, much research continues to ignore the influence of both physical and social variables on individual learners. Bligh (1977) suggests that innovations in techniques and methods should be concerned with the relation of students to other people and their adjustment rather than their relation to the academic subject matter. This area of research is challenged by the findings of Saddam (1977) concerning the efficacy of CAI in changing attitudes.

Research concerning cognitive/learning styles requires clarification of terminology. Are the constructs the same, as represented by some authors? Or are they sufficiently different to require different labels—*learning style* and *cognitive style*? Greater precision in use of the two terms, if they in reality represent different constructs, is required.

Additional research effort is also required to more adequately explicate the relationship between cognitive/learning style and achievement, changes in style, causes or origins of style, universality, and so forth.

Some problems for future consideration are also presented by the findings concerning the usefulness of advance organizers, learner involvement in planning and operating the learning program, and preferences for flexibility and permissiveness in learning activities. The challenge for the instructor is to plan for the use of advance organizers in a flexible and permissive learning environment.

Overall, the topics and related research reviewed in this chapter illustrate the need for continuing research and study of teaching in adult programs. Satisfaction is an important consideration in voluntary learning, and the small research base cited here indicates that participation in planning and operating a flexible, permissive, socially reinforcing learning activity contributes to satisfaction. Achievement is also important and may in some instances be the main basis of satisfaction, yet the research on the relative efficacy of different techniques, level of learner involvement in planning, degree of structure, and other variables is not clear.

Concern for the impact of the physical environmental conditions on the social environment and ultimately upon learning has not been adequately manifested in adult education research. Actually, too many of the studies reported in this section suffer from problems associated with small samples and inadequate specification of variables such as "structure." They are helpful, nevertheless, in pointing to areas for future research activities and thereby provide a useful point of departure for improved research design.

VI · The Field of Adult Education

12 · A Field of Study and Practice

THE EDUCATION OF ADULTS has proceeded through informal, nonformal, and, in some cases, formal means in America from early colonial days. Yet, it is only within this century, slightly more than fifty years ago, that it came to be considered as a field of study and of practice. Knowles and DuBois (1970) confirm the recency of adult education's status as a field of practice through their observations in the 1970 *Handbook of Adult Education,* concerning the content of the 1934 handbook. They note that the publication content of the first handbook reflected three concerns: (1) the need for a better public understanding of adult education as a field of practice, (2) the elimination of profitmakers, and (3) the relative emphasis to be placed on the vocational compared with the cultural or avocational content.

There is little or no reason to seriously question the proposition that adult education as a field of practice is much older than adult education as a field of study. Evidence is readily available and reasonably abundant to support the conjecture that adults were actively involved in deliberate educational activities years before a concern for adult education as a discipline emerged. After decades of experience with adult learners, however, the literature indicates teachers of adults began to inquire into ways and means of better managing the teaching-learning transaction. In the formative period of adult education as a field of practice, standards of individual performance were based upon beliefs, philosophy, and techniques learned through observation, on-the-job training, or loosely constructed communication networks. The establishment of the first American graduate program in adult education, at Teachers College, Columbia University, in the 1930s marked the formal beginning of interest in adult education as a field of study. The creation of this program gave some legitimacy to the notion that the field contained specific roles for which preentry, in-service, and postentry training was required. Such a notion has been rapidly gaining acceptance (Dickinson 1979). Acceptance of adult education as a field of study seems to have been facilitated by several factors, including the rapid expansion of the need for qualified practitioners beginning about 1965, the subsequent development of a number of additional graduate programs, and the accumulation and integration of tested knowledge. The combination of the above elements provided a foundation on which a discipline of adult education could be developed.

The rapid expansion of graduate programs in adult education in the sixties and seventies, however, did not completely remove the designation of the field as a "social movement." Some educators of adults resist and resent the suggestion that the field has become, can become, or will become a professional one. This point is well illustrated in Chapter 13. Educators opposed to a professional orientation prefer a social movement orientation. A social movement has been defined as a loosely organized or heterogeneous group of people tending toward or favoring a generalized common goal. In adult education, that common goal has been a sense of social purpose: to save souls, to free the oppressed, to feed the hungry, to school the illiterate, to clothe the naked, to equalize the distribution of wealth, and to change the social order, to cite a few examples.

Proponents of the social movement orientation are not completely opposed to the development of a body of knowledge that informs practice (Campbell 1977). Though reluctant to admit it, this group seems to be aware that without some proficiency based on selected principles of adult education, the desired social purposes are less likely to be achieved. Consequently, even though social movement oriented educators and professionally oriented educators occupy opposing ends of a philosophical continuum, both groups appear to agree on the importance of the development of a body of knowledge that is specific to the issues and challenges of educating the adult.

The various handbooks of adult education issued since 1934 serve to document the development of adult education as a field of study and practice. Their content reflects the changing concerns and emphases in the different periods. The issues and questions that have confronted educators of adults across the past fifty years have not become simpler; neither have all the early questions and concerns been fully addressed. Furthermore, some of the issues such as conceptualization of the field require continuing review and revision. A dynamic society demands a dynamic conceptualization of adult education as a field of study and practice.

Science provides some instructions that would inform the field if they are properly regarded. The strength and fragility of the scientific method reside in an openness to disproof and approximations of truth that permit the orderly construction and testing of hypotheses and paradigms that in turn yield new and improved ones. The maturity of a discipline may be measured in terms of the nature of its paradigms; hence a discipline with countless incomplete paradigms that are not popularly subscribed to by the scholars and practitioners in the field may be described as immature. This condition adequately describes adult education as a field of study: it is characterized by few widely accepted useful paradigms.

Gradually, and sometimes painfully, paradigms on which to base the further study and practice of adult education are emerging. This is not inconsistent with Verner's 1978 suggestion that the development of an academic discipline depends upon the slow and uncomfortable process of analyzing and integrating previously obtained knowledge into a higher-order structure. Verner believed that adult education, in 1970, still needed to more fully investigate additional aspects of adult learning and instruction before adult education could rightfully be identified as a discipline.

Some of the basic structural elements critical to the development of adult education as a field of study include a new look at the historical foundations of the field, agreement concerning concepts and terminology, establishment of appropriate parameters of the field, clarity of functions of adult education, and professionalization of the field based on a useful distinctive body of knowledge that contributes to specialized techniques of practice requiring appropriate preentry professional graduate programs. Each of these topics as revealed in the discursive, hortatory, and research literature is discussed in detail in the following pages.

HISTORICAL FOUNDATIONS

Compared with the British condition, the historical dimensions of adult education in the United States are impoverished. Authors in Great Britain have provided relatively extensive and intensive historical treatment of adult education in their nation. The situation in the United States is gradually improving, but the historical foundations as developed and reported are unusually weak. The "reported historical foundation" is perceived to be rather different from the real, and yet *unreported*, historical foundation.

Improved understanding of the historical experience of adult education in the different nations of the world should lead to an improved practice in those countries while also increasing the possibility for improvement at the international level. Unfortunately, North American adult educators have been slow to show a deep concern for the genesis of the field and the lessons that might be learned from history.

The American emphasis, or lack thereof, on historical foundations of adult education is adequately illustrated by the fact that the field has only one extensive historical work that attempts to recount the origins and practice of adult education from the colonial period to the present. Knowles's *History of the Adult Education Movement in the United States* was published in 1962 (and slightly revised in 1977). Without detracting from Knowles's important contribution, which has proved to be extremely durable, it should be noted that almost 200 of the 345 pages are devoted to the history of adult education from the perspective of associations of adult educators. This is useful, but it remains primarily a description of the field and does not rest heavily upon extensive or detailed historical treatment of educating adults. Indeed, Knowles is to be congratulated for successfully providing American adult educators with its best "history" over a twenty-year period.

Knowles's 1977 historical analysis resulted in some useful tentative generalizations that may have productive implications for planning in adult education:

1. Adult education institutions have typically emerged in response to specific needs, rather than as a part of a general design.
2. Developmentally, adult education is characterized by episodic growth rather than consistent growth.
3. Institutional forms for the education of adults seem to have survived to the extent that they became attached to agencies with other objectives.
4. Educational programs for adults have tended to gain stability and permanence as they have increasingly become differentiated in administration, finance, curriculum, and methodology.
5. Educational programs for adults have emerged with, and continue to occupy, a secondary status in the institutional hierarchy.
6. Institutional elements of adult education have tended to become crystallized independent of any conception of a general adult education movement.

There are, of course, a number of lesser published historical works that include Anania's exceptional 1969 dissertation, Seybolt's (1969) several works on apprenticeship, and my own cluster of investigations of adult education in colonial America. These works, independently and collectively, serve well to identify some general characteristics that are helpful in understanding adult education in the United States. Historically, adult education in the United States has reflected four important characteristics, being frequently voluntary, pluralistic, pragmatic, and dynamic (Long 1980a).

Anania's basic work concerning the concept of adult age is extremely useful and is helpful to scholars and others who seek to understand educational activities for adults in an earlier period of history. Seybolt and I provide informative discussions that help to explain the gradual institutionalization of adult education in America. This work also contains ample illustration of the importance of voluntary adult participation in the pluralistic provisions for adult education in a continually changing social setting. These works collectively provide a small but sound foundation for the investigation of emerging institutions and developing tasks in adult education across more than two hundred years of American history.

CONCEPTS, DEFINITIONS, AND TERMINOLOGY

The field of adult education contains diverse literature written by practitioners and scholars from a variety of discipline backgrounds from anthropology to zoology. Under such conditions it is not surprising that the jargon of the field is somewhat confusing; at best, communication is sometimes tentative because of the lack of clear agreement on terms used to refer to important concepts and activities. The problem is conspicuously illustrated by the difficulty with such terms as *adult education, continuing education, education permanente, life-*

long education, lifelong learning, and *recurrent education,* to name just a few, each of which is used in literature of interest to the educator of adults. The terms are used interchangeably by some, while others insist that each term has a unique meaning.

Adult Education

Brunner and his colleagues (1959) devoted little space to defining the field of adult education. They briefly commented on the youthfulness of adult education as a profession and discipline with little elaboration on the topic based on the research literature.

Coles (1978) indicates that there have been several efforts in recent years to provide a comprehensive definition of adult education to break down barriers that once existed between "adult," "further," "vocational," and "technical" education. He suggests that the move was prompted by an increasing awareness of adult education in totality. Thus, Liveright and Haygood (1969) suggested that adult education is the process whereby persons who no longer attend school on a regular full-time basis participate in sequential and organized activities with a conscious intention of bringing about changes in information, knowledge, understanding or skills, appreciation and attitudes; or for the purpose of identifying and solving personal or community problems.

Bertelsen (Coles 1978) provides a more general and less restrictive definition that takes informal education into account. He defines adult education, simply, as any learning experience designed for adults, irrespective of content, level, and methods used.

Coombs (1973) has offered one of the more useful discussions of informal, formal, and nonformal education. He says that *informal education* refers to the truly lifelong process whereby all people acquire attitudes, values, skills, and knowledge from experience and the educative influences and resources in their environment. Generally, informal education is characterized as being relatively unorganized and unsystematic. *Formal education* defines the hierarchically structured chronologically graded system of schooling running from the primary grades through the university and including, in addition to general academic studies, a variety of specialized programs and institutions and technical and professional training. *Nonformal education* refers to any organized educational activity outside the established formal system that is designed to serve identifiable learning clienteles and learning objectives.

McClusky (1974) has also commented upon the shades of difference among the kinds of concepts identified by some of the labels used in the literature of adult education. According to him, it is well to remember that the term *education permanente* refers to a concept of lifelong learning with a deliberately built-in cradle-to-grave design for interrelating the successive developmental stages of education into an integrated programmatic whole. The idea is supposed to be accomplished by a kind of "spiral curriculum," i.e., by recycling and articulating substantive material at ever-increasing levels of complexity and relevance. More familiar in Europe than in the United States, this concept forms a more inclusive background for the terms he next attempts to describe. "Continuing education" may be lifelong in character but in practice deals with intermediate and later years of learning, especially the continuation of learning once begun. By implication it does not necessarily differ in style, content, and purpose from stage to stage and does not stress the articulation of successive stages of learning as does the idea of *education permanente*. "Adult education," while yet a comprehensive domain, is more age restricted. It refers to that portion of *education permanente* and continuing and lifelong education where the adult is a client for whom educational programs deliberately oriented to the adultness of life are especially arranged.

A variety of other sources, including federal legislation, have contributed different definitions to the lexicon of adult education. One of the more frequently occurring problems posed by the various definitions concerns two views (Broschart 1977, p. 11):

> Internationally, the ISCED [International Standard Classification of Education], statement on adult education is predictably derivative from its . . . usage of the term "education." An external providing system is implied: "*Adult education* is synonymous with 'out-of-school education' and means organized programs of education provided for the benefit of and adapted to the needs of persons not in the regular school and university system and generally fifteen or over."

DeCrow (1975), in addressing the conventional definition of adult education as it is used in the United States, concurs in stipulating an organization external to the learner.

The UNESCO *Recommendation on the Development of Adult Education* (1976) contains one of the latest efforts to define adult education as an activity and field of practice (p. 2):

> —the term "adult education" denotes the entire body of organized educational processes, whatever the content, level and method, whether formal or otherwise, whether they prolong or replace initial education in schools, colleges and universities as well as in apprenticeship, whereby persons regarded as adult by the society to which they belong develop their abilities, enrich their knowledge, improve their technical or professional qualifications or turn them in a new direction and bring about changes in their attitudes or behaviour in the twofold perspective of full personal development and participation in balanced and independent social, economic and cultural development;

> adult education, however, must not be considered as an entity in itself, it is a sub-division, and an integral part of, a global scheme for life-long education and learning;

> the term "life-long education and learning," for its part, denotes an overall scheme aimed both at restructuring the existing education system and at developing the entire educational potential outside the education system;

> in such a scheme men and women are the agents of their own education, through continual interaction between their thoughts and actions;

> education and learning, far from being limited to the period of attendance at school, should extend throughout life, include all skills and branches of knowledge, use all possible means, and give the opportunity to all people for full development of the personality;

> the educational and learning processes in which children, young people and adults of all ages are involved in the course of their lives, in whatever form, should be considered as a whole.

The previous discussion does no more than lightly touch the many efforts that are reported in the literature to bring conceptual clarity to conversations on the topic of adult education. My personal preference is to use *adult education* as general lexicon that includes those informal, formal, and nonformal educational activities conducted at different grade, content, and purpose levels. The latter activities may be considered to be "continuing," "vocational," "basic," and so forth according to their content, design, and purpose. *Lifelong education, recurrent education,* and *education permanente* are terms that include adult and childhood education.

Perhaps Figure 12.1 will serve to adequately reflect the relationship of adult education and other educational concepts that include adult learners. The figure is also designed to display the association between planned and unplanned educative experiences.

Other Terms

Lack of agreement on definitions is not limited to the term *adult education*. A number of terms in use by educators of adults almost defy consensus. Three words that illustrate the challenge of communication on agreed-upon constructs are discussed in the following paragraphs. They are *adult, program,* and *process*.

Adult

Professionals and volunteers who are confused by the public conversation concerning the definition of adult education will not find the discussion of who is an adult much more helpful. Anania's 1969 work indicates that the concept of adultness has varied across centuries and probably across cultures. A number of definitions, too tedious to replicate here, appear in the literature. Critical features of the definition and concept of adult as applied to the context of adult education include (1) age as a legal requirement for civil and legal designation as an adult and age as it relates to the compulsory schooling laws of a government, (2) student status as it applies to full-time or part-time educational activity, and (3) major life role, which distinguishes between individuals whose primary role is that of student in contrast with worker, parent, and so forth.

Verner (1964) defined an adult as an individual who has come into that stage of life in which he or she has assumed responsibility for himself or herself and usually for others, and who has concomitantly accepted a functionally productive role in the community. In contrast, I have defined (Long 1967) an adult as anyone who is over eighteen years of age and not attending secondary school, or anyone who has assumed adult-like responsibilities such as marriage and parenthood. Compare these definitions with one that simply says that for purposes of adult education an adult is anyone who is beyond the compulsory school age and who is not currently enrolled in completing the normal public school curriculum. The latter two definitions evade many of the philosophical and value-laden decisions that must be made in an effort to apply Verner's definition. For some purposes, Verner's definition may be more useful, but in operationalizing data collection procedures that are important to defining the clientele for adult education, the latter two definitions seem to be more productive.

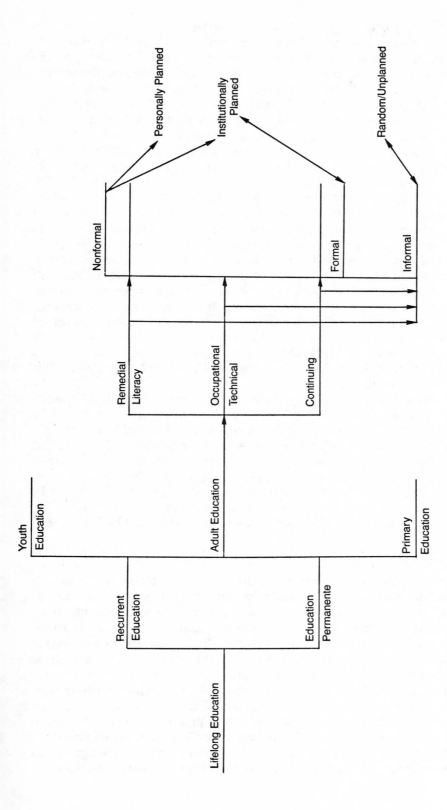

Figure 12.1 Schematic representation of the relationships of educational concepts addressed to the adult phase of life

Program

The concept of program is basic to much of the field of adult education; technically, it is comparable to the term *curriculum* as used in ordinary educational language. Verner, however, says that in adult education the term is applied to three levels of activity, only one of which parallels the term *curriculum*. First, *program* is used to include all the adult educational opportunities that exist in a community. Second, *program* may refer to the variety and extent of educational activities for adults conducted by a single institution (actually this use denotes the various individual programs provided). Third, the term is a label for the design of an educational activity that may consist of a single meeting or a series of sessions.

Schwertz (1972) conducted a philosophical conceptual analysis of the word *program* as employed in adult education discourse and discovered that the term is used in five ways: (1) in the sense of a system (organization), (2) as a verb in the sense of the process of planning, (3) in the sense of a plan, (4) in the sense of a document, and (5) in the sense of a performance or activity. Accordingly, one may be involved in a program to program a program that will lead to a program that describes a program. The consequent possibility of lack of clarity in discussing *program* as used in adult education, however, does not appear to be as severe as indicated above. The first use of the term as identified by Schwertz is infrequent, and when the term is used to refer to a document, it is obvious. Hence, the ambiguity concerns uses 2, 3, and 5: *program* as a verb in the sense of the process of planning, in the sense of a plan, and in the sense of a performance or activity.

The elaboration of the term *program* by Schwertz and Verner indicates a multidimensional concept. Verner's observations address the fifth use of the term identified by Schwertz. Hence, Verner's proposed solution of defining a program as a series of learning experiences designed to achieve, in a specified period of time, certain specific instructional objectives for an adult or a group of adults addresses only one dimension of the concept—the activity or performance dimension. Clarity in communicating the concept as restricted by Verner can be achieved by the two-word term "program planning." This solution applies the third and fifth uses of the term as identified by Schwertz to Verner's definition.

Process

Verner's 1964 conceptualization of the manner in which a relationship is established between an educator and a learner continues to influence the discussion of basic processes in adult education. According to his scheme, there are three basic components in the relationship: organizing people for learning, helping the individuals to learn, and selecting the devices that will be used to facilitate the first two components. Verner identified the three elements as methods, techniques, and devices. Collectively they are referred to as the processes of adult education. The appropriateness of the application of the term *processes* to refer to the collective integration of the three components, however, is questionable. Verner also said that these processes describe the *instrumentalities* through which learning is facilitated. These instrumentalities are distinguished from the *procedures* that an educator employs in designing and managing a learning situation. The concept would appear to be clarified if the term *processes* included the procedures at two levels: administrative procedures used by the administrator/planner/faculty to facilitate the application of the appropriate instrumentalities (methods, techniques, and devices) for the employment of optimum instructional procedures.

Method as defined by Verner refers to the way the institution relates to the learner. The methods chosen may be either individual methods or group methods. Individual methods include correspondence, tutoring, coaching, directed individual instruction, apprenticeship, and other similar patterns of relationships. Group methods are those designed to collect people into groups for learning purposes. Group methods include class meetings, lectures, seminars, and other similar patterns of simultaneously providing instruction to more than one person in the same location.

Technique is defined by Verner as the way the learner relates to the content of the teaching/learning situation. Teaching techniques thus include such patterns of people-content (learning task) relationships as lectures, panel discussions, group discussions, and role playing.

Devices, the third of the instrumentalities through which learning is facilitated according to Verner, includes that increasingly extensive array of mechanical and electronic instruments, audiovisual aids, and materials used by adult educators to augment the processes and procedures employed. Verner says that the use of a device determines its status. For example, television is a method if it is the way the institution relates to the learner, but it is a device when used in a class to provide information.

PARAMETERS OF THE FIELD

Unlike traditional childhood and university education, which are firmly identified with specific institutions with well-defined overlapping missions, adult education occurs in diverse settings with a range of dissimilar missions. Businesses, churches, and government are all engaged in adult education. The education of adults may be the only activity common to a number of the agencies, organizations, and institutions identified in some lists of purveyors of adult education.

The diversity and scope of what is referred to as the field of adult education have challenged educators to develop useful conceptualizations that adequately and accurately communicate. Hence, the literature contains several efforts in this direction. Those selected for discussion here include schemes suggested by Knowles, Schroeder, Boyd and Apps, and Peterson.

Knowles (1964) provides a useful framework for organizing the multitude of agencies, institutions, and organizations whose business in some way involves them in adult education. He indicates that all the entities involved in the provision of education to adults fall into one of four categories:

1. Agencies that were initially concerned with education of young people but have now assumed the additional task of educating adults.
2. Agencies that were created primarily to serve adults.
3. Agencies that were created to serve the entire community.
4. Agencies that are primarily concerned with other goals but which need adult education in order to achieve them.

The range of efforts by adult educators to define and describe the field prior to 1970 is admirably presented by Schroeder (1970). Writing in the 1970 *Handbook of Adult Education,* he classified efforts to define the field according to three analytical frameworks: by classification, by structural analysis, and by operational analysis. Boyd and Apps (1980a) provide a more recent effort to explicate adult education as a field. They propose that the field be conceptualized as a cube with each plane of the cube representing one of three dimensions: (1) traditional mode (the way the learner(s) interacts with content, i.e., individually or collectively in different modalities), (2) client focus (individual, group, and communities), and (3) personal, social, and cultural systems (the significant personal, social, and cultural factors that are associated with the individual's learning behavior).

Adult educators who have searched for a defensible way to fix the boundaries for purposes of study have tended to focus on one or more identifiable factors in adult education, such as institutional bases, methodological or transactional bases, client bases, function and purpose, and content.

There is little doubt that the investigator's and the philosopher's points of departure in analyzing adult education as a field of study or as a field of practice shape their conclusions. In the following pages we shall see how Clark's and Moses' investigations resulted in two persistent conceptualizations of the field; then we shall learn how Liveright's conclusions are directly related to the institutional framework. Similarly, the contributions to *Lifelong Learning in America* (Peterson et al. 1979) provide grist for Peterson's conclusions, which are influenced by governmental trends in the support of adult education.

Description

Two descriptions of the field of adult education that have received extensive attention in the literature were provided by Clark (1958) and Moses (1971). Unfortunately the descriptions applied to the field by these two writers tend to be used in negative references to adult education as a field.

While writing about a particular kind of adult education in a specific state (adult education in the public school system of California), Clark coined a phrase that was too readily accepted by American adult educators. He described adult public school education in California as being marginal because of (1) its position in the legal structure of the educational system, lacking any independent separate status, (2) its dependence upon part-time personnel who regard it as secondary to their primary occupation, (3) its lack of any of its own separate capital facilities and its subsequent need to borrow regular elementary and secondary school facilities, and (4) its identification as the first target of attack at times of budget cuts and economy drives.

Since Clark's concept of "marginality" was reported, adult educators have been inclined to apply the term indiscriminately.[1] They have failed to understand how Clark used the term and to consider the four justifications that he used for characterizing one small part of the field. Only because adult educators are inclined to be apologetic and pessimistic about their field could this have happened.

It is obvious that at least three of the four justifications identified by Clark apply to adult education sponsored by some agencies and that only one or two may apply in others. Some agencies have their own capital facilities; they have specialized personnel and are not any more subject to budget constraints than other institutional units. Furthermore, for most adult education organizations the issue of legal status as determined by compulsory school attendance laws is a moot one. This is not to negate the influence of the four factors, as noted by Clark, on public school adult education, but to generalize these same four explanations to the entire field is inappropriate. Other factors for justifying the use of the term *marginal* in describing other segments of the field must be focused on greater precision in language that should be adopted by those who use Clark's term.

Dickerman (1964) observed that "ever since John Powell told adult educators that they were in for trouble so long as their programs are sponsored by institutions whose primary function is something else, and Burton Clark gave them a name for this disease, they have been trying to find a cure. They haven't and they aren't likely to" (p. 316). Hallenbeck (1964), however, suggests two possibilities that the more pessimistic doomsayers have tended to overlook. First, adult educators should learn to exploit the advantages of "marginality." Second, they can gain greater acceptance by explicating the roles of adult education in society and demonstrating its effectiveness.

On the face of it, Moses (1971) appears to have provided a slightly more positive appellation for the field of adult education when he referred to it as the "periphery" (in contrast to the "core") of the learning force represented by the traditional school system, including the post-secondary levels. It is, however, noteworthy that both *margin* and *periphery* are words that refer to the "outer edge" or "boundary" in spatial terms. Hence, it appears that Moses selected a word parallel to the one selected by Clark. He referred to the constituent elements in the periphery as the "new educational system" that includes manpower development activities conducted by government, proprietary schools, correspondence schools, and programs of organized instruction through educational television. The major criterion for inclusion is that the program involve participation in learning through an organized, structured learning activity.

Just as it is illuminating to consider the focus of Clark's study, it is also instructive to note that Moses' work was not specifically a study of the field of adult education. Instead, he was engaged in an analysis of education writ large for the purpose of making broad education policy recommendations. Consequently, his study of the traditional educational system, which he referred to as the core, revealed that although the core was best represented in available data, it did not seem sufficiently responsive to new demands and expectations. Hence, Moses looked to that sector that seemed to possess favorable characteristics for flexibility and responsiveness. That area he called the "periphery."

Following Dickerman's observation cited earlier, it once again appears that there is some danger that the periphery may be viewed in negative terms. In contrast, there is reason to observe that qualities such as "responsiveness" and "flexibility" may be desirable attributes. How would the field have reacted if Moses had chosen to use the terms *static* and *dynamic* rather than *core* and *periphery*?

Scope and Dimensions

Knowles and DuBois's 1970 review of the 1934 *Handbook of Adult Education* indicates that the institutional dimension of the field was described in terms of sixteen kinds of agencies, which failed to include government agencies, health and welfare agencies (except for settlement houses), proprietary schools (except for correspondence schools), and voluntary organizations (except for men's and women's clubs). The content dimension was restricted to four distinct topical areas: the arts, music, political education, and vocational education. It is apparent that both institutional and content dimensions have expanded dramatically since 1934 in most countries of the world, with perhaps adult education in the Western industrialized nations experiencing the greatest expansion along both dimensions.

Several works have been selected to illustrate the scope and dimensions of adult education as a field of study and practice. These works address certain concerns of educators of adults about the definition of the field. Among other things, they examine social and economic trends affecting adult education as well as expansion and stabilization of the field. These concerns and the works addressing them are discussed in the following pages.

Social and Economic Trends

Liveright (1968) provides one of the few studies that specifically attempt to define the parameters and trends in the field. His investigation followed a discussion with Francis Keppel, then U.S. Commissioner of Education, who encouraged the study and observed that adult education was the fastest growing and most important area in U.S. education. Liveright's research was designed to determine social and economic trends affecting adult education, the impact of those trends, activity of the federal government in adult education, non-federal agency activity, and the role of the U.S. Office of Education. The study was designed to obtain answers to the research from commissioned analyses provided by selected adult education consultants. Even though there was some variation between studies and trends reviewed, there was obvious agreement that there existed a substantial and growing need for more and better programs in each of the four areas identified in the study: (1) education for vocational, occupational, and professional competence, (2) education for personal and family competence, (3) education for civic and social competence, and (4) education for self-realization.

Liveright concluded that federal activity in adult education was too overwhelming for one research associate with only five months of working time to completely and accurately inventory. The partial data, however, revealed the involvement of at least twenty-one different federal agencies or departments in fifty-five programs. The data indicated that at least $1.5 billion was available in fiscal year 1966 for activities that reportedly reached some 27 million adults in the United States. The programs supported by federal agencies varied from citizen education about civil rights, through programs for owners of small businesses, farmers, and urban dwellers, to those for professionals and specialists; and ranged from brief in-service educational programs to extended professional graduate training.

Even with the difficulties encountered in inventorying federal programs, it was much easier than obtaining accurate information on what was going on outside the national programs. The information obtained in this research phase led to the development of a classification system that included thirteen different categories of purveyors of adult education. These partial data indicated that well over 52 million adults were then involved in educational programs outside the federal government at an annual cost of $10-20 billion.

Based on the research, Liveright shared the following observations concerning adult education in 1968:

1. Adult education is fragmented, lopsided, and lacking a sense of direction.
2. More action in terms of total involvement, experimental programs, and new directions is apparent outside the regular educational establishments than within them.
3. Traditional faculty and institutions perceive adult education as being a low-priority, somewhat peripheral educational activity with limited institutional provisions for adult and continuing education.
4. The profession of adult education as it now exists and operates is not geared to meet the needs and challenges which characterize the field today.
5. Despite the numerous problems confronting the field, the climate and the prospects for a creative explosion in the field have never been better.

Expansion and Stabilization

Publication of *Lifelong Learning in America* (Peterson et al.) in 1979 is exceptional testimony to the accuracy of Liveright's fifth observation published in 1968. Just eleven short years after Liveright presented his perceptions about the status of the field, the seven-chapter work by Peterson and associates tends to confirm his optimistic assessment of the possibility of an impending "explosion" of interest in adult and continuing education. Interestingly, even though Liveright's 1968 study made no reference to adult education in countries other than the United States, adult education experienced an unusual expansion in most nations of the world during the decade following his work.

Peterson and his colleagues provide a useful review and assessment of some of the same topics addressed by Liveright. Peterson provides a valuable and conceptually sound discussion of sources of education and learning and thereby extends a major concern of Liveright's investigation. Cross examines some of the studies of participants in adult education, Valley addresses some issues associated with local programming, Powell examines state policies, Hartle and Kutner look at federal policies, and Hirabayashi provides a useful discussion on information resources, organizations, publications, and projects. Peterson concludes the work with some observations about implications and consequences for the future. The nature of the field of adult education is also confirmed by another aspect of Peterson's book. He and his colleagues had an unusual opportunity to write about adult education at the apparent end of an extended period of growth and expansion, at least as far as governmental support is concerned. The various contributors thus had an opportunity to present trend data that Peterson could use in making informed speculations about adult education in the coming years.

Peterson's theme is conservative. He indicates that the national enthusiasm for adult education, as reflected by federal and state governmental support, may have reached a peak in the passage of the Mondale Act, also known as the Lifelong Learning Act. After more than a decade of increasing governmental budgets for expanding social programs, including education, a conservative trend appears to have culminated in the Proposition-13 kinds of legislation (designed to limit governmental taxation powers) and the election of a conservative President. Moderation in governmental support for adult education, however, does not remove or seriously mitigate the social forces that encourage its development and expansion.

PURPOSES

Just as educators of adults have been challenged by the diversity of providers of learning activities designed for adults, they have also been severely tested to develop conceptual schemata for the definition of the purposes of education of adults. A number of qualified adult educators have turned their hands to the task. Consequently, the literature reports a number of slightly differing systems of classifying the purposes and objectives of educational activities for adults. Sources cited in this chapter have revealed how institutional providers have been identified and classified, how the field has been described, and how scholars have attempted to establish the parameters of the field. Ultimately, there are those who see the purposes of adult education as a means for specifying and limiting the focus of the field for purposes of study and practice.

Table 12.1 provides a comparative representation of the purposes of adult education as noted by the authors of seven studies. The identification of the objectives of educational activities for adults listed in Table 12.1 covers a period from the mid 1930s to 1982. A review of the data in the table reveals the overlap and areas of convergence and divergence.

Some authors such as Bowen (1977) and Peterson (1979) prefer larger, more inclusive categories, while others such as Lenning (1978) and Sell (1978) opt for a longer list of objectives for purposes of greater specification. For some purposes, educators would doubtless prefer Lord's (1972) five major categories with their sub-classification provisions. For example, Lord's system lists eleven sub-categories under the major heading Problems and Issues of Society, including such diverse topics as health, education, government, and business. Six sub-categories are provided for the classification Intellectual Skills Development; they include reading, writing, language, mathematics, critical and creative thinking, and listening.

The various schemata developed and used by educators of adults reflect the diversity of perceptions of the purposes of adult educators. Once again the pluralistic characteristic of the field of adult education emerges as a significant factor with which to contend. Each of the authors cited includes objectives that could be interpreted as specifically personal or individual in nature, and each includes a social/civic purpose. Scholars examining the field in an effort to establish parameters are thus once again challenged by the basic nature of American adult education.

Table 12.1
Purposes of Adult Education—Seven Studies

Bryson 1936	Lord 1972	Bowen 1977	Lenning 1978	Sell 1978	Peterson 1979	Darkenwald and Merriam 1982
Liberal education needs	Intellectual skills development	Cognitive learning	Academic	Basic education	Individual benefits	Cultivation of intellect
Occupational education needs	Occupational improvement	Emotional and moral development	Esthetic/Cultural	Civic	Personal economic	Societal advancement
Political education needs	Personal interest	Practical competence for citizenship and economic productivity	Intellectual	Family	Personal non-economic	Personal growth and maintenance/promotion of a better society
Relational needs	Personal life problems and demands		Moral	Leisure and recreation	Societal benefits	
Remedial needs	Problems and issues of society	Practical competence for family life, consumer behavior, leisure, and health	Motivation/Aspiration	Self-development		Change in social order
			Personality	Social development		Improvement in organizational effectiveness
			Social			

A Body of Content

This section addresses the issue of how well adult education meets the first criterion of a profession suggested by the American Association of Professors of Higher Education. That criterion specified that a professional field should have an organized body of intellectual theory constantly expanded by research. In a larger sense, this criterion is also addressed by the totality of this volume. Therefore, only a highly specific dimension of the issue is examined here.

Development of a body of content appropriate to the establishment of adult education as a field of study has been a critical concern for at least thirty years. During the same period, an increasing number of educators of adults seem to have recognized the close relationship between the establishment of a unique body of knowledge and the professionalization of the field. Two writers (Vollmer and Mills 1966) outside the field of adult education have provided criteria that may be appropriate for adult educators to use as they seek to determine the status of the field as a field of study and as a professional field of practice.

Vollmer and Mills identify three basic elements in the elevation of an occupation to professional status: (1) acquisition of a specialized technique supported by a body of theory, (2) development of a career supported by an association of colleagues, and (3) establishment of community recognition of professional status.

Horton (Liveright 1964) included the following in his list of ten criteria for a profession:

1. It must demand an adequate preprofessional and cultural training.
2. It must demand the possession of a body of specialized and systematized knowledge.
3. It must have developed a scientific technique that is the result of tested experience.
4. It must have a group consciousness designed to extend scientific knowledge in technical language.

Jensen (1964) was impressed that adult education was attempting to develop the kind of body of knowledge, skills, and techniques required to meet the requirements of professional and discipline status by two procedures. First, practice was informed and knowledge generated by experience obtained in dealing with past problems of adult education practice. Second, needed knowledge was derived from relevant disciplines and reformulated for use in adult education. Jensen failed, however, to include adult education research as a useful procedure.

Observations concerning the rapid expansion of research and publications concerning the education of adults have already been made in Chapter 1. Therefore, detailed discussion of the meta-research and other research in and related to adult education is not necessary here. It can be safely observed that as a field, adult education is increasingly supported by a growing research foundation.

PROFESSIONALIZATION OF THE FIELD

Whether or not adult education is a profession is one of the recurrent questions in the literature and conversation of adult educators. The issue is also related to another frequently posed query: Is adult education a discipline? The two concerns seem to be from the same bolt of cloth and, therefore, the second question is partially addressed by efforts to respond to the first. Some of the critical elements in the professionalization of the field of adult education include (1) development of a body of content, (2) identification of specialized techniques of practice, (3) realization of appropriate graduate training programs based on the first two elements, and (4) professional socialization. Following a brief review of the general literature on professionalization in adult education, research foundations for the four elements identified above are explicated.

Brunner and his associates, writing in 1959, noted four factors that contributed to mounting interest in the qualities and training needed by those who are engaged in the education of adults as employed leaders with professional status in the field. The bulk of the fourteen pages that they devote to the related research, however, focuses more on research concerned with issues and qualities of "leadership" rather than with "professional" characteristics related to specific roles in which educators function. Role analyses of administrators, teachers, professors, program planners, conference coordinators, researchers, and so forth were not conspicuous among the research reports identified by Brunner et al.

The literature on professionalization of the field of adult education has increased sufficiently since Brunner's work to provide a basic foundation so as to encourage the development of a prolific area of study. At about the time Brunner and his colleagues were working on their manuscript, Whipple (1958) identified two prominent research needs common to educators of adults: the need to search for truth, as scientists, and the competing need to improve the practice of adult education.

The "obvious" path to both goals, however, has presented the field with a dilemma. The social movement orientation requires a voluntary cadre of amateurs unfettered by institutional or statutory authority. In contrast, the needs identified by Whipple can best be met through a formal program of university study. In turn, higher education preparation tends to institutionalize and standardize practice consistent with a professional orientation. Hence, the literature reflects the tension between the adherents of the opposing views. Increasingly, however, the literature has favored the professional orientation. The trend has been sufficiently significant to cause recent writers to observe that little "movement" remains in adult education today.

Statements of criteria to distinguish occupational from professional status are abundant. One of the more appropriate ones has been issued by the American Association of Professors of Higher Education (1975). It indicates that a profession includes the following (p. 5).

1. An organized body of intellectual theory constantly expanded by research
2. An intellectual technique

3. A close-knit association of members with a high quality of communication between them
4. A period of long training
5. A series of standards and an enforced statement of ethics
6. Applications to the practical affairs of man
7. Active influence on public policy in its field

Analysis of the field of adult education indicates that six of the seven criteria identified above can be applied to it. Only the fifth criterion seems to be excluded. The seventh criterion is admittedly inadequately met; there is evidence, however, that educators of adults have become increasingly active in efforts to influence public policy over the past twenty years. Each of the remaining five criteria is addressed in this chapter. It becomes a matter of judgment whether these criteria are sufficiently met for the field of adult education to be considered a profession. There is no agreement in the literature at this time as to whether adult education has developed a unique body of knowledge. Some say yes, while others have hedged their position by saying that it is developing one.

Farmer (1974) has written on the concept of professionalization in adult education. He observes that professionalization of the field began with the acquisition of a specialized technique that increasingly has been supported by a body of theory. Gradually, according to Farmer, the role of adult education has moved in a direction away from that of the willing amateur, as also noted by Houle (1960), toward that of a trained specialist. As early as 1958, Carey stated that adult education is not a profession. He was, however, confident that the direction was toward professionalization.

Techniques of Practice

Criteria for professional status suggested by the Association of Professors of Higher Education as well as those given by Vollmer and Mills assert that acquisition of a specialized technique supported by a body of theory is one of the major elements in the emergence of a profession. This criterion has been interpreted as indicating that before adult education can be considered to be a professional area, certain techniques of practice unique to the education of adults must exist and practitioners must be competent to employ those techniques. The research literature on this topic falls into several categories that include program planning, marketing, research, and instruction. Since all these categories are covered in other chapters of this book, this section addresses the topic of competencies, proficiencies, and characteristics of educators of adults.

The concept of identifying competencies or desirable characteristics of educators of adults implies that the practitioner must manifest certain abilities or traits relevant to identifiable techniques. Furthermore, it is assumed that these desirable characteristics can be learned and developed. Frequently, identified competencies or proficiencies as defined by Knox[2] serve as a basis for the evaluation and development of graduate programs designed to prepare educators of adults. Since Houle's 1960 conceptualization of the leadership pyramid in adult education, graduate programs have been designed to prepare individuals for leadership roles through specialized advanced training. As noted by Houle, these individuals are believed to require specialized graduate education experience to qualify them to function optimally in certain leadership roles such as in the design and promotion of program, the administration of program, and the advancement of adult education as a field.

One of the first models for the development of competencies of adult educators (Dickerman 1964) was published less than twenty years ago. Table 12.2 reports that model, which contains three conceptual phases: required functions, relevant competencies, and appropriate learning activities.

Since Dickerman, many studies have been conducted throughout the world to identify the competencies and proficiencies that educators of adults should have. Campbell (1977) and Knox (1979a) provide excellent summaries of the countless efforts that have been conducted in recent years to describe the skills, knowledge, and personal characteristics required of educators of adults. Research available for review on this topic has been conducted in Canada, the United Kingdom, and the United States. There is little reason to question the generalizability of the results of these studies to other parts of the world. Reviewers of the various investigations, however, should be alert to some differences among the studies. For example, there is reason to believe that competencies and characteristics of adult basic education teachers may be different from those of the administrators of those programs, while it is equally likely that there will be preferred differences between administrators of public school programs for adults and administrators of higher education programs for adults. Some studies appear to adequately identify a special population of educators of adults, while others seek to identify "general" characteristics regardless of the arena of institutional practice.

The data collection preference reflects an important issue. Is there a so-called core area in which all educators of adults should be proficient or not? Proponents of the core concept suggest that institutional setting and educators' roles should not significantly determine the kinds of skills, knowledge, and personal characteristics required of the educator. Others would suggest that institutional setting and educator roles are variable and that, consequently, the kinds of skills, knowledge, and personal characteristics required to be a successful educator of adults will vary. Core characteristics are related to educational goals, adult development and learning, program development procedures, and general agency functioning (Knox 1979a). Specific characteristics are related to type of agency and roles such as teacher, administrator, and counselor. Knox indicates that graduate programs and other training activities designed to improve the proficiency of educators of adults can deal most effectively with a widely shared core of concepts and procedures that have been identified through previous studies.

One investigator of proficiencies of educators of adults (Knox 1979a) has suggested that regardless of the institutional and role specifications, the practitioners should benefit from three broad areas—two of them cognitive and the other affective in nature: an understanding of the field, an understanding of the adult as a learner, and the development of personal qualities such as positive attitudes toward lifelong learning, effective interpersonal relations, and innovativeness. Other lists also include both cognitive and personal characteristics that stress the appropriate combination of subject competence and per-

Table 12.2
A Model for the Development of Competencies for Adult Educators

Required Functions	Relevant Competencies	Appropriate Learning Activities
A. Formulation of policies, objectives, and programs in institutions of adult education.	1. An understanding of the function of adult education in society.	Study of the nature and scope of the adult educational field.*
	2. Ability to diagnose adult educational needs and translate these into objectives & programs.	Practice in using basic program planning processes.*
	3. An understanding of the unique characteristics and processes of adults as learners.	Systematic inquiry into research findings about adult psychology and developmental process.*
	4. Ability to plan and execute strategies of institutional and community change.	Laboratory experience in performing the role of change agent.**
B. Organization and administration of programs of adult education.	1. Same as A-2.	Same as A-2*
	2. An understanding of the theory and dynamics of organization.	Study of organizational theory and dynamics.*
	3. Skill in the selection, training, and supervision of leaders and teachers.	Laboratory and field experience in practice of supervisory skills.*
	4. Skill in institutional management.	Study and practice of principles and methods of financing, staffing, interpreting, etc.*
C. Performance of special functions required in particular adult educational roles.	Such specialized competencies as use of mass media, preparation of materials, organizational and community consultation, human relations training, etc.	Guided independent study, supervised field experience, systematic study in related fields, group projects, skill exercises, research projects, etc.

 * Most appropriate at the master's level.
** Most appropriate at the doctor's level.

Source: Dickerman 1964, p. 309. Reproduced by permission.

sonal competence. Legge (1967), commenting on the qualities desired in the educator of adults, says that the effective teacher is the "right" kind of person, who is able to kindle student response through the warmth of human contact that makes learning easier.

Table 12.3 displays the most important seven competencies identified by each of four educators of adults. A review of the twenty-eight competencies identified by the writers reveals little specific duplication. There is some generic similarity, but the specific convergence is less than might be expected. The divergence among the identified competencies can be explained partially by two factors: first, the results were obtained from different kinds of samples; second, the data were responses to slightly different questions.

Three other studies of competencies and educational needs of adult educators are discussed below to further demonstrate the specific variance that exists when different professional educational roles are considered.

Mocker (1974) studied the competencies required of the adult basic education (ABE) teacher. The identified abilities are of three kinds: knowledge, behavior, and attitude. Four activities, or topical areas, were examined according to the three kinds of abilities and at two levels of priority. The topical areas include scope and goal of adult education, curriculum, ABE learner, and instructional processes. In this complex system, twenty-four cells in a matrix are filled with anywhere from two to sixty-six items. The cell containing the fewest competencies is the one concerning attitudes about curriculum. The cell containing the largest number of desired abilities is the one on behavior concerning the instructional process.

Another study that reveals the range of differences among educators of adults concerning the desired abilities, knowledge, and attitudes of adult education practitioners was conducted at the University of Michigan (Connellan 1973). The study was designed to identify differences in the perception of competencies critical to the job success of administrators of continuing education in public community colleges. Two groups were surveyed to identify possible differences in perceptions. One group was composed of administrators of continuing education in community colleges, and the other consisted of university professors of adult/continuing education. Of ninety competencies rated by the respondents, significant differences were noted on thirty-four.

The Michigan study indicates that graduate programs in adult education reflect some differences at the masters and doctoral level. At the masters level, the emphasis is upon the teaching of adults, with a substantial number of individuals being prepared for administrative positions. At the doctoral level, there seems to be almost equal emphasis upon administrative competencies and professional competencies.

The competencies perceived to be most important to administrators reflect general administrative orientations. For example, twenty-seven of the competencies were selected by 30 percent or more of the administrators. Eleven of these were general administrative competencies, seven were related to community activities, four were marketing activities, and three related to program planning.

In contrast, 30 percent or more of the professors selected twenty-eight of the competencies. Of these, eleven were concerned with the general administrative practices. Nine were related to staff management, four focused on com-

Table 12.3
The Seven Highest-Ranked Competencies of Educators of Adults as Identified by Four Different Adult Educators

Aker 1962[1]	Chamberlain 1961a, b[2]	Robinson 1962[3]	Houle 1957[4]
Helps people control and adjust to change rather than to maintain the status quo	A belief that most people have potential for growth	Should have the qualities of a leader and should be mature enough to be accepted by adults	Should be trained to professional competence in an academic discipline
Intelligently observes and listens to what is being said or done and uses this information in guiding responses	Imagination in program development Ability to communicate effectively in both speaking and writing	Should possess initiative in program development Should understand adult psychology	Should have broad intellectual horizons Must be a socially oriented and socially adjusted person–"the right guy"
Selects and uses teaching methods, materials, and resources that are appropriate in terms of what is to be learned and in terms of the needs and abilities of individual learners	Understanding of the conditions under which adults are most likely to learn Ability to keep on learning	Should understand group leadership and be able to work with groups Should be a competent teacher	Must have creative imagination Must have competence in administrative skills
Helps clientele acquire ability for critical thinking	Effectiveness as a group leader Knowledge of one's own values, strengths, and weaknesses	Should be proficient in the use of communication media	Must have energy, and must have enthusiasm for adult education, including his or her own
Provides an atmosphere where adults are free to search, through trial and error, without fear of institutional or interpersonal threat		Should understand community organization, community power structures, and community development	Must be alert to the needs of adult individuals and of society
Identifies potential leaders and helps them to develop their potentials			
Makes use of existing values, beliefs, customs, and attitudes as a starting point for educational activities			

1. Adult educator competencies identified by diverse professionals
2. Adult educator competencies identified by educators in largely senior administrative posts
3. Optional experience and educational backgrounds of those entering the field of adult education
4. Images of adult education administrators

Source: Based on Campbell 1977.

munity activities, three concerned instruction, and one related to marketing efforts.

The investigator concluded that no relationship existed concerning the competencies favored by the two groups. At the .90 level of confidence, there were thirty-four competencies with statistically significant result differences. Analyses of the competencies selected by 60, 50, 40, and 30 percent of the respondents reveal more failure to agree than agreement, at each level.

Rossman and Bunning (1978) also report an investigation designed to assess the knowledge and skills needed by adult educators of the future to successfully fulfill their roles. They used the Delphi technique to sample 141 university professors of adult education in the United States and Canada. They obtained data on 101 skills and knowledge statements. The following skills were rated most highly:

1. Skill in diagnosing educational needs of the individual
2. Skill in continuous self-improvement
3. Skill in communicating
4. Skill in encouraging creativity
5. Skill as a competent instructor

Examples of the most highly rated knowledge statements include those concerned with knowledge of the ever changing nature of the adult and adult needs, knowledge of oneself, knowledge of the process of change, knowledge of the principles of adult education, and knowledge of learning theories in practice. Rossman and Bunning concluded that the higher rated skills and knowledge statements fell into six general categories: the adult educator, the field of adult education, the adult learner, the adult educational environment, programming, and process.

The studies concerning competencies that may be related to techniques of practice in the education of adults indicate that there are identifiable competencies required of the proficient adult educator.

Graduate Programs of Study

What is the content of a graduate program of study? How is the content determined? Is there agreement on the content of graduate study in adult education? Since the initiation of the doctoral program in adult education at Teachers College of Columbia University in 1933, university professors have been concerned with program content. Some justification for program content can be found in the various studies of abilities desired of educators of adults. The general literature of educational practice has also been a source of information. For example, Liveright (1964) made extensive comment concerning the nature and aims of graduate programs designed to equip educators to assume leadership positions in the education of adults.

Research skills are high among those competencies identified, for educators of adults, by Liveright, who cited the expectations of the medical and social work professions before concluding that the adult educator can hardly settle for less than the research requirements determined to be appropriate for the medical profession. Douglah and Moss (1968) and Boyd (1969) have also written directly to research competence. Boyd's position appears to be the more controversial, as he indicates that developing the theoretical and research skills is more important than is the development of an "excellent practicing professional."

Others such as Aker (1962) and Houle (1970) have identified desirable skills related to the professional competence of the educator of adults. Both Aker and Houle indicate that research competence is one among several important skill areas.

One of Houle's latest published comments on the activities of the adult educator (1970) reported four functions more or less common to the education of adults: direct guidance of learners, design and promotion of program, administration of program, and advancement of adult education as a field. He indicates that most part-time and volunteer workers are concerned with the "teacher role" or the guidance of learners, whereas the professional graduate adult educator is concerned with each of the four functions. According to Houle, educators who guide adult learners require two kinds of expertise: mastery of the "content" to be conveyed and mastery of the instructional techniques required in the particular setting to reach the stated objectives.

The other three functions also require specific expertise that theoretically is best achieved through graduate programs of instruction. For example, program design and promotion require competence in the knowledge and use of a basic theory of how to construct sequential learning activities, knowledge of how the theory is applied in specific settings, the capacity to guide and direct the educational program after it has been constructed, and knowledge and skill in the use of appropriate marketing techniques. Designing and promoting program require quite different knowledge and capabilities than those required for administering program. In the conduct of the first two functions, the educator is directly concerned with the learner and the design of instruction, whereas the administrator's direct activity requires skills in the areas of budgeting, staffing, organizing, controlling, and public interpretation. Finally, the fourth function identified by Houle, advancement of the field, is achieved through skills of conducting and reporting research, conceptualizing the field, training leaders, and developing other leadership qualities.

Verner (1953) did not address the competencies question directly. He used an oblique approach instead and identified four main components required in training programs for teachers of adults. He recommended the following four basic curriculum components:

1. An understanding of social change and a sound philosophy of social organization and the relationship of adult education to the social order
2. A study of the history of adult education
3. A knowledge of adult psychology
4. Study and training in teaching methods that are appropriate for adults

In 1953, he noted that there was no systematic training of adult educators that included any of these things, yet they would contribute immeasurably to the efficiency and ease with which teachers could do their job. A current review of the graduate programs in adult education reveals that Verner's 1953 complaint, with the exception of history of adult education, no longer applies. The presence of most of the four components in some degree in most graduate programs, however, confirms their importance and the accuracy of Verner's insight.

Verner's 1953 conceptualization of the objectives of training teachers of adults is slightly different from the one proposed by Houle in 1960. Houle indicated that the educational programs designed for educators of adults should address six main areas. He identifies these areas as (1) philosophy, (2) psychological and sociological foundations, (3) an understanding of the agency or institutional framework within which the individual will practice, (4) the ability to carry out and supervise the basic processes of education, (5) leadership skills, and (6) a concern for continuing personal development. Houle's third and sixth objectives seem to address concerns not mentioned by Verner. In some instances, some of the agencies in which adult education specialists function are addressed in graduate programs, whereas it is likely that detailed analysis is not always possible. The sixth objective appears to be addressed by processes other than classroom instruction—processes related to socialization as discussed elsewhere.

Campbell (1977) has offered yet another way of conceptualizing the content for graduate studies in adult education. Based on his research on the topic, he identified six elements of a graduate program designed to develop the kinds of competencies identified by Aker and others:

1. Adult Education: Provision to a Particular Clientele/Environment
2. Adult Education: The Philosophical-Historical Context
3. Adult Education: Methods and Resources
4. Adult Education Systems: Organization and Administration
5. The Adult Learner: The Psychological Context
6. The Adult Learner: The Sociological Context

The above topics, as suggested by Campbell, are easily subsumed by three subject areas: adult psychology, adult education methodology, and the sociology of adulthood. Especially significant and salient is how well the subject matter conforms to White's 1956 central conclusion that even among adult educators in diverse fields there is a common core of training interests. Two additional comments are generated by Campbell's observations. First, the identification of a central core of common interests among educators of adults serves as constraint agaist the proliferation of training content; second, it supports the proposition that adult education is a unique and prospective field of study. Elsdon (1977) cogently underscores the point by observing that even with the range in provision, structure, and content, the basic staff functions and activities of adult educators cut across the differences.

Professional Socialization

The fourth basic element in the elevation of an occupation to professional status is the development of a career supported by an association of colleagues (Vollmer and Mills 1966). One of the best research projects related to the importance of occupational socialization factors to adult educators is reported by Ashford (1978). While her study was not designed to examine the issue of professional status for adult educators, her findings are instructive to those interested in the question. The importance of Ashford's investigation resides in the conceptualization and findings relative to the importance of factors associated with socializing adult educators to the occupation.

Merton's definition of socialization as the process through which individuals are inducted into their culture and which involves the acquisition of attitudes and values, of skills and behavior patterns making up social roles established in the social structure (Merton, Reader, and Kendal 1957) served as Ashford's basic point of departure. Within this framework, she studied the impact of three variables on the socialization of adult educators to the broader field. The variables were organizational socialization, professional association membership, and colleague interaction. Organizational settings included institutions of higher education, public schools, state departments of education, and the federal government.

Ashford's findings and conclusions suggest that organizational setting is an important variable in the ocupational socialization of adult educators. For example, those in higher education seem to be more affected by prestigious peers, informal networks, and other factors identified in the survey instrument than educators of adults in other settings. Other differences among the respondents were noted on variables such as sex, number of years at present location, and age. Interactions among the variables were also noted.

OBSERVATIONS

This chapter is basically concerned with questions concerning the status of adult education as a field of study and a field of practice. It is obvious that adult education as a field of practice preceded its emergence as a field of study. In fact, a number of questions and issues concerning the field of study dimension continue to be discussed.

Throughout this chapter, one theme has tended to be reflected in the status and substance of each of the topics examined; that theme is diversity. Limited consideration of this basic characteristic of adult education confounds almost any discussion of any topic related to the education of adults. In one sense, adult education as a field of study is an abstraction. It is an organizational construct upon which adult education as a field of practice rests. As a structural concept, its purpose is not to overly restrain the field of practice; it derives its structure from the field while providing the foundation for the diverse activities, agencies, and goals of adult education.

This review of research indicates that the historical foundations of the education of adults in North America have been inadequately examined. Failure to develop the historical dimension of educational activities of adults almost ensures repetition and insufficient understanding of roles and trends. The absence of historical knowledge leads to erroneous conclusions and assumptions about the status and role of adult education in other periods. Consequently, old problems are constantly rehashed, and development of the field is circular rather than linear.

The literature concerning how the basic concepts and terminology are determined reveals that attention to this topic has been limited, with only a few researchers such as Verner systematically seeking to clarify concepts and terms. He is particularly noted for his work in the areas of processes, program methods, techniques, and devices of adult education as well as for his efforts to define *adult learners* and *the field of adult education.* The definitions that he provided for each of the above terms have met with some criticism. Yet, with the exception of his definitions of *adults, the field of adult education,* and *methods,* his terminology has been widely accepted. Even though Verner enjoyed the benefits of a popular platform in the publications of the Adult Education Association of the U.S.A., his definition of *method* has not been generally accepted in the field (Dickinson 1979). Knowles (1970) provides a better term, *formats,* to define the institutional relationship with learners. More recently, Boyd and Apps (1980a) have provided yet a different term—*transactions*—that seems to cover the same concept. However, if it can be of solace to adult educators, they can always cite the difficulty psychology has had with such basic concepts as intelligence, learning, personality, and motivation.

Conceptual and analytic philosophical methods have been used with some success to capture the essence of terms such as *program* and *involvement.* As noted by Dickerman (1964), others are now needed to continue Verner's efforts.

Verner was impressed by an urgency for the necessity of establishing appropriate parameters before adult education could become a field of study. In essence, the "problem" has to be adequately defined. In the complex milieu known as adult education, the parameters of the field must be sufficiently broad to provide for the diversity of activities, agencies, and goals, yet narrow enough to be meaningful. The consequences of too narrowly defining the field are almost as severe as those of too broadly defining it. The issue is both a philosophical and a scientific one.

The issue of marginality of adult education as discussed in the literature is associated with at least two assumptions that require debate and discussion. First, the concept was applied to a specific institutional provision of educational activities: the public schools in California. The justifications provided by Clark (1958) for designating public school adult education in that state are reasonable and logical. However, analysis of different institutions indicates that all Clark's elements do not universally apply.

Second, the idea of marginality also seems to be related to the tendency to conceptualize adult education in relationship to the "core" education institutions such as the public school, community colleges, and higher education. Two points need to be made concerning this. First, information released by the National Center for Education Statistics (1980) indicates that adult education is rapidly expanding in the activities of community colleges and universities and four-year colleges, with the greatest percentage of growth in the community colleges. Other information in this area released in the early part of the 1970s reveals that the majority of college and university students are adult part-time students. Thus, in terms of clientele and programs, shifts have occurred in the past decade to require further discussion of the concept of marginality. Second, when adult education is discussed solely in terms of its relationship to the "core" educational institutions, some of the significant distinguishing characteristics such as the field's dynamic, flexible, and plural-istic qualities are neglected. Hallenbeck (1964) provides a short but useful comment on this particular dimension of the issue.

Numerous ideas concerning the purposes of education for adults parallel the diversity of concepts and perceived limits of the field. Ultimately, all pur-poses seem to be of one of two kinds: individual or social.

Does adult education possess a distinctive body of knowledge? The answer to this question is not found in the research literature as readily as it is discov-ered in the philosophy of the writer. A case may be made, based on the litera-ture, to support either an affirmative or negative response. Indeed, quite differ-ent opinions are expressed by highly respected scholars. Some (Jensen, Liveright, and Hallenbeck 1964) indicate that adult education has been accu-mulating a unique body of theory, knowledge, and practice, while others (Dickinson 1979) hedge on the question by observing that a sufficient body of knowledge has been established to qualify for the appellation "emerging disci-pline." It should be observed that the sources for the above observation were published prior to 1970. In contrast, Elsdon's comment (1977) supports the opinion that there is a single body of knowledge that is appropriate for the education and development of adult educators. Even more recently, Boyd and Apps (1980) indicate that adult education has a unique structure and func-tion. Finally, in support of the proposition that adult education has a special-ized content, Campbell (1977) observes that the processes of adult learning and motivation to learn are sufficiently specialized to justify special training for those involved in the education of adults.[3]

Finally, the answers to questions of professional status as revealed by the literature are very similar to those concerning adult education as a field of study. The same kinds of caveats and cautiously optimistic positions character-ize the literature. It is clear that definite occupational and career roles now characterize adult education as a field of practice in the United States. Camp-bell (1977) says that while adult education cannot be classified as a profession in the conventional sense, it can be perceived as one because of the continu-ously acquired competence based on theory and related to skills derived from the field of practice.

Several elements associated with the development of a profession were identified and examined in this and other chapters of this book. Research concerning the question of professionalization has been extensive and the philosophical debate sometimes heated. Nevertheless, research concerning the core competencies and specialized competencies associated with particular agencies and roles needs to be continued and creatively designed.

NOTES

1. Darkenwald and Merriam (1982) say, "While adult education never was a marginal part of the education of the American public, today its significance is greater and more widely acknowledged than ever before" (p. 6).

2. Knox (1979a) uses the term *proficiencies* to refer to a desirable level that most of the highly effective practitioners would be expected to achieve. He describes a proficient person as one who has the capability and the reserve power to perform well in a

specific situation and to meet the demands or requirements of a situation or work demand. The concept links understanding and performance. Proficiency, according to Knox, contrasts with competence, which emphasizes minimum, satisfactory, or moderate levels of capability.

3. Hermanowicz (1976) provides an interesting alternative view. He is of the opinion that adult education is not developing the characteristics of an academic discipline. Furthermore, he denies the desirability of such a goal. This does not, according to Hermanowicz, preclude or obviate the development of a corpus of knowledge unique to the education of adults. Instead, he believes that the field will acquire the characteristics of what he calls an interdiscipline. He defines an interdiscipline, following Robert Merton, as an inter- or multi-disciplinary field that addresses problems or practices that by their nature cannot reside in a single area of knowledge.

13 • Philosophy

THE DIVERSITY OF ADULT EDUCATION as a field of practice and a field of study contributes to a complex philosophical situation. The purpose of education for adults is defined according to the philosophical bases of the institutional providers of educational opportunities. Naturally, different providers will have different objectives and, hence, different philosophical orientations. For example, certain social and religious organizations tend to cast their educational mission in terms that are consistent with their overall organizational mission, which may be to bring about some social or religious change in society and individuals. In contrast, business and professional groups often define the objectives of their educational activities in terms of organizational efficiency and individual proficiency. To complicate matters further, there is no uniform agreement about the purpose of adult education even within any one class of organizational sponsors. Among religious institutions, for example, one finds a variety of programs that range from the secular to the spiritual in terms of content and purpose—from literacy to theology.

Despite the range of organizations, agencies, and institutions involved in the education of adults, some general philosophical parameters are emerging. Historically, adult education has been taken to task for lack of philosophical attention to issues and dimensions of the education of adults. Some of the criticism is well deserved, while some appears to be based on inappropriate assumptions. The criticisms of the philosophical dimensions of adult education as a field of study fall into two general groups: the first group includes negative observations that have condemned the field because there is no one general unifying philosophical position that clearly establishes a central position on the critical issues in adult education; the second concerns the lack of attention given by individual educators to the development of explicit personal philosophies.

One's position concerning the first group of criticisms may very well be philosophical in origin. Individuals who support the drive for one philosophical position concerning the purpose of adult education, for example, are quite likely to promote the central position to which the organization that they serve subscribes. The second group of criticisms is more pragmatic. It recognizes the possibility that the field is indeed as diverse as represented in this volume and that the likelihood of developing a central unifying philosophy is no greater than that of obtaining agreement among the world's religions concerning the spiritual nature of humanity. This chapter does not extensively address the first group of criticisms. Instead, attention is directed to (1) some explanations for the limited efforts to develop several personal philosophical positions, (2) the developing nature of philosophy in adult education, and (3) some of the typologies or descriptions of different orientations identified, including a brief review of selected literature to illustrate the visibility of different philosophical perspectives in the general literature, a review of the application of analytic philosophy to adult education, and a quick look at some general issues. A few summary observations conclude the discussions.

EXPLANATIONS

Educators of adults have been reluctant to develop and publish systematically based alternative philosophical positions concerning the education of adults. Because of the absence of a variety of thoughtfully presented philosophical rationales for such issues as the purpose of education for adults, the nature of humanity, the nature of reality, instruction, and similar subjects, the literature generally reflects only shadows and vague partial outlines of the philosophical bases of authors' views on given topics.

Several reasons can be proposed to explain why educators of adults have failed to systematically develop alternative philosophical positions. These explanations include the following:

1. Limited appreciation for philosophy as a means for guiding behavior
2. Limited appreciation for philosophy as a means for understanding
3. Expectations that adult education should be guided by one monolithic philosophical system
4. The expectation that one's philosophy must be rigorously mature and complete in all aspects
5. The perception that action and philosophy are mutually exclusive—that one is doing and the other is thinking

A Means for Guiding Behavior

Even those individuals who strongly deny the existence of a personal philosophy usually demonstrate the rudimentary elements of philosophy, which can be defined as a set of motivating beliefs, concepts, and principles. The educator who fails to reflect some philosophical orientation to some important topic or issue of concern to other educators does not exist. In contrast, there are many individuals who may have conflicting philosophies. These individuals believe one thing about a topic such as the nature of humanity, while they have a conflicting view of society or the purpose of education. In each event, the denying and the conflicting behavior are counterproductive, and the educator fails to appreciate the value of philosophy as a means for guiding educational behavior. Examples of conflicting philosophies in educational practice may be found among educators who subscribe to humanistic developmental concepts and yet design instructional activities in accordance with a mechanistic concept. Further sources of conflict may include goals of education and teacher-learner relations.

A Means for Understanding

A second explanation for the absence of systematically developed philosophical positions concerning the education of adults lies in a lack of appreciation for philosophy as a means for understanding. Even some who readily appreciate philosophy as a means for guiding behavior fail to consider philosophy as a means for informing practice. Greater awareness of the relationship between one's philosophy and one's search for understanding requires the recognition and resolution of several issues. These issues include assumptions about humanity, reality, and the nature of knowledge. Commonly, *research* is a term used to describe activities designed to obtain answers to questions. Adult educators often seek to answer questions by inappropriate means. For example, the purposes of education for adults cannot be addressed adequately by the scientific approach. It is a philosophical issue that should be examined within a philosophical framework using philosophical analysis. Furthermore, the adoption of teaching-learning processes ultimately should rest upon a consistent philosophy concerning several areas of concern, including one's concepts about the nature of humanity, the nature of knowledge, the purpose of education, the purpose of a specific learning activity, and so forth. While some aspects of some of the above concerns may be clarified by science, philosophical inquiry would be expected to provide the point of departure for scientific inquiry. Apps (1979) suggests two important guidelines for alternative approaches to some of the issues that confront us: first, the educator should recognize that knowledge does not exist independent of values; second, researchers should be aware of the relationship between their research and their assumptions about such issues as the nature of humanity, reality, and knowledge.

Two prominent approaches to seeking understanding through philosophy are identified in the literature of adult education (Collins 1981). They are described as linguistic (or conceptual) analysis and phenomenology. Collins observes that linguistic analysis is based on the fundamental assumption that the proper role of philosophy is to analyze language use—to analyze concepts. Consequently, the goal is for conceptual clarification through analysis of the way we use language.

Phenomenology is described as criticism based on a rigorous process of setting aside ontological judgments on the nature and essence of phenomena. In the analysis, the object of one's experience and the experiencing of it is explored. This process requires clarification through careful description.

Current philosophical inquiry in adult education seems to favor the linguistic approach in the mode of the British philosophers (Patterson 1979; Lawson 1975). Examples found in North American literature include the work of Schwertz (1972) and Snyder (1969).

Monolithic System

It is incongruous that adult educators, of all people, should expect unanimous agreement upon one "creed" for the field. The pluralistic origins and practice settings are effective and real obstacles to such agreement. However, the nature of the criticism leveled at many aspects of the field of adult education seems to suggest the desirability of one unified philosophy wherein all educators agree on the purpose of adult education and the means by which it is to be provided to which people. Human nature suggests that such general agreement is not possible.

Maturity and Completeness

Is a philosophy ever rigorously mature and complete? It is unlikely that even the best of thinkers have successfully addressed the multitude of possible conflicts and contradictions in their philosophies. As suggested by Apps (1979), however, such a state should not deter the individual from the daily meditation required to examine behavior and beliefs about such topics as the meaning of life, the roles of the adult educator, and the purposes to which one is committed.

Action Orientation

Adult educators are traditionally action-oriented individuals who often appear to equate history and philosophy with a more passive pattern of behavior. The limited number of philosophical inquiries reported in *Adult Education* and addressed by research conferences and dissertations seems to support the observation. Yet, there is no doubt that individual adult educators are at least partially and implicitly guided by some set of motivating beliefs, concepts, and principles that collectively constitute their philosophy of adult education. The difficulty in identifying adult education philosophies lies in two areas: the nature of one's philosophy and its substance.

As action-oriented individuals, adult educators do not appear to have been overly concerned with the incomplete, intuitive, and unarticulated nature of their personal philosophies. They have been perhaps even less concerned with a systematic critical development of a formal philosophy. In other words, philosophizing about philosophy has not been a popular activity. In contrast, the abiding interest that adult educators have in such issues as purposes, procedures, and content of the field is clear evidence of a direct concern for important topics that must be addressed philosophically as well as empirically.

Perhaps adult educators, as action-oriented individuals, have tended to view philosophy as emphasizing esoteric concepts and jargon for purposes of argumentation. This is to caricature an honorable and highly useful discipline. Unwittingly, then, adult educators have ignored a useful means of addressing important concerns that are central to the field. Philosophy is concerned with general principles. Principles are general if they include a large number of phenomena, and the philosopher of adult education considers the general principles that are related to the process of educating adults. These include the aims and objectives of education, curriculum or subject matter, general methodological principles, analysis of the teaching-learning process, and the relationship between education and the society in which education takes place.

DEVELOPING PHILOSOPHY

The reluctance of adult educators to engage in philosophical analysis of the field has not completely prevented the gradual accumulation of an instructive body of literature on the topic. Even though a review of adult education dissertations, *Adult Education,* and the two primary research conferences for educators of adults in the United States reveals that only a few philosophically oriented works are published annually, the general literature is not as sterile as might be suggested. First, the field has been enriched by general education philosophy as elucidated by John Dewey, Sydney Hook, Alfred North Whitehead, and others. This dimension has been supplemented by historical and contemporary literature ranging from Rousseau and Jefferson to Freire and Illich (1970, 1971). Other, more specific, adult education philosophy has reached the printed page through the efforts of Apps and others who are cited in the following pages. The vitality and diversity of the field are apparent in the philosophical literature of adult education. For example, it quickly becomes obvious that there is a range of philosophical perspectives concerning major elements in the education of adults. Positions on these topics are as remote as are the missions of the different agencies, institutions, and organizations that populate the field. Yet, they are critical and focus on some of the major issues confronting adult educators. Disagreement on the solutions is sometimes obvious, but so is agreement on the problems. Several of the issues that strike straight at the heart of the field are these:

1. How is adult education to be defined?
2. What is the purpose, mission, or aim of adult education?
3. Is the focus to be on the individual or on society?
4. What is the nature of the learner?
5. What is to be the relationship between the learner and the teacher?
6. What is the subject matter or content?

The magnitude of the division among adult educators concerning some of the above questions is illustrated by a recent published exchange between Carlson

(1980) and Boyd and Apps (1980b) concerning the Boyd and Apps model of adult education.

Carlson identifies the model as a "utopian philosophy of education that emphasizes professional practice," among other descriptions. In turn, Boyd and Apps reject the charge of utopianism while agreeing that four implicit assumptions are evident in their work: (1) that education is planned individual and social growth and progress through a scientific, rational, problem-solving process, (2) that people have the right and power to change the condition of everyone, (3) that one can trust institutions to bring about change in the interest of all people, and (4) that adult education is a helping profession that includes practitioners who seek to diagnose educational problems and prescribe appropriate educational treatment for them.

REVIEW OF TYPOLOGIES

The extant philosophical literature in adult education is of three kinds: (1) reviews, examinations, and explications of philosophical positions, (2) analytical efforts that are usually applied to specific issues, concepts, or terms as a means of generating a fuller and more accurate understanding of the topic, and (3) general discursive and hortatory writing that reveals one individual's philosophy but is not specifically designed to systematically develop a philosophical position.

Philosophical Typologies

The literature clearly reveals that educators of adults do not necessarily agree on important philosophical points. The diversity of opinion among adult educators has stimulated several reviewers of the scene to offer typologies or other conceptual means for differentiating among the positions. The works cited below reveal some of the areas of agreement and disagreement identifiable in the literature.

Powell and Benne (1960) identify two conspicuous philosophical orientations among educators of adults as developmentalist and rationalist. Each of these is represented by one or more philosophical camps. For example, the salient foci for the developmentalists include fundamental education and community development, while the rationalists are represented by human relations and group dynamics advocates.

Miller (1967) dichotomizes philosophical orientations according to objectives. He implies that objectives of adult education focus on one of two concepts; the purpose of adult education is either to improve society or to improve the individual. Aristotle and Dewey are quite frequently used by supporters of both positions in arguments to support their views.

Miller enlarges on the horizontal continuum reflected in the above debate to indicate that educators also fall along another dimension concerning the distinction between education for "knowing" and education for "doing." Thus, he conceptually represents the philosophical parameters of adult education on two perpendicular dimensions that characterize objectives of adults according to the individual-social/knowing-doing orientations. Figure 13.1 illustrates Miller's concept.

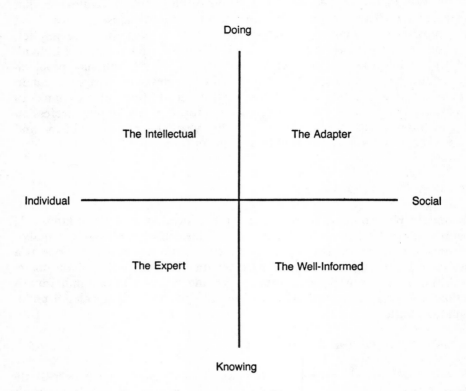

Figure 13.1   Modification of Miller's model of objectives of adult education

It is believed that each adult learner is likely to fit one of the four models in Figure 13.1 according to his or her particular situation. Miller expands on each model as follows:

1. The Adapter. Goals that emphasize active behavior change to conform to social role-demands belong in this sector of objectives. If the general view of the social function of adult education is correct, one would expect to find these kinds of objectives dominating the field. Because technical skills are instrumental rather than essential to the good individual, it is reasonable to include them here along with other more purely social role adaptations.

2. The Well-Informed. This model suggests the kind of person who seeks knowledge and understanding of essentially social role problems without particularly assuming an active role in relation to them. In its noblest terms, the aim is expressed as the humanization of knowledge, which infused much of the early impulse of general university extension. Historically, this has been a significant objective for American adult education. (The extraordinary recent

increase in the availability of informative reading material in paperbacks and popular magazines, however, as well as the public affairs activities of commercial television networks, seems likely to replace the functions formerly performed by adult education programs in this area.)

3. The Expert. Concentrating on individual growth through relatively passive acquisition of knowledge tends to produce this type of person. Programs to keep professionals up-to-date, where the occupation itself is more than instrumental (medicine, law, science, and so forth) fall into this category, as well as recreational pursuits that emphasize knowing rather than doing. The Civil War buff and the amateur archeologist are familiar examples.

4. The Intellectual. The behaviors that form this model are the active cognitive skills of rationality and judgment (Aristotle's virtuous person, Dewey's thinker).

It is in the Intellectual sector that our objectives are highest and our performance least creditable. It is here that the service character of the field does the most disservice to our pretensions because, in a society oriented to instrumentality, people themselves seldom perceive the need for their own intellectual growth.

Elias and Merriam (1980) suggest that adult education and individual educators are influenced by six different philosophical schools: liberal adult education, progressive adult education, behavioristic adult education, humanistic adult education, radical adult education, and the analytical philosophy of adult education. Each of these philosophies subscribes to particular concepts of humanity, education, instruction, society, and knowledge. Consequently, individual educators or groups of adult educators guided by the principles derived from these disparate philosophical schools are likely to see the various issues in the field from different perspectives and recommend diverse solutions according to their philosophical orientation.

Apps (1979) emphasizes yet another treatment of some of the philosophical concepts reflected in adult education. His view begins with two conceptualizations of human beings. The first orientation is identified as organismic, or mechanistic, which is based on the belief that human beings are essentially related to other life forms. The second position, based on the opinion that humans are essentially different from other life forms, is identified as a humanistic orientation. These two orientations are also embedded in the different philosophical schools identified by Elias and Merriam.

Other scholars provide yet a different typology of views concerning the nature of humanity. Langer (1969), for example, provides a three-cell typology: mechanical mirror theory, organic lamp theory, and psychoanalytic theory. Both psycholanalytic and mechanical mirror theories would be included in Apps's organismic (mechanistic) classification. Each of Langer's classes is described below.

1. Mechanical mirror. According to this view, the human being grows to be what he or she is made to be by the environment.
2. Organic lamp. Subscribers to this view believe that individuals develop to be what they make themselves by their own actions.

3. Psychoanalytic. This view represents the human as a conflicted being who is driven to action and growth both by his or her own passions or instincts and by external demands.

Yet other philosophies based on religious concepts would introduce additional models to explain the nature of human beings. For example, the doctrine of vitalism is sometimes used to account for a spiritual force to describe the nature of humankind.

According to Cotton (1968), three general philosophical orientations are distinctly revealed in the literature of adult education published between 1919 and 1968. He identified them as social reformist, professional, and eclectic orientations.

The oldest of the traditions is the social reformist view, which dominated the field through the mid thirties. Subscribers to the social reformist philosophy have been extremely critical of the status quo, special interests of those other than the "oppressed," traditional education, and the prevailing cultural environment. Adult educators who respond to this orientation generally believe that individual and social intelligence have to be mobilized, on a large scale, to address critical social, economic, and political problems. Representatives include Joseph K. Hart, W. H. Kilpatrick, Harold Laski, and Eduard C. Lindeman.

In contrast, the professional tradition is more recent. It seems to have emerged as a reaction against the social reformist orientation and is temporally associated with the development and expansion of graduate programs in adult education. Adherents of this philosophical tradition perceive the function of adult education more in educational terms than in social terms. The emphasis has been on the establishment of adult education as an additional level of education on some parity with other levels of the traditional educational structure. Consequently, individuals identified with the professional tradition have been most concerned with professionalization, establishment of the discipline, and institutionalization of adult education. They include Lyman Bryson and Wilbur Hallenbeck. Adult educators identified as having an eclectic philosophical orientation tend to fall somewhere between the views of social reformists and professionals as discussed above. Robert J. Blakely, Dorothy Canfield Fisher, Alvin Johnson, Sir Richard Livingstone, and Harry Overstreet are examples.

Several issues that tend to discriminate among the social reformist, professional, and eclectic orientations relate to the audience to whom adult education is justified, the purpose for which the justification is made, the approach used in setting forth the philosophy, and the extent to which adult education is perceived to be needed.

Table 13.1 illustrates the distinctive aspects of the philosophical orientations of the reformist and professional traditions as revealed in the literature.

General Issues

Merriam's 1977 review of the philosophical perspectives revealed in the literature of adult education provides some support for Cotton's classification system. However, she selected and focused on three variables different from those selected by Cotton: (1) aims and objectives of adult education, (2) the teacher, the learner, and the instructional process, and (3) the content of adult education. Merriam's review was limited to publications that specifically addressed the philosophy of adult education—fewer than a dozen books and twenty articles, according to her count. Her review includes both American and British works.

Philosophical thought regarding the aims and objectives of adult education is distributed along a continuum from the "liberation of the mind" to various forms of political/economic/social liberation. Related positions taken by other authors deal with the issue identified earlier by Miller: individual growth versus social concerns. While Miller favors the former, Lindeman (1961) and Bergevin (1967) discuss the aims of adult educators in terms of societal improvement: Bergevin encourages adult education because it promotes the democratic way of life, while Lindeman thinks of adult education as a way to democratize life. Knowles, with his emphasis on individual development apart from external concerns, is represented by Merriam as holding to a position similar to Miller's. From Knowles's perspective, the aim and mission of adult education is to help adults become liberated, with the individual adult determining what he or she will be when "free."

The philosophies of British philosophers Patterson (1973) and K. H. Lawson (1970) line up with the orientation of Miller and Knowles and seem to totally reject the idea that adult education should be in some way linked to social change. Patterson argues that when social change is an objective of adult education, one of two "abhorrent" consequences will result. Either the field of adult education will become a political arena, or it will become a "political closed shop." Patterson is convinced that no one professional group such as educators should promote social change. The major point of his argument is a telling one: The educational process should be as objective as possible—it neither promotes social change nor defends the status quo.

Table 13.1
Rationales of Reformist and Professional Orientations in
Adult Education on Four Selected Topics

Philosophical Orientation	Audience	Purpose of Writing	Approach	Extent of Need
Social Reformist	National audience	To gain public support	Rational-normative arguments	Crucial
Professional	Restricted audience (mainly professional colleagues)	To clarify why adult education is needed	Empirical documentation of the case for adult education	Important

Source: Based on Cotton 1968.

Just as there is a range of philosophical opinions concerning the aims and objectives of adult education, there are diverse orientations concerning philosophical issues that focus on the teacher, the learner, and the instructional process. This dimension is illustrated by the vertical dimension in Miller's model. The degree to which the learner is perceived to be autonomous, intrinsically motivated, disciplined, and self-directing has direct consequences for the instructor's role and the techniques applied in the instructional process. The issues included here are numerous and range from concepts of humanity as perfectable to concepts of humanity as basically depraved with little redeeming value.

While not directly related, there are a number of tangentially associated instructional issues that are influenced by one's view of human nature. It is not sufficient, for example, to identify one's philosophical position as in the humanistic tradition rather than among the organismic philosophies; one must be informed by a view of the human race concerning worth, dignity, and other concepts such as the extent to which the human is creative, self-directed, curious, and so forth. These constellations of ideas about human beings must then interact with one's concept of learning and education. Hence, the adult education literature reflects a range of philosophies from those of Lindeman and Knowles to those of Lawson. The former support discovery and experiential, self-responsible learning techniques, while Lawson favors more traditional expert input techniques.

Who selects the content of adult education? This question is closely related to how one feels the content is to be learned. It is not surprising, therefore, that those who place a heavy responsibility on the teacher for "teaching," in contrast with those who place similar emphasis on the learner for learning, focus on the instructor's role in content selection. Those whose instructional philosophies are more teacher centered, such as Lawson and Patterson, also seem to have more traditional concepts about the content of education. In contrast, others, as Freire (1970), believe that the life of the learner provides the content.

All the problems of adult education are subject to philosophical analysis. Points of departure or perceptions of the nature of selected problems are influenced by the philosophical orientation of each educator. Philosophical issues in the field include many of the topics that are also issues that have been the subject of empirical research as discussed throughout this book. They include, for example, the definition of adult education and the needs and interests of adults, and the importance of these two topics in educational activities such as methods, techniques, and content; the adult as a learner; and other related issues.

Analytic Philosophy

Analytic philosophy concentrates on the careful analysis of arguments, concepts, language, and policy statements in order to develop a philosophical foundation. While it is a recent addition to American adult education, it is a little older in British literature. Over the last twenty years, a number of adult education doctoral dissertations in the United States have been written using the procedures of analytic philosophy.

In a sense, analytic philosophy has been around since Plato and Aristotle. In the Middle Ages, Aquinas, Duns Scotus, and others resorted to careful analysis and argumentation to examine philosophical issues. Although the clarification of concepts through philosophical analysis dates from the earliest origins of philosophy, it is only in our own century that a distinctive analytic approach has emerged. This approach differs from those of the past in its abandonment of metaphysical statements about the nature of the world and other key concepts such as God and reality. It concentrates on the analysis of language as the exclusive function of philosophy.

Analytic philosophy includes a number of different forms of philosophy: scientific realism, logical analysis or logical atomism, logical positivism, and conceptual analysis. Only conceptual analysis is prominent in educational philosophy. The philosopher's role, according to proponents of conceptual analysis procedures, is not to construct explanations about reality but to eliminate language confusion. Philosophy becomes a method of investigation that results in pure description. Accordingly, all language, no matter how abstract, metaphysical, or theological, is to be subjected to analysis in the philosopher's efforts to determine its meaning for those who use it.

Conceptual analysts recognize that there is not necessarily only one right answer when it comes to the analysis of concepts. The concept of education has a variety of meanings or usages in language. These usages are not totally arbitrary. For example, the concept of education is more appropriately applied to persons than to animals or plants. Furthermore, education is usually distinguished from training and indoctrination. Thus, there are some senses of the term that are more central to the concept than others. It is getting to the core of the concept as it is ordinarily used that is one of the principal tasks of the conceptual analyst.

In isolating questions of concept while avoiding a search for the "right" meaning of a concept, conceptual analysts use a number of techniques. They look for model cases where the concept is used in such a way that everyone agrees that it is a good use. For example, some liberal adult educators present liberal adult education as a model case for adult education. They examine the key characteristics of liberal adult education and compare other forms with it. They have also made the debatable point that the term *education* in adult education should be restricted only to liberal adult education.

Besides model cases, analysts examine concepts through the use of contrary cases—cases in which the term clearly cannot be appropriately used. Contrary cases have value in conceptual analysis especially in the preliminary stages when one is first setting out to establish parameters of usages of the concept.

Conceptual analysis is not always a value-free or neutral philosophical activity. Peters (1967) believes that there is a trend for those who do conceptual analysis to go beyond the analytic process to make normative proposals about what education should be like. He justifies the trend by observing that since education is concerned with questions of values, educational philosophers cannot ignore the issue of values.

Philosophical writing in adult education in the tradition of conceptual analysis includes the work of Snyder (1969), who used the procedure to clarify the concept of *involvement,* a term frequently used by adult educators.

Schwertz (1972) also turned to conceptual analysis to address the definition of *program* as used in adult education. Other, more recent, contributions have been made by Monette (1977), who turned to the concept of needs as noted in the literature of the field. The most comprehensive work, however, is of British origin. Lawson (1975) and Patterson (1979) provide the most sophisticated illustrations of analytic philosophy as applied in the field of adult education.

The most extensive example of analytic philosophy as yet available in adult education is Patterson's *Values, Education, and the Adult.* Patterson addresses a number of critical philosophical issues in his nine chapters. He seems to have arrived at organizing concepts similar to those used by Cotton and by Apps, discussed earlier. For example, he divided the focus of his inquiry into four segments: the concept of adult education, educational objectives, educational processes, and adult education and society. Briefly, he defines *education* in a traditional British manner, with its liberal arts orientation, as the development of individuals as independent centers of value whose development is seen to be intrinsically worthwhile. He continues to discriminate between teaching something only because it is good in itself (education) and teaching something only because acquisition of that knowledge or skill will help produce some extrinsic social or economic benefit. The former, according to Patterson, the learner *ought* to learn because it is inherently worthwhile, while the latter is worth doing only if the social and economic benefit cannot be achieved in some more direct way.

This brief introduction to Patterson's lengthy and interesting exercise serves well to illustrate the orientation of his philosophy of adult education as developed through analytic means. His book is provocative and should generate additional discussion among adult educators in America and the United Kingdom. It also serves well to illustrate the scholarly liberal arts philosophical tradition. No comparable analysis is available concerning other philosophical orientations that define education for adults according to an applied objective in contrast to Patterson's knowledge-centered objectives.

General Literature

The general literature, as revealed by Cotton's 1968 review (cited earlier), is instructive in identifying the range of philosophical orientations among educators of adults. A sampling of this body of literature is all that is required to make this point.

Some of the most heated debates concerning the philosophical formulations of adult education have concerned issues of "schooling," mandatory continuing education (MCE), professionalism, and the mission of adult education. Educators who have made known part of their philosophy on these and related issues include Gueulette, Carlson, Irish, Ohliger, Broschart, Verner, Boone, and Rauch. Some observations concerning the positions taken by these authors provide a good introduction to this body of literature.

Gueulette (1976) is one of several writers who have expressed deep and emotional objections to concepts associated with lifelong learning. He represents a sizable number of educators who have been quite strident in their warnings about the dangers of lifelong learning, *education permanente,* career education, mandatory continuing education, and other labels given to educational activities that are often interpreted as lifelong schooling.

Carlson (1977), who seems to agree with Gueulette, links the efforts to make adult education more of a profession to the schooling movement. He interprets several apparently independent events that occurred during the 1960s as being related to a desire among adult educators to achieve professional status. These events include a commitment of the Canadian Association of Adult Education, efforts of the Commission of Professors of the Adult Education Association of the U.S.A. to define the field of adult education, and efforts to improve theory building in adult education. Carlson implicitly and explicitly questions the motives of the professors and the effects of professionalization. He suggests that professionalization of the field will have negative consequences that are directly related to issues concerning the purpose of adult education and the relationship between learner and teacher.

Irish (1975) provides a useful specimen of the philosophical orientation which asserts that adult education has a social mission. She frequently raises questions about human nature, the right of personal control, the major purpose of adult education, and the individual as the source of content and educational processes.

The most radical position concerning institutionalization, professionalization, credentialization, and mandatory requirements for adult participation in education is reflected in the comments of Ohliger (1975). Much of Ohliger's recent writing on these topics is fugitive in nature and not widely reported in major adult education publications. The following quote, however, seems to capture the spirit of his objections (p. 39).

> This is *not* to say that we [adult educators] are any more evil than any other group in this country. But we are, like almost every other professional group, caught in the near tragic grip of the spiraling dilemma that the more we contribute, in the name of "helping people," to the trend . . . , the less we can live the best ethics of our profession.

Ohliger indicates that one of those ethics about which he is concerned is the partnership working relationship between adult educators and individuals and groups to help them increase their responsible control over their lives. Such a relationship, according to him, is undermined by large expenditures on adult education by both government and enterprise, which ultimately results in the shift of voluntary action to centralized control.

In contrast to the work of Gueulette, Carlson, and Irish, Broschart (1977) cites a series of documents that are supportive of lifelong learning and education of the individual for personal rather than social goals. However, like Bergevin's, Broschart's position concerning the purpose of education is not always clear. Broschart promotes the concept of lifelong learning as a way to enable each person to take charge of his or her life while developing individual potential, social participation, and citizenship.

Verner's position (Verner and Booth 1966) concerning the purpose of adult education seems to weigh more heavily in favor of individual goals, emphasizing formal instruction, the role of the teacher (agent in Verner's language), and programs that help individuals keep abreast of vital changes. Verner does not, however, oppose citizenship and basic education for adults.

In the introduction to a recently published anthology of comments on the mission of adult education, Boone (1980) also focuses on the individual. Even though his comments, in part, justify the education of adults in terms of social change, the individual as the key element in the educational mission is clear. Boone shares the opinion that from the earliest years adult education (which he describes as a movement) has emphasized the planned acquisition of knowledge and coping skills by individuals. Accordingly, he identifies the purpose for which knowledge and skills were achieved not as to change society but as to address personal needs.

Rauch (1972) also supports the view of the adult educator that some would refer to as the professional philosophical orientation in contrast to the social movement orientation. He indicates a belief in society's responsibility to provide as much education to all people as they want at all points in their lives. He further notes some of the many ways that people may benefit from their educational opportunity, including improved agricultural practices, art, occupational improvement, and political action. Rauch says, "Education, and particularly adult education, can offer a person only learning. What he does with that learning is partially in his own hands and partially in the hands of society" (p. 24). In addition to revealing something about his philosophy concerning the general mission of adult education, Rauch also shared something about his views of the relationship between the individual and society.

This brief and general sampling of adult education literature in the United States serves to sufficiently illustrate an extensive range of philosophical orientations. The comments from the works cited here generally address only the issue of the mission of adult education. They reveal how such adult educators as Carlson, Gueulette, and Irish subscribe to a social movement philosophy, while such others as Boone, Rauch, and Verner tend to identify more with what has been referred to as a professional orientation that focuses on education for individual goals. Other equally revealing statements can be found in the literature concerning the nature of the adult learner, instructional techniques, and content. Usually, however, the philosophical orientations of writers are not systematically and explicitly developed in the general literature. Writers who have written across a span of years may also reveal some changes over the period. Complete analysis of the corpus of the contributions of selected leaders of the field such as Hallenbeck, Houle, Kidd, Knowles, Knox, Kreitlow, Sheats, and Verner may be helpful in further explication of the philosophical foundations of the field.

OBSERVATIONS

This review of philosophical foundations for the education of adults reveals that the topic has been the subject of some censure for two reasons: first, the field of adult education lacks a coherent single unifying philosophy; second, educators of adults have tended to refrain from efforts to develop and publish alternative philosophical analyses. The first justification for criticism was identified as inappropriate because the diversity of the field seems to preclude the possibility of framing a broadly inclusive central philosophical rationale. The second evaluation is appropriate and was discussed in some detail. Accordingly, a variety of reasons that might be given by adult educators to explain their reluctance to engage in publishing philosophical works were cited.

The material examined and referred to in this chapter substantiates several points that should be remembered:

1. Different agencies, institutions, and organizations have disparate missions that are reflected in the definition of their educational goals and purposes.
2. The missions of diverse agencies, institutions, and organizations reflect different basic philosophies that are integral to their origin, structure, and survival.
3. As the field of adult education includes extremely diverse agencies, institutions and organizations reflecting different basic philosophical positions concerning the major issues in the education of adults will show a similar variety.
4. Major issues on which educators of adults fail to agree include, but are not limited to, the following.

   How the field of adult education should be defined
   The purpose of adult education
   Whether the focus is to be on the individual or on society
   The nature of the adult learner
   The relationship between the learner and the teacher
   The subject matter or content of the learning activity
5. The adult educator is interested not only in what is but why it is, and what it ought to be.

The various positions of educators of adults on the above and related topics reveal a certain degree of tension in the field on several other concerns. For example, is adult education a "social movement," or is it a profession? Another general question that influences how the practitioners and scholars line up concerns the political dimension. How politically sensitive is adult education? When does education become politicized?

Educators of adults struggling with the above issues, conflicts, and perspectives are also widely separated on the answer to the question "How shall we know?" Now that adult education is a university-based field of study, there are extreme pressures upon educators of adults to discover and generate new knowledge by empirical procedures. There does not appear to be pressure of equal strength upon the educator to seek to know through the method of philosophical analysis.

Other chapters in this volume, which report various research findings and related criticisms of the field of adult education, should be considered in a framework that includes the content of this chapter. Many of the perspectives on the different topics are not independent of the values and philosophical orientation of the investigators and reviewers.

14 · Foundations for the Future

THE PRECEDING THIRTEEN CHAPTERS are based upon hundreds of research reports concerning the education of adults. A very large number of studies were reviewed, but because of redundancy or questions concerning their validity, they were not all cited. The impressive feature of this extensive research concerning the education of adults is its total volume and increasing sophistication. Adult educators generally seem to be quite cautious about saying favorable things about the research conducted by other adult educators. The conservatism of reviewers probably derives from the "marginal" identification used to label adult education as a field of practice and study. Because adult educators perceive themselves to be engaged in what the literature has defined as marginal or peripheral educational activities, there is possibly a psychological explanation for a harsh self-critical attitude. Unfortunately, it appears that the self-flagellation has at times approached masochism.

My perception of the vast array of research reviewed for the purposes of this volume leads to a more optimistic view. This perception is also influenced by appreciation for some of the issues that confront the older disciplines such as anthropology, psychology, and sociology. Yes, adult education as a field is challenged to clean up its terminology, to establish parameters, to improve the rigor of its research, and to create new and creative concepts to guide both research and practice. The same kinds of challenges are posed for most fields of study. Even the most cursory reviews of the history of science or the evolution of theories in most of the disciplines indicate that similar calls are typical.

We are reminded of two proverbs that should guide our thinking in the assessment of the research reviewed here. First, volume is not sufficient cause for satisfaction. The Russian proverb about one hundred rabbits not making a horse addresses this point. But a second proverb from Turkey also should restrain us in our criticism and rejection of research in the field: Don't burn your blanket to kill the fleas. Such an act will rid us of the fleas, perhaps, but it will also eliminate our blanket.

In the first thirteen chapters of this volume an effort is made to judiciously present research that has implications for the study and practice of adult education in a variety of institutional settings. The studies and their findings were not selected to apply to one institution only or to one kind of educational context or structure. As it is possible from a precise scientific position to criticize many, if not all, of the research studies reported here from a position of theoretical rigor or purity, I have purposely chosen to consider the overall quality of specific studies rather than to focus on a questionable procedure. For example, research designs are perceived as a series of compromises, and few studies are sufficiently immune to the exigencies of budgets, time, sampling requirements, instrumentation quality, and other concerns to free them completely of critical comment. The study of adults is a particularly challenging activity because of the nature of the population. The availability of a sample with desirable characteristics for sufficient time to adequately study various phenomena is rare indeed.

Thus, with the confession that alternative hypotheses are not excluded by much of the research reviewed here, it should be observed that even so, the findings reported are encouraging. In essence, they provide adult educators with some acceptable foundations for practice. Let us review some of the more salient findings that have implications for the practice of adult education in the future.

LEARNING ABILITY

Five general conclusions concerning adult learning ability derived from the literature reviewed are noted below:

1. Age does not seem to be an important variable in the learning ability of adults. In other words, adults can continue to learn at an acceptable level of efficiency at least into the seventh decade of life.

2. Variables that may be associated with learning ability, and which are frequently associated with age, include health and other physiological changes. The concept of fluid intelligence (in contrast with crystallized intelligence) provides an explanatory framework for further analysis of biological and morphological variables in learning performance.

3. Concepts such as cognitive structure and cognitive style appear to be more meaningful and useful than age in explaining learning performance.

4. There is an increasing body of evidence that suggests that biological and morphological factors place certain limitations upon learning activities.

5. Mental functioning may be associated with certain chemical elements that may be emphasized or deemphasized through nutrition or the use of drugs.

ENROLLING THE ADULT

Five propositions based on the review of literature concerning participation and dropout of adults in educational activities are as follows:

1. Participation in educational activities seems to be more likely among adults who have an above-average educational achievement level and income, who work at white-collar types of jobs, and who live in urban areas.

2. Participation of blacks and other minority members does not appear to be a factor of race per se; low participation rates among these groups seem to be associated with socioeconomic factors.

3. Explanations for attrition among adult learners remain difficult to disentangle. In some ways, some of the personal, social, and institutional variables examined indicate that the same kinds of variables that are associated with original enrollment may also be associated with an adult's persistence in a learning situation.

4. Educators of adults appear to be increasingly sensitive to the desirability of explaining participation in such a way that the interaction of social (situational), personal (dispositional), and institutional structures is considered.

5. Models of participation are based on a rational concept of humanity rather than on psychoanalytical explanations.

PROGRAM BUILDING

Five salient observations based on the literature concerning program building activities include findings concerning procedures, needs assessment, marketing, recruiting, and physical surroundings. The summary observations on these topics are noted here:

1. Although there is general agreement in the literature concerning the broad outlines of the program planning procedure, the procedure itself remains a complex constellation of many action steps that are difficult to evaluate.

2. It is generally accepted that needs assessment is a desirable activity. Procedures to conduct needs assessment vary; conceptually the topic is unclear, but progress seems to characterize the research.

3. Marketing, promoting, and recruiting learners for educational purposes have been subjects of increasing research attention over the past five years though all the variables in these areas of concern have not been studied.

4. Recruitment activities in the Nordic countries indicate that workplace enrollment contacts may be relatively more successful than residential enlistment procedures.

5. There is some indication that one's physical surroundings associated with architectural and other environmental variables influence feelings, attitudes, and social interaction, but how this may affect learning is not known.

TEACHING-LEARNING TRANSACTIONS

The literature reviewed on teaching-learning transactions in adult education indicates that educators of adults are looking for more general explanatory concepts for teaching-learning effectiveness than a continuing emphasis on comparative studies. Findings that appear to be useful in conceptualizing some issues and research programs on this topic are noted below:

1. Intelligence and prior educational experience are important factors that are associated with learning performance.

2. Usefulness of the learning activity appears to be associated with interest in specific programs.

3. There are variables other than age that seem to be more important in explaining adult learning performance. Some of these include motivation and meaningfulness of the learning experience.

4. Teaching techniques are numerous and varied. There is, however, reason to believe that comparisons of teaching techniques without more stringent control will not be as productive in the near future as experimental work with given techniques in clearly identified circumstances.

5. Electronic formats and techniques appear to be as effective as face-to-face teaching techniques for a number of purposes.

6. Findings that computer-assisted instruction is more effective in attitude change than group discussion is represent a challenging area of study that seems to pose an important threat to concepts concerning social learning theories.

7. There are a number of personality variables that remain to be adequately studied before their association with learning performance becomes clear.

8. There is preliminary evidence that suggests that an individual who believes that he or she can make a difference in the outcome of life will make a greater effort to learn.

9. Personal characteristics that represent promising areas of research concerning learning performance include cognitive/learning styles.

10. Involvement of the adult learner in planning and conducting educational activities is believed to be associated with achievement, attendance, and

favorable attitudes. *Involvement* and *satisfaction,* however, are poorly defined terms.

11. Social dimensions of the learning activity seem to be important to many learners; some appear to be affected by social interactions with other learners, while for others, social relations with the teacher are more important.

12. Structure in learning seems to be poorly defined. Perhaps as a consequence, we discover that some learners opt for structure, and others prefer unstructured learning.

13. Teacher behaviors seem to have different consequences according to certain cognitive orientations of learners.

14. Preexisting attitudes toward education are often associated with participation and learning.

15. Independent self-directed learning is perceived to be a rather common phenomenon in most cultures studied.

16. Much learning is associated with an individual's perceived need to adjust to one of life's many transitions.

FIELD OF PRACTICE AND PHILOSOPHY

The issue of whether adult education is a field of practice and study seems to have been resolved in a *de facto* manner. In the meantime, a convincing body of research has developed that supports the idea that there is a legitimate field of practice identified as adult education. Parallel to the discussion of the legitimacy of adult education's status as a field of practice and study is wide concern about its philosophical underpinnings.

Literature reviewed here encouraged the formulation of the following statements concerning the status of adult education and its philosophical condition:

1. There is increasing acceptance of adult education as a field of professional practice that has a distinctive body of knowledge.

2. There is increasing agreement that professionals engaged in the education of adults require specific competencies.

3. For a number of years, the field of adult education has tended to be described as marginal and peripheral. Moses, however, opted for *peripheral* as the term to designate adult education, while he selected *core* to describe the other educational institutions of American society.

4. The philosophies that guide the practitioners in the field are as diverse as the agencies, institutions, and organizations that provide educational opportunities for adults.

5. The philosophies of adult education have been the object of increasing attention of philosophers and practitioners in the field, which will probably help sharpen some of the discussion concerning the purposes, parameters, and content of the field.

6. Analytic philosophy offers promise in helping to clarify some of the questions concerning the use of terms in adult education; it may thereby also be helpful in identifying parameters for the field.

7. Philosophical inquiry is a potentially valuable procedure for examining some basic questions in adult education that may not be adequately addressed through scientific empiricism.

CONTRIBUTIONS

The preceding statements and the research from which they are derived are instructive. When one assesses the status of the field and the research concerning the education of adults in 1959, when Brunner and his associates made their worthy contribution, and considers these findings collectively, they become more impressive. For example, the participation studies provide us with a useful profile of the individual likely to participate in educational activities designed for adults. Program planners, through demographic and psychosocial analyses, can, with a margin of error, predict the potential audience for specific kinds of general adult educational programs. Botsman's work and the Nordic experience emphasize certain characteristics of blue-collar workers that should be considered in enlistment campaigns for them. Challenges remain in the recruitment of minority members of society, but the evidence concerning participation patterns at least provides the program planner with advance awareness of the difficulty that such programs may encounter.

Various models reported in this review illustrate that there is no absence of theoretical frameworks for the study of certain phenomena of interest to educators of adults, such as participation motives, program development procedures, and learning. The various methods of determining needs of individuals, target groups, and communities also provide the practitioner and the researcher with points of departure that have been described in diverse ways and great quantity.

It is obvious that the field of adult education is, has been, and will continue to be dependent upon a number of the social and behavioral sciences and related disciplines for basic research and theory building. This should be seen as one of the positive dimensions of the field. We are not restricted to one kind of explanatory option. For example, questions of participation and persistence may be examined from a psychological, sociological, or psychosocial perspective. Researchers and practitioners thus can develop their models from the work of a variety of scholars, as Bergsten and Rubenson have done. Such a dependence upon social science disciplines does not reduce the challenge before theoreticians, researchers, and teachers of adults. We are greatly challenged to discover fruitful ways of applying the theory and basic research data derived from related disciplines. Some believe that this is the most difficult task.

QUESTIONS

Despite the progress made in the research in adult education, or because of it, a number of questions yet remain. Some years ago Kreitlow (1970) observed that researchers in adult education were interested in the question of "what" to the exclusion of the question of "why." To an important degree, it appears that we also have tended to neglect the questions of "when" and "how." Ultimately, all these kinds of questions must be answered in a comprehensive manner. For example, philosophical support exists for the practice of involving the adult learner in planning and conducting the learning activity. This is a "what" question that has a philosophical "why" dimension and which, to a limited degree, has been addressed in a "why" manner that justifies involvement on the basis that it may contribute to learner achievement, attendance, and positive attitudes. Vedros and Pankowski (1980) have addressed the "how" question from at least one perspective that recommends the nominal group approach. The "when" and "who" questions, however, have yet to be addressed through research.

The continuing emergence of new questions is not a cause for alarm. Instead, it should be a source of satisfaction. Theories are frequently judged by their fruitfulness. Thus, new theories and research findings should generate additional efforts to obtain more answers that will contribute to improved practice. The generation and development of knowledge through the several ways that we have of creating knowledge are seen as a positive and constructive process for educators of adults to continue to improve the foundations for the practice of adult education.

SUMMARY

This chapter provides a concluding comment on the volume. Here I have made some comments about the nature of the research reviewed and some general guidelines that influenced my inclusion and selection of research reports. It is noted that most areas of scientific inquiry fail to measure up to the highest possible requirements of rigor and that alternative hypotheses can be offered for most of the research cited in this volume, regardless of the discipline of the original investigator. However, rather than focus on the weaknesses of various research designs and procedures the overall quality of selected works was considered.

I believe that the value of the findings reported in the chapter is to be found in the simultaneous consideration of a number of these findings. Such a holistic perception of the research data represents an impressive advancement in knowledge concerning questions of lifelong learning over the last twenty years.

Questions remain. New concepts and new questions have emerged from research conducted over the last twenty years. The expansion in the number of questions, however, is seen as a positive sign that will contribute to the strengthening of the foundations for future practice in the education of adults.

References

As a convenience for the reader, abstract sources are included in dissertation references. Abbreviations are explained below:

AEDA, 1970: DeCrow, Roger, and Loague, Nehume (Eds.). *Adult Education Dissertation Abstracts, 1963–67.* Washington, D.C.: Adult Education Association of the U.S.A., 1970.

AEDA, n.d.: Grabowski, S. M., and Loague, Nehume (Eds.). *Adult Education Dissertation Abstracts, 1968–69.* Washington, D.C.: Adult Education Association of the U.S.A., n.d.

DAI: *Dissertation Abstracts International.*

RAE: Charnley, Alan H. (Ed.). *Research in Adult Education in the British Isles: Abstracts and Summaries Principally of Masters and Doctoral Theses Presented Since 1945.* London: National Institute of Adult Education, 1974.

Adams, J. S. "Reduction of Cognitive Dissonance by Seeking Consonant Information." *Journal of Abnormal and Social Psychology*, 1961, 62, 75–78. (Cited by Zahn 1969.)

Aker, George F. "The Identification of Criteria for Evaluating Programs in Adult Education." Doctoral dissertation, University of Wisconsin–Madison, 1962. [*DAI*, 1962, 22, 3914.]

Aker, George F.; Jahns, I. R.; and Schroeder, W. L. *Evaluation of an Adult Basic Education Program in a Southern Rural Community.* Tallahassee, Fla.: Florida State University, Department of Adult Education, 1968.

Al-Adasany, Haskamiah. "Reasons for Drop-out as Seen in the Center for Illiteracy in Kuwait." Cairo: UAR Government Press, 1972. (Cited by Hamidi 1978, p. 35.)

Allerton, Thomas D. "Selected Characteristics of the Learning Projects Pursued by Parish Ministers in the Louisville Metropolitan Area." Doctoral dissertation, University of Georgia, 1974. [*DAI*, 1975, *35*, 6422-A.]

Altman, I. *Environmental and Social Behavior*. Belmont, Calif.: Wadsworth, 1975.

American Association of Professors of Higher Education. *Newsletter*. Washington, D.C.: American Association for Higher Education, 1975, *30*, 5.

Anania, Pasquale. "Adult Age and the Education of Adults in Colonial America." Doctoral dissertation, University of California–Berkeley, 1969. [*DAI*, 1970, *30*, 4247-A.]

Anders, Terry R.; Fozard, James L.; and Lillyquist, Timothy D. "Effects of Age Upon Retrieval from Short-Term Memory." *Developmental Psychology*, 1972, *6* (2), 214–217.

Anderson, Darrell, and Niemi, John A. *Adult Education and the Disadvantaged Adult*. Syracuse, N. Y.: ERIC Clearinghouse on Adult Education, 1969.

Anderson, J. R. *Language, Memory, and Thought*. Hillsdale, N. J.: Lawrence Erlbaum Associates, 1976.

Anderson, Richard, and Darkenwald, Gordon. *Participation and Persistence in American Adult Education*. New York: Future Directions for a Learning Society, College Board, 1979.

Andrulus, Richard S., and Bush, David. "Adult Cognitive Styles and Test Performance." *Educational Gerontology*, 1977, *2*, 173–182.

Apps, Jerold W. "Toward a Broader Definition of Research." *Adult Education*, 1972, 23 (1), 59–64.

Apps, Jerold W. *Problems in Continuing Education*. New York: McGraw-Hill, 1979.

Apps, Jerold W. *The Adult Learner on Campus*. Chicago: Follett Publishing Company, 1981.

Archambault, Reginald D. "The Concept of Need and Its Relation to Certain Aspects of Educational Theory." *Harvard Educational Review*, 1957, 27, 38–62.

Arlin, P. K. "Cognitive Development in Adulthood: A Fifth Stage?" *Developmental Psychology*, 1975, *5*, 602–606.

Armstrong, David. "Adult Learners of Low Educational Attainment: The Self-Concepts, Backgrounds, and Educative Behavior of Average and High Learning Adults of Low Educational Attainment." Doctoral dissertation, University of Toronto, 1971. [*DAI*, 1972, *33*, 944–945-A.]

Armstrong, Leslie H. "A Survey of Adult Education Classes in the State of Washington." Doctoral dissertation, Washington State University, 1965. [*AEDA*, 1970, p. 36.]

Ashford, Mary. "A Comparative Analysis of the Perceived Importance of Selected Occupational Factors to Adult Educators." Doctoral dissertation, University of Georgia, 1978. [*DAI*, 1979, *39*, 4654-A.]

Aslanian, Carol B., and Brickell, Henry M. *Americans in Transition*. New York: College Entrance Examination Board, 1980.

Atwood, Mason, and Ellis, Joe. "The Concept of Need: An Analysis for Adult Education." *Adult Leadership*, 1971, *19*, 210–212.

Auch, F. L. "The Differential Effects of Age Upon Human Learning." *Journal of Genetic Psychology*, 1934, *11*, 261.

Ausubel, D. P. "The Fascination of Meaningful Verbal Learning in the Classroom." *Educational Psychologist*, 1977, *12*, 168.

Bagnall, R. G. "Principles of Adult Education in the Design and Management of Instruction." *Australian Journal of Adult Education*, 1978, *18* (1), 19–28.

Baldwin, J. M. *Genetic Theory of Reality*. New York: G. P. Putnam's Sons, 1915.

Baltes, Paul B., and Schaie, K. Warner. "Aging and I. Q.: The Myth of the Twilight Years." *Psychology Today*, March 1974, 35–40.

Barnes, Robert F., and Hendrickson, Andrew. *A Review and Appraisal of Adult Literacy Materials and Programs*. Columbus: Ohio State University Research Foundation, 1965.

Barnett, Ellen. "Comparative Effectiveness of Three Instructional Formats in Small-Group Continuing Education for Physicians in Community Hospitals." Doctoral dissertation, University of Southern California, 1973. [*DAI*, 1973, *34*, 547-A.]

Baron, R. M.; Cowan, G.; Ganz, R. L.; and McDonald, M. "Interaction of Control and Type of Performance Feedback: Considerations of External Validity." *Journal of Personality and Social Psychology*, 1974, *30*, 285–292.

Baron R. M., and Ganz, R. L. "Effects of Locus of Control and Type of Feedback on the Task Performance of Lower Class Black Children." *Journal of Personality and Social Psychology*, 1972, *21*, 124–130.

Bayley, Nancy, and Oden, M. H. "The Maintenance of Intellectual Ability in Gifted Adults." *Journal of Gerontology*, 1955, *10*, 91–107.

Beatty, Jackson. "Activation and Attention in the Human Brain." In M. C. Wittrock et al. (Eds.), *The Human Brain*. Englewood Cliffs, N.J.: Prentice-Hall, 1977.

Beatty, Paulette T. "A Process Model for the Development of an Information Base for Community Needs Assessment: A Guide for Practitioners." ERIC, 1976, ED 128 616.

Bennett, Nancy L. "Learning Styles of Health Professionals Compared to Preference for Continuing Education Program Format." Doctoral dissertation, University of Illinois at Urbana-Champaign, 1978. [*DAI*, 1979, *39*, 7109-A.]

Berg, Clay N., Jr. "Relationship Among Teachers' Knowledge and Application of Principles of Adult Teaching and Student Satisfaction." ERIC, 1969, ED 052 454.

Bergevin, Paul. *A Philosophy for Adult Education*. New York: Seabury Press, 1967.

Bergevin, Paul; McKinley, John; and Smith, Robert M. "The Adult Education Activity: Content, Processes, and Procedures." In Gale Jensen, A. A. Liveright, and Wilbur Hallenbeck (Eds.), *Adult Education: Outlines of an Emerging Field of University Study*. Washington, D.C.: Adult Education Association of the U.S.A., 1964.

Bergevin, Paul; Morris, Dwight; and Smith, Robert. *Adult Education Procedures*. New York: Seabury Press, 1963.

Bergsten, U. "Interest in Education Among Adults with Short Previous Formal Schooling." *Adult Education*, 1980, *30* (3), 131–151.

Berry, Dick. "A Multi-Phasic Motivational Paradigm for Adult Education." *Adult Education*, 1971, *22* (1), 48–56.

Bertelsen, Paul H. "Adult Education: A Position Paper." Unpublished report to UNESCO, 1974, p. 4. (Cited by Coles 1978, p. 5.)

Bertinot, Elizabeth A. "Choice of Learning Format as a Function of Three Constructs: Personality Variables, Cognitive Style, and Locus of Control." In Gene C. Whaples and D. Merrill Ewert (Eds.), *Proceedings: Lifelong Learning Research Conference.* College Park, Md.: Cooperative Extension Service, University of Maryland, 1979.

Birren, Faber. *New Horizons in Color.* New York: Reinhold, 1958.

Birren, Faber. *Light, Color, and Environment.* New York: Van Nostrand Reinhold, 1969.

Birren, J. E., and Botwinick, J. "The Relation of Writing Speed to Age and to the Senile Psychoses." *Journal of Consulting Psychology,* 1951, *15,* 243–249.

Bittner, W. S. "Adult Education." In W. S. Monroe (Ed.), *Encyclopedia of Educational Research* (rev. ed.). New York: Macmillan, 1950.

Blackburn, Donald J., and Douglah, Mohammed. "Method Orientation of Adults for Participation in Educative Activities." Paper presented at the National Adult Education Research Conference, 1968.

Blackwell, Gordon. "The Needs of the Community as a Determinant of Evening College." In Gordon Blackwell, *Purposes of the Evening College.* Boston: Center for the Study of Liberal Education for Adults, 1967.

Blakely, Robert J. "Adult Education Needs a Philosophy and a Goal." *Adult Education,* 1952, *3,* 1–10.

Blaney, John P., and McKie, Douglas. "Knowledge of Conference Objectives and Effect Upon Learning." *Adult Education,* 1969, *19* (2), 98–105.

Bligh, Donald M. "Are Teaching Innovations in Post-Secondary Education Irrelevant?" In Michael J. A. Howe (Ed.), *Adult Learning: Psychological Research and Applications.* New York: John Wiley and Sons, 1977.

Blum, J. E., and Jarvik, L. F. "Intellectual Performance of Octogenarians as a Function of Educational Initial Ability." *Human Development,* 1974, *17,* 364–375.

Bock, Linda K. "Participation." In Alan B. Knox et al., *Developing, Administering, and Evaluating Adult Education.* San Francisco: Jossey-Bass, 1980.

Bogen, J. E. "Some Education Aspects of Hemispheric Specialization." *UCLA Educator,* 1975, *17* (2).

Bogen, J. E. "Some Educational Implications of Hemispheric Specialization." In M. C. Wittrock et al., *The Human Brain.* Englewood Cliffs, N.J.: Prentice-Hall, 1977.

Bohman, Lee Garrison. "The Effects of Variations in Educational Behavior on the Learning Process in Laboratory Human Relations Training." ERIC, 1968, ED 039 476.

Bolton, E. B. "Cognitive and Noncognitive Factors That Affect Learning in Older Adults and Their Implications for Instruction." *Educational Gerontology,* 1978, *3,* 331–344.

Boone, E. J. "Introduction: Serving Needs Through Adult Education." In Edgar J. Boone et al. (Eds.), *Serving Personal and Community Needs Through Adult Education.* San Francisco: Jossey-Bass, 1980.

Boone, E. J.; Dolan, R. J.; and Shearon, Ronald W. *Programming in the Cooperative Extension Service: A Conceptual Schema.* Raleigh, N.C.: North Carolina Agricultural Extension Service, North Carolina State University, 1971.

Boshier, Roger. "Motivational Orientations of Adult Education Participants: A Factor Analytic Exploration of Houle's Typology." *Adult Education,* 1971, *21* (2), 3–26.

Boshier, Roger. "The Development and Use of a Dropout Prediction Scale." *Adult Education,* 1972, *22* (2), 87–99.

Boshier, Roger. "Educational Participation and Dropout: A Theoretical Model." *Adult Education*, 1973, 23 (4), 255–282.

Boshier, Roger, and Baker, Gary. "Effects of Fees on Clientele Characteristics and Participation in Adult Education." *Adult Education*, 1979, 29 (3), 151–169.

Boshier, Roger, and Collins, John. "Education Participation Scale Factor Structure and Norms for Thirteen Thousand Learners." Paper presented at the Adult Education Research Conference, Lincoln, Nebraska, April 1982.

Boshier, Roger, and Riddell, Gail. "Education Participation Scale Factor Structure for Older Adults." *Adult Education*, 1978, 28 (3), 165–175.

Botsman, Peter B. *The Learning Needs and Interests of Adult Blue Collar Factory Workers.* Ithaca, N.Y.: New York State College of Human Ecology, March 1975.

Botwinick, Jack. *Cognitive Processes in Maturity and Old Age.* New York: Springer, 1967.

Bowen, H. R. *Investment in Learning: The Individual and Social Value of American Higher Education.* San Francisco: Jossey-Bass, 1977.

Boyd, Robert D. "Basic Motivations of Adults in Non-Credit Programs." *Adult Education*, 1961, 11 (2), 92–94.

Boyd, Robert D. "New Designs for Adult Education Research Programs." *Adult Education*, 1969, 19 (3), 186–196.

Boyd, Robert D. "A Model for the Analysis of Motivation." *Adult Education*, 1965, 16 (1), 24–33.

Boyd, Robert D., and Apps, Jerold W. "A Conceptual Model for Adult Education." In Robert D. Boyd and Jerold W. Apps (Eds.), *Redefining the Discipline of Adult Education.* San Francisco: Jossey-Bass, 1980a.

Boyd, Robert D., and Apps, Jerold W. "Response." In Robert D. Boyd and Jerold W. Apps (Eds.), *Redefining the Discipline of Adult Education.* San Francisco: Jossey-Bass, 1980b.

Boyd, Rosemond R., and Oakes, Charles E. (Eds.). *Foundations of Practical Gerontology.* Columbia, S.C.: University of South Carolina Press, 1969.

Boyle, Patrick G. "Planning with Principles." In Coolie Verner and Thurman White (Eds.), *Administration of Adult Education.* Washington, D.C.: Adult Education Association of the U.S.A., 1965.

Boyle, Patrick G. *Planning Better Programs.* New York: McGraw-Hill, 1981.

Boyle, William Joseph. "Adult Participation in Educational Activities." Doctoral dissertation, University of Wisconsin, 1967. [*AEDA*, 1970, p. 34.]

Bradshaw, Jonathan. "The Concept of Social Need." *Ekistics*, March 1974 (220), 184–187.

Brady, Henry G., and Long, Huey B. "Differences in Perceptions of Program Planning Procedures." *Adult Education*, 1972, 22 (2), 122–135.

Brieger, Karen L. "Older Adults Learning Productivity in Team and Individual Settings Utilizing Criterion Referenced Instructional Modules." Doctoral dissertation, University of San Francisco, 1980. [*DAI*, 1980, 41, 3834-A.]

Broadwell, M. M. "Classroom Instruction." In R. L. Craig (Ed.), *Training and Development Handbook.* New York: McGraw-Hill, 1976.

Brodey, W. M. "Soft Architecture: The Design of Intelligent Environments." *Landscape*, 1967, 17 (1), 8–12.

Brookfield, Stephen. "Adult Education Research: A Comparison of North American Theory and Practice." *International Journal of Lifelong Education,* 1982, *1* (2), 157–168.

Broschart, James R. *Lifelong Learning in the Nation's Third Century.* Washington, D.C.: U.S. Department of Health, Education, and Welfare, Office of Education. U.S. Government Printing Office, 1977.

Brown, Robert D., et al. "Adult Learner Characteristics and Their Responsiveness to Multi-Media Instructional Programs Designed for an Open University System." ERIC, 1973, ED 086 158.

Brunner, Edmund deS.; Wilder, David S.; Kirchner, Corinne; and Newberry, John S., Jr. *An Overview of Adult Education Research.* Washington, D.C.: Adult Education Association of the U.S.A., 1959.

Bryson, Lyman. *Adult Education.* New York: American Book Company, 1936.

Buchanan, W. Wray, and Barksdale, H. C. "Marketing's Broadening Concept Is Real in University Extension." *Adult Education,* 1974, *25* (1), 34–46.

Buchsbaum, Monte S. "Tuning in on Hemispheric Dialogue." *Psychology Today,* January 1979, p. 100.

Buckley, Margaret B. "A Field Study Comparing Closed-Circuit Television and Face-to-Face Instruction for an Adult Reading Improvement Course." Doctoral dissertation, University of South Carolina, 1962. [*DAI,* 1962, *23,* 2780.]

Burgess, Paul. "Reasons for Adult Participation in Group Educational Activities." *Adult Education,* 1971, *22* (1), 3–29.

Busse, E. W. "Theories of Aging." In E. W. Busse and E. Pfeiffer (Eds.), *Behavior and Adaptation in Later Life.* Boston: Little, Brown, 1969.

Butler, John L. "A Study of the Effectiveness of Lecture Versus Conference Teaching Techniques in Adult Learning." Doctoral dissertation, New York University, 1965. [*DAI,* 1966, *26,* 3712.]

Buttedahl, Knute, and Verner, Coolie. "Characteristics of Participants in Two Methods of Adult Education." *Adult Education,* 1965, *15,* 67–73.

Campbell, Duncan D. *Adult Education as a Field of Study and Practice.* Vancouver: Centre for Continuing Education, University of British Columbia, 1977.

Carey, J. T. "Is University Adult Education a Profession?" *Adult Education,* 1958, *8* (2), 76–81.

Carlson, Robert A. "Professionalization of Adult Education: An Historical-Philosophical Analysis." *Adult Education,* 1977, *28* (1), 53–63.

Carlson, Robert A. "The Foundation of Adult Education: Analyzing the Boyd-Apps Model." In Robert D. Boyd and Jerold W. Apps (Eds.), *Redefining the Discipline of Adult Education.* San Francisco: Jossey-Bass, 1980.

Carp, Abraham; Peterson, Richard; and Roelfs, Pamela. "Adult Learning Interest and Experiences." In K. Patricia Cross and John R. Valley (Eds.), *Planning Non-Traditional Programs.* San Francisco: Jossey-Bass, 1974.

Carpenter, W. L. "The Relationship of Age to Information Processing Capacity of Adults." Paper presented at the annual Adult Education Research Conference, New York, New York, 1971.

Carson, Raymond P. "Factors Related to the Participation of Selected Young Males in Continuing Education." Doctoral dissertation, Florida State University, 1965. [*AEDA,* 1970, pp. 36–37.]

Carter, C. Sue, and Greenough, William T. "Sending the Right Sex Messages." *Psychology Today*, September 1979, p. 112.

Carter, G. W. "Action Research." In Ernest B. Harper and Arthur Dunham (Eds.), *Community Organization in Action: Basic Literature and Critical Comments*. New York: Association Press, 1959.

Cartwright, D., and Harary, F. "Structural Balance: A Generation of Heider's Theory." *Psychological Review*, 1956, *63*, 277–293.

Cassirer, E. *Philosophy of Symbolic Forms*. Vol. 3: Phenomenology of Knowledge. 1929. Reprint. New Haven: Yale University Press, 1957.

Castillo, Gregoria A. G. "Student and Teacher Performance in Adult Basic Education." Doctoral dissertation, University of Missouri–Columbia, 1976. [*DAI*, 1977, *38*, 591-A.]

Castle, David. "The Effect of Participation Training on the Self-System." Doctoral dissertation, Indiana University, 1965. [*AEDA*, 1970, p. 73.]

Cattell, Raymond B. *The Scientific Analysis of Personality*. Baltimore: Penguin Books, 1965.

Cawley, Richard; Miller, Sheila; and Milligan, James. "Cognitive Styles and the Adult Learner." *Adult Education*, 1976, *26* (2), 101–116.

Chamberlain, M. N. "The Competencies of Adult Educators." *Adult Education*, 1961a, *11* (2), 78–83.

Chamberlain, M. N. "The Professional Adult Educator: An Examination of His Competencies and of the Programs of Graduate Study Which Prepare Him for Work in the Field." Doctoral dissertation, University of Chicago, 1961b.

Chiapetta, E. L. "A Perspective on Formal Thought Development." Paper presented at the 48th annual meeting of the National Association for Research in Science Teaching, Los Angeles, California, March 1975. ERIC, ED 108 862.

Chu, G. H., and Schramm, W. "Learning from Television What the Research Says." Palo Alto, Calif.: Stanford Institute for Communications Research, 1967.

Clark, Burton R. *Adult Education Transition: A Study of Institutional Insecurity*. Berkeley: University of California Press, 1958.

Clark, L. E., and Knowles, J. B. "Age Differences in Dichotic Listening Performance." *Journal of Gerontology*, 1973, *28*, 173–178.

Coates, Paul M. "Integration of Evaluation and Instructional Methodology." Doctoral dissertation, Iowa State University, 1980. [*DAI*, 1981, *41*, 3835-A.]

Cochran, George Clark. "Relation Between Preference for Delayed Gratification and Behavior in an Industrial Training Program." Doctoral dissertation, Stanford University, 1967. [*AEDA*, 1970, p. 31.]

Cocking, W. D. "Environment Teaches." In H. C. Hunsaker and R. Pierce (Eds.), *Creating a Climate for Adult Learning*. Lafayette, Ind.: Purdue University, 1958.

Coggins, Chere S. "Application of the Freire Method in North America: An Exploratory Study with Implications for Adult Education." Masters thesis, University of Wisconsin–Madison, 1973.

Cohen, Rosalie. "Conceptual Styles, Culture Conflict, and Non-Verbal Tests of Intelligence." *American Anthropologist*, 1969, *7*, 828–856.

Cole, J. William, and Glass, J. Conrad, Jr. "The Effects of Adult Student Participation in Program Planning on Achievement, Retention, and Attitudes." *Adult Education*, 1977, *27* (2), 75–88.

Coleman, Sandra B. "The Effects of Aging on Piaget's Developmental Stages: A Study of Cognitive Decline." Doctoral dissertation, Temple University, 1973. [*DAI*, 1973, *34*, 1122-A.]

Coles, Edwin K. Townsend. *Adult Education in Developing Countries* (2nd ed.). New York: Pergamon Press, 1978.

Collins, A. M., and Quillian, M. R. "How to Make a Language User." In E. Tulving and W. Donaldson (Eds.), *Organization of Memory*. New York: Academic Press, 1972.

Collins, Mike. "Doing Philosophical Research in Adult Education." *Perspectives in Adult Learning and Development*, 1981, 2 (1), 20–27.

Commander, Frank. "A Study of Attitudes and Achievement in Adult Basic Education Teacher Training Programs." Doctoral dissertation, University of Georgia, 1971. [*DAI*, 1972, *32*, 5523-A.]

Commission of Professors of Adult Education, Adult Education Association of the U.S.A. *Adult Education: A New Imperative for Our Times*. Washington, D.C.: Adult Education Association of the U.S.A., 1961.

Commission on Non-Traditional Study. *Diversity by Design*. San Francisco: Jossey-Bass, 1973.

Committee for Economic Development. *Innovation in Education: New Directions for the American School*. New York: Committee for Economic Development, 1969.

Conlin, Bernard J., et al. "The Comparison of Telelecture and Regular Lecture in the Transfer of Knowledge to Adults." ERIC, 1973, ED 070 946.

Connellan, Thomas K. Personal correspondence with T. K. Connellan, Editorial Director, Graduate School of Business Administration, Division of Management Education, University of Michigan, Ann Arbor, Michigan, April 3, 1973.

Coolican, Patricia M. "The Learning Styles of Mothers of Young Children." Doctoral dissertation, Syracuse University, 1973. [*DAI*, 1975, *35*, 4958-A.]

Coombs, P. H. *New Paths to Learning for Rural Children and Youth*. New York: International Council for Educational Development, 1973.

Cotton, Webster E. *On Behalf of Adult Education*. Boston: Center for the Study of Liberal Education for Adults, 1968.

Cravens, R. W., and Worchel, P. "The Differential Effects of Rewarding and Coercive Leaders on Group Membership Differing in Locus of Control." *Journal of Personality*, 1977, *45*, 150–168.

Cronback, Lee J. "How Can Instruction Be Adapted to Individual Differences?" In R. M. Gage (Ed.), *Learning and Individual Differences*. Columbus, Ohio: Merrill, 1967.

Cronback, Lee J., and Suppes, Patrick (Eds.). *Research for Tomorrow's Schools: Disciplined Inquiry for Education*. New York: Macmillan, 1969.

Cross, K. Patricia. "When Will Research Improve Education?" *The Research Reporter*, 1967, *11* (4), 1–4.

Cross, K. Patricia. *Accent on Learning*. San Francisco: Jossey-Bass, 1976.

Cross, K. Patricia. "Adult Learners: Characteristics, Needs, and Interests." In Richard E. Peterson et al., *Lifelong Learning in America*. San Francisco: Jossey-Bass, 1979.

Cross, K. Patricia. *Adults as Learners*. San Francisco: Jossey-Bass, 1981.

Curle, A. "A Theoretical Approach to Action Research." *Human Relations*, 1949, 2, 269–280.

Curtis, John A. "Instructional Television Fixed Service: A Most Valuable Educational Resource." In John A. Curtis and Joseph M. Biedenback (Eds.), *Educational Telecommunications Delivery Systems*. Washington, D.C.: American Society for Engineering Education, 1979.

Czarnecki, Karen Gordon. "Adult Performance on the Test of General Educational Development as a Function of Field Dependent-Independent Cognitive Style." Doctoral dissertation, Rutgers University, 1980. [*DAI*, 1981, *41*, 3836-A.]

Darkenwald, Gordon G., and Merriam, Sharan B. *Adult Education: Foundations of Practice*. New York: Harper and Row, 1982.

David, T. G., and Wright, B. E. *Learning Environments*. Chicago: University of Chicago Press, 1975.

Davis, George S. "A Study of Classroom Factors Related to Dropouts in Adult Education." Doctoral dissertation, Florida State University, 1963. [*AEDA*, 1970, pp. 45–46.]

Davis, George S. "A Study of Classroom Factors Related to Dropouts." *Adult Education*, 1966, *17* (1), 38–40.

Davison, Catherine V. "The Effects of Goal Specifications and Instructor Behavior on Information Acquisition by Adult Learners." Doctoral dissertation, University of British Columbia, 1972. [*DAI*, 1973, *34*, 548-A.]

DeCosmo, Richard D. "A Study of Field Dependence-Independence: Selected Curricula Choices and Preferred Guidance Strategies of Adult Evening Community College Students." Doctoral dissertation, Loyola University of Chicago, 1977. [*DAI*, 1977, *38*, 112-A.]

DeCrow, Roger. "Programs and Providers of Adult Education: A National Overview." Washington, D.C.: Adult Education Association of the U.S.A., 1975. (Cited by Broschart 1977, p. 12.)

Denis, Margaret. "Intuitive Learning Among Adults." Paper presented at the annual Adult Education Research Conference, Ann Arbor, Michigan, 1979.

Denys, Laurent O. J. "The Major Learning Efforts of Two Groups of Accra Adults." Doctoral dissertation, University of Toronto, 1973. [*DAI*, 1975, *35*, 5759-A.]

DeVries, James. "Agricultural Extension and the Development of Ujamaa Villages in Tanzania: Toward a Dialogical Agricultural Extension Model." Doctoral dissertation, University of Wisconsin–Madison, 1978. [*DAI*, 1978, *39*, 1991-A.]

Dewey, John. *Democracy and Education*. New York: Macmillan, 1916. Copyright renewed 1944 by John Dewey.

Diamond, Marian C. "Aging and Cell Loss: Calling for an Honest Count." *Psychology Today*, September 1978, p. 126.

Dickerman, Watson. "Implications of This Book for Programs of Graduate Study in Adult Education." In Gale Jensen, A. A. Liveright, and Wilbur Hallenbeck (Eds.), *Adult Education: Outlines of an Emerging Field of University Study*. Washington, D.C.: Adult Education Association of the U.S.A., 1964.

Dickinson, Gary. "Educational Variables and Participation in Adult Education: An Exploratory Study." *Adult Education*, 1971, *22* (1), 36–47.

Dickinson, Gary. *Contributions to a Discipline of Adult Education: A Review and Analysis of the Publications of Coolie Verner*. Vancouver: Centre for Continuing Education, University of British Columbia, 1979.

Dickinson, Gary, and Clark, K. M. "Learning Orientations and Participation in Self-Education and Continuing Education." *Adult Education*, 1975, *26* (1), 3–15.

Dickinson, Gary, and Verner, Coolie. "Attendance Patterns and Drop-outs in Adult Night School Classes." *Adult Education*, 1967, *19* (1), 24–33.

Diekhoff, John S. "The Teachers of Adults." In Marilyn V. Miller (Ed.), *On Teaching Adults: An Anthology*. Boston: Center for the Study of Liberal Education for Adults, 1960.

Dietrich, J. E. "A Conference to Stimulate Research and Development on Curriculum and Instructional Innovation at Large Schools and Universities." Washington, D.C.: U.S. Department of Health, Education, and Welfare, Office of Education, 1966.

Diggins, Dean, and Huber, Jack. *The Human Personality*. Boston: Little, Brown, 1976.

Dobbs, Ralph C. "Self Perceived Educational Needs of Adults." *Adult Education*, 1966, *16* (2), 92–100.

Donnarumma, Theresa; Cox, David; and Beder, Hal. "Success in a High School Completion Program and Its Relation to Field Dependence-Independence." *Adult Education*, 1980, *30* (4), 222–232.

Dooley, Bobby J., and White, W. F. "Motivational Patterns of a Select Group of Adult Evening College Students." *Journal of Educational Research*, 1968, *62* (2), 65–66.

Douglah, Mohammed A. "Factors Affecting Adult Participation in Educational Activities and Voluntary Formal Organizations." Doctoral dissertation, University of Wisconsin, 1965. [*AEDA*, 1970, pp. 35–36.]

Douglah, Mohammed. "Some Perspectives on the Phenomenon of Participation." *Adult Education*, 1970, *20* (2), 88–98.

Douglah, Mohammed, and Moss, Gwenna. "Differential Participation Patterns of Adults of Low and High Educational Attainment." *Adult Education*, 1968, *18* (4), 247–259.

Dow, J. "Characteristics of Noncredit University Extension Students." Doctoral dissertation, University of California–Berkeley, 1965. [*DAI*, 1966, *26*, 3734.]

Doyle, W. "Paradigms for Research on Teacher Effectiveness." In L. S. Shulman (Ed.), *Review of Research in Education*, Vol. 5. Itasca, Ill.: F. E. Peacock, 1978.

Drane, Richard Steven. "The Effects of Participation Training on Adult Literacy in a Mental Hospital." Doctoral dissertation, Indiana University, 1967. [*AEDA*, 1970, p. 75.]

Dubin, Samuel S., and Okun, Morris. "Implications of Learning Theories for Adult Instruction." *Adult Education*, 1973, *24* (1), 3–19.

DuCette, J., and Wolk, S. "Cognitive and Motivational Correlation of Generalized Expectancies for Control." *Journal of Personality and Social Psychology*, 1973, *26*, 420–426.

Dugger, James G. "Motivation and Factors Characterizing Adult Learners Enrolled in Evening Courses at Drake University." Doctoral dissertation, Iowa State University of Science and Technology, 1965. [*AEDA*, 1970, p. 37.]

Dulit, Everett. "Adolescent Thinking à la Piaget: The Formal Stage." *Journal of Youth and Adolescence*, 1972, *1*, 281–301.

Easting, Geoffrey. "Programme Research and Its Application to Adult Education." *Studies in Adult Education*, 1979, *11* (1), 62–66.

Eigen, L. D. "A Comparison of Three Models of Programmed Instruction Sequence." *Journal of Educational Research*, 1962, *55*, 453–460.

Eisdorfer, C., and Cohen, D. "The Issue of Biological and Psychological Deficits." In E. G. Borgatta and N. G. McClusky (Eds.), *Aging and Society: Current Research and Perspectives.* Beverly Hills, Calif.: Sage Publications, 1980.

Eisdorfer, C., and Lawton, M. P. *The Psychology of Adult Development and Aging.* Washington, D. C.: American Psychological Association, 1973.

Eisdorfer, C.; Nowlin, J.; and Wilkie, F. "Improvement of Learning in the Aged by Modification of Autonomic Nervous System Activity." *Science,* 1970, *170,* 1327–1329.

Elias, John L., and Merriam, Sharan. *Philosophical Foundations of Adult Education.* Huntington, N.Y.: Robert E. Kreiger Publishing Company, 1980.

Elias, Merrill F.; Elias, Penelope K.; and Elias, Jeffery W. *Basic Processes in Adult Developmental Psychology.* St. Louis: C. V. Mosby Company, 1977.

Elkind, David. "Quantity Conceptions in College Students." *Journal of Social Psychology,* 1962, *57,* 459–465.

Elliott, Paul H. "An Exploratory Study of Adult Learning Styles." ERIC, 1975, ED 116 016.

Elsdon, K. T. "Some Practical Implications for Training and Professional Development." Paper presented at the conference "Explorations in Adult Learning and Training for Adult Educators." (Cited by Campbell 1977, p. 71.)

Erikson, Erik. *Childhood and Society.* New York: W. W. Norton, 1943.

Even, Mary Jane. "An Overview of Cognitive Styles and Hemispheres of the Brain Research." Paper presented at the annual Adult Education Research Conference, San Antonio, Texas, 1978.

Even, Mary Jane. "The Adult Learning Process." *Perspectives in Adult Learning and Development,* 1981, *1* (1), 13–19.

Everitt, Jack McLarin. "Perceptions of the Importance of Adult Education Program Planning Procedures." Doctoral dissertation, University of Georgia, 1974. [*DAI,* 1975, *35,* 6425-A.]

Farmer, James A., Jr. "Impact of 'Lifelong Learning' on the Professionalization of Adult Education." *Journal of Research and Development in Education,* 1974, *7* (4), 57–65.

Festinger, Leon. *The Theory of Cognitive Dissonance.* New York: Harper and Row, 1957.

Fincher, Cameron. "A Minimax Principle for Educational Research." *Research in Higher Education,* 1974, *2,* 99–107.

Finkel, Coleman L. "The Supportive Environment: A New Dimension in Meetings." *Training and Development Journal,* 1975, *29* (1), 26–36.

Fisher, Ralph Alan. "Influence of Selected Environmental Phenomena on Social Interactions of Adult Learners." Doctoral dissertation, University of Georgia, 1980. [*DAI,* 1981, *41,* 4252-A.]

Flaherty, Mary J. "The Prediction of College Level Academic Achievement in Adult Extension Students." Doctoral dissertation, University of Toronto, 1968. [*DAI,* 1970, *31,* 997-A.]

Flavell, J. H. *The Developmental Psychology of Jean Piaget.* Princeton, N.J.: D. Van Nostrand and Company, 1963.

Flavell, J. H. "Cognitive Changes in Adulthood." In L. R. Goulet and P. B. Baltes (Eds.), *Lifespan Developmental Psychology: Research and Theory*. New York: Academic Press, 1970.

Fogel, Max. "Warning: Auto Fumes May Lower Your Kid's I.Q." *Psychology Today*, January 1980, p. 108.

Forest, L. B. "Beyond Scientific Empiricism in Adult Education Research." Paper presented at the annual Adult Education Research Conference, Chicago, Illinois, 1972.

Fox, Robert D. "An Analysis of the Role of Special Interest Groups in the Formation of the Cooperative Extension Service." *Adult Education*, 1982, 32 (3), 156–164.

Fozard, J. L., and Nuttall, R. L. "GATB Scores for Men Differing in Age and Socioeconomic Status." *Journal of Applied Psychology*, 1971, 55 (4), 372–379.

Freire, Paulo. *Pedagogy of the Oppressed*. New York: Herder and Herder, 1970.

Freire, Paulo. *Education for Critical Consciousness*. New York: Seabury Press, 1973.

Friedman, S., and Juhasz, J. B. *Environments: Notes and Selections on Objects, Spaces, and Behaviors*. Monterey, Calif.: Brooks/Cole Publishing Company, 1974.

Fromm, Erich. *The Sane Society*. New York: Rinehart, 1955.

Froomkin, J., and Wolfson, R. J. *Adult Education 1972: A Re-analysis*. Washington, D.C.: Froomkin, 1977. (Cited by Cross 1979, p. 87.)

Frye, Roye Melton. "The Theory of Training and the Trainer Role in the Indiana Plan Institute." Doctoral dissertation, Indiana University, 1963. [*AEDA*, 1970, pp. 254–255.]

Fryer, Douglas. *The Measurement of Interests*. New York: Henry Holt and Company, 1931. (Cited by Brunner et al., 1959, p. 65.)

Furry, C. A., and Baltes, P. B. "The Effects of Age Differences in Ability: Extraneous Performance Variables in the Assessment of Intelligence in Children, Adults, and the Elderly." *Journal of Gerontology*, 1973, 28, 73–80.

Gage, N. L. *The Scientific Basis of the Art of Teaching*. New York: Columbia University, Teachers College Press, 1977.

Gans, H. J. *The Urban Villagers*. Glencoe: Ill.: The Free Press, 1962.

Gauvin, M. T. "Students' Perceptions of Behavior and Instructional Practices in Open Space Schools." Paper presented at the annual meeting of the American Education Research Association, New York, New York, April 1977.

Gazzaniga, Michael S. "Review of the Split Brain." In M. C. Wittrock et al., *The Human Brain*. Englewood Cliffs, N.J.: Prentice-Hall, 1977.

Getzels, J. "Images of the Classroom and Visions of the Learner." *School Review*, 1974, 82, 527–540.

Gill, Everett, III. "The Learning Activities of Illiterate Adults." Doctoral dissertation, University of Georgia, 1982.

Gilliland, J. W. "How Environment Affects Learning." *American School and University*, 1969, 42, 48–49.

Glennan, Thomas. "National Institute of Education: Personal View." *Educational Researcher*, 1973, 2, 13–16.

Glynn, Shawn M., and DiVesta, Francis J. "Outline and Hierarchical Organization as Aids for Study and Retrieval." *Journal of Educational Psychology*, 1977, 69 (2), 89–95.

Glynn, Shawn M., and Muth, K. Denise. "Text-Learning Capabilities of Older Adults." *Educational Gerontology*, 1979, *4*, 252–269.

Goodnow, Betsy. "Increasing Enrollment Through Benefit Segmentation." *Adult Education*, 1982, *32* (2), 89–103.

Goodnow, Jacqueline. "A Test of Milieu Differences with Some of Piaget's Tasks." *Psychological Monographs*, 1962, *76*, no. 36 (Whole no. 555).

Gordon, George K. "A Q-Sort Instrument for Measuring Attitudes Toward the Educational Conditions of the Indiana Plan." Doctoral dissertation, Indiana University, 1965. [*AEDA*, 1970, p. 118.]

Grabowski, Stanley M. "Motivational Factors of Adult Learners in a Directed Self-Study Bachelor's Degree Program." Paper presented at the annual Adult Education Research Conference, Montreal, Quebec, 1973.

Grabowski, Stanley M., and Loague, Nehume. *Adult Education Dissertation Abstracts, 1968–69.* Washington, D.C.: Adult Education Association of the U.S.A., n.d.

Graves, A. J. "Attainment of Conservation of Mass, Weight, and Volume in Minimally Educated Adults." *Developmental Psychology*, 1972, *1*, 223.

Gray, W. M. "Development of a Written Test Based Upon the Model of Piaget." University of Dayton, Project No. 2-E-052, Grant No. OEG-5-72-0044 (509), National Center for Research and Development. Final report, September 1973.

Griffith, William S. "Adult Educators and Politics." *Adult Education*, 1976, *26* (4), 270–297.

Griffith, William S. "Needs, Definition, Assessment, and Utilization." *School Review*, 1978, *86* (3), 382–394.

Griffith, William S. "Adult Education Research—Emerging Developments." *Studies in Adult Education*, 1979, *11* (2), 125–144.

Griffith, William S. "Personnel Preparation." In Harold J. Alford (Ed.), *Power and Conflict in Continuing Education.* Belmont, Calif.: Wadsworth Publishing Company, 1980.

Griffith, William S., and Cervero, Ronald M. "The Adult Performance Level Program: A Serious and Deliberate Examination." *Adult Education*, 1977, *27* (4), 209–224.

Griffith, William S., and Dhanidina, Lutaf. "Costs and Benefits of Delayed High School Completion." *Adult Education*, 1975, *25* (4), 217–230.

Grotelueschen, Arden D. "Introductory Material Structure and Principle Knowledge Effects on Adult Learning." *Adult Education*, 1979, *29* (2), 75–82.

Grotelueschen, Arden, and Caulley, Darrel N. "A Model for Studying Determinants of Intention to Participate in Continuing Professional Education." *Adult Education*, 1977, *28* (1), 22–37.

Guetzkow, H.; Kelly, E. L.; and McKeachie, W. J. "An Experimental Comparison of Recitation, Discussion, and Tutorial Methods in College Teaching." *Journal of Educational Psychology*, 1954, *45*, 193–207.

Gueulette, David E. "Exorcising the Spectre of Permanent Schooling." *Adult Education*, 1976, *27* (1), 48–53.

Guilford, J. P. "Development of a Theory." In Robert A. Weisgerber (Ed.), *Perspectives in Individualized Learning.* Itasca, Ill.: F. E. Peacock, 1971.

Haldane, I. R. "Workers' Education: A Psychological Survey." Doctoral dissertation, University of London, 1962. [*RAE*, 1974, pp. 169–171.]

Hall, Budd. *Creating Knowledge: Breaking the Monopoly.* Toronto: International Council for Adult Education, n.d.

Hall, C. S., and Lindzey, G. *Theories of Personality.* New York: John Wiley and Sons, 1957.

Hall, E. T. *The Hidden Dimension.* Garden City, N.Y.: Anchor Books, 1969.

Hallenbeck, Wilbur. "The Role of Adult Education in Society." In Gale Jensen, A. A. Liveright, and Wilbur Hallenbeck (Eds.), *Adult Education: Outlines of an Emerging Field of University Study.* Washington, D.C.: Adult Education Association of the U.S.A., 1964.

Hamidi, Abdulvahman, "Motivational Aspects of Literacy Education for Adults in Saudi-Arabia." *Adult Literacy and Basic Education,* 1978, *1* (4), 27–38.

Hammer, Bernard. "Grade Expectations, Differential Teacher Comments, and Student Performance." *Journal of Educational Psychology,* 1972, *63,* 454–458.

Hand, Samuel. *Community Study as a Basis for Program Planning in Adult Education.* Tallahassee: The Florida State University, 1960, p. 15.

Hanna, I. "A Socio-Psychological Survey of Student Membership of Adult Education Classes in Leeds and Changes in the Adult Student Population Since 1945." Masters thesis, University of Leeds, 1964. [*RAE,* 1974, pp. 131–134.]

Hansl, Nicholas, and Hansl, Adele B. "Learning and Memory Improvement Through Chemistry: Dream or Reality in the Offing?" *Phi Delta Kappan,* 1979, *61* (4), 264–265.

Hare, P. A. "Study of Interaction and Consensus in Different Sized Groups." *American Sociological Review,* 1952, *17,* 261–267.

Harris, Raymond. "Biological and Psychological Factors in Aging." In E. F. Borgatta and Neil G. McClusky (Eds.), *Aging and Society.* Beverly Hills, Calif.: Sage Publications, 1980.

Hartley, James, and Davies, Ivor K. "Programmed Learning and Educational Technology. In Michael J. A. Howe (Ed.), *Adult Learning: Psychological Research and Applications.* New York: John Wiley and Sons, 1977.

Havighurst, Robert J. *Developmental Tasks and Education.* New York: David McKay, 1952.

Havighurst, Robert J. "Changing Status and Roles During the Adult Life Cycle: Significance for Adult Education." In H. W. Burns (Ed.), *Sociological Backgrounds of Adult Education* (2nd ed.). Syracuse, N.Y.: Center for the Study of Liberal Education for Adults, 1964.

Havighurst, R. J., and Orr, Betty. *Adult Education and Adult Needs.* Chicago: Center for the Study of Liberal Education for Adults, 1965.

Heider, F. "Attitudes and Cognitive Organizations." *Journal of Psychology,* 1946, *21,* 107–112.

Herem, Maynard A. "Adult Motivation to Learn." *Lifelong Learning: The Adult Years,* 1978, *2* (4), 9.

Hermanowicz, Henry. "Some Realities of Adult Education: One Rhetorician's View." In Joseph F. Blake and Erma D. Keyes (Eds.), *From Rhetoric to Reality.* Harrisburg, Pa.: Division of Continuing Education, Bureau of Vocational Education, Pennsylvania Department of Education, 1976.

Hertling, James. "Market Research: A Guide to Adult and Continuing Education Program Planning." *Adult Leadership,* 1973, *21* (6), 217–219.

Hiemstra, Roger P. "Continuing Education for the Aged: A Survey of Needs and Interests of Older People." *Adult Education,* 1972, 22 (2), 100–109.

Hiemstra, Roger P. "The Older Adult and Learning." Lincoln, Neb.: Department of Adult and Continuing Education, University of Nebraska, 1975. ERIC Document Reproduction Service, ED 117 371.

Hiemstra, Roger P., and Penland, P. R. "Self-Directed Learning." Paper presented at the annual meeting of the Commission of Professors of Adult Education, Anaheim, California, 1981.

Hill, J. E. *The Educational Sciences.* Bloomfield Hill, Mich.: Oakland Community College Press, 1971.

Hoddes, Eric. "Does Sleep Help You Study?" *Psychology Today,* June 1977, p. 69.

Hodges, W. F. "The Effects of Success, Threat of Shock, and Failure on Anxiety." Doctoral dissertation, Vanderbilt University, 1967. [*DAI,* 1968, 28, 4296-B.]

Hooper, F. H.; Fitzgerald J.; and Papalia, D. E. "Piagetian Theory and the Aging Process: Extensions and Speculations." *Aging and Human Development,* 1971, 2 (1), 3–20.

Hopper, Earl, and Osborn, Marilyn. *Adult Students: Education Selection and Social Control.* London: Frances Printer, 1973.

Horn, John L. "Organization of Data on Life-Span Development of Human Abilities." In L. R. Goulet and P. B. Baltes (Eds.), *Life-Span Development Psychology: Theory and Research.* New York: Academic Press, 1970.

Horn, John L., and Donaldson, Gary. "On the Myth of Intellectual Decline in Adulthood." *American Psychologist,* October 1976, pp. 701–719.

Houle, Cyril O. *Proceedings of the Fifth Leadership Conference for University Adult Educators.* Chicago: Center for the Study of Liberal Education for Adults, 1957.

Houle, Cyril O. "The Education of Adult Educational Leaders." In Malcolm S. Knowles (Ed.), *Handbook of Adult Education in the United States.* Chicago: Adult Education Association of the U.S.A., 1960.

Houle, Cyril O. *The Inquiring Mind.* Madison: University of Wisconsin Press, 1961.

Houle, Cyril O. "The Educators of Adults." In Robert Smith, George Aker, and J. Roby Kidd (Eds.), *Handbook of Adult Education.* New York: Macmillan, 1970.

Houle, Cyril O. *The Design of Education.* San Francisco: Jossey-Bass, 1972.

Howe, Michael J. A. "Learning and the Acquisition of Knowledge by Students: Some Experimental Investigations." In Michael J. A. Howe (Ed.), *Adult Learning: Psychological Research and Applications.* New York: John Wiley and Sons, 1977.

Hulicka, I. M., and Weiss, R. L. "Age Differences in Retention as a Function of Learning." *Journal of Consulting Psychology,* 1965, 29, 125–129.

Hull, Clark L. "Primary Motivation." In Richard C. Teevan and Robert C. Birney (Eds.), *Theories of Motivation in Learning.* New York: D. Van Nostrand, 1964.

Hultsch, D. F. "Adult Age Differences in Retrieval: Trace Dependent and Cue Dependent Forgetting." *Developmental Psychology,* 1975, 11, 197–201.

Hunter, Walter E. "The New Generation Gap: Involvement vs Instant Information." ERIC, 1977, ED 148 412.

Hurkamp, Rosemary Crosby. "Differences in Some Initial Attitudes of Students Who Complete and Students Who Drop Out in the Wellesley, Massachusetts, Adult Education Program." Doctoral dissertation, Boston University, 1969. [*AEDA,* n.d., p. 48.]

Illich, Ivan D. *Celebration of Awareness: A Call for Institutional Revolution.* Garden City, N.Y.: Doubleday, 1970.

Illich, Ivan D. *Deschooling Society.* New York: Harper & Row, 1971.

Illinois, State of, Board of Higher Education. "Study of Adult Learners." Springfield, Ill.: Illinois Board of Higher Education, State Advisory Council on Adult Vocational and Technical Education, 1978.

Illinois, State of, Board of Higher Education. *Report on the 1978-79 Survey of Adult Learners.* Springfield, Ill.: Illinois Board of Higher Education, July 1980.

Imbler, Irene I. "The Effects of Participation Training on Closed-Mindedness, Anxiety, and Self-Concept." Doctoral dissertation, Indiana University, 1967. [*AEDA*, 1970, p. 69.]

Inhelder, B., and Piaget J. *The Growth of Logical Thinking from Childhood to Adolescence.* New York: Basic Books, 1958.

Irish, Gladys H. "Reflections on Ends and Means in Adult Basic Education." *Adult Education*, 1975, 25 (2), 125–130.

Jenkins, David S. "Conditions Underlying Good Learning." In Marilyn V. Miller (Ed.), *On Teaching Adults: An Anthology.* Boston: Center for the Study of Liberal Education for Adults, 1960.

Jensen, Gale. "Social Psychology and Adult Education Practice." In Gale Jensen, A. A. Liveright, and Wilbur Hallenbeck (Eds.), *Adult Education: Outlines of an Emerging Field of University Study.* Washington, D.C.: Adult Education Association of the U.S.A., 1964.

Jensen, Gale; Liveright, A. A.; and Hallenbeck, Wilbur (Eds.). *Adult Education: Outlines of an Emerging Field of University Study.* Washington, D.C.: Adult Education Association of the U.S.A., 1964.

Joe, V. C. "A Review of the Internal-External Control Construct as a Personality Variable." *Psychological Reports*, 1971, 28, 619–640.

Johns, Will E. "Selected Characteristics of the Learning Projects Pursued by Practicing Pharmacists." Doctoral dissertation, University of Georgia, 1973. [*DAI*, 1974, 34, 4677-A.]

Johnson, D. M., and Smith, H. C. "Democratic Leadership in the College Classroom." *Psychological Monographs*, 1953, 27, no. 11 (Whole no. 361).

Johnson, E. A. "Selected Characteristics of the Learning Projects Pursued by Adults Who Have Earned a High School Diploma and/or a High School Equivalency Certificate." Doctoral dissertation, University of Georgia, 1973. [*DAI*, 1973, 34, 3004-A.]

Johnstone, John W. C., and Rivera, Ramon. *Volunteers for Learning.* Chicago: Aldine, 1965.

Jones, H. E., and Conrad, H. S. "The Growth and Decline of Intelligence: A Study of Homogeneous Populations Between the Ages of Ten and Sixty." *Genetic Psychology Monographs*, 1933, 13, 233–298.

Julian, J. W., and Katz, S. B. "Internal Versus External Control and the Value of Reinforcement." *Journal of Personality and Social Psychology*, 1968, 8, 89–94.

Kagan, Jerome. "Reflection-Impulsivity and Reading Ability in Primary Grade Children." *Child Development*, 1965, 36, 609–628.

Kagan, Jerome; Moss, Howard A.; and Siegel, Irving E. "Psychological Significance of Styles of Conceptualization." In J. C. Wright and J. Kagan (Eds.), *Basic Cognitive Processes in Children.* Monographs of the Society for Research in Child Development. Lafayette, Ind.: Child Development Publications, 1963.

Kalus, Richard A., and Patchner, Michael A. "Sources of Stress Encountered by Adults Enrolled in a Statewide MSW Degree Program." In Gene C. Whaples and William M. Rivera (Eds.), *Lifelong Learning Research Conference Proceedings*. College Park, Md.: Department of Agricultural and Extension Education, University of Maryland, 1982.

Karabel J., and Halsey, A. H. (Eds.). *Power and Ideology in Education*. New York: Oxford University Press, 1977.

Karmel, L. J. "Effect of Windowless Classroom Environment on High School Students." *Perceptual and Motor Skills*, 1965, *20*, 277–278.

Kekkonen, Helena. "Outreaching Work in Finland." Unpublished paper. Also personal correspondence with the author, April 1980.

Kempfer, Homer. "Identifying Educational Needs and Interests of Adults." In Coolie Verner and Thurman White (Eds.), *Administration of Adult Education*. Washington, D.C.: Adult Education Association of the U.S.A., 1965.

Keogh, B. K., and Donlon, G. McG. "Field Dependence, Impulsivity, and Learning Disabilities." *Journal of Learning Disabilities*, 1972, *5*, 16–21.

Kerwin, Michael. "Student Involvement as a Dimension of the Student's Perceived Teaching Behavior of Post-Secondary Educators." *Adult Education*, 1981, *31* (2), 85–92.

Keys, A., et al. *The Biology of Starvation*. 2 volumes. Minneapolis: University of Minnesota Press, 1950.

Kidd, J. R. *How Adults Learn*. New York: Association Press, 1975.

Kight, H. R., and Sassenrath, J. M. "Relation of Achievement Motivation and Test Anxiety to Performance in Programmed Instruction." *Journal of Educational Psychology*, 1966, *57*, 14–17.

Killeen, John, and Bird, Margaret. *Education and Work: A Study of Paid Educational Leave in England and Wales (1976/77)*. London: National Institute of Adult Education, 1981.

Kimura, Doreen. "The Asymmetry of the Human Brain." *Scientific American*, 1973, *228* (3), 70–78.

Kinsbourne, Marcel. "Why Is the Brain Biased?" *Psychology Today*, May 1979, p. 150.

Knowles, Malcolm S. "Philosophical Issues that Confront Adult Educators." *Adult Education*, 1957, *7* (4), 234–239.

Knowles, Malcolm S. (Ed.). *Handbook of Adult Education in the United States*. Chicago: Adult Education Association of the U.S.A., 1960.

Knowles, Malcolm S. "The Field of Operations in Adult Education." In Gale Jensen, A. A. Liveright, and Wilbur Hallenbeck (Eds.), *Adult Education: Outlines of an Emerging Field of University Study*. Washington, D.C.: Adult Education Association of the U.S.A., 1964.

Knowles, Malcolm S. *The Modern Practice of Adult Education*. New York: Association Press, 1970.

Knowles, Malcolm S. *The Adult Learner: A Neglected Species*. Houston, Tex.: Gulf Publishing Company, 1973.

Knowles, Malcolm S. *A History of the Adult Education Movement in the United States* (rev. ed.). Huntington, N.Y.: Kreiger Publishing Company, 1977.

Knowles, Malcolm S., and DuBois, Eugene E. "Prologue." In Robert Smith, George Aker, and J. R. Kidd (Eds.), *Handbook of Adult Education*. New York: Macmillan, 1970.

Knox, Alan B. *Adult Development and Learning*. San Francisco: Jossey-Bass, 1977a.

Knox, Alan B. *Current Research Needs Related to Systematic Learning By Adults*. Occasional Paper No. 4. Urbana, Ill.: Office for the Study of Continuing Education, College of Education, University of Illinois at Urbana-Champaign, 1977b.

Knox, Alan B. "Helping Adults to Learn." In *Yearbook of Adult and Continuing Education*. Chicago: Marquis Academic Media, 1978–79.

Knox, Alan B. *Enhancing the Proficiencies of Continuing Educators: New Directions for Continuing Education*. San Francisco: Jossey-Bass, 1979a.

Knox, Alan B. "The Nature and Causes of Professional Obsolescence." In Preston P. LeBreton et al. (Eds.), *The Evaluation of Continuing Education for Professionals: A Systems View*. Seattle: University of Washington, 1979b.

Knox, Alan B.; Grotelueschen, Arden; and Sjogren, Douglas D. "Adult Intelligence and Learning Ability." *Adult Education*, 1968, *18* (3), 188–196.

Knox, Alan B., and Sjogren, D. D. "Research on Adult Learning." *Adult Education*, 1965, *15*, (3), 133–137.

Knox, Alan B., and Videbeck, Richard. "Adult Education and Adult Life Cycle." *Adult Education*, 1963, *13* (2), 102–121.

Knudsen and Skaalvik. 1979. (Cited by Kjell Rubenson. *Recruitment to Adult Education in the Nordic Countries—Research and Outreaching Activities*. Stockholm: Stockholm Institute of Education, 1979, p. 9. Additional bibliographical information on Knudsen and Skaalvik not provided by Rubenson.)

Kobler, J. "The Environment Is the Meeting." *Best's Insurance Convention Guide*, 1974.

Kolb, David A. "Disciplinary Inquiry Norms and Student Learning Styles: Diverse Pathways for Growth." Cleveland, Ohio: Case Western Reserve Working Paper Series in Organizational Behavior, n.d.

Koplowitz, H. *Unitary Operations: A Projection Beyond Piaget's Formal Operations Style*. Amherst: University of Massachusetts Center on Humanistic Education, 1978.

Korman, A.; Greenhaus, J. H.; and Badin, I. J. "Personal Attitudes and Motivation." *Annual Review of Psychology*, 1977, *28*, 175–196.

Kotler, Philip. "Strategies for Introducing Marketing into Non-profit Organizations." *Journal of Marketing*, 1979, *43*, 37–44.

Kotler, Philip, and Levy, Sidney J. "Broadening the Concept of Marketing." *Journal of Marketing*, 1969, *33*, 10–15.

Kovach, John A. "Issues and Problems in the Needs Assessment of Unique Target Groups: The Adult American Indian." In Gene W. Whaples and D. Merrill Ewert (Eds.), *Proceedings: Lifelong Learning Research Conference*. College Park, Md.: Department of Agricultural and Extension Education, University of Maryland, 1980.

Krech, David. "The Chemistry of Learning." *Saturday Review*, 20 January 1968, p. 48.

Kreitlow, Burton W. "Research in Adult Education" In Malcolm S. Knowles (Ed.), *Handbook of Adult Education in the United States*. Chicago: Adult Education Association of the U.S.A., 1960.

Kreitlow, Burton W. *Research Priorities in Adult Education*. Madison: University of Wisconsin, 1964.

Kreitlow, Burton W. "Needed Research." *Review of Educational Research*, 1965, *35*, 240–245.

Kreitlow, Burton W. "Research and Theory." In Robert M. Smith, George F. Aker, and J. Roby Kidd (Eds.), *Handbook of Adult Education*. New York: Macmillan, 1970.

Krumboltz, J. D. "Needed Research in Programmed Instruction." *Educational Leadership*, 1963, *21*, 30–33.

Kuhlen, Raymond. "Motivational Changes Through the Adult Years." In R. Kuhlen (Ed.), *Psychological Backgrounds of Adult Education*. Chicago: Center for the Study of Liberal Education for Adults, 1963.

LaForest, J. R. *A Model for Program Planning in Adult Education*. Atlanta: Southern Regional Education Board, 1973.

Lam, Yee-Lay Jack, and Wong, Andrew. "Attendance Regularity of Adult Learners: An Examination of Content and Structural Factors." *Adult Education*, 1974, *24* (2), 130–142.

Langer, Jonas. *Theories of Development*. New York: Holt, Reinhart, and Winston, 1969.

Laurence, Mary W. "Memory Loss With Age: A Test of Two Strategies for Its Retention." *Psychonometric Science*, 1967, *9* (4), 209–210.

Lawson, K. H. "The Concept of Purpose." *Adult Education* (NIAE), 1970, *43*, 165–170.

Lawson, K. H. *Philosophical Concepts and Values in Adult Education*. Nottingham (England): Barnes and Humby, 1975.

Leagans, J. P. "Educational Interests of Farm Operators in North Carolina as Related to Work of Agricultural Extension Service." Doctoral dissertation, University of Chicago, 1948.

Lefcourt, H. M. "Recent Developments in the Study of Locus of Control." In B. A. Maher (Ed.), *Progress in Experimental Personality Research*, Vol. 6. New York: Academic Press, 1972.

Lefcourt, H. M.; Lewis, L.; and Silverman, I. W. "Internal Versus External Control of Reinforcement and Attention in Decision Making Tasks." *Journal of Personality*, 1968, *36*, 663–682.

Legge, C. Derek. "Training Adult Educators." *Journal of the International Congress of University Adult Education*, 1967, *6* (1), 2.

Legge, C. Derek. "Research for Higher Degrees." *Studies in Adult Education*, 1979, *11* (1), 56–62.

Lenning, O. T. *The Outcomes Structure: An Overview and Procedures for Applying It in Post-Secondary Education Institutions*. Boulder, Colo.: National Center for Higher Education Management Systems, 1978.

Levinson, Daniel J. et al. *The Seasons of a Man's Life*. New York: Ballantine Books, 1978.

Lewin, Kurt. "Forces Behind Food Habits." *Bulletin of the Nation's Research Council*, No. 108, 1943, 35–65.

Lewin, Kurt. "Frontiers in Group Dynamics: Concept, Method, and Reality in Social Science." *Human Relations*, 1947, *1* (1).

Lindeman, Eduard. *The Meaning of Adult Education*. 1926. Reprint. Montreal: Harvest House, 1961.

List, E. Frederick. *The Community Attitude Self-Survey*. Columbia, Mo.: Department of Regional and Community Affairs, School of Social and Community Services, University Extension Division, University of Missouri–Columbia, 1969.

Liveright, A. A. "The Nature and Aims of Adult Education as a Field of Graduate Education." In Gale Jensen, A. A. Liveright, and Wilbur Hallenbeck (Eds.), *Adult Education: Outlines of an Emerging Field of University Study*. Washington, D.C.: Adult Education Association of the U.S.A., 1964.

Liveright, A. A. *A Study of Adult Education in the United States*. Boston: Center for the Study of Liberal Education for Adults, 1968.

Liveright, A. A., and Haygood, N. (Eds.). *The Exeter Papers*. Boston: Center for the Study of Liberal Education for Adults, 1969.

London, Jack. "Attitudes Toward Adult Education by Social Class." *Adult Education*, 1963, *13* (4), 226–233.

London, Jack. "The Relevance of the Study of Sociology to Adult Education Practice." In Gale Jensen, A. A. Liveright, and Wilbur Hallenbeck (Eds.), *Adult Education: Outlines of an Emerging Field of University Study*. Washington, D.C.: Adult Education Association of the U.S.A., 1964.

London, Jack. "The Influence of Social Class Behavior Upon Adult Education Participation." *Adult Education*, 1970, *20* (3), 140–153.

London, Jack, and Wenkert, R. "Leisure Styles and Adult Education." *Adult Education*, 1969, *20* (1), 3–22.

Londoner, Carroll A. "Perseverance Versus Non-Perseverance Patterns Among Adult High School Students." *Adult Education*, 1972, *22* (3), 179–195.

Londoner, Carroll A. "Sources of Educational Funds as Motivations for Participating in Adult Secondary Education." *Adult Education*, 1974, *25* (1), 47–63.

Long, Huey B. "A Summary Report: Adult Education Participation in Brevard County, Florida." *Adult Education*, 1967, *19 [17]* (1), 34–42.

Long, Huey B. *Are They Ever Too Old To Learn?* Englewood Cliffs, N.J.: Prentice-Hall, 1971.

Long, Huey B. *The Psychology of Aging: How It Affects Learning*. Englewood Cliffs, N.J: Prentice-Hall, 1972.

Long, Huey B. *Continuing Education of Adults in Colonial America*. Syracuse, N.Y.: Syracuse University Publications in Continuing Education, 1976.

Long, Huey B. "Publication Activity of Selected Professors of Adult Education." *Adult Education*, 1977, *27* (2), 173–186.

Long, Huey B. "Historical Characteristics of Adult Education in the United States." Briefing paper delivered to visiting Chinese adult educators, Belmont, Maryland, September 1980a.

Long, Huey B. "A Perspective on Adult Education Research." In Huey B. Long, Roger Hiemstra, et al. *Changing Approaches to Studying Adult Education*. San Francisco: Jossey-Bass, 1980b.

Long, Huey B.; Anderson, R. C.; and Blubaugh, Jon A. *Approaches to Community Development*. Washington, D.C.: National University Extension Association and the American College Testing Program, 1973.

Long, Huey B.; McCrary, Kay; and Ackerman, S. "Adult Cognition: Piagetian-Based Research Findings." *Adult Education*, 1979, *30* (1), 3–18.

Lord, Charles B. "A Classification System for Continuing Education Programs." *Adult Leadership*, 1972, *20* (10), 357–359.

Lorge, Irving, "The Influence of Tests Upon the Nature of Mental Decline as a Function of Age." *Journal of Educational Psychology*, 1936, *27*, 100–110.

Lorge, Irving. *Effective Methods in Adult Education: Report of the Southern Regional Workshop for Agricultural Extension Specialists.* Raleigh: North Carolina State College, June 1947.

Lorge, Irving. "The Adult Learner." In Irving Lorge, Howard Y. McClusky, Gale E. Jensen, and Wilbur C. Hallenbeck (Eds.), *Adult Education: Theory and Method.* Washington: Adult Education Association of the U.S.A., 1963.

Love, Robert A. "The Use of Motivational Research to Determine Interest in Adult College-Level Training." *Educational Record,* 1953, 34, 212–213.

Lumsden, D. Barry. "Adult Learning and the Application of Modern Educational Technology." In D. Barry Lumsden and Ronald H. Shearon (Eds.), *Experimental Studies in Adult Learning and Memory.* New York: John Wiley and Sons, 1975.

Lumsden, D. Barry, and Shearon, Ronald H. (Eds.). *Experimental Studies in Adult Learning and Memory.* New York: John Wiley and Sons, 1975.

Lyne, Noreen. "The Relationship Between Adult Students' Level of Cognitive Development and Their Preference for Learning Format." In Gene C. Whaples and D. Merrill Ewert (Eds.), *Lifelong Learning Research Conference Proceedings.* College Park, Md.: Department of Agriculture and Extension Education, University of Maryland, 1981.

McClelland, David C. "Methods of Measuring Motivation." In John W. Atkinson (Ed.), *Motives in Fantasy, Action, Society.* New York: D. Van Nostrand Company, 1958.

McClelland, David C., et al. *The Achievement Motive.* New York: Appleton-Century, 1953.

McClusky, Howard Y. "The Relevance of Psychology for Adult Education." In Gale Jensen, A. A. Liveright, and Wilbur Hallenbeck (Eds.), *Adult Education: Outlines of an Emerging Field of University Study.* Washington, D.C.: Adult Education Association of the U.S.A., 1964.

McClusky, Howard Y. "An Approach to a Differential Psychology of the Adult Potential." In Stanley M. Grabowski (Ed.), *Adult Learning and Instruction.* Syracuse, N.Y.: ERIC Clearinghouse on Adult Education, 1970.

McClusky, Howard Y. "The Adult as a Learner." In Stanley E. Seashore and Robert J. McNeil (Eds.), *Management of Urban Crises.* New York: Free Press, 1971.

McClusky, Howard Y. "The Coming of Age of Lifelong Learning." *Journal of Research and Development in Education,* 1974, 7 (4), 97–98.

McGee, Paul A. "Merchandising Adult Education." *Adult Education,* 1959, 9, 75–79.

McGinnies, E., and Ward, C. D. "Persuasibility as a Function of Source Credibility and Locus of Control: Five Cross-Cultural Experiments." *Journal of Personality,* 1974, 42, 360–371.

McGrane, Helen F. "Effects of Anxiety State and Differentially Structured Content on Achievement and a Measure of Compliance in an Adult Education Program." Doctoral dissertation, University of Southern California, 1979. [*DAI,* 1979, 39, 5343-A.]

McGuigan, F. J., and Peters, R. J., Jr. "Assessing the Effectiveness of Programmed Texts: Methodology and Some Findings." *Journal of Programmed Instruction,* 1965, 3, 23–34.

McKenzie, Leon R. "Participation Training: Introduction and Analysis." *Viewpoints,* 1975, 51 (4), 1–34.

McKinley, John. "A Participation Training Program in a Mental Hospital: An Experiment in Adult Education." Doctoral dissertation, Indiana University, 1960. [*DAI,* 1960, 21, 1119-A.]

McKinley, John. "Perspectives on Diagnostics in Adult Education." *Viewpoints*, 1973, *49*, 69–83.

McKinnon, J. W., and Renner, J. W. "Are Colleges Concerned with Intellectual Development?" *American Journal of Physics*, 1971, *39*, 1047–1052.

McLoughlin, D. "Participation of the Adult Learner in Program Planning." *Adult Education*, 1971, *22* (1), 30–35.

McMahon, Ernest E. *Needs of People and Their Communities and the Adult Educator.* Washington, D.C.: Adult Education Association of the U.S.A., 1970.

McNulty, J. A. "An Analysis of Recall and Recognition Processes in Verbal Learning." *Journal of Verbal Learning and Verbal Behavior*, 1965, *4*, 430.

McNulty, J. A., and Caird, W. "Memory Loss with Age: Retrieval or Storage?" *Psychological Reports*, 1966, *19*, 229–230.

McNulty, J. A., and Caird, W. "Memory Loss with Age: An Unsolved Problem." *Psychological Reports*, 1967, *20*, 283–288.

Madsen, K. B. *Modern Theories of Motivation.* New York: John Wiley and Sons, 1974.

Maier, N. R. F. "An Experimental Test of Effects of Training on Discussion Leadership." *Human Relations*, 1953, *5*, 161–173.

Main, Keith. "The Power-Load-Margin Formula of Howard Y. McClusky as a Basis for a Model of Teaching." *Adult Education*, 1979, *30* (1), 19–33.

Mandler, G., and Sarason, S. B. "A Study of Anxiety and Learning." *Journal of Abnormal and Social Psychology*, 1952, *47*, 166–173.

Marieneau, Catherine, and Klinger, Karla. "An Anthropological Approach to the Study of Educational Barriers of Adults at Postsecondary Level." ERIC, 1977, ED 141 511.

Marsh, G. R., and Thompson, L. W. "Psychophysiology of Aging." In J. E. Birren and K. W. Shaie (Eds.), *Handbook of the Psychology of Aging.* New York: Van Nostrand Reinhold, 1977.

Martindale, Colin. "What Makes Creative People Different?" *Psychology Today*, July 1975, pp. 44–50.

Maslow, A. H. *Motivation and Personality.* New York: Harper and Row, 1954.

Maslow, A. H. *Toward a Psychology of Being.* New York: Van Nostrand, 1968.

Maslow, A. H. *Motivation and Personality* (2nd ed.). New York: Harper and Row, 1970.

Maslow, A. H., and Mintz, N. L. "Effects of Esthetic Surroundings: Initial Effects of Three Esthetic Conditions Upon Perceiving Energy and Well-Being in Faces." *Journal of Psychology*, 1965, *41*, 247–254.

Mazmanian, Paul E. "A Decision-Making Approach to Needs Assessment and Objectives Setting in Continuing Medical Education Program Development." *Adult Education*, 1980, *31* (1), 3–17.

Mead, G. H. *The Self and Society.* Chicago: University of Chicago Press, 1934.

Melton, A. W. "Implications of Short-Term Memory for a General Theory of Memory." *Journal of Verbal Learning and Verbal Behavior*, 1963, *2*, 1–21.

Merriam, Sharan B. "Philosophical Perspectives on Adult Education: A Critical Review of the Literature." *Adult Education*, 1977, *27* (4), 195–208.

Merton, R. K.; Reader, G. G.; and Kendal, P. L. (Eds.). *The Student Physician.* Cambridge: Harvard University Press, 1957.

Messick, S. "The Criterion Problem in the Evaluation of Instruction: Assessing Possible, Not Just Probable, Intended Outcomes." In M. C. Wittrock and D. E. Wiley (Eds.), *The Evaluation of Instruction: Issues and Problems.* New York: Holt, 1970.

Mezirow, Jack. "Toward a Theory of Practice." *Adult Education,* 1971, *21* (3), 135–147.

Mezirow, Jack; Darkenwald, Gordon G.; and Knox, Alan B. *Last Gamble on Education.* Washington, D.C.: Adult Education Association of the U.S.A., 1975.

Miles, Catherine C. "The Influence of Speed and Age on Intelligence Scores of Adults." *Journal of Genetic Psychology,* 1934, *10,* 208–210.

Miles, W. R., and Miles, C. C. "Mental Changes with Normal Aging." In Edward J. Stieglitz (Ed.), *Geriatric Medicine.* Philadelphia: W. B. Saunders Company, 1949.

Miller, Charles E. "The Utilization of an Adult Education Program of Group Discussion with Participation Training to Meet Selected Needs of Aged Persons." Doctoral dissertation, Indiana University, 1963. [*AEDA,* 1970, p. 66.]

Miller, Harry L. *Teaching and Learning in Adult Education.* New York: Macmillan, 1964.

Miller, Harry L. *Participation of Adults in Education: A Force-Field Analysis.* Occasional Paper No. 14. Brookline, Mass.: Center for the Study of Liberal Education for Adults, 1967.

Mirza, M. S. "A Study of Cognitive Structure Among Adults: Piaget's Formal Operations Stage." Doctoral dissertation, University of Georgia, 1975. [*DAI,* 1976, *36,* 7811–7812-A.]

Misanchuk, Earl R. "A Proportionate Reduction in Error Approach to the Analysis of Needs Identification Data." Unpublished paper, April 1981.

Mocker, Donald W. *A Report on the Identification, Classification, and Ranking of Competencies Appropriate for Adult Basic Education Teachers.* Kansas City, Mo.: Center for Resource Development in Adult Education, University of Missouri–Kansas City, 1974.

Monette, Maurice L. "The Concept of Educational Need: An Analysis of Selected Literature." *Adult Education,* 1977, *27* (2), 116–127.

Monette, Maurice L. "Needs Assessment: A Critique of Philosophical Assumptions." *Adult Education,* 1979, *29* (2), 83–95.

Monge, Rolf H., and Gardner, E. F. "A Program of Research in Adult Differences in Cognitive Performance and Learning: Backgrounds for Adult Education and Vocational Retraining. Syracuse University, Project No. 6, 1963, Grant No. OEG-1-706193-014a. Final report, 1972.

Monge, Rolf H., and Gardner, E. F. "Education as an Aid to Adaptation in the Adult Years." In K. F. Riegel and S. A. Meachun (Eds.), *The Developing Individual in a Changing World,* Vol. 2: Social and Environmental Issues. The Hague: Morton, 1976.

Moorehead, Robert D. "The Effect of Learner Participation in Planning an Adult Learning Experience and Acquisition of Knowledge." Doctoral dissertation, The Ohio State University, 1977. [*DAI,* 1977, *38,* 593-A.]

Morris, L. W., and Liebert, R. M. "Relationship of Cognitive and Emotional Components of Test Anxiety to Physiological Arousal and Academic Performance." *Journal of Consulting and Clinical Psychology,* 1970, *35,* 332–337.

Morstain, Barry R., and Smart, John C. "Reasons for Participation in Adult Education Courses: A Multivariate Analysis of Group Differences." *Adult Education,* 1974, *24* (2), 83–98.

Moses, Stanley. *The Learning Force.* Syracuse, N.Y.: Syracuse University Publications in Continuing Education, 1971.

Murgatroyd, Steve. "Observing Adult Learning Groups." *Studies in Adult Education,* 1977, *9* (2), 177–196.

Murphy, Gardner. *Human Potentialities.* New York: Basic Books, 1958.

Myrick, R., and Marx, B. S. *An Exploratory Study of the Relationship Between High School Building Design and Student Learning.* Washington, D.C.: U.S. Department of Health, Education, and Welfare, Office of Education, and George Washington University, 1968.

National Center for Education Statistics. *Participation in Adult Education: Final Report, 1975.* Washington, D.C.: U.S. Government Printing Office, 1978.

National Center for Education Statistics. *The Condition of Education–1980.* Washington, D.C.: U.S. Government Printing Office, 1980.

Neidt, Charles O., and Baldwin, Lionel V. "Use of Videotape for Teaching In-Plant Graduate Engineering Courses." *Adult Education,* 1970, *20* (3), 154–167.

Newcomb, Theodore. *Social Psychology.* New York: Dryden Press, 1950.

Newcomb, T. M. *The Acquaintance Process.* New York: Holt, Rinehart, and Winston, 1961.

Niemi, John A. "Concerns and Trends in ABE: Signposts of the Past and Future." Address to the annual conference of the Commission on Adult Basic Education, Adult Education Association of the U.S.A., 16 April 1976.

O'Connor, Andrea B. "Reasons Nurses Participate in Continuing Education." In Gene C. Whaples and D. Merrill Ewert (Eds.), *Proceedings: Lifelong Learning Research Conference.* College Park, Md.: Department of Agricultural and Extension Education, University of Maryland, 1980.

Ohliger, John. "Prospects for a Learning Society." *Adult Leadership,* 1975, *24* (1), 37–39.

Olmstead, Joseph A. "Theory and State of the Art of Small Group Methods of Instruction." ERIC, 1970, ED 040 345.

Orme, Maynard E. "Effects of Community College Broadcast Television with Self-Directed Group Discussion Activity in the Home." Doctoral dissertation, University of California–Los Angeles, 1978. [*DAI,* 1979, *39,* 3984-A.]

Ornstein, Robert. "Eastern Psychologies: The Container vs. the Content." *Psychology Today,* September 1976, pp. 36–43.

Osgood, C. E.; Suci, G. J.; and Tannenbaum, P. H. *The Measurement of Meaning.* Urbana: The University of Illinois Press, 1957.

Owens, W. A. "Age and Mental Ability: A Second Adult Follow-up." *Journal of Educational Psychology,* 1966, *57,* 311–325.

Palmer, Robert E., and Verner, Coolie. "A Comparison of Three Instruction Techniques." *Adult Education,* 1959, *9* (4), 236–237.

Pantzar, Eero. "Shift Work, Leisure and the Leisure Time Studying of Adults." *Adult Education in Finland,* 1977, *14* (2), 13–26. (Translated by Brad Absetz.)

Papalia, D. E. "The Status of Several Conservation Abilities Across the Life Span." *Human Development,* 1972, *15,* 229–243.

Papalia, D. E., and Bielby, D. D. "Cognitive Functioning in Middle and Old Age Adults." *Human Development,* 1974, *17,* 424–443.

Parsons, Talcott. *The Social System*. Glencoe, Ill.: Free Press, 1951.

Partin, James J. "A Study of Two Group Discussion Procedures for Changing Accept-ance of Self and Others." Doctoral dissertation, Indiana University, 1967. [*AEDA*, 1970, p. 73.]

Patterson, R. W. K. "Social Change as an Educational Aim." *Adult Education* (NIAE), 1973, *45*, 353–359.

Patterson, R. W. K. *Values, Education, and the Adult*. Boston: Routledge and Kegan Paul, 1979.

Patton, M. O. *Qualitative Evaluation Methods*. Beverly Hills, Calif.: Sage Publications, 1980.

Peluffo, Nicola. "Cultural and Cognitive Problems." *International Journal of Psychol-ogy*, 1967, *2*, 187–198.

Penland, Patrick R. "Self-Initiated Learning." *Adult Education*, 1979, *29* (3), 170–179.

Pennington, Floyd, and Green, Joseph. "Comparative Analysis of Program Develop-ment Processes in Six Professions." *Adult Education*, 1976, *27* (1), 13–23.

Perkins, Hugh V. *Human Development and Learning*. Belmont, Calif.: Woodsworth, 1974.

Peters, John M. "Internal-External Control, Learning, and Participation in Occupa-tional Education." *Adult Education*, 1969, *20* (1), 23–43.

Peters, John M., and Gordon, Susan. "Adult Learning Projects: A Study of Adult Learn-ing in Urban and Rural Tennessee." Knoxville: University of Tennessee, 1974. ERIC Document Reproduction Service, ED 102 431.

Peters, R. S. *Ethics and Education*. Atlanta: Scott, Foresman, 1967.

Peterson, Richard E., et al. *Lifelong Learning in America*. San Francisco: Jossey-Bass, 1979.

Phares, E. Jerry. *Locus of Control: A Personality Determinant of Behavior*. Morristown, N.J.: General Learning Press, 1973.

Phares, E. Jerry. *Locus of Control in Personality*. Morristown, N.J.: General Learning Press, 1976.

Piaget, Jean. "The Theory of Stages of Cognitive Development." In D. R. Green, M. P. Ford, and G. B. Flamer (Eds.), *Measurement and Piaget*. New York: McGraw-Hill, 1971.

Piaget, Jean. "Intellectual Evolution from Adolescence to Adulthood." *Human Devel-opment*, 1972, *15*, 1–12.

Pigg, Kenneth E.; Busch, Lawrence; and Lacy, William B. "Learning Styles in Adult Education: A Study of County Extension Agents." *Adult Education*, 1980, *30* (4), 233–244.

Pine, William S. "The Effect of Foreign Adult Student Participation in Program Plan-ning on Achievement and Attitude." Doctoral dissertation, Auburn University, 1980. [*DAI*, 1981, *41*, 2405-A.]

Plotnikoff, N. "Magnesium Pemoline: Enhancement of Memory After Electroconvul-sive Shock in Rats." *Life Sciences*, 1966, *5*, 1495.

Powell, John W., and Benne, Kenneth D. "Philosophies of Adult Education." In Mal-colm S. Knowles (Ed.), *Handbook of Adult Education in the United States*. Chi-cago: Adult Education Association of the U.S.A., 1960.

Pressey, Sidney L. "Major Problems—and the Major Problem: Motivating Learning and Education in the Later Years." In J. E. Anderson (Ed.), *Psychological Aspects of Aging*. Washington, D.C.: American Psychological Association, 1956.

Pressey, Sidney L., and Kuhlen, R. G. *Psychological Development Through the Life-span*. New York: Harper Brothers, 1957.

Preston, M. G., and Heintz, R. K. "Effects of Participatory versus Supervisory Leadership on Group Judgment." In Dorwin Cartwright and Alvin Zander (Eds.), *Group Dynamics*. Evanston, Ill.: Row, Peterson, 1956.

Pribram, Karl H. "The Neurophysiology of Remembering." *Scientific American*, 1969, *220*, 73–87.

Propst, R. "Human Needs and Working Places." In T. G. David and B. E. Wright (Eds.), *Learning Environments*. Chicago: University of Chicago Press, 1975.

Rauch, David B. "New Priorities for Adult Education." In David B. Rauch (Ed.), *Priorities in Adult Education*. Washington, D.C.: Adult Education Association of the U.S.A., 1972.

Rees, J. N., and Botwinick, J. "Detection and Decision Factors in Auditory Behavior of the Elderly." *Journal of Gerontology*, 1972, *26*, 361–363.

Rees, M. B., and Paisley, W. J. "Social and Psychological Predictions of Information Seeking and Media Use: A Multivariate Re-Analysis." Palo Alto, Calif.: Institute for Communication Research, 1967.

Renner, J. W., and Stafford, D. G. *Teaching Science in the Secondary School*. New York: Harper and Row, 1972.

Restak, Richard M. "Brain Potentials: Signaling Our Inner Thoughts." *Psychology Today*, March 1979, pp. 42–54.

Rice, Joy K. "Self-Esteem, Sex-Role Orientation, and Perceived Spouse Support for a Return to School." *Adult Education*, 1979, *29* (4), 215–233.

Riegel, K. F. "Dialectic Operations: The Final Period of Cognitive Development." *Human Development*, 1973, *16*, 346–370.

Riegel, K. F. "The Dialectics of Human Development." *American Psychologist*, 1976, *31*, 689–700.

Ritchie, E., and Phares, E. J. "Attitude Change as a Function of Internal-External Control and Communication Status." *Journal of Personality*, 1969, *37*, 429–443.

Robbins, J. Nevin. "Analysis of Human Need: New Concepts for Practice and Research." In Gene C. Whaples and D. Merrill Ewert (Eds.), *Lifelong Learning Research Conference Proceedings*. College Park, Md.: Department of Agriculture and Extension Education, University of Maryland, 1981.

Roberson, Howard Bennett. "A Study of Selected Attitudes as Influential Forces in Adult Learning Environments." Doctoral dissertation, The Florida State University, 1980. [*DAI*, 1980, *41*, 901-A.]

Roberts, Thomas B. "Consciousness, Psychology and Education." *Journal of Transpersonal Anthropology*, 1981, *5* (1), 86.

Robinson, C. O. "Criteria for the Education of Adult Educators." *Adult Education*, 1962, *12* (4), 243–245.

Robinson, John. "Exploring the Range of Adult Interests." In R. L. Collison (Ed.), *Progress in Library Science*. London: Butterworths, 1965.

Robinson, Russell D. "Adult Education Participation in the Industrial Suburb of West Milwaukee, Wisconsin." *Adult Education*, 1970, *20* (4), 226–232.

Robson, B. T. "The Human Ecology of Sunderland: A Study of Social Structure and Attitudes Toward Education." Doctoral dissertation, Cambridge University, 1966. [*RAE*, 1974, pp. 182–184.]

Roelfs, Pamela J. T. "Teaching and Counseling Older College Students." ERIC, 1975, ED 130 737.

Rogers, Carl R. "The Self-Actualization Tendency." In David C. McClelland (Ed.), *Studies in Motivation.* New York: Appleton-Century-Crofts, 1955.

Rogers, Jennifer. *Adults Learning.* Baltimore: Penguin Books, 1973.

Rokeach, M. *The Open and Closed Mind.* New York: Basic Books, 1960.

Rossman, Mark H., and Bunning, Richard L. "Knowledge and Skills for the Adult Educator: A Delphi Study." *Adult Education,* 1978, *28* (3), 139–155.

Rotter, J. B., and Mulry, R. C. "Internal versus External Control of Reinforcements and Decision Time." *Journal of Personality and Social Psychology,* 1965, *2,* 598–604.

Royce, J. R. *The Encapsulated Man.* New York: D. Van Nostrand, 1964.

Rubenson, Kjell. *Recruitment to Adult Education in the Nordic Countries: Research and Outreaching Activities.* Stockholm: Stockholm Institute of Education, Paper presented at ICAE's and the Swedish National Federation of Adult Educational Associations' Conference on Research in Adult Education, June 25–27, 1979, Kungälv, Sweden. Department of Educational Research, 1979.

Rubenson, Kjell. "Adult Education Research: In Quest of a Map of the Territory." *Adult Education,* 1982, *32* (2), 57–74.

Rubin, K. H. "Extinction of Conservation: A Life-Span Investigation." *Developmental Psychology,* 1976, *12* (1), 51–56.

Ruja, H. "Outcomes of Lecture and Discussion Procedures in Three College Courses." *Journal of Experimental Education,* 1954, *22,* 368–394.

Rusnell, Albert D. "Development of an Index of Quality for the Planning of Management Training Programs." Doctoral dissertation, University of British Columbia, 1974. [*DAI,* 1975, *35,* 7018-A.]

Saddam, Alma M. "The Effects of Three Instructional Approaches on Knowledge Gain and Attitude Change of Paraprofessionals in the Expanded Food and Nutrition Education Program." Doctoral dissertation, The Ohio State University, 1977. [*DAI,* 1978, *38,* 4518-A.]

Sahakian, William S., (Ed.). *Psychology of Learning: Systems, Models, and Theories.* Chicago: Markham Publishing Company, 1970.

Sainty, Geoffrey E. "Predicting Drop-Outs in Adult Education Courses." *Adult Education,* 1971, *21* (4), 223–230.

Sarason, I. G. "Test Anxiety and the Intellectual Performance of College Students." *Journal of Educational Psychology,* 1961, *52,* 201–206.

Scanland, Francis W. "An Investigation of the Relative Effectiveness of Two Methods of Instruction, Including Computer Assisted Instruction, as Techniques for Changing the Parental Attitudes of Negro Adults." Doctoral dissertation, Florida State University, 1970. [*DAI,* 1971, *31,* 4443-A.]

SCB. Levnadsförhållanden. Rapport 14. Utbildning, vuxenstudier förvärvsarbetande 1975. 1978. (Cited by Rubenson 1979, p. 9.)

Schact, Robert H. "When Programs Fail, Find Out Why." *Adult Leadership,* 1971, *20* (3), 91–92.

Scharles, Henry G., Jr. "The Relationship of Selected Personality Needs to Participation, Dropout, and Achievement Among Adult Learners." Doctoral dissertation, The Florida State University, 1966. [*AEDA*, 1970, p. 29.]

Schillace, Ralph. "Theory and Research in Adult Education." Paper presented at the annual Adult Education Research Conference, Montreal, Quebec, 1973.

Schonfield, David. "Memory Loss with Age: Acquisition and Retrieval." *Psychological Reports*, 1967, *20*, 223–226.

Schonfield, David, and Robertson, Betty-Anne. "Memory Storage and Aging." In D. Barry Lumsden and Ronald H. Shearon (Eds.), *Experimental Studies in Adult Learning and Memory*. New York: John Wiley and Sons, 1975.

Schroeder, Wayne L. "Adult Education Defined and Described." In R. M. Smith, George F. Aker, and J. R. Kidd (Eds.), *Handbook of Adult Education*. New York: Macmillan, 1970, 25–44.

Schroeder, Wayne L. "Typology of Adult Learning Systems." In John M. Peters et al., *Building an Effective Adult Education Enterprise*. San Francisco: Jossey-Bass, 1980.

Schwertman, John B. "The Intellectual Challenge of Adult Education." In Marilyn V. Miller (Ed.), *On Teaching Adults: An Anthology*. Boston: Center for the Study of Liberal Education for Adults, 1960.

Schwertz, Courtney. "An Analysis of the Denotations of 'Program' as Employed in Ordinary Language and Adult Education Discourse, with a Typology of Program Based on the Denotations." Paper presented at the annual Adult Education Research Conference, Chicago, Illinois, 1972.

Scissons, Edward H. "Psychometric Needs Assessment: Theory and Practice." *Canadian Journal of University Continuing Education*, 1980, *6* (2), 14–19.

Seaman, Don F., and Schroeder, Wayne L. "The Relationship Between Extent of Educative Behavior by Adults and Their Attitudes Toward Continuing Education." *Adult Education*, 1970, *20* (2), 96–106.

Seeman, Melvin. "Alienation and Social Learning in a Reformatory." *American Journal of Sociology*, 1963, *69*, 270–284.

Seeman, Melvin, and Evans, J. W. "Alienation Learning in a Hospital Setting." *American Sociological Review*, 1962, *27*, 772–781.

Sell, Roger. *A Handbook of Terminology for Classifying and Describing the Learning Activities of Adults* (draft). Boulder, Colo.: National Center for Higher Education Management Systems, 1978.

Sequin, Barbara R. "Piagetian Cognitive Levels of Adult Basic Education Students Related to Teaching Methods and Materials." *Journal of Research and Development in Education*, 1980, *13* (3), 44–51.

Seybolt, Robert F. *Apprenticeship and Apprenticeship Education in Colonial New England and New York*. 1917. Reprint. New York: Arno Press and the New York Times Report Edition, 1969.

Sharon, Ameil T. "Adult Academic Achievement in Relation to Formal Education and Age." *Adult Education*, 1971, *21* (4), 231–237.

Sharpe, D. *The Psychology of Color and Design*. Chicago: Nelson-Hall Company, 1974.

Shaw, A. "Characteristics and Opinions of Part-Time GCE Students in Manchester Colleges of Further Education." Masters thesis, University of Manchester (England), 1972.

Shay, Earl R. "Self Concept Changes Among Alcoholic Patients in Madison (Indiana) State Hospital Resulting from Participation Training in Group Discussion." Doctoral dissertation, Indiana University, 1963. [*AEDA*, 1970, p. 68.]

Sheasha, Taha. "A Definition of Needs and Wants." *Adult Education*, 1961, *12* (1), 52–53.

Sheffield, Sherman B. "The Orientations of Adult Continuing Learners." In Daniel Solomon (Ed.), *The Continuing Learner*. Chicago: Center for the Study of Liberal Education for Adults, 1964.

Sheridan, Edmund, and Shannon, Daniel W. "A Comprehensive Model of Assessing the Training Needs of Local Governmental Staff." In Preston P. LeBreton et al. (Eds.), *The Evaluation of Continuing Education for Professionals: A Systems Review.* Seattle: University of Washington, 1979.

Sheriff, Denis F. "A Critical Analysis of Hill's 'Cognitive Style Inventory.' " Paper presented at the annual Adult Education Research Conference, Ann Arbor, Michigan, 1979.

Sherman, Mark A., and Glore, George R. "Attitudes of Adult Basic Education Students Toward Computer Aided Instruction." ERIC, 1970, ED 041 203.

Sherman, S. J. "Internal-External Control and Its Relationship for Attitude Change Under Different Social Influence Techniques." *Journal of Personality and Social Psychology*, 1973, *23*, 23–29.

Shipp, Travis. "The Marketing Concept and Adult Education." *Lifelong Learning: The Adult Years*, March 1981, pp. 8–9.

Shipp, Travis, and McKenzie, Leon. "Utilization of Market Research Analytical Techniques for Educational Research." Paper presented at the annual Adult Education Research Conference, San Antonio, Texas, 1978.

Shipp, Travis, and McKenzie, Leon. "Marketing Parish Adult Education." *Today's Parish*, January 1981, pp. 29–30.

Siegel, Laurence, (Ed.). *Instruction: Some Contemporary Viewpoints*. San Francisco: Chandler Publishing Company, 1967.

Simutis, Zita M. "CAI as an Adjunct to Teach Basic Skills." ERIC, 1979, ED 171 326.

Smith, A. "Aging and Interference with Memory." *Journal of Gerontology*, 1975, *30*, 319–325.

Smith, J. "Locating, Designing, and Equipping the Ideal Training Room—Part I." *Training*, 1978a, *15* (8), 21–26.

Smith, J. "Locating, Designing, and Equipping the Ideal Training Room—Part II." *Training*, 1978b, *16* (9), 91–98.

Smith, Robert; Aker, George; and Kidd, J. R. *Handbook of Adult Education*. New York: Macmillan, 1970.

Snow, R. E.; Tiflin, J.; and Seibert, W. F. "Individual Differences and Instructional Film Effects." *Journal of Educational Psychology*, 1969, *60*, 153–157.

Snyder, Robert E. "An Analysis of the Concept *Involvement*, with Special Reference to Uses Found in Ordinary Language, Adult Education, and in Empirical Research." Doctoral dissertation, The Florida State University, 1969. [*DAI*, 1970, *30*, 5223-A.]

Sommer, R. *Personal Space: The Behavioral Basis of Design*. Englewood Cliffs, N.J.: Prentice-Hall, 1969.

Sorenson, Herbert. *Adult Abilities*. St. Paul: University of Minnesota Press, 1938.

Sork, Thomas, J. "Meta-Research in Adult Education: An Historical Analysis and Critical Appraisal." Paper presented at the annual Adult Education Research Conference, Vancouver, British Columbia, 1980.

Sovie, M. D. "The Relationships of Learning Orientation, Nursing Activity, and Continuing Education." Paper presented at the annual Adult Education Research Conference, Montreal, Quebec, 1973.

Spear, George E., and Mocker, Donald W. "The Organizing Circumstance: Environmental Determinants in the Non-Formal Learning." Unpublished paper, November 1981. [Available from the authors, Center for Research Development in Adult Education, School of Education, University of Missouri–Kansas City.]

Spence, R. B. "Lecture and Class Discussion in Teaching Educational Psychology." *Journal of Educational Psychology*, 1928, *19*, 454–462.

Spence, R. B., and Evans, L. H. "Dropouts in Adult Education." *Adult Education*, 1956, *6* (4), 221–225. (Cited by Brunner et al. 1959, p. 251.)

Spencer, Barbara B. "Non-Directive Group Interviews: A Needs Assessment Approach for Older Adults." In Gene C. Whaples and D. Merrill Ewert (Eds.), *Proceedings: Lifelong Learning Research Conference*. College Park, Md.: Department of Agricultural and Extension Education, University of Maryland, 1980.

Spielberger, C. D.; Gorsuch, R. L.; and Lushene, R. E. *The State-Trait Anxiety Inventory (STAI)*. Tallahassee, Fla.: The Florida State University, 1968.

Sprouse, Betty M. "Participation Motivations of Older Learners." In Gene C. Whaples and D. Merrill Ewert (Eds.), *Lifelong Learning Research Conference Proceedings*. College Park, Md.: Department of Agricultural and Extension Education, University of Maryland, 1981.

Stern, Bernard H. "The Teaching of Adults." In Marilyn V. Miller (Ed.), *On Teaching Adults: An Anthology*. Boston: Center for the Study of Liberal Education for Adults, 1960.

Stern, Milton R. "Promotion and Recruitment of Adult Students." In Coolie Verner and Thurman White (Eds.), *Adult Education Theory and Method: Administration of Adult Education*. Washington, D.C.: Adult Education Association of the U.S.A., 1965.

Sternberg, S. "Memory-Scanning: Mental Processes Revealed by Reaction-Time Experiments." *American Scientist*, 1969, *57*, 421–457.

Stevens-Long, Judith. *Adult Life: Developmental Processes*. Palo Alto, Calif.: Mayfield Publishing Company, 1979.

Stewart, David W. "Systems Theory as a Framework for Analysis of the Politics of Adult Education." *Adult Education*, 1981, *31* (3), 142–154.

Stock, Arthur K. "Teaching Styles and Learning Research Strategies and Models with Special Reference to the Part-Time Teacher of Adults." *Studies in Adult Education*, 1974, *6* (2), 115–124.

Storck, P. A. "Cross-Sequential Assessment of Quantative and Qualitative Changes in Cognitive Behavior Across the Life-Span: The Interrelationships of Piagetian Theory to Fluid and Crystallized Intelligence." Doctoral dissertation, University of Wisconsin, 1974. [*DAI*, 1975, *35*, 3406–3407-B.]

Storck, P. A.; Lott, W. R.; and Hooper, F. H. "Interrelationships Among Piagetian Tasks and Traditional Measures of Cognitive Abilities in Mature and Aged Adults." *Journal of Gerontology*, 1972, *27* (4), 461–465.

Strayer, Paula J. R. "The Effect of Simulation versus Traditional Instructional Strategies on the Achievement and Attitude of Baccalaureate Nursing Students." Doctoral dissertation, The Ohio State University, 1979. [*DAI*, 1979, *40*, 67-A.]

Strolurow, L. M. "Programmed Instruction and Teaching Machines." In P. H. Rossi (Ed.), *The New Media and Education*. Chicago: Aldine Publishing Company, 1966.

Stubblefield, Harold W. "Installing the Participation Training System: Common Problems." *Viewpoints*, 1975, *51* (4), 59–66.

Talland, G. A. "Initiation of Response and Reaction Time in Aging and with Brain Damage." In A. T. Welford and J. E. Birren (Eds.), *Behavior, Aging, and the Nervous System*. Springfield, Ill.: Charles C. Thomas, 1965.

Taub, H. A. "Effects of Coding Cues Upon Short-Term Memory of Aged Subjects." *Developmental Psychology*, 1975, *11*, 254.

Taylor, Fitz J. "Acquiring Knowledge from Prose and Continuous Discourse." In Michael J. A. Howe (Ed.), *Adult Learning: Psychological Research and Application*. New York: John Wiley and Sons, 1977.

Taylor, John E., et al. "The Interrelationships of Ability Level, Instructional System, and Skill Acquisition." Symposium presentation, American Psychological Association Convention, September 1970.

Teevan, Richard C., and Smith, Barry. *Motivation*. New York: McGraw-Hill, 1967.

Tesch, S.; Whitbourne, S. K.; and Nehrke, M. F. "Cognitive Egocentricism in Institutionalized Adult Males." *Journal of Gerontology*, 1978, *33* (4), 546–552.

Teyler, Timothy J. "An Introduction to the Neurosciences." In M. C. Wittrock et al. (Eds.), *The Human Brain*. Englewood Cliffs, N.J.: Prentice-Hall, 1977.

Thibodeau, Janice. "Adult Performance on Piagetian Cognitive Tasks: Implications for Adult Education." *Journal of Research and Development in Education*, 1980, *13* (3), 25–32.

Thorndike, E. L. *Adult Learning*. New York: Macmillan, 1928.

Thorndike, Edward L. et al. *Adult Interests*. New York: Macmillan, 1935.

Thorndike, Robert L., and Hagen, Elizabeth P. *Measurement and Evaluation in Psychology and Education* (4th ed.). New York: John Wiley and Sons, 1977.

Tognoli, J. "The Effect of Windowless Rooms and Unembellished Surroundings on Attitudes and Retention." *Environment and Behavior*, 1973, *5* (2), 191–201.

Tough, Allen. "The Assistance Obtained by Adult Self-Teachers." *Adult Education*, 1966, *17* (1), 30–37.

Tough, Allen. "Some Major Reasons for Learning." Paper presented at the annual Adult Education Research Conference, University of Wisconsin, 1969. ERIC, ED 033 251.

Tough, Allen. *The Adult's Learning Projects: A Fresh Approach to Theory and Practice in Adult Learning*. Toronto: Ontario Institute for Studies in Education, 1971.

Tough, Allen. "Major Learning Efforts: Recent Research and Future Directions." *Adult Education*, 1978, *28* (4), 250–263.

Tough, Allen. "Choosing to Learn." In Grace M. Healy and Warren L. Ziegler (Eds.), *The Learning Stance: Essays in Celebration of Human Learning*. Syracuse Research Corporation, National Institute of Education Project No. 400-78-0029. Final report. Washington, D.C.: National Institute of Education, 1979.

Trenaman, S. J. M. "Attitudes to Opportunities for Further Education in Relation to Educational Environment and Background in Samples of the Adult Population." Baccalaureate thesis, Oxford University, 1957. [*RAE*, 1974, pp. 161–164.}

Tubb, A. "The Bearing of Modern Analytical Philosophy on Education Theory: A Critical Exploration of the Literature, 1942–1965." Masters thesis, University of Durham, 1966. [*RAE*, 1974, pp. 182–184.]

Ulmer, R. Curtis, and Verner, Coolie. "Factors Affecting Attendance in a Junior College Adult Program." In Coolie Verner and Thurman White (Eds.), *Participants in Adult Education*. Washington, D.C.: Adult Education Association of the U.S.A., 1965.

UNESCO. *Recommendation on the Development of Adult Education*. Paris: UNESCO, 1976.

Vedros, Kathy, and Pankowski, Mary L. "Participatory Planning in Lifelong Learning." In Gene C. Whaples and D. Merrill Ewert (Eds.), *Proceedings: Lifelong Learning Research Conference*. College Park, Md.: Department of Agriculture and Extension Education, University of Maryland, 1980.

Verduin, John R., Jr.; Miller, Harry G.; and Greer, Charles E. *Adults Teaching Adults*. Austin, Texas: Learning Concepts, 1977.

Veres, Helen C., and Carmichael, Mary M. "Learning Interests of Urban and Rural Adults: Implications for Planning Continuing Education Services." In Gene C. Whaples and D. Merrill Ewert (Eds.), *Proceedings: Lifelong Learning Research Conference*. College Park, Md.: Department of Agricultural and Extension Education, University of Maryland, 1980.

Verner, Coolie. "Tutors Need Tutoring Too." *The Tutor's Bulletin*, 1953, 92, 11–14.

Verner, Coolie. "Definition of Terms." In Gale Jensen, A. A. Liveright, and Wilbur Hallenbeck (Eds.), *Adult Education: Outlines of an Emerging Field of University Study*. Washington, D.C.: Adult Education Association of the U.S.A., 1964.

Verner, Coolie. "Organizing Graduate Professional Education for Adult Education." In J. Roby Kidd and Gordon R. Selman (Eds.), *Coming of Age: Canadian Adult Education in the 1960's*. Toronto: Canadian Association of Adult Education, 1978. (Dickinson 1979, p. 31).

Verner, Coolie, and Booth, Alan. *Adult Education*. New York: Center for Applied Research in Education, 1966.

Verner, Coolie, and Davis, George S., Jr. "Completions and Drop-Outs: A Review of Research." *Adult Education*, 1964, 14 (3), 157–176.

Verner, Coolie, and Dickinson, Gary. "The Lecture: An Analysis and Review of Research." *Adult Education*, 1967, 17 (2), 85–100.

Villaniel, F. J. A. "The Comparative Effectiveness of Two Different Methods of Teaching Technical Farm Credit and Total Money Management to Tenth Grade Vocational Agriculture Students and Adult Farmers in Puerto Rico." Doctoral dissertation, University of Connecticut, 1979. [*DAI*, 1980, 40, 4394-A.]

Vollmer, H. M., and Mills, D. L. *Professionalization*. Englewood Cliffs, N.J.: Prentice-Hall, 1966.

Voth, Donald E. "Social Action Research in Community Development." In Edward J. Blakely (Ed.), *Community Development Research: Concepts, Issues, and Strategies*. New York: Human Sciences Press, 1979.

Walker, Delker. "A Naturalistic Model of Curriculum Development." *School Review*, 1971, 80, 51–65.

Walker, Franelo R. "Some Aspects of Adult Learning Theory Tested in a Continuing Education Model." Doctoral dissertation, Purdue University, 1978. [*DAI*, 1979, *40*, 68-A.]

Wallace, S. Gerald, Jr. "The Effects of Cognitive Style and Modality of Study in Achievement in Self-Paced Auto-Tutorial Instruction." Doctoral dissertation, Texas A&M University, 1980. [*DAI*, 1981, *41*, 4255-A.]

Walsh, R. P.; Engbretson, R. O.; and O'Brien, B. A. "Anxiety and Test Taking Behavior." *Journal of Counseling Psychology*, 1968, *15*, 572–575.

Wason, P. C. "Reasoning About a Rule." *Quarterly Journal of Experimental Psychology*, 1968, *20*, 273–281.

Wegner, Wallace W. "Opsimathic Styles of Adults." Doctoral dissertation, University of Southern Mississippi, 1980. [*DAI*, 1980, *41*, 1898-A.]

Weil, M., and Joyce, B. *Information Processing Models of Teaching*. Englewood Cliffs, N.J.: Prentice-Hall, 1978.

Welden, Eugene J. "Program Planning and Program Effectiveness in University Residential Centers." Doctoral dissertation, University of Chicago, 1966.

Welford, A. T. *Skill and Age: An Experimental Approach*. New York: Oxford University Press, 1951.

Werner, H. "The Concept of Development from a Comparative and Organismic Point of View." In D. B. Harris (Ed.), *The Concept of Development*. Minneapolis: University of Minnesota Press, 1957.

Westfall, R. S. "Newton and the Fudge Factor." *Science*, 1973, *179*, 751–758.

Whipple, J. B. "University Training for Adult Educators." *Adult Education*, 1958, *8* (2), 93–97.

Whitbourne, S. K., and Weinstock, C. S. *Adult Development: The Differentiation of Experience*. New York: Holt, Rinehart, and Winston, 1979.

White, Sally. "Physical Criteria for Adult Learning Environments." Syracuse, N.Y.: ERIC Clearinghouse on Adult Education. Adult Education Association of the U.S.A., 1973.

White, Thurman. "Some Common Interests of Adult Education Leaders." *Adult Education*, 1956, *6* (3), 151–161.

Wientge, Kingsley M.; Dubois, Philip H.; and Gaffney, H. "An Evaluation of Elective Class Participation." *Adult Education*, 1970, *21* (1), 44–51.

Wilkie, F., and Eisdorfer, C. "Intelligence and Blood Pressure in the Aged." *Science*, 1971, *172*, 959–962.

Willsey, Frank R. "An Experimental Study of an Adult Learning Situation Involving Three Levels of Training in the Group Discussion Process." Doctoral dissertation, Indiana University, 1962. [*DAI*, 1963, *23*, 2407-A.]

Wilson, Russell C. "Personological Variables Related to GED Retention and Withdrawal." *Adult Education*, 1980, *30* (3), 175–185.

Windham, D. M.; Kurland, N. D.; and Levinsohn, F. H. (Eds.). *School Review*, 1978, *86* (3).

Witkin, H. A. *The Role of Cognitive Style in Academic Performance and in Teacher-Student Relations*. Princeton, N.J.: Educational Testing Service, 1973.

Witkin, H. A., and Berry, J. W. *Psychological Differentiation in Cross-Cultural Perspective*. Princeton, N.J.: Educational Testing Service, 1975.

Witkin, H. A., Dyk, R. B., et al. *Psychological Differentiation.* New York: John Wiley and Sons, 1962.

Wittrock, M. C., et al. *The Human Brain.* Englewood Cliffs, N.J.: Prentice-Hall, Inc., 1977.

Wohlwill, J. F. "The Physical Environment: A Problem for a Psychology of Stimulation." *Journal of Social Issues,* 1966, 22 (4), 29–38.

Woodruff, Diana S. "Biofeedback Control of the EEG Alpha Rhythm and Its Effect on Reaction Time in the Young and Old." Doctoral dissertation, University of Southern California, 1972. [*DAI,* 1972, *33,* 1833-B.]

Wuerger, William W. "Mailing Lists: How Effective Are They?" *Adult Leadership,* 1971, *20* (3), 89–90.

Youse, Clifford F. "Promotion and Recruitment of Part-Time Students." *Adult Leadership,* 1973, *21* (8), 246–249.

Zahn, Jane. "Some Adult Attitudes Affecting Learning Powerlessness, Conflicting Needs, and Role Transition." *Adult Education,* 1969, *19* (2), 91–97.

Name Index

Subject Index

ABOUT THE AUTHOR

Huey B. Long is Professor of Adult Education and former Director of Graduate Studies in the College of Education at the University of Georgia, where he has been on the faculty since 1969. He also is former Acting Associate Dean for Research and Graduate Studies in the College. His special research interests are in the history of adult education, particularly during the colonial period in America, in adult development, and in community development.

Long is a past president of the Adult Education Association of the U.S.A. and has served on several of its committees and in other leadership positions with the National University Extension Association (now the National University Continuing Education Association), the Community Development Society, and the Commission of Professors of Adult Education. He served as a member of the International Adult Education Committee of the American Association of Community and Junior Colleges and has served on the Executive Committee for the International Council for Adult Education. His studies and teaching in adult education have taken him to Canada, Europe, India, China, and the Caribbean in recent years. While Director of the Urban Research Center at Florida State University in the late 60s, Long studied social change in the Cape Canaveral area during the height of the space program activities there. He received his Ph.D. in Higher Adult and Continuing Education from Florida State in 1966.

Published contributions by Long to professional journals and books have covered such topics as Piagetian theory and adult learning, aging and adult learning, adult education in colonial America, the mentally retarded adult and adult basic education, adult religious education, and community education, and have included many works on research and adult education. He is a co-author of the book *Changing Approaches to Studying Adult Education* (1980).